Stalking

Perspectives on Victims and Perpetrators

Keith Davis, PhD, is Professor of Psychology and former chair of the Department of Psychology at the University of South Carolina, Columbia. He earned his PhD in social-personality psychology at Duke University in 1962, and has taught at Princeton, Rutgers, and the University of Colorado, Boulder. He is a Fellow of the American Psychological Association (Division 9), The American Psychological Society, and a recent winner of the University's Educational Foundation Award for Research in the Humanities and the Social Sciences. He was a founding associate editor of *Personal Relationships.* His contributions include the foundation of attribution theory, the application of attachment theory to adult romantic relationships, the development of friendship and love relationships, and, more recently, the predictors and consequences of psychological abuse and stalking. He is the author or co-author of more than 95 articles, books, and book chapters.

Irene Hanson Frieze, PhD, is a Professor of Psychology and Women's Studies at the University of Pittsburgh. She earned her PhD in Personality Psychology from UCLA in 1973. She is a former president of the Psychology of Women division [Division 35] of the American Psychological Association. She is Editor of the "Journal of Social Issues" and a former Associate Editor of "Violence and Victims." She is the author or co-author of over 150 books, journal articles, and book chapters. Dr. Frieze has been researching violence in close relationships for nearly 30 years, looking at battered women, violence in marriage, dating violence, and, most recently, stalking.

Roland D. Maiuro, PhD, is the Director of the Anger Management, Domestic Violence, and Workplace Conflict Programs located at Harborview Medical Center in Seattle, and Associate Professor in the Department of Psychiatry and Behavioral Sciences at the University of Washington School of Medicine. Dr. Maiuro has received the Social Issues Award from the Washington State Psychological Association for his research on domestically violent men, and the Gold Achievement Award from the American Psychological Association for program development, teaching, and applied research in the areas of anger and interpersonal violence. Dr. Maiuro currently serves as Editor-in-Chief for *Violence and Victims,* an internationally distributed research journal devoted to theory, practice, and public policy related to perpetrators and victims of interpersonal violence.

Stalking

Perspectives on Victims and Perpetrators

Keith E. Davis, PhD
Irene Hanson Frieze, PhD
Roland D. Maiuro, PhD, Editors

 Springer Publishing Company

Springer Publishing Company, Inc.
536 Broadway
New York, NY 10012-3955

Acquisitions Editor: Sheri Sussman
Production Editor: Janice Stangel
Cover design by Susan Hauley

01 02 03 04 05 / 5 4 3 2 1

Library of Congress Cataloging-in-Publication-Data

Stalking : perspectives on victims and perpetrators / Keith Davis and Irene Hanson Frieze, Roland D. Maiuro, editors.
  p. cm.
Includes bibliographical references and index.
ISBN 0-8261-1535-7
  1. Stalking. 2. Stalkers—Pschology. 3. Stalking victims. 4. Man-woman relationships. 5. Conjugal violence. I. Davis, Keith E. II. Frieze, Irene Hanson. III. Maiuro, Roland D.

HV6594 .S74 2002
364.15—dc21   20011049774

Printed in the United States of America by Sheridan Books.

Contents

Contributors

April Ace, JD
Department of Psychology
University of South Carolina
Columbia, SC

Christine J. Allison, MA
WINGS Foundation
Denver, Colorado

Michelle Andra, MA
Department of Psychology
University of South Carolina
Columbia, SC

Beth Bjerregaard, PhD
Department of Criminal Justice
University of North Carolina at
   Charlotte
Charlotte, NC

Mary P. Brewster, PhD
Department of Criminal Justice
West Chester University
West Chester, PA

Jennifer Cohen
Department of Psychology
University of Nebraska—Lincoln
Lincoln, NE

William R. Cupach, PhD
Department of Communication
Illinois State University
Normal, IL

Robin M. Kowalski, PhD
Department of Psychology
Western Carolina University
Cullowhee, NC

**Jennifer Langhinrichsen-Rohling,
   PhD**
Department of Psychology
University of South Alabama
Mobile, AL

Carl Leukefeld, PhD
Center on Drug & Alcohol
   Research
University of Kentucky
Lexington, KY

TK Logan, PhD
Center on Drug & Alcohol
   Research
University of Kentucky
Lexington, KY

Amy Lyndon, MA
Department of Psychology
University of North Carolina—
   Greensboro
Greensboro, NC

Mindy B. Mechanic, PhD
Department of Psychology
University of Missouri—St. Louis
St. Louis, MO

Russel E. Palarea
Department of Psychology
University of Nebraska—Lincoln
Lincoln, NE

Patricia A. Resick, PhD
Department of Psychology
University of Missouri—St. Louis
St. Louis, MO

Martin Rohling, PhD
Department of Psychology
University of South Alabama
Mobile, AL

H. Colleen Sinclair
Department of Psychology—
   N218 Elliott Hall
University of Minnesota
Minneapolis, MN

Brian H. Spitzberg, PhD
School of Communication
San Diego State University
San Diego, CA

Patricia Tjaden, PhD
Center for Policy Research
Denver, CO

Nancy Thoennes, PhD
Center for Policy Research
Denver, CO

Mary H. Uhlmansiek, MA
Department of Psychology
University of Missouri—St. Louis
St. Louis, MO

Sherri Valentine
Department of Psychology
Western Carolina University
Cullowhee, NC

Bob Walker, PhD
Center on Drug & Alcohol Research
University of Kentucky
Lexington, KY

Terri L. Weaver, PhD
Department of Psychology
St. Louis University
St. Louis, MO

Jacquelyn W. White, PhD
Department of Psychology
University of North Carolina—
   Greensboro
Greensboro, NC

Preface

Stalking Research: Through the Looking Glass and What We Have Found There

You know a few things about me, dear sweetheart
Like my obsession with fantasy
But what the rabble don't yet understand
Is that fantasies become reality in my world.
                                    —John Hinckley Jr.

On March 30, 1981, John Hinckley Jr. fired six bullets at former president Ronald Reagan outside of the Washington Hilton hotel, wounding Reagan, a police officer, a Secret Service agent, and Press Secretary James Brady. As the investigation of the incident unfolded, a nation of concerned citizens was surprised to discover that the act had little to do with politics. Rather, the investigation revealed that the 25 year old Hinckley had a prior history of adjustment problems, strong identification with a character named Travis Bickle played by Robert DeNiro in a Martin Scorsese film titled "Taxi Driver," an obsessive pursuit of actress Jodie Foster, who also appeared in the film, and a desire to make "the greatest love offering in the history of the world" through an act of violence.

During the ensuing 10 years, a series of cases, having aspects in common with Hinckley's, captured the attention of the news media as a problem afflicting a variety of celebrity figures. It was during this time that the term "stalking" gained popular usage in the tabloid press. More commonly employed in studies of the animal kingdom whereby predators track and stealthily pursue quarry or prey, the term stalking was applied to describe what appeared to be a predatory form of pursuit during which a persistent series of intrusive violations were made by an obsessed "fan" to a well known or celebrated person's privacy and/or personal sense of safety and well-being. Many of these cases were determined to involve gross levels of delusional thinking in the form of "erotomania" and other forms of mental illness. However, soon thereafter, the term stalking was applied more generally to also describe a pattern of domestic violence and abuse in which a former intimate or partner made a series of unwanted, harassing, or threatening contacts. These contacts often followed a history of personal boundary violations and controlling tactics during the course of the relationship that later intensified during the process of relationship disengagement. We have now become keenly aware that stalking, in its various forms, is a pattern of behavior that can affect many people, crossing demographic, developmental, and gender lines.

Although there are historical references to stalking dating back to biblical times, scientific study of this pattern is a relatively new focus within the social and forensic sciences. In a recent review paper, Spitzberg and Cupach (in press) conducted a computer-assisted literature search for articles indexed in either PsycInfo or Criminal Justice Abstracts and found that there were only two citations employing the term stalking prior to 1990. After the term had been firmly established in the literature, the investigators located less than 5 empirical studies prior to 1995, and then a surge of over 60 in the 5 years subsequent. Given the fact that stalking is sometimes associated with serious levels of violence, most frequently in the course of estrangement in domestic relations, legal policy making efforts have preceded the development of an extensive empirical data base on the topic. Since 1990, the 50 states in the U.S., the U.S. Federal Government, the United Kingdom, Canada, and Australia have all passed or reinforced existing anti-stalking legislation (Gill & Brockman, 1996; Kong, 1996; Lawson-Cruttenden, 1996; National Institute of Justice, 1993, 1996; U.S. Department of Justice, 1998; Department of Justice, Victoria, 1996; Welch, 1995. These legal changes were necessitated by the inadequacy of previous laws prohibiting actions such as criminal harassment, menacing, trespassing as existing statutes had been oriented toward single actions rather than the core feature of stalking as a *pattern of behavior* over time. Moreover, the fact that stalking can manifest itself through a multitude behaviors, at times subtle and idiosyncratic to the victimized individual, is amply illustrated by the fact that newer laws also incorporate the victim's fear of danger as a criterion along with the more objectively observable criteria of repeated incidents of pursuit, threatening, or harassing behavior.

Given the vast increase in attention that stalking has received in public policy, law enforcement, and social scientific circles, it is important that the paradigm of our understanding be advanced through carefully conducted and well-documented empirical studies. In the present book, I have been honored to collaborate with Irene Hanson Frieze and Keith Davis who have done the "lions share" of the work in pulling this scholarly book together. As a research volume, it is intended to advance the descriptive, phenomenological, and forensic work previously pioneered by noted authors such as Meloy (1998) and Mullen, Pathe, and Purcell (2000). As the work in this book is based, in part, upon peer reviewed papers recently submitted to the scholarly journal, *Violence and Victims,* I am pleased that the journal has provided a forum for the latest research on this obsessive pattern of human aggression and abuse. An attempt has been made to provide a balance of papers that places stalking within a commonly experienced "everyday" and gender sensitive context without compromising an empirical rigor that demands attention to victimization of both men and women.

Clinical researchers will be edified to find that certain psychological correlates of violence such as anger and depression (cf. Davis, Ace, & Andra; Sinclair & Frieze, present volume) reappear in predictive models of stalking related violence as previously documented in studies of domestic violence (Maiuro, 2001; Maiuro, Cahn, Vitaliano et al.,1988; Maiuro, Hager, Lin, & Olsen, in press) and child abuse (Sheppard, 1997). Similarly, Brewster (present volume) reminds us that verbal threats remain a good predictor of other threatening gestures and physical violence within patterns of stalking. Heightened risks for violence and more serious levels of violence are also documented in cases involving intimate relationship break-up as has been previously researched in cross-cultural contexts (Wilson & Daly, 1993) as well as the seemingly ubiquitous exacerbating role of alcohol and drugs (cf. Logan, Leukefeld, & Walker, present volume).

Readers will be equally pleased to find new empirical support for conceptual and theoretical advances related to stalking such as the general concept of "obsessive relational intrusion" (ORI). In this respect, Cupach and Spitzberg (present volume) detail no less than 63 ORI behaviors within both a motivational and dynamic coping response framework and provide a broader framework for viewing stalking than that permitted by criminal and legal codes. Attention is also paid to stalking within important developmental (White, Kowalski, Lyndon, & Valentine, present volume) and dating-related contexts (Sinclair & Frieze, present volume; Langhinrichsen-Rohling, Palarea, Cohen & Rohling, present volume), as we are able to identify risk factors within families of origin and able to distinguish when garden variety, courtship persistence crosses the line into the darker realm of criminal trespassing, pathological obsession, terrorism, and fear. Davis and Frieze's (present volume) summary and discussion of definitional issues and measurement tools in the area should quickly bring the reader up to speed with regard to protocols for assessment of stalking. As Mechanic (present volume) cogently observes in her state-of-the-art overview of current assessment and intervention issues, there is considerable overlap between stalking and domestic battering populations, with the rate of violence among stalkers who have had prior sexually intimate relations with victims exceeding 50% (cf. Meloy, 2001). Thus, it is no coincidence that chapters that investigate and report on some of the more serious forms of stalking related violence in the present volume are based upon domestic violence samples (Mechanic, Weaver, & Resick; Mechanic, Uhlmansiek, Weaver, & Resick; Tjaden, Thoennes, & Allison). The measurement tools and methods described herein should be of great interest to domestic violence specialists as stalking is commonly and conspicuously omitted from currently used inventories of domestic abuse and risk assessment checklists. All of this material should be a worthwhile addition to the libraries of researchers, clinical practitioners, victim advocates, law enforcement workers, forensic specialists, and policy makers in the field of interpersonal violence and victimization.

Roland D. Maiuro, Ph.D.
Editor-in-Chief, *Violence and Victims*
Seattle, Washington

REFERENCES

Department of Justice, Victoria. (1996). *Crimes family violence act: 1994/95 monitoring report.* (Caseflow Analysis Section, Courts and Tribunals Services). Melbourne, Australia.

Gill, R., & Brockman, J. (1996). *A review of section 264 (criminal harassment) of the Criminal Code of Canada.* Working document WD 1996–7e. Research, Statistics and Evaluation Directorate, Department of Justice, Canada.

Kong, R. (1996). Criminal harassment. *Juristat, 16* (12, Statistics Canada: Canadian Centre for Justice Statistics), 1–13.

Lawson-Cruttenden, T. (1996). Is there a law against stalking? *New Law Journal, 6736,* 418–420.

Maiuro, R. D. (2001). Sticks and stones may break my bones, but names will also hurt me: Psychological abuse in domestically violent relationships. In K.D. O'Leary and R.D. Maiuro (Eds.) *Psychological abuse in violent domestic relations* (pp. ix—xx). New York: Springer Publishing.

Maiuro, R. D., Cahn, T. S., Vitaliano, P. P., Wagner, B. C., & Zegree, J. D. (1988). Anger, hostility, and depression in domestically violent versus generally asssaultive men and nonviolent control subjects. *Journal of Consulting and Clinical Psychology, 56,* 17–23.

Maiuro, R. D., Hager, T., Lin, H., & Olsen, N. (in press). Are current state standards for domestically violent men perpetrators treatment adequately informed by research: A question of questions? *Journal of Aggression, Maltreatment, and Trauma.*

Meloy, J. R. (1998). The psychology of stalking. In J. R. Meloy (Ed.), *The psychology of stalking* (pp. 2–23). San Diego, CA: Academic Press.

Meloy, J. R. (2001). Stalking and violence. In J. Boon & L. Sheridan (Eds.), *Stalking and psychosexual obsession.* London: Wiley.

Mullen, P. E., Pathe, M., and Purcell, R. (2000). *Stalkers and their victims,* Cambridge University Press.

National Institute of Justice. (1993). *Project to develop a model anti-stalking code for states.* Washington, DC: U.S. Department of Justice.

National Institute of Justice. (1996). *Domestic violence, stalking, and anti-stalking legislation* (Annual Report to Congress under the Violence Against Women Act, NCJ 160943). Washington, DC: U.S. Department of Justice.

Sheppard, M. (1997). Double jeopardy: the link between child abuse and maternal depression. *Child and Family Social Work, 2,* 91–107.

Spitzberg, B. H., & Cupach, W. R. (in press). What mad pursuit? Obsessive relational intrusion and stalking related phenomena. *Aggression and Violent Behavior: A Review Journal.*

U.S. Department of Justice. (1998). *Stalking and domestic violence* (Third Annual Report to Congress under the Violence Against Women Act; NCJ 172204). Washington DC: Violence Against Women Grants Office, U.S. Department of Justice.

Welch, J. M. (1995, Fall). Stalking and anti-stalking legislation: A guide to the literature of a new legal concept. *Reference Services Review, 23,* 53–58, 68.

Wilson, M. & Daly, M. (1993). Spousal homicide risk and estrangement. *Violence and Victims, 8*(1), 3–16.

1

Perspectives on Stalking Research

Irene Hanson Frieze and Keith Davis

This book examines the crime of stalking from the perspective of the researcher. There has been much attention in the media over the past few years regarding famous people who have been stalked. This may lead one to conclude that stalking is a fairly rare behavior, done by those with severe mental disorders. However, as this book discusses, once we examine stalking behaviors, we find them to be widespread.

Stalking can take many forms. Although legal definitions vary across states, from a legal point of view, stalking is willful, malicious, and consists of repeated following and harassing of another person, with fear of violence on the part of the victim (see the chapter by Tjaden, Thoennes, & Allison). The chapter by Davis and Frieze discusses some of the many other definitions of stalking used by researchers. Using the behaviors associated with stalking rather than a formal legal definition, Davis and Frieze point out that up to 62% of young adults have been victims of stalking-like behaviors after the breakup of intimate relationships. Fisher, Cullen, and Turner (2000) found that 13% of a representative sample of college women had been stalked within the previous seven months. As Tjaden, Thoennes, and Allison demonstrate in their chapter, legal definitions of stalking do not always correspond to these types of victim perceptions. Many feel they are being stalked, even though they would not be so classified under current legal definitions. College students routinely self-report higher levels of stalking than would be expected given the strict legal definition of

Tjaden et al. Sinclair and Frieze raise this same issue of defining stalking in the context of exploring many low-level behaviors engaged in before a relationship ever starts where one person is attracted and the other rejects this person. At what point do following the person, or trying to intimidate him or her into accepting one's advances become "stalking?" Many of the studies in this volume suggest that the examples of stalking seen in the popular media are only some of the most extreme of a wide range of stalking-related behaviors that are quite common and part of everyday life experiences for many people.

A second issue of concern in many of the chapters in this book is who is the stalker. Two chapters report on data showing that attachment and type of love felt by the potential stalker are both predictors of stalking during the breakup of a relationship (see chapters by Davis, Ace, & Andra and by Langhinrichsen-Rohling, Palarea, Cohen & Rohling). Sinclair and Frieze report similar findings for initial relationship stalking. Davis et al. also implicated need for control as an important personal characteristic that was predictive of stalking for both men and women. Other chapters by Brewster and by Logan et al. explore the role of alcohol and drugs in stalking behavior.

It is interesting to note that both sexes can be stalkers or their victims. This finding of both sexes engaging in this type of assaultive behavior is consistent with earlier research on dating violence (e.g., Bookwala, Frieze, Smith & Ryan, 1992; Magdol et al., 1997; Makepeace, 1983). Women are often found to engage in more low-level violence that characterizes most dating relationships that include physical violence than men (see Archer's [2000] meta-analysis). Women may also engage in more violent acts in marriages, although it is clear that the most violent forms of marital violence are much more often done by husbands to wives (e.g., Frieze & Browne, 1989; Straus, Gelles, & Steinmetz, 1981). Johnson (1995) argues that the very severe physical and emotional violence done by men is qualitatively different from the more "common" violence of men and women that occurs in marital relationships. He labels this more severe violence "patriarchal terrorism."

Similar findings of both sexes being perpetrators of stalking can be seen in the initial stages of relationships (e.g., Sinclair & Frieze). However, the dynamics may be somewhat different for women and men as victims and perpetrators (Logan et al.). Whether future research will also find qualitative differences in the milder forms of stalking and the extremely violent forms, analogous to patriarchal terrorism in marriage, is a question we cannot yet answer. It does appear that the most violent forms of stalking occur during the breakups of relationships and are most often done by men who have already been physically violent toward their female partner in other ways (see chapters by Mechanic et al. and by Tjaden & Thoennes). White, Kowalski, Lyndon and Valentine's chapter outlines some of the theory about male violence toward women and shows how stalking can be very similar to these other forms of violence.

As the chapters in this book do point out, stalking is one more form of violence and aggression in close relationships. Since the 1970's, social scientists have begun seriously to address a number of different types of violence in male-female relations. First, researchers became aware of and began to study physical violence in married couples (e.g., Pagelow, 1981; Straus, 1977; Walker, 1979). Soon it became clear that this type of marital violence sometimes included rape, and the idea of marital rape was introduced into the literature (Frieze, 1983; Russell, 1982). While researchers continued to work on marital violence, another group of social scientists were investigating another form of male-female violence—dating violence (e.g., Makepeace, 1983; Marshall & Rose, 1987; Pirog-Good & Stets, 1987).

Various forms of overlap were found in these two bodies of work, and research on marital violence and dating violence is increasingly merging. As work continued on violence in married couples and those living together, researchers came to believe that a pattern of violence was often established before marriage, during the dating period (e.g., Frieze & Browne, 1989; McLaughlin, Leonard, & Senchak, 1992; Ryan, Frieze, & Sinclair, 1999; Sigelman, Berry, & Wiles, 1984). Thus, at least some of the couples displaying violence during courtship are now believed to eventually marry and continue a pattern of violence. Recently, it has been further suggested that psychological abuse is also part of this larger pattern of physical and sexual violence (e.g., O'Leary & Mauiro, 1999).

This book continues the investigation of violence in female relationships, addressing an area in which there has as yet been little social science research—stalkers and their victims. Consistent with the clinical-forensic findings of Mullen, Pathe, and Purcell (2000), the articles in this book suggest that the most common form of stalking tends to occur during the breakup of relationships. But some cases of stalking begin before a true relationship has begun, and many of these instances also appear to involve a sense of rejection from a desired relationship (Mullen, Pathe, & Purcell, 2000; Sinclair & Frieze, 2000). Stalking is shown to occur in response to the breakup of marriages as well as of dating relationships as discussed in chapters by Brewster, Langhinrichsen-Rohling, Palarea, Cohen and Rohling; Logan, Leukefeld, and Walker; and Mechanic, Weaver and Resick. As shown in this book and in a recent study by Meloy, Davis, and Lovette (2001), stalking is most likely to become violent during breakups of intimate relationships. The research of Davis, Ace, & Andra, Logan et al. and Mechanic, Weaver, and Resick indicates that physically and psychological abusiveness during the relationship is predictive of subsequent stalking.

Another concern expressed in the chapters of this book are the reactions of victims of stalking and an analysis of how to best aid them. Cupach and Spitzberg contribute to the analysis of this issue by showing the systematic effects of specific types of intrusive behaviors on judgments of how annoying, threatening, upsetting, and violative. Mechanic addresses these clinical issues directly. We also find that women are much more likely to mention stalking in police reports than men as shown in the chapter by Tjaden and Thoennes. Women also report more stalking when victim fear is part of the definition of stalking as can be seen in Bjerregaard's chapter. The chapter by Cupach and Spitzberg further explores some of the ways in which victims respond to being stalked.

REFERENCES

Archer, J. (2000). Sex differences in aggression between heterosexual partners: A meta-analytic review. *Psychological Bulletin, 126,* 651–680.

Bookwala, J., Frieze, I. H., Smith, C., & Ryan, K. (1993). Predictors of dating violence: A multivariate analysis. *Violence and Victims, 7,* 297–311.

Fisher, B. S., Cullen, F. T., & Turner, M. G. (2000). *The sexual victimization of college women: Results from two national-level studies.* Washington DC: National Institute of Justice. (Document # NCJ 182369).

Frieze, I. H. (1983). Investigating the causes and consequences of marital rape. *Signs, 8,* 532–553.

Frieze, I. H., & Browne, A. (1989). Violence in marriage. In L. Ohlin & M. Tonry (Eds.), *Family violence* (pp. 163–218). Chicago: University of Chicago Press.

Johnson, M. P. (1995). Patriarchal terrorism and common couple violence: Two forms of violence against women. *Journal of Marriage and the Family, 57,* 283–294.

Magdol, L., Moffitt, T. E., Caspi, A., Newman, D. L., Fagan, J., & Silva, P. A. (1997). Gender differences in partner violence in a birth cohort of 21–year-olds: Bridging the gap between clinical and epidemiological approaches. *Journal of Consulting and Clinical Psychology, 65,* 68–78.

Makepeace, J. M. (1983). Life events stress and courtship violence. *Family Relations, 32,* 101–109.

Marshall, L. L. & Rose, P. (1987). Gender, stress and violence in the adult relationships of a sample of college students. *Journal of Social and Personal Relationships, 4,* 299–316.

McLaughlin, I. G., Leonard, K. E., & Senchak, M. (1992). Prevalence and distribution of premarital aggression among couples applying for a marriage license. *Journal of Family Violence, 7,* 309–319.

Meloy, J. R., Davis, B., & Lovette, J. (2001). Risk factors for violence among stalkers. *Journal of Threat Assessment, 1*(1), 3–16.

Mullen, P. E., Pathe, M., & Purcell, R. (2000). *Stalkers and their victims.* New York: Cambridge University Press.

O'Leary, K. D., & Maiuro, R. D. (Eds.). (1999). Psychological abuse in domestically violent relationships. Special issue. *Violence and Victims, 14,* 3–116.

Pagelow, M. D. (1981). *Woman-battering: Victims and their experiences.* Beverly Hills, Sage.

Pirog-Good, M. & Stets,D. (1987). Violence in dating relationships. *Social Psychology Quarterly, 50,* 237–246.

Russell, D. E. H. (1982). *Rape in marriage.* New York: MacMillan.

Ryan, K., Frieze, I. H., & Sinclair, H. C. (1999). Physical violence in dating relationships. In M. A. Paludi (Ed.), *The psychology of sexual victimization: A handbook.* (pp. 33–54). Westport, CT: Greenwood Press.

Sigelman, C. K., Berry, C. J., & Wiles, K. A. (1984). Violence in college students' dating relationships. *Journal of Applied Social Psychology, 5,* 530–548.

Straus, M. A. (1977). Wife beating: How common and why? *Victimology, 2,* 443–459.

Straus, M. A., Gelles, R. J., & Steinmetz, S. K. (1981). *Behind closed doors: Violence in the American family.* Newbury Park, CA: Sage.

Walker, L. E. (1979). *The battered woman.* New York: Harper and Row.

I

Victimization Issues

2

Comparing Stalking Victimization From Legal and Victim Perspectives

Patricia Tjaden, Nancy Thoennes, and Christine J. Allison

Because stalking has only recently been recognized as a serious social problem and criminal justice concern, it is not surprising that there is little consensus among lawmakers about what constitutes stalking. To further understanding of how legal definitions and victim definitions of stalking intersect and diverge, this study compares stalking prevalence, using a definition of stalking that is based on the model anti-stalking code for states developed by the federal government versus a definition of stalking that is victim delineated. Data for the study come from a national telephone survey that queried 8,000 men and 8,000 women about their experiences with stalking victimization, using both direct questions that contained the word "stalking" and behaviorally specific questions. Results show that prevalence estimates increase when respondents are allowed to self-define stalking victimization. However, victim definitions of stalking tend to converge with the model anti-stalking code's definition of stalking in the vast majority of cases. Only 4% of survey respondents defined themselves as stalking victims but failed to meet the legal definition of a stalking victim. A negligible proportion denied being stalked despite the fact they met the legal definition of a stalking victim.

During the past decade, stalking has emerged as a serious social problem and criminal justice concern in the United States. In 1990, California passed the nation's first antistalking law; two years later, 27 other states had enacted similar legislation and by 1995, all states and the District of Columbia had laws proscribing stalking (Hunzeker, 1992). In 1996, a federal law was enacted that prohibited stalkers from traveling across state lines in pursuit of their victims (Violence Against Women Grants Office, 1998).

Despite this flurry of legislative activity, there appears to be little consensus among legislators, policy makers, practitioners, or the public about what exactly constitutes stalking. Legal definitions of stalking vary widely from state to state, and constitutional challenges to state antistalking statutes abound.[1] While most states define stalking as the willful, malicious, and repeated following and harassing of another person, some states include in their definition such activities as lying-in-wait, surveillance, nonconsensual communication, telephone harassment, and vandalism (Hunzeker, 1992). And while most states require that the alleged stalker engage in a course of conduct showing that the crime was not an isolated event, some states specify how many acts (usually two or more) must occur before the conduct can be considered stalking. Finally, while some states require that the stalker make a credible threat of violence against the victim, others require only that the stalker's course of conduct constitute an implied threat (Hunzeker, 1992; National Institute of Justice, 1996).

To assist the states in their efforts to respond to stalking, the federal government developed a model antistalking code for states that is both constitutional and enforceable (National Criminal Justice Association, 1993). Although the model antistalking code has not been universally adopted by the states, it provides a guideline that states can use as they seek to develop constitutionally sound and effective antistalking legislation.

To further understanding of how legal definitions of stalking correspond with victims' definitions of stalking, this study compares the prevalence of stalking using a definition of stalking that is similar to the one used in the model antistalking code for states versus a victim-delineated definition of stalking. Data for the study come from the National Violence Against Women (NVAW) survey, a telephone survey that queried a national sample of 8,000 U.S. women and 8,000 U.S. men about their experiences with various forms of violent victimization, including stalking. In addition to being asked direct questions using the term "stalking," respondents were asked a series of behaviorally specific questions about whether they had ever experienced any number of acts associated with stalking. Findings from the current study suggest that a majority of men and women in the United States define stalking in a manner that is similar to the definition of stalking promulgated in the model antistalking code.

PREVIOUS RESEARCH

This study contributes to a growing body of research on stalking. Shortly after enactment of the first antistalking laws, a series of reviews examining the constitutionality and effectiveness of antistalking laws appeared in prominent legal journals around the country (e.g., Bernstein, 1993; Boychuk, 1994; Gilligan, 1992; Guy, 1993; Harmon, 1994; Lingg, 1993; McAnaney, Curliss, & Abeyta-Price, 1993; Morin, 1993; Strikis, 1993; Walker, 1993). For the most part, these reviews examine the types of antistalking laws passed by individual states and discuss ambiguities and inconsistencies in the laws that might make them unconstitutional or unenforceable. While providing much needed insight into the diversity and shortcomings of antistalking laws, these reviews do little to further understanding of the extent or nature of stalking in America or the ways in which ordinary citizens define stalking victimization.

At the same time that states were passing laws proscribing stalking, a number of psychiatrically oriented studies were conducted that treated stalking as an obsessional or delusional disorder known as erotomania (Harmon, Rosner, & Owens, 1995; Leong, 1994; Segal, 1989; Wright et al., 1995; Zona, Sharma & Lane, 1993). These studies are limited because they are based on small, unrepresentative samples of known stalkers, and because they focus on only the most extreme and pathological stalking cases.

Several case studies provide firsthand descriptions of stalking victimization (Hoffman, 1994; Lardner, 1995; Markman & Labrecque, 1994; Orion, 1997; Skalias & Davis, 1994). Although these case studies provide riveting accounts of individual victim's stalking experiences, they do not address the sociological processes by which stalking is defined.

Some previously published articles outline different typologies of stalking behaviors (e.g., Kienlen, Birmingham, Solberg, O'Regan, & Meloy 1997; Wright et al., 1996) and a few consider the connections between domestic violence and stalking (e.g., Burgess et al., 1997; Coleman, 1997). Earlier writings have also addressed prevention and intervention strategies (Gargan, 1994; Hays, Romans, & Ritchhart, 1995; Lindsey, 1993; Meloy, 1997; Snow, 1998; Williams, Lane, & Zona, 1996; Wolffe, 1995). Previous research which analyzes the victim-offender relationship has found that for a majority of stalking cases, the victim and offender had a relationship prior to the stalking's commencement (Meloy & Gothard, 1995; Tjaden & Thoennes, 1998; Tucker, 1993).

Three previous studies have examined how stalking is defined from the victim's perspective. A study by Sheridan and colleagues (1998) asked 80 women between 18 and 55 years of age in Leicester and Liverpool, England, to indicate which of 40 intrusive behaviors they considered exemplars of stalking, using a self-administered questionnaire. A cluster analysis showed a clear distinction between what study participants felt to be stalking and nonstalking behaviors. Included in the cluster of behaviors that constituted stalking-related acts were following, making threatening or mysterious phone calls, loitering outside a target's home or workplace, furtively taking photographs of the target, constantly watching or spying on the target or staring at the target or her home, sending unwanted notes, letters, or items, constantly telephoning the target's workplace, constant drive-bys, repeated personal approaches, intercepting mail deliveries, loitering in the target's neighborhood, using obscene and/or threatening language, criminal damage/vandalism, threatening suicide, death threats, uninvited visits, moving closer to where the target resides, and visiting places the target frequents. The study also found that about 14% of the sample had been the victim of one or more of the stalking-related behaviors identified by the study.

A second previous study of victims' perspectives on stalking used data collected from a variety of sources—personal interviews with persons who had been followed, observations of petitioners for temporary restraining orders, written accounts of stalking and following from students and acquaintances of the authors, and accounts of stalking published in newspapers, magazines, and books—to analyze the social processes through which victims come to recognize that they are being stalked (Emerson, Ferris, & Gardner, 1998). The study found that many forms of what the authors refer to as "relational stalking" grow out of glitches and discontinuities that are associated with normal, everyday practices for establishing, advancing, and ending relationships.

A third previous study examining stalking from the victim's perspective used a self-administered questionnaire to query 69 male and 93 female undergraduate students about their stalking victimization experiences (Spitzberg, Nicastro, & Cousins, 1998). Respondents were asked to indicate which of 23 obsessive relational intrusion (ORI) behaviors they had experienced. The researchers found that study participants who labeled themselves as stalking victims had higher ORI scores than non-victims and higher levels of angst, fear, and helplessness. The researchers report that 27% of their sample specifically identified themselves as victims of stalking.

A study of stalking victimization conducted by Tjaden and Thoennes (1998), using data from the National Violence Against Women Survey, provides the first ever national data on the extent and nature of stalking in the general population. Using a definition of stalking that is similar to the definition of stalking contained in the model antistalking code for states, Tjaden and Thoennes found that 8% of women and 2% of men in the U.S. have been stalked at some time in their life, while 1% of women and 0.4% of men are stalked annually. The current study builds on and complements this previous study by examining how many survey respondents self-define as stalking victims, and the degree of convergence that exists between prevalence estimates generated using a legal definition of stalking and those generated using a victim-delineated definition of stalking.

STUDY METHODS

Sample Generation and Conduct of the Interviews

The NVAW survey was conducted from November 1995 to May 1996 by interviewers at Schulman, Ronca and Bucuvalas, Inc. (SRBI) using a questionnaire format designed by the first author. The survey consists of telephone interviews with 8,000 U.S. women and 8,000 U.S. men, 18 years of age and older (see Table 2.1 for demographic information on the sample).

The sample was drawn by random-digit dialing (RDD) from households with a telephone in all 50 states and the District of Columbia. The sample was administered by U.S. Census region. Within each region, a simple random sample of working residential "hundreds banks" of phone numbers was drawn. (A hundreds bank is the first 8 digits of any 10-digit telephone number.) A randomly generated 2-digit number was appended to each randomly sampled hundreds bank to

Table 2.1 Demographic Characteristics of Male and Female
Respondents to the National Violence Against Women Survey

Demographic Characteristics	Male Respondents (%)[a]	Female Respondents (%)[a]
Ages	(n = 7,920)	(n = 7,856)
18–24	11.4	9.8
25–29	10.4	9.6
30–39	25.4	24.6
40–49	24.0	22.5
50–59	13.5	14.4
60–69	8.8	9.9
70–79	5.2	6.8
80+	1.5	2.5
Race	(n = 7,759)	(n = 7,850)
White	82.8	82.2
African-American	8.5	9.9
American Indian/Alaska Native	1.4	1.1
Asian/Pacific Islander	2.1	1.7
Mixed Race	5.2	5.1
Hispanic Origin	(n = 7,945)	(n = 7,945)
Hispanic	7.3	7.9
Non-Hispanic	92.7	92.1

[a]Percentages exceed 100 due to rounding.

produce the full 10-digit telephone number. Separate banks of numbers were generated for male and female respondents. SRBI interviewers called these random-digit numbers and screened out non-working
and non-residential numbers. When a residential household was reached,
eligible adults were identified. In households with more than one eligible adult, the adult with the most recent birthday was selected as the
designated respondent. The participation rate was 69% for males and
72% for females.[2]

The interviews were conducted using a computer-assisted telephone
interviewing (CATI) system. Only female interviewers surveyed female
respondents. A split sample approach was used in the male sample
whereby half the respondents were interviewed by men and half by
women. A Spanish-language translation was administered by bilingual
interviewers for Spanish-speaking respondents.

STALKING SCREENING QUESTIONS

During the introductory stage of the interview, respondents were asked whether they had ever been stalked by anyone, and if so, how many different persons had stalked them; whether that person was a spouse, ex-spouse, live-in partner, boyfriend/girlfriend or date, someone else they knew, or a stranger; and what that person did that they considered to be stalking. These questions were designed to generate information about the prevalence and characteristics of stalking from the respondents' perspectives.

Later in the interview, respondents were asked whether they had ever experienced a number of acts associated with stalking. These were: being followed or spied on; being sent unsolicited letters or written correspondence; receiving unsolicited phone calls; having someone stand outside their home, school, or place of work; having someone show up at places they frequented even though that person had no business being there; receiving unwanted items; having someone attempt to communicate with them in other ways against their will; having property vandalized or destroyed. These acts are the most commonly cited behaviors which are defined as stalking in state antistalking statutes (Hunzeker, 1992). Respondents who answered yes to one or more of these items were asked whether anyone had ever done any of these things to them *on more than one occasion.* Respondents who reported being victimized on more than one occasion were subsequently asked a series of questions, including whether they were very, somewhat, a little, or not at all frightened by their assailant's behavior; and whether they thought they or someone close to them would be seriously harmed or killed by their assailant. Information from these behaviorally specific questions was used to classify respondents as stalking victims.

For this study, responses to both the direct questions using the term "stalking" and the behaviorally specific screening questions were analyzed to determine the degree of convergence that exists between victims' perceptions of stalking victimization and a legal definition of stalking. The legal definition of stalking used in the study closely resembles the definition of stalking used in the model antistalking code for states developed by the National Institute of Justice. The study defined stalking as "a course of conduct directed at a specific person that involves repeated visual or physical proximity, nonconsensual communication, or verbal, written or implied threats, or a combination thereof, that would cause a reasonable person fear, with *repeated* meaning on two or more occasions." The model antistalking code does not require stalkers to make a credible threat of violence against victims, but it does require victims to feel a high level of fear ("fear of bodily harm"). Similarly, the legal definition of stalking used in this study does not require stalkers to make a credible threat, but it does require victims to feel a high level of fear. Thus, only respondents who reported *both*—that they had experienced one or more of the behaviors listed on more than one occasion by the same person and that they had been very frightened by their assailant's behavior or thought that they or someone close to them would be seriously harmed or killed as a result of their assailant's behavior—were classified as stalking victims, using a legal definition of stalking.

Measures of association (e.g., lambda) were calculated between nominal level independent and dependent variables, and the chi-square statistic was used to test for statistically significant differences between victims who perceived of themselves as stalking victims and those who did not (*p*-value .05). Any estimates based on fewer than 5 responses were deemed unreliable and therefore were not tested for statistically significant differences between groups and not presented in the tables. Because estimates presented in this article generally exclude "don't know," "refused," and other invalid responses, sample and subsample sizes (*n*'s) sometimes vary from table to table.

DISCUSSION OF FINDINGS

Stalking Prevalence From a Legal and Victim Perspective

Results from the study show that stalking prevalence rates increase dramatically when survey respondents are allowed to self-define stalking victimization. Using a definition of stalking that is similar to the definition of stalking used in the model antistalking code for states, and behaviorally specific questions to screen for stalking victimization, the survey found that 2.2% of surveyed men and 8.1% of surveyed women were stalked at least once in their lifetime. In comparison, the survey found that 6.2% of surveyed men and 12.1% of surveyed women responded affirmatively to the question, "Have you ever been stalked?" (see Table 2.2). Thus, male stalking prevalence rates nearly

Table 2.2 Stalking Prevalence for Men and Women Using Legal and
Victim Definitions of Stalking

| | Persons Stalked in Lifetime (%)[a] | |
	Men	Women
Type of definition	(n = 8,000)	(n = 8,000)
Legal (model antistalking code)	2.2	8.1
Victim (self-identified)	6.2	12.1

[a]Differences between men and women are statistically significant: χ^2, p-value
≤ .001.

tripled and female prevalence rates increased by 50% when respondents were given the opportunity to self-define as stalking victims.

It is important to note that women reported significantly more stalking victimization than men, regardless of the type of definition used. Depending on the definition of stalking used, women are two to four times as likely as men to be stalking victims.

Convergence of Legal and Victim Definitions of Stalking

To determine the degree to which legal and victim definitions of stalking converge, respondents were classified according to whether they fit the legal definition of stalking used in the study (and patterned after the model antistalking code for states) and whether they identified themselves as stalking victims. Four possible categories were included in this classification scheme: *Self and legally defined victims* included respondents who fit the legal definition of stalking used in the study and who also defined themselves as stalking victims. *Self-but-not-legally-defined victims* included respondents who defined themselves as stalking victims, but did not fit the legal definition of stalking.[3] *Nonvictims* included respondents who neither defined themselves as stalking victims nor fit the legal definition of a stalking victim. And *legally-but-not-self-defined victims* included respondents who fit the legal definition of a stalking victim, but did not consider themselves stalking victims.

Using this classification scheme, 1.5% of the men and 6.2% of the women were categorized as *self and legally-defined victims*; while 93.7% of the men and 87.2% of the women were categorized as *nonvictims* (see Table 2.3). Thus, the legal definition of stalking used in the study converged with respondents' definition of stalking in 95.2% of the

Table 2.3 Percentage of Men and Women Who Were Classified as Victims/Nonvictims Using Legal and Victim Definitions of Stalking

Men (*n* = 8,000)	Victim Definition	
Legal Definition	Stalked	Not Stalked
Stalked	Self & Legally-Defined Victim 1.5%	Legally-But-Not-Self-Defined Victim 0.8%
Not Stalked	Self-But-Not-Legally-Defined Victim 4.0%	Nonvictim 93.7%

Percentage of cases with convergence between legal and victim definition: 95.2%

Women (*n* = 8,000)	Victim Definition	
Legal Definition	Stalked	Not Stalked
Stalked	Self & Legally-Defined Victim 6.2%	Legally-But-Not-Self-Defined Victim 2.2%
Not Stalked	Self-But-Not-Legally-Defined Victim 4.4%	Nonvictim 87.2%

Percentage of cases with convergence between legal and victim definition: 93.4%

male cases and 93.4% of the female cases. Obviously, the high degree of convergence found between the legal definition of stalking used in the study and victims' definitions was primarily the result of the large number of respondents who neither thought they had been stalked nor fit the legal definition of a stalking victim.

Conversely, 4% of the men and 4.4% of the women were categorized as *self-but-not-legally-defined victims*, while 0.8% of the men and 2.2% of the women were categorized as *legally-but-not-self-defined victims* (see Table 2.3). Thus, the legal definition of stalking and the victim definition of stalking diverged in 4.8% of male cases and 6.6% of female cases.

Two questions emerge from this analysis: Why did 4% of surveyed men (1 out of 25) and 4.4% of surveyed women (one out of 23) consider themselves stalking victims, but fail to meet the legal requirements of a stalking victim? And why did 0.8% of surveyed men (one out of 125) and 2.2% of surveyed women (one out of 45) fit the legal definition of a stalking victim, but not identify themselves as a stalking victim? The remainder of this article will focus on these two questions.

EXPLAINING THE PHENOMENON OF SELF-DEFINED VICTIMS

As reported above, 4% of men and 4.4% of women in the sample were classified as *self-but-not-legally-defined victims*; that is, they defined themselves as stalking victims, but failed to meet the legal criteria of being a stalking victim. Further analysis showed that over 60% of these respondents did not fit the legal definition of a stalking victim because they failed to meet the fear requirement: Either they did not report feeling very frightened by their assailant's behavior or they did not think they or someone close to them would be seriously harmed or killed (see Table 2.4).

A smaller, but sizable number of *self-but-not-legally-defined victims* (38.3% of male and 36% of the female victims) did not meet the legal definition of a stalking victim because they failed to respond affirmatively to any of the behavioraly specific stalking questions used to screen respondents for stalking victimization. People who said yes to the direct question, "Have you ever been stalked by anyone?" were asked "What did they do that you considered to be stalking?" It is important to note that the answers to this second question were not substantively different from the behaviors listed in the behaviorally specific screening questions. Thus, it is difficult to explain why these self-but-not-legally-defined respondents did not respond affirmatively to the behaviorally specific stalking items. It is possible that some of these respondents were experiencing interview fatigue by the time they were administered the behaviorally specific questions used to screen for stalking victimization and therefore failed to respond affirmatively out of concern they would be asked additional follow-up questions.

Table 2.4 Percentage of Men and Women Who Were Classified as Self-But-Not-Legally-Defined Victims by Reasons They Did Not Fit Legal Definition

Reason	Men (%) ($n = 320$)	Women (%) ($n = 352$)
Did not respond affirmatively to any behaviorally specific screening question	38.3	36.0
Did not report that behaviors happened on more than one occasion	0.0	2.4
Did not meet fear requirement	61.7	61.6

Finally, a very small percentage of the women (2.4%), but none of the men, who were categorized as *self-but-not-legally-defined victims* failed to meet the legal definition of a stalking victim because they did not report that the behaviors they experienced occurred on more than one occasion (see Table 2.4).[4] This finding suggests that a small segment of the population considers being harassed or threatened on only one occasion a form of stalking.

Although the factors mentioned above explain most cases classified as *self-but-not-legally-defined victims*, it is possible there were other reasons for men and women to report they were stalked when they did not meet the legal definition of a stalking victim. Researchers Mohandie, Hatcher, and Raymond (1998) report that some persons who falsely portray themselves as victims of a violent crime have admitted in interviews that the reasons they presented themselves as actual victims have to do with a need for attention and/or a need for a meaningful identity in life. Mohandie and colleagues offer three examples of stalking cases which involved false allegations and which are most likely encountered by law enforcement. In each of these case studies, the false victim exhibited a personality disorder, most notably Borderline Personality Disorder; each had motives for their false allegations including gaining attention, sympathy, and reconciliation; and each had a dysfunctional relationship with their partner that appeared to be related to the false allegations. It is possible that some of the NVAW survey respondents who self-identified as stalking victims, but failed to meet the legal definition of a stalking victim, were motivated by a need for attention, albeit from an anonymous telephone interviewer.

It is also important to note that attitudes of one's friends and family could play an important role in influencing whether or not an individual identifies as a victim of a crime (Bourque, 1989, p. 290). However, the NVAW survey did not query individuals about their families' and friends' attitudes about crime in general or stalking in particular.

EXPLAINING THE PHENOMENON OF LEGALLY DEFINED VICTIMS

As noted above, 0.8% of men and 2.2% of women in the sample were classified as *legally-but-not-self-defined victims*; that is, they fit the legal definition of a stalking victim, but did not identify themselves as stalked. The study found that several characteristics of the victim,

Table 2.5 Percentage of Men and Women Who Met the Legal Definition of a Stalking Victim by Characteristics of the Case and Whether They Self-Identified as Stalking Victims

Characteristic	Victims Who Self-Identified (%)			
	Men	p-value	Women	p-value
Total Who Self-Identified[a]	65.9		73.3	
Victim's age when interviewed				
Less than 65	66.7	___[b]	74.1	.041
65 or older	___[b]		54.5	
Whether victim attended college				
College	69.6	.174	76.0	.061
No college	59.7		69.3	
Victim-perpetrator relationship				
Intimate	81.1	.005	77.6	.004
Non intimate	59.5		67.3	
Sex of perpetrator				
Male	60.7	.043	73.6	___[b]
Female	76.3		83.3	
Perpetrator approached victim				
Approached	69.7	.121	81.1	.000
Did not approach	57.7		57.3	
Perpetrator used an accomplice				
Yes	74.7	.011	84.7	.000
No	56.8		68.8	
Perpetrator threatened victim				
Yes	68.8	.476	83.0	.000
No	63.7		65.0	
Perpetrator violated restraining orderc				
Yes	84.6	___[b]	86.0	.011
No	___[b]		69.2	

[a]Difference between men and women is statistically significant: χ^2, p-value $\leq .052$.

[b]The number of victims is insufficient to reliably calculate estimates and/or the chi-square statistic.

[c]Estimates are based on responses from victims who had restraining orders.

perpetrator, and stalking episode differentiate these victims from those who identified themselves as stalking victims.

Foremost among these is the victim's gender: Men who met the legal definition of a stalking victim were significantly less likely to define themselves as stalking victims than their female counterparts (see Table 2.5). This finding suggests that men who find themselves targets of stalking may be less likely to seek criminal justice intervention. More research is needed to determine why men who report experiencing the same stalking behaviors and levels of fear as women are less inclined to view themselves as victims of stalking.

The study also found that age and college attendance were significant factors for women defining themselves as stalking victims (but not for men). Specifically, women who were less than 65 years old at the time of the interview were significantly more likely to identify themselves as stalking victims than were women 65 years of age and older, regardless of how long ago the stalking occurred, while women with at least some exposure to college were more likely to describe themselves as stalking victims than those with no college exposure (see Table 2.5). These findings support previous research that shows younger, more educated women are more likely to define assaultive behavior as inappropriate and worthy of sanction. For example, Skogan (1981) found that college-educated respondents report disproportionately more crimes than others, particularly in the category of assaultive violence. Sorenson and colleagues (1987) reported a significant three-way interaction between education, sex, and age on sexual assault prevalence, with the highest levels of sexual assault being reported by non-Hispanic White women aged 18 to 39 with some college education compared to White women collapsed across age and education levels. However, as Bourque (1989) points out, while younger, highly educated women are more likely to define assaultive behavior as inappropriate and worthy of sanction, they are not necessarily more likely to report sexual assaults to police or other authorities.

The victim-perpetrator relationship was also a factor in determining whether stalking victims self-identified as victims. Men and women who fit the legal definition of a stalking victim were significantly more likely to define themselves as stalking victims if their stalker was a current or former intimate (i.e., spouse, cohabiting partner, or date), rather than a nonintimate (i.e., acquaintance, stranger, or relative) (see Table 2.5). Thus, it appears that both men and women perceive of stalking as behavior that occurs primarily among persons with an intimate history.

Previously reported findings from the National Violence Against Women survey indicate that this perception is true for female victims, but not male victims. The study found that 59% of female stalking victims, but only 30% of male stalking victims, are stalked by a current or former intimate partner (Tjaden & Thoennes, 1998). It is not surprising, therefore, that women who are stalked by an intimate partner are more likely to self-define as a stalking victim than are women who are stalked by someone else. It is unclear why men who are stalked by an intimate partner are more likely to self-define as a stalking victim because, in fact, men are more likely to be stalked by strangers and acquaintances (Tjaden & Thoennes, 1998).

For men, the current study found that the gender of the perpetrator also seemed to influence whether the behaviors were labeled as stalking. Seventy-eight percent of men called the behavior stalking if the perpetrator was female, while only 56% called it stalking if the perpetrator was male. Thus, men seem to see stalking as something done by the opposite sex.

Because of the way stalking was operationalized, respondents who met the legal definition of a stalking victim experienced somewhat similar events—harassing behaviors, occurring on more than one occasion, causing great fear or a belief that the individual or someone close to him/her would be harmed. However, within this definition there was room for a wide variety of actions by a wide variety of perpetrators. Information from the study suggests that men and women decide whether they were stalking victims after taking into account all the details of the event and deciding whether they meet their definition of "stalking." For both men and women, if the behavior resulted in the perpetrator approaching the victim, it was more likely to be labeled stalking. Similarly, if the perpetrator used another person (i.e., an accomplice), such as a friend or relative, to help follow or harass the victim, the behavior was likely to be called stalking. For women, two other factors also increased the likelihood that the behavior would be perceived as stalking: overt threats and violations of restraining orders. Women who experienced threats were more likely to label the action stalking, as were women who reported the perpetrator violated a restraining order (see Table 2.5).

As with *self-but-not-legally-defined victims*, there are various psychological reasons why *legally-but-not-self-defined victims* might not define their experiences as stalking. For example, *legally-but-not-self-defined victims* might be hesitant to assume the identity of a victim or they may blame themselves for their victimization. Research of a more qualitative nature than the NVAW survey is needed to explore these psychological dynamics of victimization.

CONCLUSIONS

Self-Definitions of Stalking Victimization and Rape Victimization

Some interesting comparisons can be made between this study's findings on self-defintions of stalking victimization and previous research on self-definitions of rape victimization. Research on rape (e.g., Koss, Kinero, & Seibel, 1988) has shown that the closer the relationship between the perpetrator and the victim, the less likely the victim is going to define the sexual assault as rape. Data from the NVAW survey show the opposite is true for stalking: Victims are more likely to label their experience stalking, the closer their relationship is to the perpetrator. Thus, victims tend to perceive rape as a crime primarily perpetrated by strangers, while they perceive stalking as a crime primarily perpetrated by intimates. This finding mirrors an important shift that has occurred in public perceptions of stalking in recent years. Although stalking first came to the public's attention through publicity relating to a series of "celebrity"-stalking cases in which strangers (who were obsessed fans) stalked well-known personalities, since then stalking has come to be defined increasingly as a crime committed by an acquaintance or intimate (Dunn, 1998, pp. 143–144; Emerson, Ferris, & Gardner, 1998; Lowney & Best, 1995).

This study found that older women who met the legal definition of a stalking victim were less likely to label themselves as stalking victims than younger women (who likewise met the legal definition of a stalking victim). Previous research has shown this pattern holds true for rape victims as well. For example, Bergen (1996) found that older women in her sample who met the legal definition of having experienced marital rape were less likely to define themselves as victims of wife rape than younger women (who also met the legal definition of having experienced marital rape). Bergen argues that this was because the terms "marital rape" and "domestic violence" did not exist when the older women's experiences of marital rape began. "Stalking," like "domestic violence" and "wife rape," has only recently been recognized and labeled as a social problem. As with marital rape, women who have not heard much about the phenomenon of "stalking" would probably be less likely to define themselves as a victim of stalking than women who are more familiar with the term.

Koss (1987) has reported that only 27% of college women whose experiences meet the legal definition of rape actually label themselves as rape victims when surveyed. The NVAW study found that 73% of women whose experiences meet the legal definition of stalking victimization self-identified as stalking victims. Thus, it seems it is much easier for women to admit they have been stalked than to admit they have been raped.

POLICY IMPLICATIONS

The results of this study suggest that the vast majority of men and women in the United States define stalking in a manner similar to the definition offered by the model antistalking code for states developed by the National Institute of Justice. This convergence is due primarily to the fact that the majority of individuals surveyed neither considered themselves to have been stalking victims nor to fit the legal definition of stalking used in the study.

The previously mentioned Sheridan and associates (1998) survey of 80 women in England also found a high degree of convergence around women's definitions of what behaviors constitute stalking. Although no one behavior garnered 100% agreement that it constituted stalking, 20 of the 23 behaviors identified in the "stalking cluster" shared agreement among respondents at a rate of 70% or higher, while 11 behaviors shared agreement at a rate above 90%.

Although respondents to the NVAW survey expressed a high degree of agreement about what behaviors constitute stalking, there was a small (about 4%) but important group of respondents who considered themselves stalking victims, but failed to meet the legal (model antistalking code) definition of a stalking victim—a group that was labeled self-but-not-legally-defined victims for purposes of this study. Analyses showed that over 60% of these self-defined victims did not fit the legal definition of a stalking victim because they failed to meet the fear requirement of feeling very frightened or fearing bodily injury or death for themselves or someone close to them. Thus, much of the divergence between legal and victim definitions of stalking stems from the fact that victims may perceive of themselves as stalking victims, even if they are not extremely frightened by the perpetrator's behavior. This finding indicates that antistalking laws could provide relief to a greater number of stalking victims if fear requirements were lowered. Not all stalkers overtly threaten the well-being of their victims or those close to their victims; stalking may not necessarily invoke high degrees of fear in all stalking victims. This research indicates that a sizable number of stalking victims may experience persistent harassing behaviors which cause emotional distress and/or interfere with their daily lives but which do not cause them a high degree of fear. Legislators who wish to provide relief to such victims will need to lower fear requirements in their antistalking statutes.

Of course, lessening the fear requirement in antistalking statutes will increase stalking prevalence rates. This phenomenon was previously demonstrated in a study conducted by Tjaden and Thoennes (1998) who found that lifetime stalking prevalence rates increased from 8% to 12% for women and from 2% to 4% for men when a less stringent definition of stalking is used—one requiring victims to feel only somewhat or a little frightened by their assailant's behavior.

This study also found that 0.8% of men and 2.2% of women fit the legal definition of a stalking victim, but do not identify themselves as a stalking victim—a group that was labeled legally-but-not-self-defined victims in this study. Various attributes of the victim and perpetrator and the event can explain this divergence between victim and legal definitions of stalking among legally defined victims. These characteristics include the victim's gender; education and age (for female victims only); the relationship between the victim and perpetrator; and the gender of the perpetrator (for male victims only). Also, the existence of specific behaviors, such as the stalker repeatedly approaching the victim and the stalker's use of another person in following or harassing the victim, made victims more prone to label themselves as stalking victims. In addition, women, but not men, were more likely to self-define as a stalking victim if they received overt threats and if a restraining order was violated by their stalker.

Although this group, the *legally-but-not-self-defined victims*, is small in number, it is an important group to consider. Because they do not consider themselves stalking victims, this group would seem to be the least likely to seek outside intervention. Research on stalking has shown that stalking behaviors tend to escalate (Emerson et al., 1998) and that there is a high co-occurrence of stalking and violence (Tjaden & Thoennes, 1998). Thus, members of this group may be in serious danger, but do not consider themselves to be. The existence of this group indicates the continued need for public education focusing on what constitutes stalking and publicizing the fact that antistalking laws exist which can provide relief to individuals who are being stalked.

NOTES

1.In Colorado alone, three constitutional challenges to the state's harassment-by-stalking statute were made during 1998–99. To date, the Colorado Supreme Court has upheld the state's constitutionality in one of these challenges. Decisions are pending on the remaining two challenges.

2. The participation rate for the survey was determined by calculating the number of completed interviews, including those that were screened out as ineligible, divided by the total number of completed interviews, screened-out interviews, refusals, and terminated interviews.

3. Self-defined victims answered affirmatively to the question, "Have you ever been stalked?" They did not meet the legal definition of a stalking victim because they did not indicate they had experienced a repeated stalking behavior or behaviors on more than one occasion and/or they did not feel a high level of fear.

4. To meet a legal definition of stalking, according to the model anti-stalking code for the states, there must be a pattern of threatening behaviors. This pattern can be made up of a variety of behaviors and a specific behavior need not occur more than once in this constellation of behaviors.

ACKNOWLEDGMENTS

This research was supported jointly by the Centers for Disease Control and Prevention and the National Institute of Justice under NIJ Grant No. 93IJ-CX0012. The opinions and conclusions expressed in this document are solely those of the authors and do not necessarily reflect the views of the funding agencies.

REFERENCES

Bergen, R. K. (1996). *Wife rape: Understanding the response of survivors and service providers*. Thousand Oaks, CA: Sage.

Bernstein, S. E. (1993). Living under siege: Do stalking laws protect domestic violence victims? *Cardoza Law Review*, 15, 525–529.

Bourque, L. B. (1989). *Defining rape*. Durham and London: Duke University Press.

Boychuk, K. M. (1994). Are stalking laws unconstitutionally vague or overbroad? *Northwestern University Law Review, 88*, 769–802.

Burgess, A. W., Baker, T., Greening, D., Hartman, C. R., Burgess, A. G., Douglas, J. E., & Halloran, R. (1997). Stalking behaviors within domestic violence. *Journal of Family Violence, 12,* 389–403.

Coleman, F. L. (1997). Stalking behavior and the cycle of domestic violence. *Journal of Interpersonal Violence, 12,* 420–432.

Dunn, J. L. (1998). No place to hide: Violent pursuit in public and private. *Perspectives on Social Problems, 9,* 143–168.

Emerson, R. M., Ferris, K. O., & Gardner, C. B. (1998). On being stalked. *Social Problems, 45,* 289–314.

Gargan, J. (1994, February). Stop stalkers before they strike. *Security Management, 38*(2), 31–32.

Gilligan, M. (1992). Stalking the stalker: Developing new laws to thwart those who terrorize others. *Georgia Law Review, 27,* 285–342.

Guy, R. A., Jr. (1993). Nature and constitutionality of stalking laws. *Vanderbilt Law Review, 46,* 991–1029.

Harmon, B. K. (1994). Illinois' newly amended stalking law: Are all the problems solved? *Southern Illinois University Law Journal, 19,* 165–198.

Harmon, R. B., Rosner, R., & Owens, H. (1995). Obsessional harassment and erotomania in a criminal court population. *Journal of Forensic Sciences, 40*(2), 188–196.

Hays, J. R., Romans, J. S. C., & Ritchhart, M. K. (1995). Reducing stalking behaviors for college and university counseling services. *Journal of College Student Psychotherapy, 10,* 57–63.

Hoffman, A. (1994). *Love kills: The stalking of Diane Newton King.* New York: Avon Books.

Hunzeker, D. (1992, October). Stalking laws. *State Legislative Report,* Denver, Colorado National Conference of State Legislatures, 17(19), 1–6.

Kienlen, K. K., Birmingham, D. L., Solberg, K. B., O'Regan, J. T., & Meloy, J. R. (1997). A comparative study of psychotic and nonpsychotic stalking. *Journal of the American Academy of Psychiatric Law, 25,* 317–334.

Koss, M. P. (1987). Hidden rape: Sexual aggression and victimization in a national sample of students in higher education. In A. Burgess (Ed.), *Rape and Sexual Assault II* (pp. 3–25). New York: Garland Publishing, Inc.

Koss, M. P., Kinero, T. E., & Seibel, C. A. (1988). Stranger and acquaintance rape: Are there differences in the victim's experience? *Psychology of Women Quarterly, 12,* 1–24.

Lardner, G., Jr. (1995). *The stalking of Kristin.* New York: Onyx.

Leong, G. B. (1994). De Lerambault syndrome (erotomania) in the criminal justice system: Another look at this recurring problem. *Journal of Forensic Sciences, 39,* 378–385.

Lindsey, M. (1993). *Terror of batterer stalking: A guideline for intervention.* Littleton, CO: Gylantic Publishing Company.

Lingg, R. A. (1993). Stopping stalkers: A critical examination of anti-stalking legislation. *Saint John's Law Review, 67,* 347–381.

Lowney, K. S., & Best, J. (1995). Stalking strangers and lovers: Changing media typifiction of a new crime problem. In J. Best (Ed.), *Images of issues: Typifying contemporary social problems* (2nd ed., pp. 33–57). New York: Aldine de Gruyter.

Markman, R. M. D., & Labrecque, R. (1994). *Obsessed: The stalking of Theresa Saldana.* New York: William Morrow.

McAnaney, K. G., Curliss, L. A., & Abeyta-Price, C. E. (1993). From impudence to crime: Anti-stalking laws. *Notre Dame Law Review, 68,* 819–909.

Meloy, J. R. (1997). The clinical risk management of stalking: "Someone is watching over me . . . " *American Journal of Psychotherapy, 51*(2), 174–184.

Meloy, J. R., & Gothard, S. (1995). Demographic and clinical comparison of obsessional followers and offenders with mental disorders. *American Journal of Psychiatry, 152,* 258–263.

Mohandie, K. Hatcher, C., & Raymond, D. (1998). False victimization syndromes in stalking (pp. 227–256). In J. R. Meloy (Ed.), *The psychology of stalking: Clinical and forensic perspectives.* San Diego, CA: Academic Press.

Morin, K. S. (1993). The phenomenon of stalking: Do existing state statutes provide adequate protection? *San Diego Justice Journal, 1,* 123–162.

National Criminal Justice Association. (1993, October). *Project to develop a model anti-stalking code for states.* Washington, DC: U.S. Department of Justice, National Institute of Justice.

National Institute of Justice. (1996, April). *Domestic violence, stalking, and antistalking legislation: An annual report to congress under the violence against women act* (NCJ 160943). Washington, DC: U.S. Department of Justice.

Orion, D. (1997). *I know you really love me.* New York: MacMillan.

Segal, J. (1989). Erotomania revisited: Kraepelin to DSM-IIIR. *American Journal of Psychiatry, 146,* 1261–1266.

Sheridan, L., Gilett, R., & Davies, G. (1998). *Stalking—Seeing the victim's perspective.* Unpublished manuscript, Department of Psychology, University of Leicester, Leicester, England.

Skalias, L., & Davis, B. (1994). *Stalked: A true story.* Arlington, TX: Summit.

Skogan, W. G. (1981). *Issues in the measurement of victimization* (NCJ-74682). Washington, DC: U.S. Government Printing Office.

Snow, R. L. (1998). *Stopping a stalker: A cop's guide to making the system work for you.* New York: Plenum Press.

Sorenson, S. B., Stein, J. A., Siegel, J. M., Golding, J. M., & Burnam, M. A. (1987). Prevalence of adult sexual assault: The Los Angeles Epidemiologic Catchment Area Study. *American Journal of Epidemiology, 126,* 1154–1164.

Spitzberg, B. H., Nicastro, A. M., & Cousins, A. V. (1998). Exploring the interactional phenomenon of stalking and obsessive relational intrusion. *Communication Reports, 11*(1), 33–47.

Strikis, S. (1993). Stopping stalking. *Georgetown Law Journal, 81,* 2772–2813.

Tjaden, P., & Thoennes, N. (1998). *Stalking in America: Findings from the National Violence Against Women Survey.* Washington, DC: National Institute of Justice and Center for Disease Control and Prevention.

Tucker, J.T. (1993). Stalking the problems with stalking laws: The effectiveness of Florida stalking statutes section 784.048. *Florida Law Review, 45*(4), 609–707.

Violence Against Women Grants Office. (1998). *Stalking and domestic violence. The Third Annual Report to Congress under the Violence Against Women Act.* Washington, DC: U.S. Department of Justice.

Walker, J. M. (1993). Anti-stalking legislation: Does it protect the victim without violating the rights of the accused? *Denver University of Law Review, 71,* 273–302.

Williams, W. L., Lane, J., Zona, M. A. (1996). Stalking: Successful intervention strategies. *The Police Chief, LXIII*(2), 24–26.

Wolffe, B. (1995, May 29). Stalking workplace violence: Threats to employees require prompt and reasonable responses by management. *Legal Times,* p. 32.

Wright, J. A., Burgess, A. G., Burgess, A. W., Laszlo, A. T., McCrary, G. O.,& Douglas, J. E. (1996). A typology of interpersonal stalking. *Journal of Interpersonal Violence, 11,* 487–502.

Wright, J. A., Burgess, A. G., Burgess, A. W., McCrary, G. O., & Douglas, J. E. (1995). Investigating stalking crimes. *Journal of Psychosocial Nursing and Mental Health Services, 33,* 38–43.

Zona, M., Sharma, K., & Lane, J. (1993). A comparative study of erotomanic and obssional subjects in a forensic sample. *Journal of Forensic Sciences, 38,* 894–903.

3

Stalking Victimization: Clinical Implications for Assessment and Intervention

Mindy B. Mechanic

This chapter summarizes and evaluates existing knowledge about stalking that may have clinical implications for conceptualizing, assessing, and responding to stalking-related victimization. It emphasizes the serious implications of stalking and the inextricable links between stalking and other forms of coercion and violence in interpersonal relationships. Stalking has been described in the literature as intense, pursuit-oriented behavior targeted toward an individual, often a love object or former intimate, who experiences such behaviors as intrusive, invasive, and even threatening. Stalking can take a variety of forms. The constellation of behaviors that comprise stalking includes actions referred to by a variety of labels, including "obsessional following" (Meloy, 1996); "obsessive relational intrusion" (Cupach & Spitzberg, 1998); "unwanted pursuit behaviors" (Langhinrichsen-Rohling et al., this volume); and "obsessional harassment" (Harmon, Rosner, & Owne, 1995).

Legal definitions generally require that the victim experience fear in order for the perpetrator's behavior to be defined as "stalking." Requiring that fear occur in response to stalking dovetails with restrictions in the diagnosis of posttraumatic stress disorder (PTSD), a commonly documented consequence of interpersonal violence (Resnick,

Acierno & Kilpatrick, 1997), particularly, intimate partner violence (Golding, 1999). A diagnosis of PTSD requires that the victim experience fear, helplessness or horror in response to an event posing a risk of actual or threatened harm, or threatening the physical integrity of oneself or others (American Psychiatric Association, 1994). However, some studies have defined stalking more broadly to include behaviors that do not necessarily induce fear. Clinically, the lack of reported fear or the absence of threatened violence, may preclude the diagnosis of PTSD in some stalking cases, despite the presence of an array of frequent and disturbing symptoms from the classic PTSD triad: re-experiencing, avoidance, and hyperarousal. This issue will be taken up in greater detail later on in this chapter.

Methodological problems in the existing stalking literature limit the nature and extent of conclusions that can be drawn about stalking impact. These issues are: (1) wide variations in how "stalking" is defined; (2) the multiplicity of populations studied; (3) the anecdotal and descriptive assessment of victims' reactions; and (4) the failure to use standardized methods to assess psychological and behavioral functioning. Nevertheless, several clear-cut themes emerge from the literature—and these will be the focus of this chapter.

Recent research on stalking (this volume) supports the thesis that at least one subtype of stalking can be functionally described as a pattern of coercive control transacted in the context of existing or dissolving romantic or intimate relationships. This type of stalking is most often committed by estranged and former instead of current partners, and frequently co-exists with other dimensions of relationship abuse. Perceived loss and threatened or actual separation are strongly linked to both increased stalking and to greater risk of violence, including lethal violence.

ACTUAL AND THREATENED VIOLENCE

It is impossible to explore the scope and intensity of victim reactions apart from understanding the context of assaultive violence within which some forms of stalking take place. Without question, acts of violence against persons and property may result in physical injury and damage to possessions, yet such acts are also powerful determinants of emotional and psychological responses to trauma. For example, perceived life threat and injury, singly and in combination, substantially increase the risk of PTSD following a physical assault (Resnick et al., 1993). Moreover, both stalking and separation have been linked to elevated risk of homicide among women with histories of intimate partner victimization (e.g., Block, 2000; McFarlane et al., 1999). Thus, a brief review of violence risk associated with stalking is presented here.

While one might have the impression that stalking is a disturbing, but generally non-violent offense (e.g., Zona et al., 1993, 2.3% rate of violence), accumulating evidence derived from multivariate statistical models and more refined stalker typologies underscores the serious physical dangers posed by intimate partner stalkers, especially former and estranged partners (e.g., Meloy, 2001; Meloy et al., 2001; Mullen et al., 2000; Palarea et al., 1999). Meloy (2001) observed that former intimate partners are responsible for a disproportionate amount of stalking violence, estimated at approximately 50%. The highest rate of violence (59%) was found among the "rejected" stalkers in Mullen et al.'s (2000) five-group typology, leading to their conclusion that: "Stalkers who are strangers and overtly mentally ill produce the most fear in victims, but those who assault are most likely to be rejected ex-partners" (p. 1248).

Palarea et al. (1999) used path analysis to study the relationship among threats, violence, and prior intimacy between the stalker and the victim in a sample drawn from the records of the Los Angeles Police Department Threat Management Unit (LAPD-TMU). Compared to non-intimate stalkers, intimate stalkers were more dangerous to their victims and their property and were more likely to back up their threats to commit harm by engaging in acts of violence. Surprisingly, criminal, psychiatric, or domestic violence histories were unrelated to violence committed against persons or property, although methodological problems may explain this finding.

Meloy et al. (in press) studied a small sample ($n=59$) of "obsessional followers" charged with a stalking-related offense. Six categories of risk were studied in a multivariate predictive model to determine their contribution to stalking violence: (1) prior sexual intimacy with victim; (2) major mental disorder; (3) explicit threat toward the victim; (4) personality disorder; (5) chemical abuse/dependency; and (6) prior criminal history. Although prior sexual intimacy, absence of a major mental disorder, and explicit threats were all associated with risk of violence to persons or property in bivariate analyses, only prior sexual intimacy was retained in a multivariate analysis. Prior sexual intimacy increased the odds of violence committed by a stalking offender by a factor of 112. However, Meloy et al. (2001) note that due to skewness in the sampling distribution of odds ratios with small samples, a confidence interval must be computed. Using a 95% confidence interval the lower limit was calculated to be an 11–fold increase in violence associated with prior sexual intimacy between the victim and offenders.

In a randomly selected large sample of college students, Bjerregaard (this volume) found that nearly one-quarter of female stalking victims were physically harmed by their stalkers; threats to harm were strongly associated with the commission of violence. Unfortunately, these data were not disaggregated by the victim-offender relationship, although 42% of the females in her sample reported being stalked by an ex-spouse or ex-boyfriend. In one study of college students that collected data on three separate samples, 25%–37% of participants reported obsessive relational intrusion (ORI) that took the form of a physical assault, and 19%–30% reported ORI-property damage (Cupach & Spitzberg, this volume). Westrup et al. (1999) compared harassed with stalked female college students and found the following rates of physical assaults: 12% and 36%, respectively, and property damage: 12% and 31%, respectively. Unfortunately, the nature of the victim-offender relationship was not examined with respect to the violence variables.

In a sample of self-identified stalking victims, Hall (2000) reported that 43% suffered property damage, 38% and 28%, respectively, were physically and sexually assaulted. Brewster (chapter 4) studied a convenience sample of female former stalking victims to assess the relationship between verbal threats and physical violence. Nearly half of her sample disclosed physical violence, with two-thirds of those reporting one or two episodes of violence. High rates of assaultive violence were associated with stalking among the battered women studied by Mechanic et al. (this volume).

Among women randomly identified as battered with universal screening in medical settings, intimate partner stalking (particularly, "being followed") and morbid jealousy were associated with severe incidents of violence measured both retrospectively and prospectively. Findings remained constant after controlling for other risk and protective factors (Block, 2000). Women who asked their partners to leave were at particularly high risk of severe violence in three types of situations: (1) when their partners refused to leave; (2) when their partners threatened to kill them if they left; and (3) if the woman had already left and refused to return.

These studies highlight the sobering reality that stalking-related violence against persons and property is not uncommon and is amplified in the context of separating or estranged intimate partners when the risk of lethality escalates. Elevated risk of stalking violence has been documented in samples of battered women, help-seeking stalking victims, college students, and clinical samples of perpetrators, thus providing convergent validation for conclusions. The implications of these findings were summed up succinctly by Meloy (2001): "Risk management of prior sexually intimate stalking cases *should assume that an act of interpersonal violence toward the object of pursuit will occur* at some point in the stalking crime" (p. 23, italics added for emphasis). Stalking in concert with other forms of abuse committed by a former intimate partner is a risk factor for severe violence and lethal harm— an issue that should be considered by professionals working with abused women in medical, mental health, social service and criminal justice settings.

PHYSICAL HEALTH IMPACT OF STALKING VICTIMIZATION

Research addressing the physical health impact of stalking victimization can be divided into two categories: (1) somatic health complaints, and (2) acute physical injuries.

Physical Health/Somatic Complaints

A host of chronic somatic and physical health complaints and disproportionate utilization of primary health care services has been documented in response to all forms of violence against women, most notably sexual assault and rape, sexual abuse, and intimate partner violence (Follingstad et al., 1991; Golding, 1996; Kimerling & Calhoun, 1994; Koss, Koss & Woodruff, 1991; Lesserman et al., 1997, 1998; Resnick, Acierno & Kilpatrick, 1997; Walker et al., 1999). Diminished physical health functioning, poor health care behaviors, and increased use of hazardous tension reduction behaviors has been unequivocally demonstrated as a consequence of interpersonal victimization in many studies. However, data on the physical health status of stalking victims are virtually non-existent.

Generalized somatic complaints were reported in one study of stalking victims (Mullen et al., 2000; Pathe & Mullen, 1997). Stalking victims reported worsening of pre-existing physical conditions and the development of new somatic complaints. Victims acknowledged general deterioration in their physical health as a result of stalking. Specific types of somatic complaints were also assessed. Digestive disturbances were reported by 23%–30% of the sample; 47% complained of headaches; 45%–48% reported appetite and weight fluctuations; and 55% complained of excessive tiredness or weakness. Increased use of self-medicating/tension-reduction behaviors, such as cigarette smoking and alcohol use, were also reported by nearly one-quarter of the sample. Increased tobacco and alcohol use have been documented in other samples of victimized women, and are hypothesized to represent an indirect link between interpersonal victimization and the reduced physical health functioning observed among victimized populations (Resnick, Acierno & Kilpatrick, 1997).

Westrup et al. (1999) used the SCL-90 somatization subscale and found no differences between stalked, harassed, and control subjects in a student sample. It is possible that somatic symptoms are more apt to develop among cases with chronic exposure to stalking and other forms of interpersonal victimization, thus making it difficult to identify them in a less severe, college student sample. Unfortunately no other study of stalking victimization measured somatic and physical health complaints or medical service utilization rates.

In lieu of data directly addressing the physical health consequences of stalking, pertinent findings from the literature on other forms of violent interpersonal victimization can be offered. Golding (1996) assessed the role of sexual assault history on physical health functioning in two general population surveys (n=6,024). Greater functional impairment, including more days spent in bed and greater activity restriction, was associated with assaults committed by spouses, physically threatening assaults, and repeated assaults—all risk factors associated with chronic forms of relationship abuse. Sutherland, Bybee, and Sullivan (1998) conducted a prospective study of battered women, with assessments at three time points (immediately post-shelter, 8.5-month and 14.5-month follow-up). Results indicated that increased physical health complaints were associated with higher rates of intimate partner abuse. Moreover, the deleterious effects of abuse on women's health persisted over time, despite significant decreases in abuse levels after shelter exit. Interestingly, these investigators found that the relationship between intimate partner abuse and negative physical health was mediated by symptoms of anxiety and depression.

While the relationship between trauma and negative physical health outcomes is a complicated one, various explanatory mechanisms have been hypothesized (Lesserman et al., 1998; Resnick, Acierno & Kilpatrick, 1997). Although a lengthy discussion of this issue is beyond the scope of this chapter, brief mention of some postulated mechanisms is worthy of note. Hypothesized mechanisms include: (1) the chronic effects of stress on immune functioning, particularly the role of physiological hyperarousal; (2) increased symptoms of anxiety, depression, and posttraumatic stress; (3) chronic assault related to physical injury; (4) decreased deployment of positive health care behaviors; and (5) increased use of potentially detrimental tension reduction behaviors, such as smoking and substance abuse. Resnick, Acierno and Kilpatrick (1997) present a theoretical model specifying causal pathways and mediated relationships between violent assault and negative health outcomes.

Clearly, future research could benefit from more thorough documentation of the contribution stalking makes to diminished physical health functioning. Primary health care practitioners are in a unique position to assess and intervene with undisclosed victims of interpersonal violence through universal screening procedures followed-up with more detailed assessment and intervention as indicated (Carlson & McNutt, 1998; Cascardi, Langhinrichsen, & Vivian, 1992; Dutton, Haywood, & El-Bayoumi, 1997; Kilpatrick, Resnick, & Acierno, 1997). Because victims of violence are more apt to use (or overuse) primary health care settings instead of emergency care settings, specialized medical services, or mental health services (e.g., Walker et al., 1999), these settings are ready to offer needed attention to undisclosed victims of stalking-related violence, many of whom may continue to remain at risk for further abuse/violence. Despite the call for more attention to violence against women directed toward medical practitioners, lack of institutional support, lack of professional role socialization, and inadequate education/training have been cited as barriers to effective implementation (Carlson & McNutt, 1998; Kilpatrick et al., 1997; Resnick, Acierno, & Kilpatrick, 1997; Sugg & Innui, 1992).

Injury

Rates of injury stemming from stalking are difficult to document accurately, apart from epidemiological surveys because help-seeking samples of victims are likely to overrepresent severe victims with higher rates of physical injury. The NVAWS did not assess stalking-related physical injuries because their definition of stalking precluded measuring indices of physical harm (Tjaden & Thoennes, 2000). One statewide study of stalking among female residents of Louisiana documented a 32% injury rate among women reporting lifetime stalking victimization and who perceived their stalking to be somewhat dangerous or life threatening (CDC, 2000).[1] These injuries, resulting from assaults committed by the stalker included: swelling, cuts, scratches, bruises, strains/sprains, burns, bites, broken teeth, and knife or gunshot wounds; however, rates of each type of injury were not provided. Injury rates were *four times higher* among women stalked by current or former intimate partners than among other types of stalkers. Interestingly, there were no reported injuries among women who were stalked by strangers, even when the group was restricted to those who perceived danger or a life threat from their stalkers.

A surprisingly high rate of injuries was documented in one study of former stalking victims; 81% of assaulted stalking victims disclosed physical injuries (Brewster, this volume). No details regarding the types of injury were reported. Similarly, both Bjerregaard (chapter 5) and Hall (2000) cited physical harm as an outcome of stalking in their samples, though neither specified the nature or extent of physical injuries sustained as a result of stalking violence. Mechanic, Weaver, & Resick (this volume) reported relatively high rates of injury in their sample of battered and stalked women, with higher rates of injury, including those resulting in loss of consciousness among women with more extensive stalking histories.

Several well-conducted studies of violence-related acute injuries among women presenting to hospital emergency departments and clinics have been published. Although none of these studies reports data specifically addressing stalking-related injuries, data on risk factors for injuries associated with domestic assaults and medical screening of female patients for domestic violence exposure are nonetheless pertinent. As will be seen, the risk factors associated with injury parallel those identified for stalking-related violence (Meloy, 2001).

Abbott et al. (1995) studied a large sample (N=833) of randomly selected women presenting to one of five hospital emergency departments or walk-in clinics. More than half of the women reported having been "assaulted, threatened, or made to feel afraid by partners" during their lifetimes, although only 12% (of those with current male partners) sought care for acute domestic-violence-related illness or injury during that medical visit. Of those women with acute domestic violence, a surprising 23% sought care for an injury, whereas the remainder presented with more general somatic complaints related to the domestic violence in their lives.

Kyriacou et al. (1999) compared 256 intentionally injured women (by male partners) with 659 control participants recruited from emergency departments at eight large university-based teaching hospitals. Collectively, 434 contusions and abrasions, 89 lacerations, and 41 fractures and dislocations were documented among the women intentionally injured by their male partners. In multivariate analyses, the following risk factors were associated with increased risk of injury from intimate partner violence: 1) partner alcohol use; (2) partner drug use; (3) intermittent or unemployment of partner; (4) partner with less than a high school education; and (5) former/estranged partners. Violence by a former partner was associated with a 3.5-fold increase in injury risk, and this risk increased to 8.9 when the woman was living with her former partner. Increased risk of injury associated with partner violence was associated with partner drug use and history of previous arrests, as well as victim isolation and lack of financial and other resources in another hospital-based study of violence-exposed women (Grisso et al., 1999).

Meloy (in press) offered the following set of empirically identified risk factors associated with stalking violence: (1) prior criminal history; (2) drug use/dependence; (3) prior intimate relationship with the victim—and to a lesser extent; (4) lack of psychosis; and (5) the presence of threats. Striking similarities appear in the list of risk factors offered by Meloy based on research with stalking perpetrators and those identified by Kyriacou et al. (1999) and Grisso et al. (1999) in their studies of treatment-seeking women assaulted by their male intimate partners. Again, the symmetry in these findings obtained from two very different types of research contexts is a powerful indicator of convergent validity that underscores the nexus between stalking and other forms of intimate partner violence.

PSYCHOLOGICAL/MENTAL HEALTH IMPACT OF STALKING VICTIMIZATION

The regrettable lack of research documenting the psychological consequences of stalking victimization has been noted by others (e.g., Lewis et al., 2001; Westrup et al., 1999). Most published studies measure victim impact descriptively, without the use of standardized scales, although the findings from these studies support the conclusion that stalking has a deleterious impact on emotional and behavioral functioning, with serious decrements in the quality of life. Only three studies used standardized scales to measure symptomatology associated with stalking victimization (Brewster, this volume; Mechanic, Uhlmansiek et al., this volume; Westrup et al., 1999). These studies document a broad spectrum of emotional reactions, ranging from fear and distress and schema disruptions at the lower level—to full-fledged clinical syndromes, and participation in other life-threatening behaviors, such as alcohol abuse, drug abuse, and suicidality.

Schema disruptions or "shattered assumptions" are hallmark residues of traumatic events and have been observed among victims of various forms of interpersonal victimization, including sexual assault, sexual abuse, and domestic violence (Dutton et al., 1994; Janoff-Bulman, 1992; Mechanic & Resick, under review). Traumatic events challenge core beliefs about the meaning and predictability of the world and the trustworthiness of oneself and others—at times resulting in attempts to restore schematic structures by disavowing the traumatic event or by holding oneself accountable for the victimization, i.e., self-blame (Janoff-Bulman, 1992; Mechanic & Resick, under review). Schema disruptions centering upon themes of safety, trust, control/power and esteem have been documented among survivors of interpersonal trauma (Dutton et al., 1994; Mechanic & Resick, under review). Cognitive schemas play an important role in information processing because they function as filters for organizing information and integrating a traumatic experience into existing cognitive structures. When a traumatic event and a schematic structure are in conflict, the result can be failed information processing, resulting in traumatic stress symptoms (Resick, 1993). Moreover, disruptions in schemas about trust and safety can result in massive curtailment of life activities, including interpersonal relationships, due to fear that others are likely to cause harm or betrayal. Treatment with survivors of trauma often involves working with disruptions in cognitive schemas to integrate the traumatic experience with world views and restore functional capacities (McCann & Pearlman, 1990; Resick & Schnicke, 1993). While schema disruptions are likely to result from stalking, there is a paucity of research on the topic.

The types of serious emotional problems that might result from stalking parallel those documented in the interpersonal trauma literature, more generally (e.g., Golding, 1999; Resnick, et al., 1997). They are depression, suicidality, PTSD, and substance abuse. Of these trauma-related disorders, PTSD has received the most attention. A number of large-scale population studies have been conducted to ascertain the relative risk of developing PTSD in response to a variety of traumatic stressors. (e.g., Breslau et al., 1999; Kessler et al., 1995). Unfortunately, none of these studies queried participants about stalking as a traumatic event that might have resulted in PTSD. The NVAWS, which did assess population base rates of stalking, did not assess the presence of mental health and psychological problems attributable to stalking violence. Thus, base rates of PTSD and other disorders resulting from stalking are not part of the extant literature. Research from the more developed traumatic stress and violence literature is presented.

Fear

Fear is perhaps the most frequently reported emotional response to stalking. Overall, women stalking victims report significantly greater levels of fear compared to men (see White et al., this volume for a review of this topic). Hall's (2000) data suggest that stalking victims are plagued by a great deal of fear (52%), increased cautiousness (88%), and paranoia (41%). High levels of fear and consequent alterations in lifestyle were described by the stalking victims in several studies (e.g., Pathe et al., 1997). Stalking predicted fear of future harm or death among battered women stalked by their abusive partners (Mechanic, Weaver, & Resick, this volume). Fear of personal safety leads some stalking victims (11%–17%) to purchase guns (CDC, 2000; Tjaden & Thoennes, 1998). While purchasing a gun might provide an illusion of safety, the presence of guns raises the risk of exposure to additional violence and injuries, particularly in the context of intimate partner violence (Abbott et al., 1995). These findings suggest the importance of working with stalking victims to help manage their levels of fear and elevated safety concerns. Perhaps the use of risk assessment tools might help in working with a victim to appraise her risks of being harmed, and provide information that may assist in making choices about what risk management options to pursue. Successful prediction of re-abuse was documented in one study of battered women using the criminal justice system (Goodman et al., 2000).

General Distress

Significant levels of general distress have been reported in several studies of stalking victims, with greater distress associated with more severe stalking (Westrup et al., 1999). Spitzberg and Rhea (1999), also studying college students, examined the contributions of sexual coercion and ORI to general distress levels and sense of loss. Sexual coercion explained a greater proportion of variance than ORI symptoms in explaining general distress (38%), although ORI did account for unique variance (9%). ORI accounted for 8% of unique variance in the prediction of "sense of loss" after controlling for the effects of sexual coercion which explained 11% of the variance. It is not surprising that sexual coercion was a more potent determinant of distress and loss given the extremely high rates of distress and disorder associated with sexual trauma (e.g., Kilpatrick, Edmunds, & Seymour, 1992; Resnick et al., 1993). More than half of the female stalking victims identified in one statewide study reported chronic stress (1 month or longer) that significantly interfered with activities. Like fear, high levels of distress might be responsive to risk assessment procedures and problem solving, in addition to traditional stress management approaches to treating anxiety symptoms.

Psychological Symptomatology

PTSD consists of intrusive, avoidant and hyperarousal symptoms. Individual symptoms of PTSD, particularly hypervigilance, were extremely common among the stalking victims interviewed by Pathe and colleagues (1997). Chronic sleep disturbance, exaggerated startle response, jumpiness, recurring nightmares, intrusive recollections and flashbacks were acknowledged by more than half of the sample. Although formal structured diagnostic interview methods were not used to to diagnose PTSD, 37% of the sample met clinical criteria for PTSD, and another 18% met symptom criteria but failed to qualify for a diagnosis due to the absence of threatened or actual physical harm required by criterion A of the diagnosis. Diagnoses of full and partial PTSD were associated with the presence of violence, a former intimate relationship with the stalker, and "being followed."

PTSD symptomatology was assessed with the Posttraumatic Stress Diagnostic Scale (PDS: Foa et al., 1997) in two studies with very different populations—one comprising harassed and stalked college students (Westrup et al. 1999) and the other infrequently and relentlessly stalked battered women (Mechanic, Uhlmansiek et al., this volume). Westrup et al. (1999) reported significantly higher PTSD scores among stalked women ($M=16.84$; $SD=14.17$) compared to harassed women ($M=7.00$; $SD=6.63$) and control subjects ($M=5.79$; $SD=8.47$). Among the battered women, those reporting relentless stalking ($M=49.6$; $SD=10.4$) reported more severe PTSD than those who experienced less frequent stalking ($M=44.0$; $SD=9.3$). The less severely stalked battered women reported PTSD symptoms that were 2.6 times higher than the stalked college women, and 6.3 times higher than the harassed college students. Similarly, the relentlessly stalked battered women had PTSD scores that were nearly three times higher than those of stalked college women and about seven times higher than the college harassed women. These differences suggest the obvious—more severe stalking and associated violence results in greater psychological symptomatology. These comparisons also caution us about generalizing from findings on symptom indices obtained on college populations to clinical populations of stalking victims. Nonetheless, even at the lower levels of stalking, female victims report clinically significant symptoms of traumatic stress reactions.

To understand more about the factors influencing the development of PTSD among trauma-exposed individuals, there has been increasing attention to the empirical identification of PTSD risk factors. Increased risk for developing PTSD in response to trauma is associated with the following factors: (1) interpersonal victimization (Acierno, Kilpatrick & Resnick, 1999; Kessler et al., 1995; Norris, 1992); (2) exposure to prior traumatic events (Nishith, Mechanic & Resick, 2000; Norris & Kaniasty, 1994); (3) presence of injury, perceptions of life threat, or both (Resnick et al., 1993); (4) repeat victimization (Norris & Kaniasty, 1994); and (5) female gender (Breslau et al., 1999; Kessler et al., 1995; Stein et al., 1997). Moreover, physical and sexual assaults are among the events with greatest risk of PTSD (Kessler et al., 1995; Resnick et al., 1993). Given the symmetry between the risk factors associated with PTSD and many of the characteristics associated with stalking victimization (e.g., female victims, repeat victimization, often with concomitant abuse, physical threat, and injury), it is reasonable to hypothesize that stalking victimization poses a considerable risk for developing PTSD.

The applicability of current traumatic stress frameworks for conceptualizing, assessing, and responding to stalking victimization can be criticized in at least two ways. First, as previously indicated, because stalking does not always present an actual or perceived threat to the physical integrity of oneself or others, stalking victims may be precluded from a PTSD diagnosis. Recall that 18% of the victims in one study (Pathe et al., 1997) met symptom criteria for PTSD but did not qualify for a diagnosis due to the lack of perceived threat to physical integrity as required by Criterion A of the PTSD construct. Functional impairment and significant clinical distress has been documented to occur in response to subsyndromal forms of PTSD in community studies (Stein et al., 1997) and with stalking victims (Pathe et al., 1997). Second, and perhaps more problematic, is that the PTSD construct presumes that a traumatic event *occurred in the past* and no longer poses a threat, yet individuals respond to their environment as though the traumatic event remains a present danger. Hypervigilence and increased arousal are biologically based survival responses believed to be adaptive for surviving a dangerous situation, yet are considered maladaptive in the absence of actual threat and danger. Hence, the presence of these experiences after cessation of a traumatic event is a defining feature of PTSD, a traumatic stress "disorder."

The PTSD construct is a framework consistent with traumatic stressors that are circumscribed, such as a sexual assault, an accident, or even combat. Yet, in the context of stalking (and domestic violence) it can be argued that threatened harm has not ceased, that it hovers on the horizon causing ongoing fear and threat based on the potential for violation and violence at almost any time. Consequently, hyperarousal responses can be viewed as potentially realistic (arousal) responses to the appraisal of continuing danger instead of hyper-arousal responses to a no longer threatening event. Thus, it may be more appropriate to consider traumatic stress reactions that occur in response to unremitting forms of stalking as 'peritraumatic' rather than 'posttraumatic,' an issue that can also be raised with respect to intimate partner violence. These issues are clearly complex and merit more thorough theoretical, empirical, and clinical examination. By reconceptualizing traumatic stress reactions to ongoing serial events such as stalking and intimate partner violence, it is possible that more useful intervention strategies will be developed.

Clinically significant levels of depression are likely to be common in response to stalking victimization. Again, there is a paucity of research documenting depression among stalking victims. Suicidal thoughts or behaviors, a serious symptom of depression, were reported by nearly one-quarter of the stalking victims in one study (Pathe et al., 1997). Stalked college students reported higher levels of depression than harassed and control subjects, who did not differ from each other in their reported levels of depression (Westrup et al., 1999). The battered women studied by Mechanic and her collegaues (Mechanic, Uhlmansiek, et al., this volume) manifested levels of depression in the severe range, with more severe symptoms of depression associated with more extensive histories of stalking. Thus, while few studies of stalking have systematically assessed depression, those that have, document clinically significant levels of depression, and to a lesser extent suicidality in response to a stalking that takes place at greater and lesser levels of severity.

FUNCTIONAL IMPACT /LIFESTYLE DISRUPTION

Stalking victimization also leads to extensive restriction of activities and curtailment in lifestyle. Lifestyle changes have been assessed with greater frequency than physical or mental health outcomes in studies of stalking victims. Changes in telephone number, residence, workplace, school, or career, or daily routine are among the most oft-cited behavioral changes made by stalking victims (Bjerregaard, this volume; CDC, 2000; Fremouw et al., 1997; Hall, 2000; Pathe et al., 1997; Tjaden & Thoennes, 1998). Disruptions in occupational functioning and behavior have also been reported. More than one fourth of stalking victims surveyed in the NVAWS reported lost time from work as a result of the stalking victimizaton. It is unclear from these and other data, whether the negative impact of stalking on occupational and social functioning is a direct consequence of stalker interference in those settings, fear that the stalker might approach the victim in one of these contexts, or whether the emotional distress associated with stalking lead to decrements in levels of functioning. Future research might profit from a more systematic assessment of these competing hypotheses.

Coping and Strategic Responding

A number of studies have assessed the use of personal, informal, and formal strategies in response to stalking victimization. One consistent trend observed across studies is that exposure to greater number, type, and frequency of stalking and harassing behaviors is associated with increased coping and more extensive help-seeking efforts (Bjerregaard, this volume; Cupach & Spitzberg, this volume; Hauggard & Seri, 2000; Mechanic, Uhlmansiek, et al., this volume; Spitzberg, Nicastro, & Cousins, 1998). The same pattern has been observed among battered women (Gondolf & Fischer, 1988).

Although most studies of stalking did not measure emotional or symptomatic reactions to stalking, several report mental health service utilization, which might also be considered as a proxy variable for distress. The NVAWS (Tjaden & Thoennes, 1998) reported that approximately one-third of the stalked women and one-fifth of the stalked men reported seeking psychological counseling as a consequence of the stalking victimization. Bjerregaard (this volume) found that 9% of stalked female and 3.4% of stalked male college students sought mental health counseling for problems associated with stalking. A somewhat higher percentage of the stalking targets in the Haugaard and Seri (2000) study of college students sought assistance from mental health counselors (16% of women; 12% of men). Seeking counseling was associated with more intrusive contact; fear for personal safety; a history of previous sexual assault; and a history of childhood sexual abuse (Haugaard & Seri, 2000). Unfortunately, only 40% of those who sought counseling rated the services they received as helpful. In at least one case, minimization of the stalking experience was cited as the reason for dissatisfaction with counseling services.

Several studies report that victims sought assistance from the police or the criminal justice system in responding to the stalking, although not always with success. More than half of the females and nearly half of the male targets of stalking identified in the NVAWS reported the stalking to the police (Tjaden & Thoennes, 1998). Arrest, detainment, or prosecution of the perpetrator was reported in less than one-quarter of the cases, although police reports were filed in slightly more than 2/3 of the cases. Gender differences in police behavior were observed, with a greater likelihood of arrest, and referral for services when the stalking victim was female. Satisfaction with police response was estimated at 50% approval rate, with increased satisfaction associated with arrest of the stalker. Hauguaard & Seri (2000) found that 9% of the female targets of intrusion, and none of the males, contacted the police for assistance. Fear for physical safety, prior childhood and adolescent sexual abuse, and more extensive, more frequent intrusive contact significantly increased likelihood that a police report would be filed. Satisfaction with police intervention was reported by 57% of those who contacted the police—lack of responsiveness was cited as a reason for lack of satisfaction in two cases. Female stalking targets were significantly more likely to contact the police (35% vs. 10%) in another college student study of stalking victimization (Bjerregaard, this volume).

Seeking a restraining order is less commonly reported than seeking police assistance, with rates ranging from 0.8% of female stalking targets (Bjerregaard, this volume) to 28% of female and 10% of males surveyed in the NVAWS (Tjaden & Thoennes, 1998). Eleven percent of female stalking victims in Louisiana reported obtaining a restraining order (CDC, 2000).

These data suggest wide disparities in patterns of formal help seeking, that vary according to the type of sample studied, the definition of stalking employed, and the gender of stalking victim. Increased coping efforts were associated with greater frequency, severity, and variety of stalking and harassing behaviors targeted toward a victim, and with exposure to previous forms of sexual victimization. Reliance on more personal and informal methods of coping with stalking victimization predominates over utilization of more formal sources. It is possible that stalking victims rely on more personal and informal strategies of coping until stalking escalates in frequency and severity and such strategies are no longer sufficient. The relatively low satisfaction ratings of mental health and law enforcement highlight the lack of awareness and sensitivity to this issue, even among professionals trained to assist victims. The striking gender difference in police response to male and female stalking victims is troubling and may be indicative of insufficient education and training about stalking victimization. Increased education, beginning with dating-aged populations, about the nature and consequences of stalking and other forms of intrusive contact might lead to earlier help-seeking efforts. However, to the extent that stalking victims do seek help, it is essential that mental health and law enforcement professionals receive adequate training so that they can respond appropriately to the needs and concerns of stalking victims, without trivializing or minimizing the experience.

CLINICAL AND THREAT MANAGEMENT APPROACHES

As previously mentioned, PTSD and depression are the two clinical syndromes most likely to result from stalking. Significant gains have been made in developing empirically validated therapies (particularly, cognitive-behavioral approaches) for the treatment of PTSD arising from a variety of traumatic stressors, including sexual assault, combat, childhood sexual abuse and natural disasters (Foa, Keane, & Friedman, 2000; Follette, Ruzek, & Abueg, 1998). The International Society for Traumatic Stress Studies (ISTSS) recently published practice guidelines for the treatment of PTSD to assist practitioners in choosing validated treatments for PTSD (Foa, Keane, & Friedman, 2000). Citing competing ethical, forensic, and clinical complications faced by individuals exposed to ongoing relationship violence, the task force explicitly omitted from consideration the treatment of "currently" traumatized populations, such as battered women and stalking victims. Thus, while practice guidelines for the treatment of PTSD do exist, they are not applicable to the majority of stalking and relationship violence victims due to continued risk of violence exposure. Consequently, stalking victims facing active stalking at the time they seek treatment are not candidates for active trauma therapies.

Clinical intervention in cases with ongoing stalking should focus on a number of issues, including: documentation of stalking incidents, safety planning, risk assessment, and crisis management to deal with symptoms of distress, fear, anxiety, depression, and traumatic stress. Although a stalking victim may be unsure about whether to contact law enforcement, it is nevertheless useful to develop a paper trail documenting evidence of stalking. Caller ID records, logs of phone calls, copies of threatening letters, pictures of injuries, or of the stalker sitting outside the home, are examples of evidence that may help build a case if a victim decides to seek criminal justice system assistance. When stalking occurs without other forms of violence or without threatened violence, it may not be taken seriously by law enforcement. Similarly, stalking that takes place in the context of other forms of domestic abuse may be ignored by law enforcement (e.g., Tjaden & Thoennes, this volume). Victims should be reminded that they might consider contacting a supervisor in the police department or a prosecuting attorney if their stalking complaints are not taken seriously by the reporting officer.

A victim may also be eligible to obtain a restraining or protective order and evidence of stalking would facilitate this process. There is some controversy about whether restraining orders are useful for stalking victims (Mullen et al., 2000). It is important to recognize that restraining orders do not always prevent stalking from escalating into violence, and sometimes may contribute to the escalation of stalking and violence (Meloy, 1997). Developing a safety plan is important whether or not a victim chooses to obtain a restraining order. Informing friends, neighbors, and co-workers about the situation and showing them a photo of the stalker are also helpful strategies in responding to stalking. It might also be useful to leave a photo of the stalker with security personnel at the victim's workplace. Additional strategies for increasing the safety and security of a stalking victim in the workplace environment can be developed by working with managerial, security, and human resources staff at the workplace. While the shame and self-blame associated with stalking (and other forms of victimization) might result in social isolation and secrecy, invoking the support and involvement of other people is important for safety as well as for emotional support and validation.

If telephone harassment is a component of the stalking, it might be useful to secure an unlisted phone number for private use, and set up an answering machine to receive calls to the published number. Having easy access to a reserve set of money, credit cards, medication, important papers, keys, and other valuables is important in case a victim needs to leave quickly. It can be helpful to identify, in advance, a safe place to go in an emergency. Keeping the phone numbers of victim assistance agencies easily accessible can help if a crisis erupts. Other safety suggestions include varying the route one takes to and from work and other places, and trying to travel with others present. Cellular telephones programmed with emergency contact numbers can also provide another helpful means of accessing assistance in an emergency. Victim assistance agencies are excellent sources of support and provide detailed information about safety planning. Safety planning materials can also be obtained via several helpful stalking and victim assistance websites.

While risk assessment methods have tended to focus on perpetrator populations, such tools may be useful in working with victims of stalking. Earlier in this chapter, risk factors for the escalation of stalking into physical violence were reviewed. If stalking co-occurs in the context of relationship violence, these factors should figure into an appraisal of risk, including risk of lethal violence. Victim assistance, criminal justice, or mental health professionals can work with stalking victims in an effort to appraise risk and develop appropriate safety planning strategies that are tailored to the case-specific assessment of risk.

While active trauma treatment may not be appropriate for most stalking victims, supportive treatments aimed at reducing psychological distress, reducing self-blame, and increasing self-efficacy may be useful strategies. Several different components of supportive treatment can be identified: (1) education about trauma and traumatic responses; (2) emotional support and validation; (3) tools for managing stress and anxiety symptoms; and (4) skills training to enhance strategic responding and increase feelings of self-efficacy. Psychoeducational interventions provide basic information about the intrusive, avoidance, and arousal symptoms that comprise the PTSD triad. Information about trauma symptoms can be normalizing, given that victims sometimes feel as though they are "going crazy" when they experience some of the symptoms of PTSD. PTSD reactions are explained as normal reactions to abnormal events that occur in response to a variety of traumatic stressors that involve powerlessness, loss of control, perceived threat to life, fear, helplessness or horror (see Schiraldi, 2000, for a self-help book on PTSD). Another important component of PTSD education is to help victims understand the link between the deployment of avoidance behaviors, including suppression of thoughts and feelings, use of alcohol or drugs to numb feelings, and the development of chronic PTSD and secondary comorbid conditions, including depression, suicidality, panic, and substance use disorders. Clients are encouraged to minimize their use of avoidance behaviors to cope with distress from unbidden memories and heightened arousal and to engage in more active coping efforts that include talking about their feelings and managing symptomatic distress through relaxation or other methods. Other effects of trauma, including somatic reactions and behavioral changes are also explored. Finally, clients can be provided with information about how trauma can affect basic schemas or beliefs about the world that may contribute to self-blame, and to disruptions in beliefs about safety, trust, intimacy, esteem, and control (see Rosenbloom & Williams, 1999, for a client workbook on these themes).

Emotional support and validation can be provided by informal peer and family networks, as well as through professional relationships with service providers and participation in support of self-help groups for stalking victims and/or battered women. Rosenbloom and Williams (1999) offer guidelines for family and friends who wish to provide support to a trauma survivor. Among their suggestions are listening to the survivor instead of trying to fix the problem, and helping the survivor access other formal and informal sources of support in the community (p. 24). Professional or personal support providers should also refrain from asking questions or making statements that, for instance, might imply that the victim is responsible for the stalking that is targeted at her ("why" questions, which suggest personal responsibility/blame are generally good to avoid when providing a victim with support). Additional information on helpful hints for family and friends and other aspects of PTSD can be obtained from the National Center for PTSD (http://www.ncptsd.org) and the PTSD Alliance (1–800–877–507–PTSD or *http://www.PTSDAlliance.org*).

A number of techniques can be mobilized to assist the client with stress management. Relaxation procedures (Davis et al., 1995; Rosenbloom & Williams, 1999; Schiraldi, 2000) and breathing-retraining approaches (Barlow & Craske, 1989) can be used to reduce emotional distress and manage panic symptoms. Pharmcotherapies have also been used to manage anxiety and traumatic stress symptoms. Friedman et al. (2000) reviewed the empirical evidence supporting pharmocological intervention with PTSD. They concluded that selective serotonin reuptake inhibitiors (SSRI') are the first-line drugs for treating PTSD. Monoamine oxidase inhibitors (MAOIs) were reported to be moderately effective and tricyclic antipressant drugs were found to be mildly effective but with adverse side effects for both classes of drugs. No evidence yet exists to support the use of antiadrenergic or anticonvulsant agents due to a lack of randomized clinical trials with these medications. Friedman et al. (2000) caution against the use of benzodiazepines for treating the intrusive and avoidant symptoms of PTSD.

Stress Innoculation Training (SIT; Meichenbaum, 1993) is a cognitive-behavioral approach that combines education about stress, coping skills for managing distress, and opportunities to practice those skills. SIT has been found to be effective in managing PTSD symptoms with sexual assault survivors (Rothbaum et al., 2000). Enhanced coping skills that replace avoidant coping behaviors with more proactive engaging behaviors are likely to be effective at reducing some of the symptoms of PTSD as well as in gaining access to needed resources from community and criminal justice agencies. Moreover, the acquisition of problem-solving skills and other active coping behaviors can help a victim regain some sense of self-efficacy and control in the aftermath of victimization which tends to induce a sense of helplessness and loss of control.

For non-acute stalking cases, clinical service providers might consider adapting any one of the available cognitive behavioral therapies for treating PTSD. These therapies include prolonged exposure, cognitive therapy, cognitive processing therapy, and systematic desensitization. Empirical support for each of these therapeutic modalities, both alone and in combined approaches, can be found in Rothbaum et al. (2000).

SUMMARY AND CONCLUSIONS

Conceptualization

This chapter summarized a wealth of data indicating that stalking is associated with other forms of relationship abuse and has the potential to erupt in lethal and sub-lethal forms of violence, with greater risk of these outcomes when the stalker is a former or estranged intimate partner. Conceptualizing stalking as a variant of relationship abuse affects where, when, how, and with whom assessment and intervention is considered to be relevant.

Assessment

While many studies provide evidence for this conceptual shift, a paucity of research addresses victim reactions using standardized measures of clinical symptomatology. Use of the standardized scales across studies would facilitate the compilation of data describing the range of psychological reactions to stalking obtained with different populations of stalking victims. Comparison of stalked female college students and stalked-battered women using the PDS found considerable elevations in PTSD symptoms with greater severity of stalking. Future research might attempt to collaborate in ways that facilitate such comparative analyses. Research on college populations should move beyond the assessment of sexual coercion and dating violence and include measures of stalking as has been suggested by Belknap and colleagues (1999). In addition, research on risk assessment with stalking victims, along the lines of the Goodman et al. (2000) study appears to be a fruitful, yet untapped approach for studying stalking victimization.

At a clinical level, assessment of stalking and other forms of intrusive contact should be included as part of screening procedures for other forms of relationship abuse, such as physical violence and sexual assault. Given that stalking has been identified as a potential risk factor for severe and lethal violence, it would seem prudent to include former intimate partner stalking as a component of risk assessment procedures administered to abused women and to all women in primary care, emergency departments, and OB/GYN settings. The DAS (Campbell, 1995), one of the most popular risk assessment measures, does not include stalking as a risk factor—modifications of existing risk assessment tools should include stalking. Likewise, data from Meloy (2001) and others indicate that former intimate partner stalking should be considered as a risk factor when assessing stalking and batterer populations.

Intervention

One major dilemma for the clinician attempting to assess and treat problems presented by a stalking victim is that in all likelihood, the stalking is ongoing or threatens to continue at some point in the future. Consequently, treatment aimed at alleviating PTSD may not be viable unless the stalking has clearly ceased and the victim is out of danger. Instead, treatment goals might address the immediate issues related to safety planning, assessment of risk for serious violence, education about PTSD and trauma impact, stress management, problem solving, and affect regulation. To the extent that a stalking victim is also exposed to concomitant sexual and physical violence in the context of an ongoing relationship, these issues then may need to be addressed—along with helping the woman explore and consider her relationship decisions.

A fundamental dilemma arises when considering which clinical strategies might be viable and/or effective for stalking victims. That is, there is only so much that a victim can do in response to behavior that she has absolutely no control over. Stalking victims are left with options for managing their symptoms, decreasing their stress, or making other restricting lifestyle decisions in the hope that they will be protected from intrusion, violation, and possibly violence. Data clearly indicate that coping efforts and strategic responding are amplified in the face of more extensive, more frequent and more severe stalking—with little to no success. Hopelessness and helplessness are likely to flow from repeated unsuccessful efforts made by victims to keep themselves safe and cope with the looming threats posed by stalking. It is here that a paradigm shift may be in order. Perhaps we should shift intervention efforts from palliative attempts to reduce symptomatic distress among victims —who have no control over the stalking behaviors—to improving efforts to identify and contain stalking perpetrators. Innovative approaches for the management of stalkers are needed. The states of Iowa, Illinois, and Wisconsin recently launched a satellite tracking system to track high-risk offenders on probation, parole, and work-release (Alex, 2000). With the global positioning system, officials can determine if an offender is in a prohibited area, including a victim's address. When an offender enters an "exclusion zone" a warning message is sounded and the offender pushes a button indicating compliance with the message. Non-compliance signals authorities who can be dispatched to the area. The cost of this novel approach is estimated to be $14.00 per day, per unit.

Coordinated community responses by the criminal justice system, social service providers, mental health professionals, and existing batterer and/or stalker intervention services are needed to reduce the persistence of stalking and minimize its deleterious impact on victims. One focal point of intervention might be coordinated legal, criminal justice, and social service response to divorce when there is a history of domestic violence and stalking. Because stalking may escalate in the context of separation and stalking behaviors can be targeted directly or indirectly to the children (Mechanic et al., chapter 4), mandated visitation and custody exchange can become legally sanctioned opportunities for stalking and the eruption of violence. A coordinated, community-based approach that recognizes the true nature and implications of stalking has the best chance of alleviating this serious problem.

NOTE

1. 15% of the sample acknowledged lifetime stalking victimization ($n=176$); 75% of those believed it was somewhat dangerous or life threatening ($n=132$). The screening question was: "Have you ever been stalked, harassed or threatened with violence for more than one month by someone who would not leave you alone? (p. 653).

REFERENCES

Abbott, J., Johnson, R., Koziol-McLain, J., & Lowenstien, S. R. (1995). Domestic violence against women: Incidence and prevalence in an emergency department population. *Journal of the American Medical Association, 273* (22), 1763–1767.

Acierno, R., Kilpatrick, D. G., & Resnick, H. R. (1999). Posttraumatic stress disorder in adults relative to criminal victimization: Prevalence, risk factors, and comorbidity. In P. A. Saigh & J. D. Bremner (Eds.), *Posttraumatic stress disorder: A comprehensive text.* Boston: Allyn & Bacon, pp. 44–68.

Alex, T. (2000). Shackled by satellite. *The Des Moines Register,* September 20, 2000.

American Psychiatric Association (1994). *Diagnostic and statistical manual of mental disorders.* (4th edition). Washington DC: American Psychiatric Press.

Arias, I. & Pape, K. T. (1999). Psychological abuse: Implications for adjustment and commitment to leave violent partners. *Violence and Victims, 14* (1), 55–67.

Barlow, D. H., & Craske, M. G. (1989). *Mastery of your anxiety and panic.* Albany, NY: Graywind.

Belknap, J, Fisher, B. S., & Cullen, F. T. (1999). The development of a comprehensive measure of the sexual victimization of college women. *Violence Against Women, 5* (2), 185–214.

Block, C. R. *Chicago women's health risk study of serious injury or death in intimate violence: A collaborative research project.* Illinois Criminal Justice Authority: Revised report, June 6, 2000.

Breslau, N., Chilcoat, H. D., Kessler, R. C., Peterson, E. L., & Lucia, V. C. (1999). Vulnerability to assaultive violence: Further specification of the sex difference in posttraumatic stress disorder. *Psychological Medicine, 29* (4), 813–821.

Burgess, A. W., Baker, T., Greening, D., Hartman, C., Burgess, A. G., Douglas, J. E., & Halloran, R. (1997). Stalking behaviors within domestic violence. *Journal of Family Violence, 12,* 389–403.

Campbell, J. C. (1995). Prediction of homicide of and by battered women. In J. C. Campbell (Ed.), *Assessing dangerousness: Violence by sexual offenders, batterers, and child abusers* (pp. 99–113). Thousand Oaks, CA: Sage Publications.

Carlson, B. E., & McNutt, L. (1998). Intimate partner violence: Intervention in primary health care settings. In. A. R. Roberts (Ed.), *Battered women and their families: Intervention strategies and treatment programs*. (2ⁿᵈ Edition). NY: Springer Publishing.

Cascardi, M., Langhinrichsen, J., & Vivian, D. (1992). Marital aggression: Impact, injury and health correlates for husbands and wives. *Archives of Internal Medicine, 152,* 1178–1184.

Centers for Disease Control (2000). Prevalence and health consequences of stalking-Louisiana 1998–1999. *Morbidity and Mortality Weekly Report, 49,* 653–655.

Coleman, F. (1997). Stalking behavior and the cycle of domestic violence. *Journal of Interpersonal Violence, 12* , 420–432.

Cupach, W. R., & Spitzberg, B. H. (1998). Obsessive relational intrusion and stalking. In B. H. Spitzberg & W. R. Cupach (Eds.), *The dark side of close relationships* (pp.233–263). Hillsdale, NJ: Lawrence Erlbaum.

Davis, M., Eshelman, E. R., & McKay, M. (1995*). The relaxation & stress reduction workbook*. (4ᵗʰ edition). Oakland, CA: New Harbinger Press.

Dutton, D. G. (1998). *The abusive personality: Violence and control in intimate relationships*. New York: Guilford Press.

Dutton, D. G., Saunders, K., Starzomski, A., & Bartholomew, K. (1994). Intimacy-anger and insecure attachment as precursors of abuse in intimate relationships. *Journal of Applied Social Psychology, 24,* 1367–1386.

Dutton, M. A., Burghardt, K. J., Perrin, S. G., Chrestman, K. R., & Halle, P. M. (1994). Battered women's cognitive schemata. *Journal of Traumatic Stress, 7,* 237–255.

Dutton, M. A., Goodman, L. A., & Bennett, L. (1999). Court-involved battered women's responses to violence: The role of psychological, physical, and sexual abuse. *Violence and Victims, 14* (1), 89–104.

Dutton, M. A., Haywood, Y., & El-Bayoumi, G. (1997). Impact of violence on women's health. In S. J. Gallant, G. P. Keita, & R. Royak-Schaler (Eds.), *Health care for women: Psychological, social, and behavioral influences*. Washington, DC: American Psychological Association.

Foa, E. B., Cashman, L., Jaycox, L., & Perry, K. (1997). The validation of a self-report measure of posttraumatic stress disorder: The posttraumatic diagnostic scale. *Psychological Assessment, 9* (4), 445–451.

Foa, E. B., Keane, T. M., & Friedman, M. J. (2000*). Effective treatments for PTSD: Practice guidelines from the international society for traumatic stress studies*. New York: Guilford Press.

Follette, V. M., Ruzek, J. I., & Abueg, F. R. (1998). *Cognitive behavioral therapies for trauma*. New York: Guilford Press.

Follingstad, D. R., Brennan, A. F., Hause, E. S., Polek, D. S., & Rutledge,

L. L. (1991). Factors moderating physical and psychological symptoms of battered women. *Journal of Family Violence, 6* (1), 81–95.

Friedman, M. J., Davidson, J. R., Mellman, T. A., & Southwick, S. M. (2000). Treatment Guidelines: Pharmacotherapy. In Foa, E. B., Keane, T. M., & Friedman, M. J. (Eds.) *Effective treatments for PTSD: Practice guidelines from the international society for traumatic stress studies.* New York: Guilford Press.

Fremouw, B., Westrup, D., & Pennypacker, J. (1997). Stalking on campus: The prevalence and strategies for coping with stalking. *Journal of Forensic Sciences, 42,* 666–669.

Golding, J. M. (1996). Sexual assault history and limitations in physical health functioning in two general population samples. *Research in Nursing & Health, 19,* 33–44.

Golding, J. M. (1999). Intimate partner violence as a risk factor for mental disorders: A meta-analysis. *Journal of Family Violence, 14* (2), 99–132.

Gondolf, E. W., & Fisher, E. R. (1988). *Battered women as survivors: An alternative to treating learned helplessness.* Lexington, MA: D.C. Heath and Co.

Goodman, L. A., Dutton, M. A., & Bennett, L. (2000). Predicting repeat abuse among arrested batterers: Use of the danger assessment scale in the criminal justice system. *Journal of Interpersonal Violence, 15* (1), 63–74.

Grisso, J. A., Schwarz, D. F., Hirschinger, N., Samuel, M., Brensinger, C., Santanna, J., Lowe, R. A., Anderson, E., Shaw L. M., Bethel, C., & Teeple, L. (1999). Violent injuries among women in an urban area. *New England Journal of Medicine, 341* (25), 1899–1905.

Hall, D. M. (2000). The victims of stalking. In J. R. Meloy (Ed.), *The psychology of stalking* (pp. 113–137). San Diego, CA: Academic Press.

Harmon, R. B., Rosner, R., & Owens, H. (1995). Obsessional harassment and erotomania in a criminal court population. *Journal of Forensic Sciences, 40,* 188–196.

Haugaard, J. J., & Seri, L. G. (2000). Stalking and other forms of intrusive contact in adolescent and young adult relationships. *University of Kansas City Law Review, 69* (1), 227–238.

Holtzworth-Monroe, A., Meehan, J. C., Herron, K., & Stuart, G. L. (1999). A typology of male batterers: An initial examination. In. X.B. Arriaga & S. Oskamp (Eds.) *Violence in intimate relationships* (pp. 45–72). Thousand Oaks, CA: Sage Publications.

Holtzworth-Monroe, A., Stuart, G. L., & Hutchinson, G. (1997). Violent versus nonviolent husbands: Differences in attachment patterns, dependency, and jealousy. *Journal of Family Psychology, 11,* 314–331.

Janoff-Bulman, R. (1992). *Shattered assumptions: Toward a new psychology of trauma*. New York: Free Press.

Kessler, R. C., Sonnega, A., Bromet, E., Hughes, M., & Nelson, C. B. (1995). Posttraumatic stress disorder in the National Comorbidity Survey. *Archives of General Psychiatry, 52,* 1048–1060.

Kienlen, K. K. (1998). Developmental and social antecedents of stalking. In J.R. Meloy (Ed.), *The psychology of stalking: Clinical and forensic perspectives* (pp. 51–67). New York: Academic Press.

Kilpatrick, D. G., Edmunds, C. N., & Seymour, A. K. (1992). *Rape in America: A report to the nation.* Arlington, CA: National Victim Center.

Kilpatrick, D. G., Resnick, H. S., & Acierno, R. (1997). Health impact of interpersonal violence 3: Implications for clinical practice and public policy. *Behavioral Medicine, 23* (2), 79–85.

Kimerling, R., & Calhoun, K. S. (1994). Somatic symptoms, social support, and treatment seeking among sexual assault victims. *Journal of Consulting and Clinical Psychology, 62,* 333–340.

Koss, M.P., Koss, P.G., & Woodruff, W.J. (1991). Deleterious effects of criminal victimization on women's health and medical utilization. *Archives of Internal Medicine, 151,* 342–347.

Kurt, J.L. (1995). Stalking as a variant of domestic violence. *Bulletin of the American Academy of Psychiatry and the Law, 23,* 219–230.

Kyriacou, D., Anglin, D., Taliaferro, E., Stone, S., Tubb, T., Linden, J. A., Muelleman, R., Barton, E., & Kraus, J. F. (1999). Risk factors for injury to women from domestic violence. *New England Journal of Medicine, 341* (25), 1892–1898.

Lesserman, J.., Zhiming, L, Drossman, D, Toomey, T. C., Nachman, G., & Glogau, L. (1997). The impact of sexual and physical abuse dimensions on health status: The development of an abuse severity measure. *Psychosomatic Medicine, 29* (2), 152–160.

Lesserman, J.., Zhiming, L., Hu, Y., & Drossman, D. (1998). How multiple types of stressors impact on health. *Psychosomatic Medicine, 60* (2), 175–181.

Lewis, S.F., Fremouw, W.J., Ben, K. D. & Farr, C. (2001). An investigation of the psychological characteristics of stalkers: Empathy, problem-solving, attachment and borderline personality features. *Journal of Forensic Sciences, 46* (1), 80–84.

McFarlane, J. M., Campbell, J. C., Wilt, S., Sachs, C. J., Ulrich, Y., & Xu, X. (1999). Stalking and intimate partner femicide. *Homicide Studies, 3* (4), 300–316.

McCann, I. L., & Pearlman, L. A. (1990). *Psychological trauma and the adult survivor: Theory, therapy and transformation.* New York: Brunner/Mazel.

Mechanic, M. B. & Resick, P.A. (under review). The personal beliefs and reactions scale: Assessing rape-related cognitions.

Meichenbaum, D. (1993). Stress inoculation training: A twenty year update. In R. L. Woolfolk and P. M. Lehrer (Eds.) *Principles and practices of stress management.* New York: Guilford Press.

Meloy, J. R. (1996). Stalking (obsessional following): A review of some preliminary studies. *Aggression and Violence Behavior, 1,* 147–162.Meloy, J. R. (1997). The clinical risk management of stalking: "Someone is watching over me..." *American Journal of Psychotherapy, 51* (2), 174–184.

Meloy, J. R. (2001). Stalking and violence. In J. Boon & L. Sheridan (Eds.), *Stalking and psychosexual obsession.* London: Wiley.

Meloy, J. R., Davis, B., & Lovette, J. (2001). Risk factors for violence among stalkers, *Journal of Threat Assessment, 1*(1), 3–16.

Mullen, P., & Pathe, M (1994). Stalking and pathologies of love. *Australian and New Zealand Journal of Psychiatry, 28,* 469–477.

Mullen, P., Pathe, M., & Purcell, R. (2000). *Stalkers and their victims.* New York: Cambridge University Press.

Murphy, C. M., & Hoover, S. A. (1999). Measuring emotional abuse in dating relationships as a multifactorial construct. *Violence and Victims, 14,* 39–53.

National Criminal Justice Institute (1993, October). *Project to develop a model antistalking code for states.* Washington, DC: U.S. Department of Justice, National Institute of Justice.

Nishith, P., Mechanic, M. B., & Resick, P. A. (2000). Prior interpersonal trauma: The contribution to current PTSD symptoms in female rape victims, *Journal of Abnormal Psychology, 109*(1), 20–25.

Norris, F. H. (1992). Epidemiology of trauma: Frequency and impact of different potentially traumatic events on different demographic groups. *Journal of Consulting and Clinical Psychology, 60,* 409–418.

Norris, F. H., & Kaniasty, K. (1994). Psychological distress following criminal victimization in the general population: Cross-sectional, longitudinal, and prospective analyses. *Journal of Consulting and Clinical Psychology, 16,* 665–685.

Palarea, R. E., Zona, M. A., Lane, J. C., & Langhinrichsen-Rohling, J. (1999). The dangerous nature of stalking: Threats, violence and associated risk factors. *Behavioral Sciences and the Law, 17,* 269–283.

Pathe, M., & Mullen, P. (1997). The impact of stalkers on their victims. *British Journal of Psychiatry, 170,* 12–17.

Resick, P. A., & Schnicke, M. K. (1993). *Cognitive processing therapy for rape victims: A treatment manual.* CA: Sage.

Resnick, H. S., Acierno, R., & Kilpatrick, D. G. (1997). Health impact of interpersonal violence 2: Medical and mental health outcomes. *Behavioral Medicine, 23,* 65–78.

Resnick, H. S., Kilpatrick, D. G., Dansky, B. S., Saunders, B. E., & Best, C. L. (1993). Prevalence of civilian trauma and posttraumatic stress disorder in a representative sample national sample of women. *Journal of Consulting and Clinical Psychology, 61,* 984–991.

Rosenbloom, D., & Williams, M. B. (1990). *Life after trauma: A workbook for healing.* New York: Guilford Press.

Rosenfeld, B. (2000). Assessment and treatment of obsessional harassment. *Aggression and Violent Behavior, 5* (6), 529–49.

Rothbaum, B. O., Meadows, E. A., Resick, P. A., & Foy, D. W. (2000). Cognitive behavioral therapy. In E.B. Foa, T. M. Keane, & M. J. Friedman, (Eds.), *Effective treatments for PTSD: Practice guidelines from the international society for traumatic stress studies.* NY: Guilford.

Schiraldi, G. R. (2000). *The posttraumatic stress disorder sourcebook: A guide to healing, recovery, & growth.* Los Angeles, CA: Lowell House.

Spitzberg, B., Nicastro, A., & Cousins, A. V. (1998). Exploring the interactional phenomenon of stalking and obsessive relational intrusion. *Communication Reports, 11* (1), 33–47.

Spitzberg, B., & Rhea, J. (1999). Obsessive relational intrusion and sexual coercion victimization. *Journal of Interpersonal Violence, 14,* 3–20.

Stein, M., Walker, J. R., Hazen, A., & Forde, D. (1997). Full and partial posttraumatic stress disorder: Findings from a community survey. *American Journal of Psychiatry, 154* (8), 1114–1119.

Sugg, N. K., & Inui, T. (1992). Primary care physicians' response to domestic violence. *Journal of the American Medical Association, 267,* 3157–3160.

Sutherland, C., Bybee, D., & Sullivan, C. (1998). The long term effects of battering on women's health. *Women's Health: Research on Gender, Behavior, and Policy, 4* (1), 41–70.

Thompson, M. P., Simon, T. R., Saltzman, L. E., & Mercy, J. A. (1999). Epidemiology of injuries among women after physical assaults: The role of self-protective behaviors. *American Journal of Epidemiology, 150* (3), 235–244.

Tjaden, P., & Thoennes, N. (1998). *Stalking in America: Findings from the national violence against women survey* (NJ Report No. 169592). Washington, DC: U.S. Department of Justice.

Tjaden, P., & Thoennes, N. (2000). *Extent, nature, and consequences of intimate partner violence: Findings from the national violence against women survey.* (NJ Report No. 118167). Washington, DC: U.S. Department of Justice.

Walker, E., Unutzer, J., Rutter, C., Gelfand, A., Saunders, K., VonKork, M., Koss, M. P., & Katon, W. (1999). Costs of health care use by women HMO members with a history of childhood abuse and neglect. *Archives of General Psychiatry, 56* (7), 609–613.

Westrup, D., & Fremouw, W. J. (1998). Stalking behavior: A literature review and suggested functional analytic assessment technology. *Aggression & Violent Behavior, 3*(3), 255–274.

Westrup, D., Fremouw, W. J., Thompson, R. N., & Lewis, S. F. (1999). The psychological impact of stalking on female undergraduates. *Journal of Forensic Sciences, 44* (3), 554–557.

Wright, J. A., Burgess, A. G., Burgess, A. W., Laszlo, A. T., McCrary, G. O., & Douglas, J. E. (1996). A typology of interpersonal stalking. *Journal of Interpersonal Violence, 11,* 487–502.

Zona, M. A., Palarea, R. E., & Lane, J. C. (1998). Psychiatric diagnosis and the offender-victim typology of stalking. In J. R. Meloy (Ed.), *The psychology of stalking: Clinical and forensic perspectives* (pp. 69–84). New York: Academic Press.

Zona, M. A., Sharma, K. K., & Lane, J. (1993). A comparative study of erotomanic and obsessional subjects in a forensic sample. *Journal of Forensic Sciences, 38,* 894–903.

4

Intimate Partner Violence and Stalking Behavior: Exploration of Patterns and Correlates in a Sample of Acutely Battered Women

Mindy B. Mechanic, Terri L. Weaver, and Patricia A. Resick

Intimate partner violence has been deemed one of the most pressing public health concerns affecting women of all ethnic, racial, and socio-economic backgrounds (Biden, 1993; Koss et al., 1994; Wilson & Daly, 1993). Results of a large nationally representative survey of 8,000 adult women and 8,000 adult men underscore the fact that most violence against women is committed by current or former intimate partners or dates (Tjaden & Theonnes, 1998a). Overall, nearly 25% of female survey respondents (vs. 8% of males) reported being raped and/or physically assaulted by a current or former intimate partner or date during their adult lives. Moreover, more than three-fourths of the women reporting incidents of rape and/or physical assault during their adult lives identified current or former intimate partners or dates as the perpetrators of these acts.

In contrast to other forms of violent victimization, intimate partner violence is remarkable for its serial and repetitive nature, with acts of actual or threatened violence often continuing after separation or divorce, at times ceasing only upon the death of one or both parties (Browne, 1987; Campbell, 1992; Ellis & DeKeseredy, 1997; Kurz,

1996; Wilson & Daly, 1992, 1993). Mahoney (1991) coined the term "separation assault" to highlight the issues of power and control underlying a batterer's use of actual or threatened violence to keep his partner from physically or emotionally separating from him or to retaliate for her efforts to do so.[1] Additional support for this concept can be gleaned from research documenting increased rates of violence, particularly lethal violence upon perceived, attempted, or actual separation of women from their abusive partners (Bernard, Vera, Vera, & Newman, 1982; Campbell, 1992; Sev'er, 1997; Wilson & Daly, 1992; 1993); and from the more recent lines of research linking attachment theory to intimate partner abuse (Dutton, 1998; Dutton & Holtzworth-Monroe, 1997; Dutton, Saunders, Starzomiski, & Bartholomew, 1994; Holtzworth-Monroe, Stuart, & Hutchinson, 1997; Kesner, Julian, & McKenry, 1997; Murphy & Hoover, 1999) and stalking behavior (Kienlen, 1998).

Attachment theory provides an interesting conceptual framework for understanding the seemingly illogical persistence of pursuit/stalking behaviors by romantic partners in the face of repeated, clear-cut signs of resistance or rejection from their partners, ranging from verbal explanations to formal legal indicators of rejection (e.g., civil orders of protection, divorce decrees, or even remarriage). From an attachment perspective, the intense scrutiny, monitoring and harassing behavior engaged in by batterers can be conceptualized as proximity-seeking behavior designed to reestablish a secure base in the face of perceived or actual threats of separation (Bowlby, 1980). Histories of early attachment disruptions in childhood, as well as perceived losses or separation in the course of adult intimate relationships, have been identified as risk factors for engaging in stalking behavior (Kienlen, 1998), for committing intimate partner violence (Dutton, 1998; Dutton & Holtzworth-Monroe, 1997; Dutton et al., 1994; Holtzworth-Monroe et al., 1997), and for emotionally abusive behavior perpetrated in dating relationships (Murphy & Hoover, 1999). Murphy and Hoover (1999) found that anxious preoccupation with attachment-related issues was most strongly associated with a form of emotional abuse the authors labeled "restrictive engulfment," which consisted of restrictive, isolating behaviors and acts of jealousy and possessiveness aimed at reducing perceived threats to the relationship.

The construct of emotional/psychological abuse has begun to receive increasing attention in the literature for its deleterious impact and for its relationship to physical aggression (see O'Leary, 1999, for a review). Despite some variation in how the construct of emotional abuse has been articulated across studies and measures, one theme that emerges is the consistent reference to coercive and controlling tactics that instill fear, as well as low-level surveillance behaviors that monitor and/or restrict a partner's autonomy and freedom of movement. While recent investigations have begun to assess the many important relationships between psychological and physical aggression in female victims of intimate partner and dating abuse, stalking behavior has not been included in definitions of either construct. It is quite possible that when considered within the context of current or former romantic relationships, stalking behavior represents a severe form of emotional/psychological abuse.

In fact, recent research found that most victims of stalking are women (4 out of every 5) and that the majority of female stalking victims (59%) report being stalked by a current or former intimate partner (Tjaden & Theonnes, 1998b). Data from the only large national study of stalking (National Violence Against Women Study: NVAWS) identified a crucial link between stalking and intimate partner violence, finding that 81% of women who were stalked by a current or former (marital/cohabiting) partner also experienced physical assaults by those partners. A smaller number (31%) also reported being sexually assaulted by them. Moreover, women who were stalked by former intimate partners were significantly more likely to experience emotional abuse by those partners, compared to women who were not stalked by former partners. These findings led Tjaden and Theonnes (1998b) to conclude that there is compelling evidence of the link between stalking and controlling and emotionally abusive behavior in intimate relationships (p. 8).

To build upon the emergent literature bridging the gap between research on stalking behavior and intimate partner abuse and violence (Burgess et al., 1997; Coleman, 1997; National Institute of Justice, 1998; Tjaden & Theonnes, 1998a; Walker & Meloy, 1998), the goal of the present study was to provide a detailed picture of stalking behavior, patterns, and correlates in a sample of recently battered women. Specifically, we were interested in exploring the relationship between stalking, psychological/emotional abuse, and physical violence, in light of the considerable conceptual overlap in behaviors defined as part of the constructs of emotional/psychological abuse and stalking.

While some of the questions addressed in this paper were exploratory, we were able to offer several *a priori* hypotheses based on prior research and/or theory. First, given the findings of the NVAWS, we expected stalking behaviors to occur with a relatively high frequency within this sample of acutely battered women. Second, based on research highlighting the ongoing fear experienced by victims who are threatened with repeated violence and harassment (Dutton, 1992; Meloy, 1998), we expected to find that experiences of stalking would significantly contribute to battered women's expectations of future violence and future harm from their partners. Expectations of future harm and future violence are important dimensions to study because they affect how a victim might appraise and respond to a climate of impending violence. Moreover, such perceptions are critical in self-defense cases of battered women who have severely or lethally injured their partners. Consequently, it is important to understand whether (and how) stalking contributes to ongoing fears that violence will recur and escalate to dangerous levels.

Third, we hypothesized that emotional abuse variables would predict the severity of stalking, even after controlling for the impact of physical violence in the relationship. The prediction was based on the notion that stalking represents an extreme form of emotional abuse that would contribute to stalking behavior independent of physical violence. Clinical and empirical definitions of emotional/psychological abuse include dimensions that closely resemble stalking behavior. Specifically, isolation and domination (Marshall, 1999; Murphy & Hoover, 1999; Sonkin, 1997; Tolman, 1999), restrictive or monopolizing behavior (Murphy & Hoover, 1990; Sonkin, 1997), pathological jealousy (Follingstad et al., 1990); surveillance and monitoring behavior (Marshall, 1999) constitute forms of emotional abuse that have been found to exist both with and without co-occurring physical violence. Finally, emotionally abusive and controlling behavior was reported to occur more often among women with ex-husbands who stalked them, compared to women whose ex-husbands did not stalk them (Tjaden & Theonnes, 1998). In his discussion of research on populations with co-occurring physical and psychological abuse, O'Leary (1999) commented that "more studies assessing the relative contribution of psychological and physical aggression are needed (p. 18)." Our analyses will address the relative impact of physical and emotional abuse variables.

Finally, in light of the research on separation violence (e.g., Campbell, 1992; Mahoney, 1991) and recent loss as a precipitant to stalking (Kienlen, 1998), and the description offered by Walker and Meloy (1998) that "stalking is the name given to the combination of activities that batterers do to keep the connection between themselves and their partners from being severed (p. 142)," we predicted that separation from an abusive partner be uniquely associated with escalation in postseparation stalking behavior, even after controlling for prior stalking and prior abuse.

METHOD

Participants

Data reported in this article were collected as part of a larger study focusing on factors that influence recovery from intimate partner violence in a sample of acutely battered women. This article will present data related to stalking and intimate partner violence from the first 114 battered women who participated in the study.

Recruitment/Screening Criteria

In order to obtain a heterogeneous sample of acutely battered women, a variety of recruitment strategies were employed. All local shelter and nonshelter agencies serving battered women were provided with information about the study and were asked to assist in recruitment. They were asked to inform their clients about our project and provide them with a brief verbal or written description of the study and a telephone number to contact a member of our staff for more information. Assistance was also sought from local police departments, hospital emergency rooms and other victim service agencies that might come into contact with battered women, but do not do so exclusively. These agencies were also provided with written material that could be handed out, mailed or described verbally to battered women.

To access non-help-seeking battered women, efforts were made to work with the media to produce stories or shows about domestic violence that could be paired with information about the study that might attract potential volunteers. To this end, a number of talk radio programs, newspaper articles, and television news stories were produced as a vehicle for recruiting study participants. Finally, staff members participated at many events geared toward women (e.g., working women's survival show) or victims, (e.g., victims-rights-week rally) by staffing a booth and/or handing out informational flyers briefly describing the study.

All prospective participants, irrespective of the method of recruitment, were asked to contact our staff using a specially designated phone line to find out more about the study, and if interested, to participate in a brief screening interview over the telephone. Careful attention was paid to issues of confidentiality and safety planning at every level, from the greeting used on the telephone to leaving messages for prospective participants who phoned us.

To recruit a sample of battered women who experienced recent, serial, intimate partner violence, several screening criteria were employed. The following criteria were used to screen potential participants:

1. length of relationship;
2. recency of violence; and
3. severity of violence.

First, participants were required to have been in an intimate relationship, whether cohabiting or not, for a minimum of 3 months, effectively ruling out dating violence. Second, to improve accuracy of reporting, it was required that the most recent episode of violence occurred within the past 6 months. However, if the most recent episode occurred less than 2 weeks earlier, participants were scheduled so that there were at least 2 weeks between the most recent episode and the assessment. This was done to reduce potential inflation of scores on symptom measures as a consequence of assault recency. Finally, in order to obtain a sample of women who experienced more than an occasional episode of relationship violence, we required that participants experience at least four incidents of minor violence or two episodes of severe violence (or some combination of four incidents of minor and/or severe violence) within the past year. Minor violence items were: being pushed, shoved or grabbed; being slapped or hit; having things thrown at you that could hurt; having your arm twisted or your hair pulled. Severe violence items were: being hit or punched with a fist or with something that could hurt; anything that caused you to have physical injuries; being choked, slammed against a wall or thrown downstairs; being kicked or beaten up; threatened with a weapon; having a weapon used against you; being forced to have sex when you did not want to; and causing you to fear for your life or the lives of your family members.

Participants who were ruled out of the study based on their telephone screening were given support, thanked for their time, and were provided with information about appropriate resources in the community. Twenty-four women were screened out of the study for the following reasons: 2 women were with their partners for less than three months; 6 women reported fewer than the required number of episodes of physical violence; 15 women reported abuse that occurred more than 6 months ago (and for some women the abuse ended many years ago); and 1 woman declined to participate after hearing more about the study.

Instruments

THE STALKING BEHAVIOR CHECKLIST (SBC: COLEMAN, 1997)

The SBC is a 25–item inventory assessing a variety of unwanted harassing and pursuit-oriented behaviors. Each item is rated on a 6–point frequency scale, ranging from 1 (never) to 6 (once a day or more). On our version of the SBC, participants were asked to rate each item by focusing on unwanted contact during the past 6 months by their (most recent) abusive partner. The original version of the SBC inquired about any former dating partner's use of these tactics following the breakup of a romantic relationship. The SBC was originally developed using a small sample of college students (N = 141), 13 of whom were classified as having been stalked, 38 of whom were classified as having been harassed, with 90 serving as control subjects on the basis of their responses to the author's screening questions. The SBC was factor-analyzed resulting in two subscales, Violent Behavior (VB) with 12 items accounting for 34.7% of the variance, and Harassing Behavior (HB) with 13 items, accounting for 10.8% of the variance. The Violent Behavior subscale consists of items addressing overt acts of violence (e.g., broke into your home or car, violated a restraining order, etc.). The Harassing Behavior subscale consists of items reflecting nonviolent harassment, such as unwanted telephone calls, gifts or visits, being followed, and so forth.

Due to our modest sample size, we were unable to evaluate whether the factor structure could be replicated within our sample of battered women. Consequently, we decided to combine the subscales into a single measure of stalking for analyses using continuous scales. Because of the considerable conceptual and empirical overlap between 3 of the violence items on the SBC, and the items assessing physical . violence (described later), 3 violence items were dropped from the SBC in all analyses using the SBC. The 3 deleted items were "threatened to cause you harm," "attempted to harm you," and "physically harmed you." Coefficient alpha for the 23–item measure was .90.

THE STANDARDIZED BATTERING INTERVIEW

This interview consists of a variety of questions assessing demographic and abusive relationship characteristics, including recent (past month) stalking behavior experienced by women who left their partner. Embedded within the interview are two questions focusing on a woman's appraisal of future violence (Dutton, 1992). The first question asks the woman to rate her appraisal of the likelihood that violence by her partner will recur in the future (APV-FV). The second item asks the woman to estimate her likelihood of experiencing serious physical harm or death by her partner at some point in the future (APV-FH). Both appraisal questions are rated on a 7–point scale, anchored from 1 (not at all likely) to 7 (very likely). The interview also contains 10 questions assessing the frequency of recent (past month) stalking behaviors assessed only among women who have left the relationship. Postseparation stalking items include: threats to life, threats to children's lives, threats of custody, threats to kidnap children, telephone and in-person harassment at work, harassment at home, stalking, physical assault, and sexual assault. Items are rated on a 5–point scale for the past month (0 = never; 1 = once or twice; 2 = once or twice a week; 3 = several times a week; 4 = daily or almost every day).

A summary of postseparation stalking was created by dichotomizing (and then summing) each of the seven non-child-related stalking items. The items were dichotomized before summing because of the restricted range on the individual items. The child-related items were left off because of missing data for the women without children living with them. Internal consistency as measured by coefficient alpha was .80 for the 7–item measure of postseparation stalking.

PSYCHOLOGICAL MALTREATMENT OF WOMEN INVENTORY— ABBREVIATED VERSION (PMWI)

The abbreviated 14–item version of the PMWI (Tolman, 1998, 1999) consists of 2 factor-derived subscales that measure dominance/isolation (DI) and emotional and verbal abuse (EV). Evidence of reliability and validity are presented in Tolman (1999). The scale is a self-report measure, and each item is rated on a 5–point frequency scale, ranging from never (1), to very frequently (5). Each subscale consists of 7 items. Coefficient alphas for both subscales in the present sample were .88.

Revised Conflict Tactics Scale-2 (CTS-2)

Three subscales of the revised CTS-2 (Straus, Hamby, Boney-McCoy, & Sugarman, 1995) were administered to assess the frequency and severity of physical assault (CTS-PA; 12 items), injury (CTS-I; 6 items), and psychological aggression (CTS-PSYCH; 8 items). Ratings are made in terms of frequency (0 = never 1 = one in past year, 2 = twice in past year; 3 = 3–5 times in past year; 4 = 6–10 times in past year; 5 = 11–20 times in past year; 6 = more than 20 times in past year). The authors of the CTS-2 suggest creating a severity index by adding the midpoint for each item and creating a summed score for each subscale. The midpoint equals the rating for ratings of 0, 1, and 2. Scores of 3 are recoded to 4, scores of 4 are recoded to 8 and scores of 5 are recoded to 15, and scores of 6 are recoded to 25. Coefficient alphas for the CTS-PA and CTS-PSYCH were .90 and .80, respectively. Coefficient alpha for the 6–item injury scale was .62, with one item having an item-total scale correlation of -.03 ("I had a broken bone from a fight with my partner"). This item was dropped, resulting in a 5–item scale with an alpha of .66.

Procedure

Participants who met study criteria and agreed to participate completed the study in two visits that typically occurred within several days of each other. On day 1, women first completed several symptom-based measures programmed onto a laptop computer in order to reduce the likelihood that symptom scores would be elevated as a consequence of discussing traumatic material. Next, they were interviewed by trained master's-or doctoral-level clinicians with extensive experience dealing with traumatized populations. On day 2, participants completed a battery of nonsymptom-based self-report instruments that were programmed onto a laptop computer. Debriefings were conducted with participants following completion of all instruments.

RESULTS

Demographic and Relationship Characteristics of the Sample

Battered women in our sample averaged 35 years of age (SD = 7.9), ranging from 18 to 59 years old. In terms of race, 68% of the participants were African American; 25% were Caucasian; 2% were Latino; 3% were Native American; and 3% identified their ethnicity as "other." On average, the women completed slightly more than a high school education (M = 12.9; SD = 2.0), with education ranging from 8 through 19 years. Annual household income was reported by a subgroup of participants (n = 111) and was as follows:

1. less that $5,000 (12%);
2. $5,000–$10,000 (20%);
3. $10,001–20,000 (17%);
4. $20,001–$30,000 (22%);
5. $30,001–$50,000 (14%); and
6. $50,000+ (14%).

The length of time women reported being in a relationship with their abusive partners ranged from a minimum of 6 months to a maximum of 27 years, with 7.3 years being the mean duration of the relationship (SD = 6.4). The duration of abuse averaged 5.37 years (SD = 5.79 years), and ranged from 2 months to more than 24 years. Three women identified their abusive partners as female, whereas the remainder reported male partners. Sixty percent of the battered women had one or more children under age 18 residing with them, with a mean of 1.2 (SD = 1.3) children per woman (range = 0–6).

At the time of the interview, 35% of the women were married to their abusive partners, 13% were separated/divorced; 40% were cohabiting; and 11% described a non-cohabiting dating relationship. However, only 14% of the sample reported that they were currently living with their partners at the time of study participation, and a total of 17% indicated that they had not yet left the relationship. Of the 95 women who left their partners, the average length of time since leaving was 3 months (SD = 7.2 months), ranging from 4 days to 14 years. Women reported making many prior attempts to leave the abusive relationship, with 16% of the sample (n = 18) reporting that they left the relationship more times than they could count. Only 3 women

(2.6%) reported making no attempts to leave their partners. Forty percent of the sample made 1 to 5 attempts to leave; almost one-quarter (23.2%) left 6–10 times, and 10% of the sample made 11–40 attempts to leave. Slightly more than half of the sample (52%) resided in a shelter for battered women at the time of participation in the study.

Stalking Behavior Frequencies

To obtain a detailed picture of how often each type of stalking behavior occurs, frequencies for each of the 12 items on the Violent Behavior subscale of the SBC are presented in Table 4.1. The time frame for these questions referred back to the past 6 months. To ascertain the relative frequency of violent behaviors, each item was recoded into a dichotomous score (never vs. at least once in the past 6 months). The stalking behaviors most commonly reported were: threatened harm (94%); physical harm (89%); attempts to harm (88%)2; and stole/

Table 4.1 Frequencies of Violent Behavior Items on the Stalking Behavior Checklist

Item	Never (%)	< 1 Month (%)	2–3 Month (%)	1–2 Week (%)	3–6 Week (%)	>1 Day (%)
(8) Broke into your home	71	23	5	1	1	0
(5) Violated a restraining order	64	13	13	2	5	3
(9) Attempted to break into your car	71	24	3	1	1	0
(1) Threatened to cause you harm	6	25	28	17	13	11
(11) Broke into you car	79	17	4	0	1	0
(3) Attempted to harm you	13	28	26	15	9	10
(2) Physically harmed you	11	38	27	13	5	6
(7) Attempted to break into your home	68	20	5	2	4	2
(10) Physically harmed himself	73	18	7	1	0	2
(4) Stole/read your mail	39	22	10	6	12	11
(12) Damaged the property of your new partner	89	8	1	0	2	0
(6) Threatened to harm himself	67	21	5	4	4	0

Numbers in parentheses refer to the rank ordering of the item; N = 112.

read mail (61%). Less commonly experienced events were: violated orders (36%); threats of self-harm (33%); attempted and actual home break-ins (31%, 30%, respectively); attempted car break-ins (29%), physical acts of self-harm (28%); and damage to property of a new partner (11%). Rank ordering of these acts is presented in parentheses in Table 4.1. Numbers in parentheses refer to the rank ordering of the item; *N* = 112.

Frequencies for each of the 13 items on the Harassing Behavior subscale are listed in Table 4.2. Each harassing behavior item was also recoded to obtain the relative ranking of behaviors. Very commonly reported behaviors were: being watched (71%); receiving unwanted

Table 4.2 Frequencies of Harassing Behavior Items on the Stalking Behavior Checklist

	Frequency					
Item	Never (%)	< 1 Month (%)	2–3 Month (%)	1–2 Week (%)	3–6 Week (%)	>1 Day (%)
(2) Made calls to you at home when you didn't want him to	34	15	11	9	14	17
(4) Came to your home when you didn't want him to	38	16	10	15	11	10
(3) Followed you	38	21	14	10	10	8
(5) Made hang-up telephone calls	43	13	11	10	5	18
(9) Sent you unwanted gifts	71	16	4	5	3	2
(7) Made calls to you at work/school when you didn't want him to	49	16	7	10	9	9
(1) Watched you	29	18	12	12	16	14
(8) Came to your workplace/school when you didn't want him to	58	13	11	6	5	7
(6) Left unwanted messages on answering machine, voice mail or e-mail	44	9	11	4	16	17
(12) Sent photographs when you didn't want him to	92	5	2	0	2	0
(11) Made threats to your new partner	82	7	2	4	4	2
(10) Sent letters to you when you didn't want him to	73	13	6	1	3	4
(13) Harmed your new partner	94	4	1	1	1	0

Numbers in parentheses refer to the rank ordering of the item; *N* = 112.

calls at home (66%); being followed (63%); unwanted visits at home (62%); hang-up calls (58%); unwanted messages (56%); and unwanted visits at work (42%). Less frequent forms of harassment were: unwanted gifts (29%); unwanted letters (27%); threats made to a new partner (18%); unwanted photos (8%); and harm to a new partner (6%). Rank ordering of these acts is presented in parentheses in Table 4.2.

Dichotomized SBC items were summed to create an index reflecting the total number of different stalking and harassing behaviors experienced by a woman over the past 6 months. With 25 items, the possible range of scores was from 0–25. On average, women reported experiencing 11 (SD = 5.4) different acts of stalking and harassing behaviors during the past 6 months, with scores ranging from 0–23. Finally, frequencies of stalking behavior experienced within the last month were assessed for all women who left the relationship. These data are presented in Table 4.2.

In addition to the stalking items from the SBC that were measured for the past 6 months, separated women (n = 94) were also asked about the frequency of stalking over the course of the past month (see Table 4.3). They were most likely to report experiencing threats to

Table 4.3 Frequencies of Stalking Behavior for Separated Women in Past Month

Item n = 94	Never (%)	1–2* (%)	1–2/wk (%)	Several/wk (%)	Daily (%)
Threatened your life/well-being	63	23	3	6	4
Threatened the life or well-being of your children	90	8	0	2	0
Threatened to gain custody of your children	70	15	3	5	7
Threatened to kidnap your children	83	12	0	3	2
Harassed you at work by phone	80	9	1	7	3
Harassed you at work in person	86	9	4	1	0
Harassed you at home by phone	66	12	7	7	9
Stalked you	71	15	5	5	3
Physically assaulted you	84	14	1	1	0
Sexually assaulted you	94	4	2	0	0

their lives (37%) and being harassed at home on the telephone (34%) within the past month. For 9% of the women, telephone harassment at home occurred every day or nearly every day. When asked directly whether they were "stalked" within the past month, slightly more than one-quarter of the separated women (29%) endorsed that label. Fifteen percent reported one or two incidents of stalking, 5% reported being stalked one to two times per week, 5% indicated several times per week, and 3% reported being stalked on a daily or near daily basis.

Several analyses were conducted to determine whether demographic characteristics and shelter status were associated with stalking rates. There were no differences in the rates of stalking as a function of shelter status, $t(110) = 1.0$, ns. There were also no differences in stalking for African American and Caucasian women, $t(102) = 1.0$, ns. Similarly, rates of stalking were comparable among dating, married, cohabiting, and separated or divorced battered women, $F(3, 111) = 1.5$, ns. Stalking did not differ as a function of economic status, $F(5, 107) < 1.0$, ns.

Data Analysis Plan

First, we will present descriptive findings on the continuous measures, followed by correlations between the variables used in regression models. Next, the findings from a series of regression analyses will be presented to test hypothesized relationships between stalking and its effect on expectations of future violence and future harm:

1. more extensive stalking will significantly predict women's expectations of future violence;
2. more extensive stalking will predict battered women's expectations of future harm from their partners.

Next, we evaluated the hypothesis that emotional abuse variables would predict the severity of stalking, even after controlling for the impact of physical violence in the relationship. Finally, we examined the prediction that separation from an abusive partner be uniquely associated with escalation in postseparation stalking behavior, even after controlling for prior stalking and prior abuse. Hierarchical multiple regression analyses were chosen to examine and isolate:

Table 4.4 Means, Standard Deviations for Continuous Measures

Scale	M	SD	Min.	Max.
SBC	42.62	16.80	22	97
PMWI-EV	28.71	6.04	12	35
PMWI-DI	26.46	7.35	10	35
CTS-I	27.16	22.34	5	87
CTS-PA	82.84	65.49	12	256
CTS-PSYCH	106.90	48.49	11	200
APV-FV	4.45	2.47	1	7
APV-FH	5.16	2.26	1	7
Postseparation stalking	1.49	1.80	0	6

Note. SBC = Stalking Behavior Checklist; PMWI-EV = Psychological Maltreatment of Women Inventory-Emotional Violence Subscale; PMWI-DI = Psychological Maltreatment of Women Inventory-Dominance/Isolation Subscale; CTS-I = Conflict Tactics Scale 2–Injury Subscale; CTS-PA = Conflict Tactics Scale 2–Physical Assault Subscale; CTS-PSYCH = Conflict Tactics Scale 2–Psychological Aggression Subscale; APV-FV = Appraisal of Violence-Future Violence Item; APV-FH = Appraisal of Violence-Future Serious Harm/Death.

1. the unique role of stalking in contributing to the ongoing fear of future violence and serious harm, and
2. the unique predictors of past and recent stalking behavior.

Means and standard deviations for all measures used in the study are presented in Table 4.4. Modest correlations were obtained between the emotional abuse and stalking variables. Stalking was most strongly correlated with the dominance/isolation subscale of the PMWI ($r = .47$). As expected, the highest correlation was found between the physical assault and injury variables ($r = .79$). Correlations among the predictor variables used in the regression analyses are presented in Table 4.5.

Prediction of Expectations of Future Violence and Future Serious Harm/Death

To examine the relative contributions of stalking, emotional abuse and physical violence to expectations of future violence (APV-FV) and to expectations of future harm (APV-FH), two hierarchical multiple regression analyses were conducted on each dependent measure. First, physical assault (CTS-PA) and injury (CTS-I) were entered, followed

Table 4.5 Correlations Among Abuse and Stalking Predictor Variables

Scale	1	2	3	4	5
1. SBC					
2. PMWI-EV	.36**				
3. PMWI-DI	.47**	.63**			
4. CTS-I	.32**	.41**	.46**		
5. CTS-PA	.35**	.38**	.44**	.79**	
6. CTS-PSYCH	.38**	.67**	.40**	.48**	.59**

Note. SBC = Stalking Behavior Checklist; PMWI-EV = Psychological Maltreatment of Women Inventory-Emotional Violence subscale; PMWI-DI = Psychological Maltreatment of Women Inventory-Dominance/Isolation Subscale; CTS-I = Conflict Tactics Scale 2–Injury Subscale; CTS-PA = Conflict Tactics Scale 2–Physical Assault Subscale; CTS-PSYCH = Conflict Tactics Scale 2–Psychological Aggression Subscale. **$p < .01$.

by the addition of psychological abuse variables on the second step (DI, EV, CTS-PSYCH). Finally, stalking was added (SBC) once the effects of prior emotional abuse and violence were controlled. Then, the order of entry was reversed to test for unique variance associated with the addition of each set of variables.

Expectations of Future Violence

In the first analysis assessing expectations of future violence, physical assault and injury were added into the model first, followed by the emotional abuse variables and finally, the stalking measure. Entered first, physical assault and injury did not significantly contribute to women's expectations that future violence will recur, $F(2, 106) = 1.3$, ns; $R^2 = .02$. Consistent with predictions, the addition of the emotional abuse variables significantly increased the amount of variance explained, $F(3,106) = 4.0$, $p = .01$, R^2 change $= .10$; cumulative $R^2 = .127$. The addition of the SBC on the final step did not account for a significant increase in explained variance, $F(1,106) = 2.8$, $p = .10$, R^2 change $= .02$; cumulative $R^2 = .15$.

Reversing the order of entry, when entered first, stalking explained 10% of the variance in expected future violence, $F(1,106) = 11.8$, $p = .000$, $R^2 = .10$. The addition of the set of emotional abuse variables contributed a nonsignificant increase of 4% of explained variance,

$F(3,106) = 2.8$, ns, R^2 change = .04, cumulative R^2 = .15. The final entry of the physical abuse and injury variables did not contribute additional variance to the predictive model, once the effects of stalking and emotional abuse were accounted for, $F(2,106) = 1$, ns, R^2 change = .00, cumulative R^2 = .15. None of the variables entered into the model were significant individual predictors, although stalking evidenced a trend in that direction ($t = 1.7$, $p = .09$, $\beta = .19$).

Expectations of Future Harm/Death

In the second analysis assessing expectations of serious harm or death, physical assault and injury were added into the model first, followed by the emotional abuse variables and finally, the stalking measure. Entered on the first step, the physical assault and injury variables made significant contributions to explained variance in women's expectations that they will experience future serious harm or death at the hands of their abusive partners, $F(2,106) = 5.4$, $p = .006$, $R^2 = .09$. As expected, the emotional abuse variables contributed unique variance to the predictions of expectations of future harm, even after controlling for the effects of physical violence, $F(3,106) = 6.6$, $p = .000$, R^2 change = .15; cumulative $R^2 = .24$. Finally, the addition of stalking contributed a nonsignificant increase of 3% of explained variance in expected future harm, $F(1,106) = 3.8$, $p = .055$, R^2 change = .03, cumulative $R^2 = .27$.

When the order of entry was reversed and stalking was entered into the model first, stalking explained 14% of the variance in expected future harm, $F(1,106) = 16.4$, $p = .000$, $R^2 = .14$. An additional 12% of variance was accounted for by the addition of the emotional abuse variables, $F(3,106) = 5.7$, $p = .001$; R^2 change = .12; cumulative $R^2 = .26$. No significant improvement in the prediction of expected future harm was made when the physical violence variables were added after controlling for the effects of stalking and emotional abuse, $F(2,106) = 1$, ns; R^2 change = .01; cumulative $R^2 = .27$. The stalking (SBC), $t(106) = 1.9$; $p = .055$, $\beta = .20$ and PMWI-emotional/verbal abuse scales were significant independent predictors of expected future harm/death, $t(106) = 2.9$; $p = .00$; $\beta = .42$.

Prediction of Stalking

A hierarchical multiple regression was conducted on the Stalking Behavior Checklist with the physical assault and injury variables entered as predictors in the first step, followed by the emotional abuse variables on the second step. These physical violence variables accounted for 14% of the variance, $F(2,106) = 8.7$, $p = .000$, $R^2 = .14$, in SBC scores. Consistent with expectations, the addition of the three emotional abuse variables into the equation contributed additional unique variance to the prediction of stalking, $F(3,106) = 9.8$, $p = .000$, R^2 change $= .19$, cumulative $R^2 = .34$.

Reversing the order of entry into the equation, we first forced in the three emotional abuse variables, which accounted for 33% of the variance in stalking behavior, $F(3,106) = 17.24$, $p = .000$. Next, the physical assault and injury variables were forced into the equation, but they did not account for a significant increase in explained variance after controlling for the effects of emotional abuse, $F(2,106) = 1.0$, ns, R^2 change $= .003$, cumulative $R^2 = .34$. The dominance/isolation subscale was the only one of the predictor variables that emerged as an independent predictor of SBC scores, ($t = 4.5$; $p = .00$, $\beta = .51$).

Separation and Postseparation Stalking

To look at predictors of postseparation stalking, we conducted a hierarchical regression analysis with the women who had left their partners a minimum of 2 weeks ago ($n = 75$). This cutoff was chosen with the idea that there would be insufficient time to measure postseparation stalking in women who had been out of the relationship less than 2 weeks, and consequently that there would be restricted variance on the range of possible scores for the recently separated women. We tested the effects of prior stalking, length of time out of the relationship, emotional abuse, and physical violence and injury on the prediction of reported stalking over the past month. The predictor variables were entered in the model in the order stated above, and then reversed to assess for unique variance. Due to considerable positive skew, the amount of time since the woman left the relationship was transformed using a log transformation (Tabachnick & Fidell, 1996).

When entered into the equation on the first step, prior stalking accounted for 7% of the variance in postseparation stalking, $F(1, 68) = 4.8$, $p = .03$, $R^2 = .069$. The log of time since leaving was added next, and it contributed an additional 44% of explained variance, $F(1, 68) = 59.5$; $p = .000$, R^2 change $= .44$; cumulative $R^2 = 51$. The emotional abuse variables made no significant addition to the variance explained, $F(3, 68) = 1.3$, ns, R^2 change $= .03$, cumulative $R^2 = .54$.

The final addition of physical violence and injury contributed 6% of explained variance, $F(2, 68) = 4.6$, $p = .01$; R^2 change $=.06$, cumulative $R^2 = .60$.

Reversing the entry order, the physical violence and injury variables accounted for only 4% of the variance, $F(2, 68) = 1.3$, ns, cumulative $R^2 = .04$. The emotional abuse variables contributed unique variance to the prediction of postseparation stalking, $F(3, 68) = 3.4$ $p = .02$; R^2 change $= .13$; cumulative $R^2 = .17$. The log of the amount of time since the woman left her partner added 41% to the explained variance, $F(1, 68) = 62.2$, $p = .000$, R^2 change $= .41$; cumulative $R^2 = .59$. Prior stalking made no additional contribution to the explained variance once the other predictors were entered into the model, $F(1, 68) = 2.1$, ns, R^2 change $= .01$, cumulative $R^2 = .60$. Significant individual predictors of postseparation stalking were CTS-PSYCH, $t(67) = 2.9$; $\beta = .37$) and (log) length of time out of the relationship $t(67) = 7.7$; $\beta = .65$).

DISCUSSION

The aims of this paper were to describe the frequencies and patterns of stalking behaviors experienced in a heterogeneous sample of acutely battered women and to examine the relationship of stalking to emotional abuse and physical violence in battered women. The battered women who participated in this research were in fairly long-term relationships with their abusive partners, though most were not currently living with, or romantically involved with, their partners at the time of study participation. Because of the stringency of screening criteria, participants can be described as "battered women" based on the number and severity of abusive incidents they experienced. Moreover, unlike many samples of battered women, only about half of our sample were shelter residents at the time they participated in this research.

Examination of the individual violent and harassing stalking behavior items revealed the staggering number, type, variety, and frequency of stalking behaviors to which battered women are subjected. These behaviors range from the typical types of behaviors expected in a sample of acutely battered women (i.e., threatened, attempted, and actual physical harm), to the more typical pursuit-oriented behaviors generally conceptualized as stalking (e.g., being followed, watched, or receiving unwanted contact). With the number and range of stalking behaviors reported by these women, it is not surprising that many battered women report feeling terrorized. It was distressing to find that nearly half of the battered women reported that their partner violated an order of protection within the past 6 months. This finding is consistent with the 69% of women who reported having an order of protection violated by their male stalker in the NVAWS. The absolute differences in rates may be a function of the shorter interval (6 months) used in our study, compared to the life time criterion used in the NVAWS.

In contrast to the findings from the National Violence Against Women Study (Tjaden & Theonnes, 1998b), in which less than half of the female victims reported receiving overt threats of violence, nearly all of the battered women in our study (94%) reported being threatened by their partners. It is possible that this difference is due to the fact that our participants rated stalking behaviors occurring over the past 6 months, which may have included a period of time in which they were still involved with their partner. However, this is not a likely explanation because the NVAWS reported only 43% of women stalked by intimate partners experienced stalking only after leaving the relationship. The remainder reported being stalked only before the relationship ended (21%) or both before and after it ended (36%). It is more likely that these findings are a consequence of the differences in samples between the studies. Nonetheless, both sets of findings underscore the very high rates of stalking in intimate relationships that occur across the life span of an abusive relationship.

Physical Abuse, Emotional Abuse, and Stalking: Topographical and Functional Overlap

Topographical similarities between these three constructs include the fact that battering, emotional abuse, and stalking tend to be serial and ongoing and can occur during and after the termination of the romantic relationship. Additionally, aspects of violent stalking (e.g., physical harm, threatened harm) have been historically characterized as battering, while aspects of harassing behavior (e.g., unwanted calls at work, unwanted visits at home, following you) have been historically characterized as emotional abuse. Functional similarities include findings that battering, stalking, and some aspects of emotional abuse appear to be motivated by attempts to control and intimidate the victim and may increase in frequency and/or severity in the context of actual or perceived threats to the security of the attachment. With the increasing

acknowledgment of the pervasiveness of stalking within battering relationships, future research will need to examine the heterogeneity of the
stalking phenomena and grapple with conceptual/definitional issues
and delimit lines of demarcation between these forms of abuse.

Correlations between stalking and the emotional and physical abuse
variables tended to be modest, with the strongest relationship occurring between the stalking and the dominance/isolation subscale of the
PMWI. In light of the considerable conceptual overlap between these
two constructs, this is not a surprising result. Perhaps, stalking represents an extreme form of dominance and control when it occurs in the
context of physically violent relationships. Results of our analyses provide support for the idea that stalking is more closely linked with
emotional/psychological abuse than it is with physical violence, at least
when studied within a sample of acutely battered women. First, the
measures of physical violence and injury were unable to predict stalking, once we controlled for the effects of emotional and psychological
abuse. Moreover, the dominance/isolation scale emerged as the only
significant individual level predictor of stalking. Second, stalking did
not uniquely predict fear of future violence and expectations of future
serious harm or death, once the effects of emotional abuse were controlled. These results highlight the considerable crossover between stalking and emotional abuse and support the notion that stalking might be
conceptualized under the rubric of emotional and psychological abuse.
Taken together, the experiences of stalking and emotional abuse create
a climate of unrelenting fear that haunts battered women even after
they separate from their abusive partners. Undoubtedly, the severe
physical violence perpetrated against many of these women by their
partners serves to legitimize their fears that stalking behavior may
escalate into more serious, life-threatening violence.

Quite possibly, these findings might not be replicated in samples of
women who experienced emotional abuse without physical violence,
or in samples of less severely battered women, or women exposed to
courtship violence. Future research needs to address the topographical
overlap between stalking, emotional abuse, and physical violence in
samples that are constructed more broadly than ours. Nonetheless, we
believe that the results of this study provide compelling support for the
close ties between emotional abuse and stalking behavior.

Our results are consistent with the emergent literature focusing on
the pivotal role of emotional and psychological abuse in the lives of
physically battered women. Sackett and Saunders (1999) found that

psychological abuse was a stronger predictor of battered women's fear of abuse than was physical violence. Marshall (1999) also measured contributors to battered women's fear of death/serious harm and found that both subtle and overt forms of psychological abuse made independent contributions to fears of future harm. In a study of emotional abuse in dating relationships, Murphy and Hoover (1999) examined a multifactorial model of emotional abuse, comprised of four factors, (dominance/intimidation; denigration; hostile withdrawal; and restrictive engulfment) and found that while all four forms of emotional abuse were associated with coercive control in interpersonal relationships, the dominance/isolation and denigration scales were the most strongly related to physical aggression.

Descriptions of nonintimate partner stalking are characterized solely by a multiplicity of unwanted pursuit behavior experienced as (nonphysical contact) harassment. In fact, at least one literature review has defined a subset of stalking as "obsessional following" with relatively low incidence of actual physical violence (Meloy, 1996). Future research needs to examine the possibility that there are subtypes of stalking that appear topographically similar, but that may be functionally different. This may be particularly true when comparing cases of stranger stalking with stalking that takes place in the context of current or former romantic and intimate partnerships.

Our findings, in concert with the developing literature on stalking and emotional abuse, underscore the importance of developing and testing comprehensive theoretical models that incorporate multiple dimensions of coercive and controlling behavior that are studied prospectively in a variety of populations exposed to romantic and intimate partner coercion, abuse, and violence.

Although the impact of battering has often included the effects on physical, emotional, and psychological functioning, little research has addressed the occupational impact. One notable finding in this study was that battered women reported frequent harassment by phone or in person in their places of employment or where they attend school. Historically, most workplaces have been relatively unresponsive to and unaware of the dynamics and impact of intimate partner violence, resulting in battered women losing their jobs as a result of workplace interference by their partners (Friedman, Tucker, Neville, & Imperial, 1996). Losing a job further hinders a battered woman's efforts to achieve the financial independence necessary to establish a life without her partner. Loss of employment as well as missed workdays were also reported by stalked victims in the NVAWS. To provide education and training on stalking and intimate partner violence in employment settings may be an important next step.

Stalking and Separation

In support of the literature highlighting separation as a risk factor for battered women, we too found that stalking behavior escalated among women who left their abusive partners. Even more notable was the finding that the length of time a woman was out of the abusive relationship was the single strongest predictor of postseparation stalking, even after accounting for previous levels of stalking in the relationship. Perhaps, once a woman has left the relationship, it is more difficult (due to proximity) to commit acts of violence against her, but acts of stalking, such as harassment via phone and e-mail are achieved rather easily. Among the women who left their abusive relationships, many continued to experience recent harassing, threatening and stalking behaviors, and these women reported significant fears that their partners would commit lethal or sublethal acts of violence against them. Thus, in spite of the oft heard "Why doesn't she just leave?" these data support the growing consensus that leaving does not end the violence, and in some cases escalates it. In her discussion of separation violence, Mahoney (1991) redirects us from attending solely to battered women's efforts to separate from abusive partners. She argues that we need to reframe the question from why doesn't she just leave, to "why doesn't he let her go?" Future research and intervention strategies may need to focus on understanding and ameliorating the attachment disruptions in perpetrators of relationship abuse, as it appears that one function of pursuit-oriented behaviors, of which stalking is a particularly virulent form, is to regulate attachment and proximity seeking via coercive control strategies.

Unfortunately, we were unable to document the type, number, and frequency of stalking behaviors that might have emerged as women engaged in the process of extricating themselves from relationships with their abusive partners. Future research might address this by using qualitative and quantitative methods to study in more detail the experience of women in the course of negotiating exits from battering relationships. Findings from this study suggest that stalking of acutely battered women has been a neglected dimension in most studies of battered women and needs to be considered as a pivotal component of intervention and prevention efforts with batterer and victim populations.

NOTES

1. For ease of language the feminine pronoun will be used to refer to the victim, and the masculine pronoun to the batterer, although it is recognized that intimate partner violence does occur in same-sex relationships, and with female perpetrators and male victims.

2. It should be noted that these items were removed from analyses using the SBC as a continuous scale, but are included here for descriptive purposes only.

ACKNOWLEDGMENT

This work was supported by National Institute of Mental Health Grant RO1 MH 55542. We are grateful for the efforts of many people on our staff who made significant contributions to this project: Jenifer Bennice, Dana Cason, Michael Griffin, Anouk Grubaugh, Catherine Feuer, Debra Kaysen, Leslie Kimball, Linda Meade, Meg Milstead, Miranda Morris, Angie Waldrop, Amy Williams and Mary Uhlmansiek. Terri Weaver is now in the Department of Psychology at Saint Louis University.

REFERENCES

Bernard, G. W., Vera, H., Vera, M., & Newman, G. (1982). Till death do us part: A study of spouse murder. *Bulletin of the American Academy of Psychiatry and the Law, 10,* 271–280.

Biden, J. (1993). Violence against women: The congressional response. *American Psychologist, 48,* 1059–1061.

Bowlby, J. (1980). *Attachment and loss: Vol. III. Loss, sadness and depression.* New York: Basic Books.

Browne, A. (1987). *When battered women kill.* New York: Free Press.

Burgess, A. W., Baker, T., Greening, D., Hartman, C. R., Burgess, A. G., Douglas, J. E., & Halloran, R. (1997). Stalking behaviors within domestic violence. *Journal of Family Violence, 12,* 389–403.

Campbell, J. C. (1992). If I can't have you, no one can: Power and control in homicide of female partners. In J. Radford & D. H. Russell (Eds.), *Intimate femicide: The politics of woman killing.* New York: Twayne.

Coleman, F. (1997). Stalking behavior and the cycle of domestic violence. *Journal of Interpersonal Violence, 12,* 420–432.

Dutton, D. G. (1998). *The abusive personality: Violence and control in intimate relationships.* New York: Guilford Press.

Dutton, D. G., & Holtzworth-Monroe, A. (1997). The role of early trauma in males who assault their wives. In D. Cicchetti & S. Toth (Ed.), *Developmental perspectives on trauma: Theory, research, and intervention* (Vol. 8, pp. 379–401). Rochester symposium on developmental psychology. Rochester, NY: University of Rochester Press.

Dutton, D. G., Saunders, K., Starzomski, A., & Bartholomew, K. (1994). Intimacy-anger and insecure attachment as precursors of abuse in intimate relationships. *Journal of Applied Social Psychology, 24,* 1367–1386.

Dutton, M. A. (1992). *Empowering and healing the battered woman: A model of assessment and intervention.* New York: Springer Publishing Co.

Ellis, D., & DeKeseredy, W. S. (1997). Rethinking estrangement, interventions, and intimate femicide. *Violence Against Women, 3,* 590–610.

Follingstad, D. R., Rutledge, L. L., Berg, B. J., Hause, E. S., & Polek, D. S. (1990). The role of emotional abuse in physically abusive relationships. *Journal of Family Violence, 1,* 37–49.

Friedman, L. N., Tucker, S. B., Neville, P. R., & Imperial, M. (1996). The impact of domestic violence in the workplace. In G. R. Vandenbos & E. Q. Bulato (Eds.), *Violence on the job: Identifying risks and developing solutions.* Washington, DC: American Psychological Association.

Holtzworth-Monroe, A., Stuart, G., & Hutchinson, G. (1997). Violent versus nonviolent husbands: Differences in attachment patterns, dependency, and jealousy. *Journal of Family Psychology, 11,* 314–331.

Kesner, J. E., Julian, T., & McKenry, P. C. (1997). Application of attachment theory to male violence towards female intimates. *Journal of Family Violence, 12,* 211–228.

Koss, M. P., Goodman, L. A., Browne, A., Fitzgerald, L. F., Keita, G. P., & Russo, N. F. (1994). *No safe haven: Male violence against women at home, at work, and in the community.* Washington, DC: American Psychological Association.

Kienlen, K. K. (1998). Developmental and social antecedents of stalking. In J. Reid Meloy (Ed.), *The psychology of stalking: Clinical and forensic perspectives* (pp. 51–67). San Diego, CA: Academic Press.

Kurz, D. (1996). Separation, divorce, and woman abuse. *Violence Against Women, 2,* 63–81.

Marshall, L. L. (1999). Effects of men's subtle and overt psychological abuse on low income women. *Violence and Victims, 14*(1), 69–88.

Mahoney, M. R. (1991). Legal images of battered women: Redefining the issue of separation. *Michigan Law Review, 90,* 1–94.

Meloy, J. R. (1996). Stalking (obsessional following): A review of some preliminary studies. *Aggression and Violence Behavior, 1,* 147–162.

Murphy, C. M., & Hoover, S. A. (1999). Measuring emotional abuse in dating relationships as a multifactorial construct. *Violence and Victims, 14,* 39–53.

National Institute of Justice. (1998). *Stalking and domestic violence: The third annual report to congress under the violence against women act.* (NCJ Report No. 172204). Washington, DC: U.S. Department of Justice.

O'Leary, K. D. (1999). Psychological abuse: A variable deserving critical attention in domestic violence. *Violence and Victims, 14,* 3–23.

Sackett, L. A., & Saunders, D. G. (1999). The impact of different forms of psychological abuse on battered women. *Violence and Victims, 14,* 105–117.

Sev'er, A. (1997). Recent or imminent separation and intimate violence against women. *Violence Against Women, 3,* 566–590.

Straus, M. A., Hamby, S. L. Boney-McCoy, S., & Sugarman, D. B. (1996). The revised conflict tactics scales (CTS2). *Journal of Family Issues, 17*(3), 283–316.

Sonkin, D. J. (1997). *Domestic violence: The perpetrator assessment handbook.* (Available from Damiel J. Sonkin, PhD, 1505 Bridgeway, Sausilito, CA 94965).

Tabachnick, B. G., & Fidell, L. S. (1996). *Using multivariate statistics* (3rd ed.). New York: Harper Collins College Publishers.

Tjaden, P., & Theonnes, N. (1998a). *Prevalence, incidence, and consequences of violence against women: Findings from the national violence against women survey* (NCJ Report No. 172837). Washington, DC: U.S. Department of Justice.

Tjaden, P., & Theonnes, N. (1998b). *Stalking in America: Findings from the national violence against women survey* (NCJ Report No. 169592). Washington, DC: U.S. Department of Justice.

Tolman, R. (1989). The development of a measure of psychological maltreatment of women by their male partners. *Violence and Victims, 4,* 173–189.

Tolman, R. (1999). The validation of the maltreatment of women inventory. *Violence and Victims, 14,* 25–35.

Walker, L. E., & Meloy, J. R. (1998). Stalking and domestic violence. In J. Reid Meloy (Ed.), *The psychology of stalking: Clinical and forensic perspectives* (pp. 140–164). San Diego, CA: Academic Press.

Wilson, M., & Daly, M. (1992). Till death do us part. In J. Radford & D. H. Russell (Eds.), *Intimate femicide: The politics of woman killing.* New York: Twayne.

Wilson, M., & Daly, M. (1993). Spousal homicide risk and estrangement. *Violence and Victims, 8,* 3–16.

5

The Impact of Severe Stalking Experienced by Acutely Battered Women: An Examination of Violence, Psychological Symptoms and Strategic Responding

Mindy B. Mechanic, Mary H. Uhlmansiek,
Terri L. Weaver, and Patricia A. Resick

The compelling link between stalking and intimate partner abuse was first made evident by publication of data from the National Violence Against Women Study (NVAWS; Tjaden & Theonnes, 1998). The nexus between stalking and other forms of intimate partner abuse has been relatively understudied, particularly in the context of burgeoning research on intimate partner abuse. Consequently, many unexplored questions remain about both the topography and impact of stalking as it co-occurs with other forms of intimate partner emotional, physical, and sexual violence.

At least in the context of intimate partner violence, stalking has been identified as a risk factor for severe, even lethal violence. One recent study identified stalking as a lethal precursor to attempted and completed femicides (McFarlane et al., 1999). More than 75% of the murdered or nearly murdered women were stalked, and two-thirds were physically assaulted by their partners in the 12 months preceding the lethal or sublethal assaults. Abused women were also more likely than nonabused women to have been stalked by their partners, with former partners more likely than current partners to perpetrate stalking. While stalking and partner abuse were more likely to co-occur, 19% of attempted or completed femicides were associated with histories of recent stalking in the absence of physical violence, suggesting that there might be subtypes of partner abuse both with and without co-occurring stalking.

To look at the relationship between stalking and intimate partner abuse, Mechanic, Weaver, and Resick (this volume) studied stalking behaviors as reported by recently battered women. Extremely high rates of harassing and violent forms of stalking were reported by battered women, and relative to physical violence, emotional abuse was a stronger predictor of stalking. Stalking also predicted women's fears that their partners would lethally harm them in the future, despite the fact that most of the women had separated from their abusive partners. Moreover, consistent with the literature identifying separation as a period of risk for increased violence (Mahoney, 1991; Sev'er, 1997), stalking did not cease upon separation.

PSYCHOLOGICAL AND FUNCTIONAL RESPONSES TO INTIMATE PARTNER ABUSE

Emerging evidence documents the deleterious impact of intimate partner abuse on women's physical, psychological and emotional well-being (Campbell & Soeken, 1999a, 1999b; Campbell, Kub, Belknap & Templin, 1997; Gleason, 1993; Golding, 1999; Koss et al., 1994; Sutherland, Bybee & Sullivan, 1998; Weaver & Clum, 1995). Post-traumatic stress disorder (PTSD), depression, suicidality, substance abuse, diminished self-esteem, along with diminished physical health status occur at extremely elevated levels among women with histories of intimate partner abuse, with even more severe problems found among currently or recently abused women and among women living in poverty (Browne, Salomon & Bassuk, 1999). Rates of PTSD in battered women range from 31% to 84%, with a weighted mean prevalence estimate of 64% (Golding, 1999). These rates are considerably higher than the rates of PTSD found among general community samples of women, which range from 1% to 12%, and are also considerably higher than the PTSD rates found among community samples of women with histories of criminal victimization (Golding, 1999). Research on PTSD with community samples indicate that more than half of the individuals diagnosed with PTSD continue to suffer from the disorder for more than one year, underscoring the chronicity of the problem (Breslau & Davis, 1992; Kessler et al., 1995).

A recent meta-analysis reviewing 18 studies assessing depression among battered women estimated the weighted mean prevalence of depression as 48% (Golding, 1999), again a rate considerably higher than found in epidemiological samples of women. Depression among battered women has been found to be chronic, with symptoms continuing to exist over time for some battered women, even in the absence of recent reabuse (Campbell & Soeken, 1999b; Campbell, Kub, Belknap & Templin, 1997; Campbell, Sullivan & Davidson, 1995; Sutherland, Bybee, & Sullivan, 1998).

DISENTANGLING THE IMPACT OF CONCOMITANT FORMS OF PARTNER ABUSE

While the constructs of stalking, physical violence, sexual coercion, and emotional abuse are tied by the common thread of "coercive control tactics," few studies have addressed the full range of coercive control strategies used against women by their partners. An inclusive approach to the study of partner abuse is necessary in order to delineate the inter-relationships among different forms of abuse and to decipher their relative impacts on behavioral, psychological, and strategic outcomes. When multiple dimensions of abuse are studied conjointly, complex, sometimes contradictory findings pertaining to battered women's psychological and strategic responses to abuse emerge. Dutton (1993, 1996) defined strategic responses as those behaviors battered women deploy to respond to, cope with, or merely survive the abuse directed toward them. Emergent literature has begun to tackle these complex issues by studying both symptomatic and strategic responses to abuse in the context of co-occurring physical, emotional, and sexual abuse. However, stalking has not been included as a dimension of partner abuse. Dutton and her colleagues (1999) found varying patterns of psychological and strategic responding as a function of different types of partner abuse, with strategic responses more likely to be influenced by physical aggression whereas symptomatic responses were more closely associated with emotional and verbal abuse. Other research on battered women's help-seeking has shown that more severe abuse is associated with increased efforts to seek help (Gondolf & Fisher, 1988). The complexity of the relationship between abuse, symptoms and strategic responding is highlighted by a recent study by Arias and Pape (1999), finding that psychological symptoms moderated the relationship between abuse and strategic responding (defined as intentions to terminate the relationship) for both physical and psychological abuse. Specifically, only women who were least distressed felt able to disengage from their abusive relationships. Consistent with the findings of Dutton and colleagues (1999), psychological symptoms, such as PTSD and depression, were better accounted for by psychological abuse than physical violence (Arias & Pape, 1999). None of these studies included stalking as a component of the spectrum of abuse.

Empirical data documenting the impact of stalking are virtually nonexistent. Increased help-seeking, increased fear, and days lost from work are among the few documented findings (Tjaden & Theonnes, 1998). The purpose of the present study was to build upon our previous work on stalking in battered women (Mechanic, Weaver & Resick, this volume) and to begin to understand more about the phenomenon and impact of severe forms of stalking experienced by women who are also subjected to high levels of co-occurring physical and psychological aggression. To achieve this aim, we compared battered women reporting high rates of unremitting, multimodal stalking with a group of battered women reporting relatively infrequent stalking. Our recruitment of an acutely exposed sample of severely battered women permitted us to obtain a relatively large subsample of women experiencing extremely high frequency, multibehavior stalking episodes. We focused on evaluating whether serial stalking might be a "risk factor" for additional severe violence by evaluating both concomitant and (subsequent) post-separation aggression and examining the relationship between relentless stalking, psychological functioning, and strategic responding. On the basis of our previous work (Mechanic, Weaver, & Resick, this volume), we expected relentlessly stalked battered women to evidence more severe forms of co-occurring and post-separation psychological and physical aggression, and more severe psychological symptoms (Arias & Pape, 1999; Dutton et al, 1999). However, given conflicting findings regarding the impact of severe abuse on strategic responding, the direction of effects could not be specified a priori.

METHOD

Participants

Data reported in this article were collected as part of a larger, ongoing study focusing on factors that influence recovery from intimate partner violence in a sample of acutely battered women. The data presented in the present article were drawn from the sample used in Mechanic, Weaver, and Resick, this volume. We will present data on 65 battered women, 35 who were classified as relentlessly stalked, and 31 who were identified as infrequently stalked. This sample was drawn from a pool of 114 battered women who participated in the larger study. The classification procedure for determining stalking status is outlined in the results section.

Recruitment/Screening Criteria

Participants were recruited from local agencies serving battered women, including shelters, police departments, legal assistance agencies, hospital emergency departments, and other support service agencies. To access non-help-seeking battered women, efforts were made to contact participants through media and community outreach events targeting women. Referrals were also made directly by study participants to other battered women acquaintances.

Prospective participants contacted us and were screened for eligibility on the telephone. To recruit a sample of battered women who experienced recent, serial, intimate partner violence, several screening criteria were employed. The following criteria were used to screen potential participants:

1. length of relationship;
2. recency of violence; and
3. severity of violence.

First, participants were required to have been in an intimate relationship, whether cohabiting or not, for a minimum of three months, effectively ruling out dating violence taking place within the context of casual dating relationships. Second, to improve reporting accuracy, we required that the most recent episode of violence had occurred within the past six months. However, if the most recent episode had occurred less than two weeks earlier, participants were scheduled so that there were at least two weeks between the most recent episode and the assessment. This was done in order to reduce potential inflation of scores on symptom measures as a consequence of assault recency. Finally, in order to obtain a sample of women who experienced more than an occasional episode of relationship violence, we required that participants experience at least four incidents of minor violence or two episodes of severe violence (or some combination of four incidents of minor and/or severe violence) within the past year. Minor violence items were: pushed, shoved or grabbed you; slapped or hit you; threw things at you that could hurt; twisted your arm or pulled your hair. Severe violence items were: hit or punched you with a fist or with something that could hurt; caused you to have physical injuries; choked you; slammed you against a wall or threw you down stairs; kicked you or beat you up; threatened you with a weapon; used a weapon against you; forced you to have sex when you did not want to; caused you to fear for your life or the lives of your family members.

Participants who were ruled out of the study based on their telephone screening were given support, thanked for their time, and were provided with information about appropriate resources in the community. Twenty-four women were screened out of the study for the following reasons: two women were with their partners for less than three months; six women reported fewer than the required number of episodes of physical violence; 15 women reported abuse that occurred more than six months ago (and for some women the abuse ended many years ago); and one woman declined to participate after hearing more about the study.

Sample Demographic and Relationship Characteristics

The sample ($N = 114$) was predominantly African American (69%; 31% White), and relatively financially disadvantaged. More than half of the women (51%) reported that their own incomes were $10,000 per year or less. Thirty-nine percent of the women made between $10,000 and $30,000, and 9% earned more than $30,000. The women in our sample averaged 35 years in age ($SD = 7.9$), and ranged from 19–59. A sizable percentage of the women were married to their abusers (41%); 38% were cohabitating; 14% were separated or divorced, and 8% identified their relationships as dating. Battered women in this sample were in fairly long-term relationships with their abusive partners (M = 7.4 years; SD = 6.0 years), ranging from 10 months to 27 years. These women experienced abuse in their relationships for an average of 5.3 years (SD = 5.3 years), with duration of abuse ranging from two months to 21 years.

Instruments

THE STALKING BEHAVIOR CHECKLIST (SBC; COLEMAN, 1997)

The SBC is a 25–item inventory assessing a variety of unwanted harassing and pursuit-oriented behaviors. Each item is rated on a 6–point frequency scale, ranging from 1 = never; 2 = once a month or less; 3 = 2–3 times per month; 4 = once or twice per week; 5 = 3–6 times per week; and 6 = once per day or more. Participants rated each item for the period of time covering the past 6 months.

THE STANDARDIZED BATTERING INTERVIEW

This interview consists of a variety of questions assessing demographic and abusive relationship characteristics, including recent (past month) stalking behavior experienced by women who left their partner. Post-separation stalking items include: threats to life, threats to children's lives, threats of custody, threats to kidnap children, telephone and "stalking." One item queries respondents about whether their partners physically assaulted them after having left the relationship. Items are rated on a 5–point scale for the past month (0 = never; 1 = once or twice; 2 = once or twice a week; 3 = several times a week; 4 = daily or almost every day).

Participants were asked about their use of a number of different strategic responses to the abuse using a dichotomous (yes/no) scale: hotline, counselor, therapist; police; order of protection; shelter medical care; and clergy.

Supplemental questions were asked about injuries. Because we are interested in the role of stalking as a possible risk factor for lethality, we will use the data collected on one of the injury variables, loss of consciousness. The item was measured on a frequency scale anchored to the abuse in the relationship (0 = 0; 1 = 1–3 times; 2 = 4–10 times; 3 = 11–49 times; 4 = 50 + times).

PSYCHOLOGICAL MALTREATMENT OF WOMEN INVENTORY—
ABBREVIATED VERSION (PMWI; TOLMAN, 1989; 1999)

The abbreviated 14–item version of the PMWI consists of two factor-derived subscales that measure dominance/isolation (DI) and emotional and verbal abuse (EV). Evidence of reliability and validity are presented in Tolman (1999). The scale is a self-report measure, and each item is rated on a 5-point frequency scale, ranging from never (1), to very frequently (5). Each subscale consists of 7 items. Coefficient alphas for both subscales in the present sample were .88.

REVISED CONFLICT TACTICS SCALE-2 (CTS-2; STRAUS, HAMBY, BONEY-McCOY & SUGARMAN, 1995)

Two subscales of the revised CTS-2 were administered to assess the frequency and severity of physical assault (CTS-PA; 12 items) and injury (CTS-I; 6–items). Ratings are made in terms of frequency (0 = never, 1 = once in past year; 2 = twice in past year; 3 = 3–5 times in past year; 4 = 6–10 times in past year; 5 = 11–20 times in past year; 6 = more than 20 times in past year). The authors of the CTS-2 subscale suggest creating a severity index by adding the midpoint for each item and creating a summed score for each subscale. The midpoint equals the rating for ratings of 0, 1, and 2 for items rated with those scores. Scores of 3 are recoded to 4, scores of 4 are recoded to 8, scores of 5 are recoded to 15 and scores of 6 are recoded to 25. Coefficient alpha for the CTS-PA was .90. Coefficient alpha for the 6–item injury scale was .62, with one item having an item-total scale correlation of-.03 (I had a broken bone from a fight with my partner). This item was dropped, resulting in a 5–item scale with an alpha of .66.

To assess sexual coercion, we used a modification of the CTS-2 items, by using two separate questions to assess:

1. use of threats or force to coerce oral or anal sex; and
2. use of threats or force to coerce vaginal intercourse.

CTS-2 scoring was used. The alpha for the two items was .64.

THE POSTTRAUMATIC DIAGNOSTIC SCALE (PDS: FOA, CASHMAN, JAYCOX, & PERRY, 1997)

The PDS is a 34–item measure of PTSD symptoms that can be used to compute a continuous severity score, severity scores for each of the 3 clusters of symptoms, and for making a formal diagnosis of PTSD. Seventeen items assess symptom frequency, rated for the past month using a 4–point scale (0 = not at all or only one time; 1 = once a week or less/once in a while; 2 = 2–4 times per week/half the time; 3 = five or more times a week/almost always). Coefficient alpha for the 17–point scale was .90. Consistent with DSM-IV criteria requiring functional impairment or clinically significant distress for a diagnosis, the PDS assesses functional impairment secondary to PTSD symptoms with nine dichotomously scored items (yes/no) addressing:

1. work;
2. household chores and duties;
3. fun and leisure activities;
4. relationships with friends;
5. schoolwork;
6. relationships with family;
7. sex life;
8. general satisfaction with life; and
9. overall level of functioning in all areas of life.

The PDS has been found to possess excellent psychometric properties, including internal consistency, test-retest reliability, and convergent validity with other well-established measures of PTSD.

BECK DEPRESSION INVENTORY—SECOND EDITION (BDI-II; BECK, STEER, & BROWN, 1996)

The BDI-II is an updated version of its widely used predecessor, the BDI (Beck et al., 1961), which measures depressive symptoms. The BDI-II contains 21 items assessing depressive symptoms corresponding to the Diagnostic and Statistical Manual of Mental Disorders, Fourth edition (DSM-IV; American Psychiatric Association, 1994) criteria for major depressive disorder. Items are rated on a 4–point severity scale. Coefficient alpha for the scale was .92 in the present sample. Total scores are obtained by summing the items and scores can be clinically evaluated using the following cut score guidelines: 0–13 = minimal; 14–19 = mild; 20–28 = moderate; 29–63 = severe. Evidence of construct validity and reliability has been obtained, and the BDI-II has been successfully used in cross-sectional and longitudinal studies of battered women (Campbell, Kub, Belknap & Templin, 1997).

Procedure

Participants who met study criteria and agreed to participate completed the study in two visits that typically occurred within several days of each other. On day 1, women first completed several symptom-based measures programmed onto a laptop computer in order to reduce the likelihood that symptom scores would be elevated as a consequence of discussing traumatic material. Next, they were interviewed by trained clinicians with extensive experience dealing with traumatized populations. The second day consisted of non-symptom-based self-report instruments that were programmed onto a laptop computer. Debriefings were conducted with participants following completion of all instruments.

RESULTS

Classification Into Stalked Groups

To address our interest in studying the impact of relentless stalking experienced by battered women, we first defined the groups conceptually and then developed empirical criteria to operationalize the conceptual criteria. Two dimensions were part of our conceptual definition: high frequency of occurrence, plus repeated exposure to multiple types of stalking events. Thus, we defined our group of relentlessly stalked women as those who experienced a multiplicity of stalking events, each occurring with very high frequency. Defined in this way, our relentlessly stalked group represents a qualitatively and quantitatively distinct group.

To operationalize this definition, we first rescored the SBC to reflect very high frequency, defined as a minimum of weekly occurrence. Items scored as four or higher were recoded with a score of one. Items with a frequency of monthly or less frequent occurrence (scores of 3 or less) were recoded as zero. The items were then summed, resulting in a 25–item index with a possible range from zero to 25. Twenty-eight percent of the sample ($n = 31$) received a score of zero. This group was identified as the infrequently stalked subgroup. It is important to note that there were only two women in the full sample who reported no incidents of stalking, therefore identification of a "nonstalked" comparison group was not possible.

The relentlessly stalked group was defined as those participants reporting a minimum of six different stalking events that each occurred once per week or more (n = 35). Thus, this group could be said to represent a group of relentlessly stalked women exposed to a multiplicity of stalking events. The cutoff score of six was selected by examining the distribution of scores and selecting the top third of the distribution. This enabled us to generate two roughly equal comparison groups comprising approximately the bottom and top thirds of the distribution's 27th and 73rd percentile, respectively. Battered women who scored in the middle third of the distribution were eliminated from analyses in order to focus on severely stalked women, and to contrast them with a much lower frequency comparison group. The frequency scores on the full scale SBC were approximately one standard deviation below the mean of the full sample (N = 114) and one standard deviation above the mean for the infrequently and relentlessly stalked groups, respectively. For the relentlessly stalked group, the women reported experiencing an average of 10.2 different stalking events at the minimum level of at least one weekly (SD = 3.3). The number ranged from a minimum of six (fixed by design) to a maximum of 19.

Data Analysis Plan

First we will present descriptive findings on the relentlessly and infrequently stalked battered women. Next, we will present univariate analyses focusing on co-occurring abuse, postseparation abuse, psychological impact, and strategic responding.

Descriptive Findings

No statistically significant differences were obtained between relentlessly stalked and infrequently stalked battered women in terms of race, age and income. A nonsignificant difference in marital status was found between the groups. Dating relationships longer than three months in duration were reported by 7% of the infrequently stalked and 9% of the relentlessly stalked women. Married couples comprised 36% of the infrequently stalked and 46% of the relentlessly stalked groups. Nearly one-third (29%) of the relentlessly stalked women were cohabiting with their partners, whereas 48% of the infrequently stalked women reported cohabiting status. It is interesting to note that nearly twice as many relentlessly stalked women (17%) were separated or divorced from their abusive partners, compared to 9% of the infrequently stalked women. There were no statistically significant differences in the relentlessly stalked (M = 8.0 years; SD = 5.9 years; Minimum = 10 months, Maximum = 23 years) and infrequently stalked (M = 6.8 years; SD = 6.2 years; Minimum = 12 months, Maximum = 73 years) women in terms of the length of their relationships. The groups were also comparable in terms of the duration of the abuse they experienced. Infrequently stalked women were abused by their partners for an average of 4.7 years (SD = 5.3 years; minimum = 2 months, maximum = 20 years), and relentlessly stalked women reported abuse lasting an average of 5.8 years (SD = 5.3 years; minimum = 4 months, maximum = 21 years).

At the time of participation in the study, 85% of the women identified their status as having left the abusive relationships. Although 91% of the relentlessly stalked women, compared to 78% of the infrequently stalked women had left their partners, this difference did not reach statistical significance [χ^2 (1) = 2.5, p = .11]. At the time of the assessment 41% of the sample was housed in a shelter for battered women. No differences in shelter status was found between the stalked groups [χ^2 (1) = < 1, ns].

Relentless Stalking in Relation to Other Forms of Abuse

We compared the relentlessly stalked battered women with the infrequently stalked group on dimensions of co-occurring forms of intimate partner abuse to ascertain whether, as predicted, relentless stalking would be associated with more severe physical, sexual, and emotional abuse. A one-way MANOVA was conducted on the two psychological abuse variables (Emotional/Verbal Abuse, Dominance/Isolation), one measure of sexual coercion, and the three measures of physical violence and injury (CTS-PA, CTS-I, loss of consciousness). A significant overall effect was found for the relentlessly stalked group on the abuse measures using Wilks's Lambda = .57, $F(6, 59)$ = 11.6; p = .000. Follow-up univariate tests indicated that the relentlessly stalked group reported significantly greater abuse, violence and injuries on all indices of concomitant abuse. These findings are presented in Table 5.1.

We were interested in whether women who were relentlessly stalked during the prior 6–month period experienced additional abuse and stalking once they separated from their partners. To examine this question, we compared the women on several indicators of post-separation abuse and stalking unrelated to the stalking measure used to classify

Table 5.1 Group Comparisons on Indices of Concomitant Abuse

Measure	Relentlessly Stalked n = 35				Infrequently Stalked n = 31					
	M	SD	Min.	Max.	M	SD	Min.	Max.	F	p
PMWI-D/I	31.2	6.2	10	35	21.50	6.4	11	34	38.5	.000
PMWI-E/V	31.9	4.7	17	35	26.90	6.0	12	35	14.8	.000
CTS-PA	120.0	65.0	13	256	53.80	47.2	12	194	21.9	.000
CTS-I	39.2	20.6	5	74	17.60	18.0	5	71	20.2	.000
Sexual Coercion	17.0	17.5	2	50	8.80	13.8	2	50	4.4	.040
Lost Consciousness	1.0	1.0	0	4	.32	.6	0	2	10.3	.002

Note. PMWI-EV = Psychological Maltreatment of Women Inventory-Emotional Violence subscale; PMWI-DI = Psychological Maltreatment of Women Inventory-Dominance/Isolation Subscale; CTS-I = Conflict Tactics Scale 2–Injury Subscale; CTS-PA-Conflict Tactics Scale 2–Physical Assault Subscale. High scores reflect higher endorsement of the construct. Possible ranges for the scales are as follows: PMWI-EV and DI (7–35); CTS-PA (0–300); CTS-I (0–150); Sexual Coercion (0–50); and Lost Consciousness (0–4). Degrees of freedom for the univariate F's (1,64).

the sample. Only the 56 separated women were included in these analyses. The results of these analyses are presented in Table 5.2. As expected, relentlessly stalked battered women reported higher rates of post-separation stalking than infrequently stalked battered women. Women who reported having children who lived with them were asked about post-separation threats to harm, abduct or take custody of their

Table 5.2 Group Comparisons on Indices of Post-Separation Stalking

Measure	Relentlessly Stalked				Infrequently Stalked					
	M	SD	Min.	Max.	M	SD	Min.	Max.	t	p
General Stalking	3.2	3.4	0	10	1.0	1.8	0	7	−2.89	.005
Child Threats	2.0	2.4	0	8	0.4	1.1	0	4	−2.33	.026
	%	n	%	n	χ^2	p	df			
Physical Assault	22	7	4	1	3.5	.06	1			

Note. These analyses were restricted to women who were separated (*n* = 56), and the numbers responding to the child-related questions were smaller due to the lack of children for some women (child threats, *n* = 22). Possible ranges for both scales are 0–12.

children. Threats targeted toward children were more commonly reported by relentlessly stalked rather than infrequently stalked battered women. Finally, women were asked if they were physically assaulted by their partners after having left the relationship. Relentlessly stalked women were five and one-half times more likely (22%) than infrequently stalked (4%) women to report at least one incident of post-separation physical assault, χ^2 (1) = 3.5, p = .06.

Strategic Responses to Abuse

The use of strategies to respond to relationship abuse were compared among the relentlessly stalked and infrequently stalked battered women. The findings from these analyses are presented in Table 5.3. Relentlessly stalked women were more likely than infrequently stalked women to obtain an order of protection and to seek medical care. There was a non-significant trend for relentlessly stalked battered women being more likely to have gone to a battered woman's shelter. No differences were found in the likelihood of having contacted the police, having sought assistance from mental health sources, including hotlines, counselors and therapists, or from members of the clergy. We computed a simple sum of the seven dichotomously scored help-seeking behaviors to assess differences in global strategic responding. Overall, relentlessly stalked battered women engaged in a greater number of help-seeking behaviors (M = 4.3; SD = 1.3) than infrequently stalked battered women (M = 3.5; SD = 1.3), t(64) =-2.39, p = .02.

Table 5.3 Group Comparisons on Strategic Responses to Abuse

Variable	Relentlessly Stalked n = 35		Infrequently Stalked n = 31		χ^2	p
	%	n	%	n		
Obtain Order of Protection	74%	26	45%	14	5.8	.02
Seek Medical Care	77%	27	55%	17	3.7	.05
Seek Shelter	71%	25	52%	16	2.7	.09
Contact Police	86%	30	81%	25	< 1	ns
Seek Mental Health Care	77%	27	81%	25	< 1	ns
Seek Clergy	43%	15	39%	12	< 1	ns

df = 1 for all analyses.

Finally, a greater number of prior attempts to leave the relationship were reported by relentlessly stalked than infrequently stalked battered women (5 or fewer attempts: 35% vs. 71%; 6–15 attempts: 41% vs. 19%; 16+ attempts: 24% vs. 10%, respectively, χ^2 (2) = 8.3, p = .02.

Mental Health Consequences of Relentless Stalking

A MANOVA was used to evaluate whether relentlessly stalked women were more psychologically distressed than those who reported infrequent stalking. The overall MANOVA was significant, Wilks's Lambda = .89, $F(2, 62)$ = 3.9, p = .025. Follow-up univariate tests were conducted to evaluate the significance of the individual distress measures. At a univariate level, symptoms of both posttraumatic stress disorder (Infrequent: M = 44.0; SD = 9.3; Relentless: M = 49.6; SD = 10.4, $t(63)$ =-2.26, p < .05) and depression (Infrequent: M = 27.1; SD = 10.9; Relentless: M = 34.9; SD = 11.9, $t(63)$ =-2.75, p < .01) were more severe among women reporting relentless stalking. An index of impairment was created by summing the nine dichotomously scored impairment items from the PDS. PTSD-related impairment was very high among both groups of women, endorsing an average of nearly seven out of a total of nine indices of impairment (M = 6.9; SD = 2.4), $t(63)$ = < 1.0, ns.

Within-Group Correlations

To explore the possibility that the stalking groups might be differentiated on qualitative as well as quantitative dimensions, within-group correlations among several mental health, strategic responding and abuse variables were computed. Increased strategic responding was associated with greater symptoms of PTSD (r = .42, p = .02), and increased symptoms of depression (r = .28, p = .12) for the infrequently stalked women, but not for those who were relentlessly stalked (r's =-.10, .03, respectively). Symptoms of depression were more strongly associated with dominance/isolation (r = .43, p = .01) among the relentlessly stalked, compared to the infrequently stalked women (r = .16, n.s.), as were injuries (r = .41, p = .02; p = .16, n.s., respectively). Emotional/verbal abuse was moderately correlated with depression (r's = .35, .36; p = .04) in both groups.

Both forms of psychological abuse were more strongly associated with increased PTSD symptoms among the infrequently stalked than the relentlessly stalked battered women: emotional verbal: r = .44, p = .01; r = .27, p = .13, respectively; dominance/isolation: r = 45, p = .01; r = .31, p = .08, respectively. Finally, sexual coercion was highly correlated with injuries (r = .42, p = .01) among the relentlessly stalked, but was unrelated to injuries among the infrequently stalked women (r = .07, ns)

DISCUSSION

This article represents one of the first efforts to examine the experiences of relentless stalking among battered women who were also subjected to high levels of concomitant and subsequent emotional, physical and sexual abuse. The sheer magnitude of stalking faced by the battered women was notable, particularly given the relative lack of attention accorded to stalking in the research literature and in assessment and intervention practices targeted toward battered women. Findings from this article highlight the experiences of a subsample of battered women that could be distinguished *a priori* based on the qualitative and quantitative patterns of stalking they experienced. Relentlessly stalked women in our sample were defined by having experienced a minimum of six different stalking events occurring *at least* weekly, yet it is notable that the mean number of such events was 10, and only two women reported no incidents of stalking by their partners during a six-month period for which stalking was assessed. For some women, stalking events were daily occurrences.

The staggering persistence and relentless pursuit of battered women during and after leaving their relationships is alarming and aptly fitting within the rubric "obessional following" (Meloy, 1996) that has been applied as a label to describe unwanted, unremitting pursuit by romantic partners. Results provide growing support for the conceptualization of stalking (among battered women) as a particularly virulent form of the dominance and isolation component of emotional abuse (Mechanic, Weaver, & Resick, this volume). Research suggests that it is psychological abuse rather than physical violence that appears to instill the greatest amount of fear in battered women (Mechanic, Weaver & Resick, this volume; Sackett & Saunders, 1999). Despite the emerging associations between stalking and psychological abuse, and at the severe end, between stalking and high levels of violence, assessment of stalking-related behaviors has been relatively underrepresented on all measures of psychological abuse and physical violence used for both research and for screening purposes in victim assistance, medical, mental health care settings. These findings underscore the need to include an assessment of stalking-related behaviors in measures of abuse used in all contexts: screening, intervention, and research. Future research needs to continue to explore the nexus between stalking and emotional/ psychological abuse by focusing on women reporting little or no co-occurring physical violence in order to more clearly delineate the inter-relationships among these overlapping constructs.

Relentlessly stalked women reported extremely high levels of con-current emotional abuse, sexual assault, and physical violence result-ing in severe injuries such as loss of consciousness. While this study was not explicitly designed to assess lethality per se, our data suggest that it might be fruitful to consider the type of relentless stalking experienced by the battered women in this sample as a possible risk factor for lethality. The severely stalked women were exposed to mul-tiple episodes of life-threatening violence that resulted at times in loss of consciousness, which might be considered a good proxy variable for lethality. The severity and frequency of the violence continued to per-sist and escalate despite repeated efforts at help-seeking and separat-ing, and these acts may have even elevated the risk of the violence erupting in ways that have lethal potential. Our findings are consistent with those of our previous report which found that stalking was relat-ed to fears of future lethal violence perpetrated against battered wom-en who left their abusive partners (Mechanic, Weaver, & Resick, this volume). Given the data linking stalking, partner abuse, and femicide (McFarlane et al., 1999) it may be prudent to consider including an assessment of stalking in lethality assessment screening tools such as the Danger Assessment Scale (Campbell et al., 1999c) which does not include stalking behaviors as part of the assessment.

Given the extraordinarily high levels of co-occurring abuse, it is not surprising that the relentlessly stalked women also evidenced greater psychological distress as indexed by symptoms of PTSD and depres-sion. Depression scores for women in the complete sample were in the "severe" range of the scale and were higher than those reported in some other studies of battered women (Orava, McLeod, & Sharpe, 1996; Sackett & Saunders, 1999). However, it is notable that the magnitude of the distress was significantly greater among the relent-lessly stalked, even relative to a severe comparison group. Impairment could not be adequately examined due to ceiling effects on the impair-ment measure due to the generally high levels of impairment reported by all of the battered women in this sample. A more detailed under-standing of the multiplicity of ways in which stalking and other forms of intimate partner abuse affects functional impairment would be useful information to gather for both researchers and direct care providers.

Despite the pervasiveness, severity, and multiplicity of abuse perpetrated upon the women in the sample identified as "relentlessly stalked," they evidenced remarkable resilience in their efforts to respond to the abuse in their lives. In spite of greater psychological distress, these women managed to access resources at higher rates than the women exposed to less severe abuse. However, the high rates of help-seeking in both groups support the emerging consensus that battered women are active in their efforts to strategically respond to the violence they experience (e.g., Gondolf & Fischer, 1988). Moreover, the relentlessly stalked battered women reported having made a greater number of attempts to leave their partners, which may have been a trigger for increased violence (e.g., Mahoney, 1991). However, these findings do not address the extent to which existing services are adequate for dealing with the extreme and unremitting violence faced by stalked and battered women.

While the relentlessly stalked women reported more severe abuse, greater psychological distress, and increased strategic responding, preliminary examination of within-group correlations suggest some complicated findings with respect to the inter-relationships among these variables within each group. Greater psychological distress was associated with increased strategic responding, only for the women who experienced relatively lower levels of stalking. In concert with the findings of Arias and Pape (1999), these results indicate that strategic responding is may be differentially affected by the presence of abuse-related symptomatology. Psychological abuse evidenced stronger relationships with symptoms of PTSD and depression among the infrequently stalked women, a relationship also documented in other studies of battered women (e.g., Dutton et al., 1999). It is likely that the diminished relationship between psychological abuse and symptoms among the relentlessly stalked women is a function of the extremely high levels of psychological abuse in this group, thus restricting the range of scores suppressing the correlation for that subgroup. Not only was sexual coercion reported more frequently by the severely stalked women, but these experiences associated with injuries only among women who reported relentless stalking.

Despite numerous efforts to leave and seek help, the relentlessly stalked women were more likely to be physically assaulted and stalked after they left their abusive partners. The post-separation stalking was not confined to the women themselves. Threats to harm, abduct or threaten child custody were more often experienced by the relentlessly stalked women. The continued use of coercive control via threats to children or child custody is another arena of intervention that has not been successfully navigated for many battered women (Doyne et al., 1999). Court-ordered visitation can serve as a potent means for a batterer to continue a reign of terror and coercive control against his partner, via the children. These data underscore the need to better assist battered women, especially those also experiencing high levels of stalking with finding safety as they make efforts to exit abusive relationships. Moreover, we may need to broaden our conceptualization of "assistance," by considering other strategies for intervening with abusers who commit these relentless acts of continued pursuit.

Although the relentlessly stalked women did report a higher level of symptoms, these findings pale in the face of the extreme levels of concomitant and subsequent violence they face. The literature on PTSD indicates that each form of abuse experienced by these women is by itself a "high magnitude" event, meaning it carries with it a high risk of developing PTSD upon exposure. Consequently, disentangling the independent contributions of physical aggression, injuries, sexual assault, and psychological abuse to the development of posttraumatic symptoms in this sample of severely and acutely battered women did not seem to be a meaningful approach to understanding the phenomenon. However, this is an important task and should be completed in a considerably more heterogeneous sample with respect to the dimensions of intimate partner abuse experienced.

Limitations of this study include the small sample sizes of women in each of the two stalking groups, coupled with the homogeneity of abuse experiences that limited our ability to study these phenomena with respect to abuse occurring at lower levels of the severity spectrum. These methodological issues resulted in ceiling effects leading to diminished power to detect differences on some measures, especially those with a very low or very high base rate of occurrence in the sample. Nonetheless, these encouraging results can serve as a springboard to evaluate these important questions in samples of women with considerably greater heterogeneity with respect to stalking, psychological abuse and physical violence.

Miller, Cohen and Wiersema (1996) estimated that intimate partner violence costs $67 billion dollars per year (estimated in 1993 dollars), accounting for nearly 15% of total crime costs. These costs accrue from medical expenses, other tangible losses and reductions in quality of life and functional impairment as a consequence of partner abuse. Clearly the reduction of quality of life and functional impairment stemming from severe intimate partner abuse and stalking can be profound (Byrne, Resnick, Kilpatrick, Best, & Saunders, 1999; Fairbank, Ebert, & Zarkin, 1999). Finding ways to decrease the deleterious impact of stalking and other forms of intimate partner violence on women's lives must be considered our highest priority.

ACKNOWLEDGMENTS

This work was supported by National Institute of Mental Health Grant RO1 MH 55542. We appreciate the support of many people on our staff without whom this project would not have been possible. They are: Jenifer Bennice, Dana Cason, Michael Griffin, Anouk Grubaugh, Catherine Feuer, Debra Kaysen, Leslie Kimball, Linda Meade, Meg Milstead, Miranda Morris, Angie Waldrop, and Amy Williams.

We also would like to acknowledge the help of many battered women's, victim assistance, and law enforcement communities in the greater St. Louis metropolitan region. Finally, our most sincere appreciation is extended to the battered women who were willing to share their experience of adversity and survival with us.

REFERENCES

American Psychiatric Association (1994). *Diagnostic and statistical manual of mental disorders* (4th ed.). Washington, DC: Author.

Arias, I., & Pape, K. T. (1999). Psychological abuse: Implications for adjustment and commitment to leave violent partners. *Violence and Victims, 14*(1), 55–67.

Beck, A. T., Ward, C. H., Mendelson, M., Mosk, J., & Erbaugh, J. (1961). An inventory for measuring depression. *Archives of General Psychiatry, 4,* 561–571.

Beck, A. T., Steer, R. A., & Brown, G. K. (1996). *Manual for the Beck Depression Inventory* (2nd ed.). San Antonio, TX: The Psychological Corporation.

Breslau, N., & Davis, G. (1992). Posttraumatic stress disorder in an urban population of young adults: Risk factors for chronicity. *American Journal of Psychiatry, 149,* 671–675.

Browne, A., Salomon, A., & Bassuk, S. S. (1999). The impact of recent partner violence on poor women's capacity to maintain work. *Violence Against Women, 5*(4), 393–426.

Byrne, C. A., Resnick, H. S., Kilpatrick, D. G., Best, C. L., & Saunders, B. E. (1999). The socioeconomic impact of interpersonal violence on women. *Journal of Consulting and Clinical Psychology, 67*(3), 362–366.

Campbell, J. C., & Soeken, K. (1999a). Women's responses to battering: A test of the model. *Research in Nursing and Health, 22,* 49–58.

Campbell, J. C., & Soeken, K. L. (1999b). Women's responses to battering over time: An analysis of change. *Journal of Interpersonal Violence, 14*(1), 21–40.

Campbell, J. C., Harps, P. W., & Glass, N. E. (1999c). Risk of intimate partner homicide. In L. Pagani (Ed.), *Clinical assessment of dangerousness: Empirical contributions.* Cambridge: University Press.

Campbell, R., Sullivan, C. M., & Davidson, W. S. (1995). Depression in women who use domestic violence shelters: A longitudinal analysis. *Psychology of Women Quarterly, 19,* 237–255.

Campbell, J. C., Kub, J., Belknap, R., & Templin, T. N. (1997). Predictors of depression in battered women. *Violence Against Women, 3*(3), 271–293.

Coleman, F. (1997). Stalking behavior and the cycle of domestic violence. *Journal of Interpersonal Violence, 12,* 420–432.

Comrey, A. L., & Lee, H. B. (1992). *A first course in factor analysis* (2nd ed.). Hillsdale, NJ: Erlbaum.

Doyne, S. E., Bowermaster, J. M., Meloy, J. R., Dutton, D., Jaffe, P., Temko, S., & Mones, P. (1999, Spring). Custody disputes involving domestic violence: Making children's needs a priority. *Juvenile and Family Court Journal, 50,* 1–12.

Dutton, M. A. (1992). *Empowering and healing the battered woman: A model of assessment and intervention.* New York: Springer Publishing.

Dutton, M. A. (1993). Understanding women's responses to domestic violence: A redefinition of battered woman syndrome. *Hofstra Law Review, 21*(4), 1191–1242.

Dutton, M. A. (1996). Battered women's strategic response to violence: The role of context. In J. L. E. Z. Eisikovits (Ed.), *Future interventions with battered women and their families* (pp. 105–124). Thousand Oaks, CA: Sage Publications.

Dutton, M. A., Goodman, L. A., & Bennett, L. (1999). Court-involved battered women's responses to violence: The role of psychological, physical, and sexual abuse. *Violence and Victims, 14*(1), 89–104.

Fairbank, J. A., Ebert, L., & Zarkin, G. A. (1999). Socioeconomic consequences of traumatic stress. In P. A. Saigh & J. D. Bremner (Eds.),

Posttraumatic stress disorder: A comprehensive text (pp. 180–198). Boston: Allyn & Bacon.

Foa, E. B., Cashman, L., Jaycox, L., & Perry, K. (1997). The validation of a self-report measure of posttraumatic stress disorder: The posttraumatic diagnostic scale. *Psychological Assessment, 9*(4), 445–451.

Gleason, W. J. (1993). Mental disorders in battered women: An empirical study. *Violence and Victims, 8,* 53–68.

Golding, J. M. (1999). Intimate partner violence as a risk factor for mental disorders: A meta-analysis. *Journal of Family Violence, 14*(2), 99–132.

Gondolf, E. W., & Fischer E. R. (1988). *Battered women as survivors: An altternative to treating learned helplessness.* Lexington, MA: Lexington Books.

Kessler, R. C., Somega, A., Bromet, E., Hughes, M., & Nelson, C. B. (1995). Posttraumatic stress disorder in the National Comorbidity Survey. *Archives of General Psychiatry, 52,* 1048–1060.

Koss, M. P., Goodman, L. A., Browne, A., Fitzgerald, L. F., Keita, G. P., & Russo, N. F. (1994). *No safe haven: Male violence against women at home, at work, and in the community.* Washington, DC: American Psychological Association.

Mahoney, M. R. (1991). Legal images of battered women: Redefining the issue of separation. *Michigan Law Review, 90,* 1–94.

McFarlane, J. M., Campbell, J. C., Wilt, S., Sachs, C. J., Ulrich, Y., & Xu, X. (1999). Stalking and intimate partner femicide. *Homicide Studies, 3*(4), 300–316.

Meloy, J. R. (1996). Stalking (obsessional following): A review of some preliminary studies. *Aggression and Violence Behavior, 1,* 147–162.

Miller, T. R., Cohen, M. A., & Wiersema, B. (1996). *Victim costs and consequences: A new look* (NCJ Report no. 155282). Washington, DC: National Institute of Justice.

Orava, T. A., McLeod, P. J., & Sharpe, D. (1996). Perceptions of control, depressive symptomatology, and self-esteem of women in transition from abusive relationships. *Journal of Family Violence, 11,* 167–186.

Sackett, L. A., & Saunders, D. G. (1999). The impact of different forms of psychological abuse on battered women. *Violence and Victims, 14,* 105–117.

Sev'er, A. (1997). Recent or imminent separation and intimate violence against women. *Violence Against Women, 3,* 566–590.

Straus, M. A., Hamby, S. L. Boney-McCoy, S., & Sugarman, D. B. (1996). The revised conflict tactics scales (CTS2). *Journal of Family Issues, 17*(3), 283–316.

Sutherland, C., Bybee, D., & Sullivan, C. (1998). The long-term effects of battering on women's health. *Women's health: Research on Gender. Behavior, and Policy, 4*(1), 41–70.

Tjaden, P., & Theonnes, N. (1998). *Stalking in America: Findings from the national violence against women survey* (NCJ Report No. NCJ 169592). Washington, DC: U.S. Department of Justice.

Tolman, R. (1989). The development of a measure of psychological maltreatment of women by their male partners. *Violence and Victims, 4,* 173–189.

Tolman, R. (1999). The validation of the maltreatment of women inventory. *Violence and Victims, 14,* 25–35.

Weaver, T. L., & Clum, G. A. (1995). Psychological distress associated with interpersonal violence: A meta-analysis. *Clinical Psychology Review, 15*(2), 115–140.

6

An Empirical Study of Stalking Victimization

Beth Bjerregaard

The crime of stalking has generated widespread public and media attention in recent years. Much of this attention has resulted from several highly publicized stalking incidents including the deaths of a few well-known celebrities such as Rebecca Schaeffer and singer Selena. As a result of this attention, legislatures in all 50 states have enacted new laws designed to criminalize stalking behaviors.

In the majority of the legislation stalking is typically defined as the "willful, malicious and repeated following and harassing of another person" (N.I.J. Project, 1993, p. 13). Antistalking legislation requires that the offending behavior be repetitive and most statutes require that the behavior be accompanied by the specific intent to cause fear in the victim and that such behavior both objectively and subjectively results in fear or emotional distress to the victim. Further, a number of states require the presence of a credible threat to the victim (for a general discussion of state stalking laws see Bjerregaard, 1996, p. 310). Thus far, the vast majority of these laws have withstood constitutional challenge.

At the time these laws were drafted, little was known about the victims of this offense or the nature of the offense itself. At that time, much of the information available concerning stalking victims was predominately anecdotal and frequently derived from the popular media. Many authors discussing the issue of stalking relied on news reports and/or television shows for their information (Kurt, 1995, p. 21; Wallace, 1995).

Since the enactment of this legislation and the recognition of this type of behavior as an important topic of study, research has been conducted examining both the types of offenders who engage in this behavior and the victims of such offenses. However, such research is still in the preliminary stages and we are just beginning to understand the nuances of this type of behavior. While we have a much more comprehensive understanding of the phenomenon of stalking, there are certain aspects of this behavior that are still not well understood.

The purpose of this research was to empirically examine the phenomenon of stalking and its victims utilizing a random sample of college students. This research was designed to estimate the prevalence of stalking among this population and to describe the characteristics of both stalking victims and their offenders. More important, this research sought to examine the relationships among the various behaviors engaged in by stalkers, specifically their methods of contact and threatening behaviors, and the levels of fear felt by the victims and harm to the victims. For example, were offenders who threatened their victims more likely to make face to face contact with those victims and/or to physically harm their victims?

This research contributes to the existing research in a number of important ways. First, very few studies have been conducted examining the college population and even fewer have utilized a random sample (McCreedy & Dennis, 1996; Fremouw, Westrup & Pennypacker, 1997; Spitzberg, Nicastro & Cousins, 1998). The college setting provides a unique arena in which to study these behaviors. First, there is considerable evidence at this point that stalkers are better educated than the average criminal offender (Harmon, Rosner & Owens, 1995; Meloy & Gothard, 1995). Second, this is a unique time in an individual's life where the opportunity to interact with a wide variety of individuals, oftentimes in the dating setting, is plentiful.

Further, this research is novel in that it seeks to empirically validate many of the elements that legislatures have utilized to define the stalking event as a crime. For example, many states require the presence of a credible threat in order to classify the behavior as stalking. Other states require that the victim experience "reasonable" fear before the behavior is considered to be a criminal offense. By examining the impact of threats and approaching behaviors on both the level of fear felt by the victim and the risk of harm to the victim, we can determine if these restrictions are reasonable and more important, whether the assumptions underlying these criteria are correct.

PREVALENCE OF STALKING

In one of the most comprehensive empirical studies conducted to date, the National Institute of Justice (N.I.J.) discovered that approximately 1.4 million persons were stalked annually (Tjaden, 1997). Extrapolating the findings, it was projected that 8.2 million females and 2 million males experience stalking during their lifetime (Tjaden, 1997, p.1). This estimate is significantly higher than previous estimates. For instance, Sen. Joseph R. Biden (1992) testified before an anti-stalking legislation hearing that as many as 200,000 persons are stalked each year. Other scholars, often relying on anecdotal sources, provide estimates that range from 5 to 20 percent of all women as stalking victims (Puente, 1992, p. 9A; Strikis, 1993, p. 2772; Welch, 1995, p. 54).

Studies examining college students have reported equally impressive rates. A study examining students in West Virginia found that 34% of the females and 17% of the males indicated that they had been stalked (Fremouw, Westrup & Pennypacker, 1997). Likewise, Spitzberg, Nicastro & Cousins (1998, p. 34) state that between 4% and 40% of college students have experienced some form of obsessive relational intrusion into their lives. Their study revealed that 27% of students recruited from a Communications Class indicated that they had been stalked. McCreedy & Dennis (1996), studying sex-related offenses on a college campus, found that an unexpectedly large number of students (6.1% of their sample) reported having been stalked. They point out that the college campus is in many ways an "ideal hunting ground" for potential offenders as it is easily accessible and is typically comprised of large numbers of women. Similarly, Fisher, Cullen & Turner (1999) also studying sexual victimizations found that 13.1 percent of the women indicated that they had been stalked with the average incident lasting 60 days. However, only one of these studies utilized non-random samples (Fisher et al., 1999) and it is unclear the extent to which these findings are generalizable. Nevertheless it is clear that the available evidence indicates that a significant number of persons in the United States have been or are being stalked.

CHARACTERISTICS OF STALKING VICTIMS

To date, few empirical studies have focused on the victims of stalkers. Nevertheless, there is widespread consensus that the vast majority of all stalking victims are women (Tjaden, 1997, p.2; David, 1994, p. 207; Faulkner and Hsiao, 1993, p.5; Hall, 1998, p. 117; McCreedy and Dennis, 1996, p. 76; Strikis, 1993, p. 2772; Thomas, 1993, p. 126; Welch, 1995, p. 54; Zona, et al., 1993). Studies have also consistently found that stalking victims usually know their offenders (Kienlen, 1998; Mullen, Pathe, Purcell and Stuart, 1999). Poling (1994, p. 285) reports that most victims know their stalkers and that only ten to twenty percent of all stalking cases involve situations where the stalker is a stranger. The National Institute of Justice also found that only 21 percent of the female victims in their study were stalked by strangers (Tjaden, 1997, p. 1).

Frequently, the victims were intimately involved with their stalkers at some point. Mullen and Pathe (1994, p. 469) state that the majority of stalkers are ex-husbands/ex-lovers. Similarly, Tjaden & Thoennes (1998) report that most that most victims were previously involved with their stalkers. Further, it is estimated that the vast majority, as many as 90%, of women who are murdered each year by their husbands/boyfriends were stalked prior to the fatal attack (Browne, 1987, p. 10; David, 1994, p. 208; Guy, 1993, p. 996; Morin, 1993, p. 125; Poling, 1994, p. 286; Thomas, 1993, p. 126). Even more disturbing, statistics from Kansas City and Detroit reveal that 90% of these women contacted the police for assistance at least once prior to the killing and that over 50% had called a minimum of five times (Morin, 1993, p. 125).

In contrast, Wright et al. (1995, p. 39) found that stalking victims frequently have no knowledge of their stalker's identity. McCreedy and Dennis (1996, p. 77), surveying college students, found that although 40% of the victims reported that they knew the offender well, 53.5% of their stalking victims did not know their offenders. This may indicate that college students are vulnerable to different types of stalking events than the general population. This may again be due to the fact that a college student is much more likely to be exposed to a wide variety of individuals on a daily basis. It may be that in many cases, stalkers are approaching their victims in this setting prior to developing any type of relationship with that person. Similarly, Meloy and Gothard (1995) found that 45% of the victims of their sample of obsessional followers were strangers. However, this finding may be due to the fact that they were studying a sample of mentally ill offenders.

Overall, it appears that women are far more likely to be stalking victims and that the majority of victims are at least acquainted with their stalkers.

CHARACTERISTICS OF STALKING OFFENDERS

Most experts agree that it is difficult to develop a single profile for stalkers (Perez, 1993, p. 273; see Holmes and Gerberth for typologies). A large number of these studies that have examined the characteristics of offenders have not utilized random samples of offenders (Gerberth, 1992; Harmon, Rosner & Owens, 1995; Holmes, 1993; Leong, 1994; Meloy; 1996; Meloy & Gothard, 1995; Mullen & Pathe, 1994; Rudder, Sweeney & Frances, 1990; Zona, Sharma, & Lane, 1993). Further, these studies typically employ very small sample sizes, usually less than 10 cases (for a review see Meloy, 1996).

It is believed that most stalking offenders are males who stalk women(Attinello, 1993; Guy, 1993; Hall, 1998; Harmon, et al., 1995; Meloy and Gothard, 1995; Mullen, Pathe, Purcell & Stuart, 1999; Zona et al., 1993). Few studies have examined the race of stalking offenders. Harmon et al. (1995) and Hall (1998) both reported that two-thirds of their sample was white. Meloy and Gothard (1995), on the other hand, found that only 35% of their sample was white. Meloy (1996, p. 151) found that in 57% of the cases the race of the offender was not reported and therefore it was very difficult to draw any conclusions with regards to race.

Researchers studying obsessional followers have found these individuals to be slightly older than most other criminal offenders (Harmon et al., 1995; Meloy, 1996, p. 151; Mullen & Pathe, 1994; Mullen, Pathe, Purcell & Stuart, 1999; Schwartz-Watts, Morgan, & Barnes, 1997; Zona et al., 1993). This finding was confirmed by Meloy and Gothard (1995) who also found the average age of their sample of obsessional followers was thirty-five. Harmon et al. (1995), studying both obsessional harassment and erotomania, actually found the average age of their offenders to be slightly older (40). Leong (1994, p. 384), also studying individuals diagnosed with erotomania, found that the average age at which these persons enter the criminal justice system was in their thirties. In addition, researchers examining obsessional followers and/or individuals diagnosed with erotomania found their offenders to be better educated than other types of offenders. Harmon et al. (1995) found that all of their offenders had at least a high school degree. Similarly, Meloy and Gothard (1995) discovered that the majority of their sample had a high school education.

In addition to discovering that stalkers often share common demographic characteristics, researchers have also noted additional shared characteristics. Perez (1993, p. 273) believes that most stalkers exhibit an intense interest in the media, the inability to develop meaningful relationships and a desire for both recognition and attention. Meloy and Gothard (1995), Mullen, Pathe, Purcell & Stuart (1999) and Zona et al. (1993) all report finding a high proportion of stalkers experienced failed relationships. Likewise, Zona et al. (1993, p. 898) found that only one of their erotomania subjects was married, and that only two of their obsessional followers were married.

Perhaps the most difficult to assess is the extent to which stalking behaviors are the manifestation of a mental illness. While a number of emotional problems have been identified with stalking offenders, it is unclear which types of mental illnesses are most common or most problematic (Gerberth, 1992, pp. 138–143; Guy, 1993, p. 995; Kienlen, Birmingham, Solbert, O'Regan, and Meloy, 1997; Morin, 1993, pp. 127–130). Meloy (1996, p. 153), reviewing previous studies on obsessional followers, concludes that the "psychodiagnostic picture of the obsessional follower that emerges . . . is complex and varied," but clearly suggests that at least a minority of offenders have a diagnosable mental disorder, most frequently including erotomania and personality disorder.

CHARACTERISTICS OF THE STALKING EVENT(S)

Research has examined several different aspects of the stalking event. Meloy (1996, p. 154), reviewing past studies, suggests that stalking behaviors persist for relatively lengthy periods of time that are best measured in months and years rather than in weeks. Meloy (1992) found in an earlier study that the average length of time between the commencement of the obsessional following and the culmination of violence was five years. Mullen and Pathe (1994) found an average time span of 25 months. Other estimates were found to range from about 5 months to 12 years (Zona et al., 1993).

During the course of the stalking event, stalkers utilized a variety of methods to contact or communicate with their victims. These methods include letters, telephoning and various approaching behaviors (Goldstein, 1987; Hall, 1998; Leong, 1994; Mullen & Pathe, 1994; Mullen, Pathe, Purcell, and Stuart, 1999; Noone & Cockhill, 1987; Taylor et al, 1983; Zona et al., 1993). Meloy and Gothard (1995) found that over two-thirds of their sample had visited their victim's home, while 40% had telephoned and 25% had written letters. Zona et al. (1993, p. 899) report that among the erotomanics in their study 85% telephoned their victims, 100% wrote their victims and 43% made either location or home visits. Harmon et al. (1995, p. 192) and Hall (1998) report that the primary method of contact in their sample was telephone calls. However, they also report that a significant percentage of their offenders approached their victims in person. Recently, Mullen, Pathe, Purcell & Stuart (1999) found that while telephoning was the most frequent method of contact, 86% of their stalkers repeatedly approached their victims in public situations.

Dietz and his colleagues in their examination of threatening letters sent to celebrities and members of Congress (Dietz et al., 1991a; Dietz et al., 1991b), documented a mean number of 7.1 communications over a 12–month period for Congressional members and over an 18–month period for entertainment celebrities. Fifty-five percent of the celebrities' stalkers and 31% of the Congressional stalkers provided enclosures with their letters including photographs, media clippings, poetry, blood and other assorted items.

Threats of violence by the stalkers also appear to be rather common. Meloy and Gothard (1995) found that the majority of their obsessional followers threatened their victims and that 55% of them had threatened physical violence. Meloy (1998) and Mullen, Pathe, Purcell and Stuart (1999) report that over half of the stalkers had explicitly threatened their victims and that 36% of the stalkers attacked their victims. All in all they found that 77% of those who assaulted their victims had previously threatened them. Dietz et al. (1991a & 1991b) found that 23% of their celebrity cases and 58% of their congressional cases involved threats to the victim. They found that most of the threats to victims were considered to be indirect, veiled or conditional threats rather than direct threats. Further, Harmon et al. (1995, p. 192) found that two-thirds of those who threatened violence also made face to face contact with their victims. However, Meloy (1998), reviewing a number of previous studies, found that only 9% of the subjects mentioned or possessed a weapon and that even fewer threatened subjects with a weapon. He concludes that such behaviors are rare.

Researchers have also found that rates of violent behaviors among stalkers also vary dramatically (see Meloy, 1996, p. 157). Meloy (1998, p. 5) states that the frequency of violence among stalkers toward their objects averages in the 25–25% range. For example, Zona et al (1993) found that only 2.3% of their sample had assaulted their victims. Meloy (1996, p.157) found that of the 180 subjects reviewed, 2% committed homicides as a direct result of their obsessional following. In contrast, Mullen and Pathe (1994) discovered that 36% of their sample assaulted their victims. Harmon et al. (1995) report that 21% of their sample exhibited aggressively assaultive behaviors.

The relationships between threats to victims, face to face contact between victims and stalkers, and actual violence is not clear cut. Dietz et al. (1991a, 1991b), among their sample of Representatives, actually found an inverse relationships between making threats and approaching the subjects of those threats. Meloy (1998, p. 7) states that although explicit threats are more frequent where the stalkers actually become violent, the majority of such threats are not acted out. Meloy and Gothard (1995, p. 262) conclude that "threats may be completely unrelated to a risk of physical assault." In contrast, Pathe and Mullen (1997), examining 100 stalking victims, did discover evidence that threats are associated with actual violence. Of the 34 victims that had experienced an assault, 76% of them had been threatened.

CURRENT STUDY

The purpose of this study is to help expand our understanding of the crime by empirically studying the phenomenon of stalking and its victims among a large sample of college students. This research contributes to the existing literature in a number of ways. First, it utilizes a randomly drawn sample of individuals allowing for generalization. Second, the sample including both male and female victims allows the researcher to examine gender differences in the phenomenon of stalking. Lastly, this analysis examines the impact of threats and approaching behaviors on both the level of fear felt by the victim and the risk of harm to the victim. Specifically, this research is designed to address the following questions:

1. What is the prevalence of stalking victimization among this sample and what are the common characteristics of stalking victims?
2. What are the common characteristics of stalking offenders?
3. What are the common characteristics of the stalking events/behaviors of stalkers?
4. What are the relationships between threats, approaching behaviors, the fear of the victim and physical attacks?
5. How did these victims react to their experiences and what were their common responses?
6. Does the gender of the victim influence the characteristics of the stalking event or the responses of the victims?

METHOD

The population for this study consisted of all students in a large southeastern public university. Classes were randomly selected from a list, generated by the registrar's office, of all classes offered during the spring semester of 1997. For pragmatic purposes, classes containing fewer than 5 students were eliminated from the sampling frame. When a class was selected, the instructor was notified and their participation was solicited. This procedure yielded a total sample size of 788 undergraduate and graduate students. Surveys were administered in class by the researchers to the respondents who participated anonymously. The survey took approximately twenty minutes to complete. The survey included basic demographic characteristics of the respondents and then asked if they had ever been a victim of stalking. Respondents were provided with a general definition of stalking and then asked if they believed that they had ever been stalked. Once respondents self-identified themselves as stalking victims, they were asked a series of questions that characterized the stalking event.

Of the 788 students, 65% were female and 35% were male. The majority of the sample was white (75%). This is almost identical to the student population as a whole. Most of the students were between the ages of 18 and 25 (80%) and the vast majority were single (85%). Twenty-six percent of the sample had at least a four-year degree and therefore was either pursuing a second degree or was in graduate school.

FINDINGS

Prevalence of Stalking Victimization/Profile of Victims

Table 6.1 describes the sample in terms of its demographic character-istics. Table 6.1 shows that females are significantly were likely to be stalked than males. Twenty-five percent of the females were stalked compared to eleven percent of the males (χ^2 = 20.86, df = 1, p <.0001). Chi-square significance tests were also run comparing females who were stalked with those who were not across the various demographic characteristics and likewise for males. This analysis revealed no signif-icant differences between those who were stalked and those who were not stalked in terms of their race, education, marital status, or house-

Table 6.1 Description of the Sample

	Stalking Victims		Non-Victims	
	Females (N = 122) (24.7%)	Males (N = 29) (10.9%)*	Females (N = 372) (75.3%)	Males (N = 238) (89.1%)
Race				
White	92 (75.4%)	21 (72.4%)	259 (69.6%)	190 (79.8)
Non-White	30 (24.6)	8 (27.6)	113 (30.4)	48 (20.2)
Age				
18–25	97 (79.5)	20 (69.0)	293 (78.8)	195 (81.9)
Above 25	25 (20.5)	9 (31.0)	79 (21.2)	43 (18.1)
Education				
High School Diploma or Some College	70 (57.9)	13 (44.8)	222 (60.5)	154 (64.7)
2 Yr. College Degree	21 (17.4)	8 (27.6)	35 (9.5)	34 (14.3)
4 Yr. Degree/Graduate	30 (24.8)	8 (27.6)	111 (30.0)	50 (21.0)
Marital Status				
Married	15 (12.5)	3 (10.3)	49 (13.3)	25 (10.5)
Other	105 (87.5)	26 (89.7)	319 (86.7)	213 (89.5)
Household Income				
40,000 or Less	59 (54.1)	16 (55.2)	204 (59.6)	143 (63.3)
Over 40,000	50 (45.9)	13 (44.8)	138 (40.4)	83 (36.7)
Currently Being Stalked	7 (5.7)	3 (10.3)		
Average Length of Stalking	83.4 days (SD = 89.1)	182 days (SD = 278.4)		

*Chi-square significance p < .05 within gender across stalked and not stalked.

hold income. The majority of stalking victims, both male and female, are white. Although all respondents are currently attending college, a large portion of both groups posses either a two-year or a four-year degree. Very few of either the male or female victims indicated that they were married (10.3% & 12.5%). Male and female stalking victims also look very similar to the non-victims in terms of their household incomes. Slightly over half of the victims and non-victims, regardless of gender, reported that they earned $40,000 or less.

Of those individuals who indicated that they had been stalked at some point in their lives, 5.7% of the females and 10.3% of the males indicated that they were currently being stalked. This difference was not statistically significant. Females reported being stalked for an average of 83.4 days, while males reported that their stalking incidents lasted for approximately 99 days longer (mean = 182 days). An F-test was utilized to examine the differences in the mean number of days males and females were stalked. The analysis revealed no significant difference between these two groups.

Overall, the demographic characteristics of those who reported being stalked and those who reported that they had never been stalked, are very similar regardless of gender. The only significant difference to emerge was that females are more likely than males to become stalking victims.

Profile of Stalking Offenders

Information regarding the stalking offenders was collected by asking the respondents who had identified themselves as stalking victims to report on the characteristics of their stalkers. The analysis reveals that most victims are stalked by members of the opposite sex. As reported in the previous literature, the overwhelming majority of female victims are stalked by males (96%). While the majority of males victims are also likely to report being stalked by a member of the opposite sex, almost one-third of the male victims reported being stalked by another male. Males were significantly more likely than females to report being stalked by someone of the same sex (χ^2 = 66.68, df = 1, p < .0001) (see Table 6.2).

Both genders report that the majority of their stalkers were white. Sixty-seven percent of the female victims and 81.5% of the male victims were stalked by white stalkers.[5] Female victims were significantly more likely to report being stalked by an older stalker (χ^2 = 5.23, df = 1, p = .02). Both genders reported that very few of their stalkers were married. Somewhat surprisingly, when asked the occupation of their stalkers, only 25.7% of the females and 39.1% of the males

Table 6.2 Profile of Stalking Offenders as Reported by Victims

	Female Victims		Male Victims	
Gender				
Male	113	(95.8%)	9	(32.1)*
Female	5	(4.2%)	19	(67.9)
Race				
White	76	(67.9)	22	(81.5)
Nonwhite	36	(32.1)	5	(18.5)
Age				
25 or Under	84	(72.4)	26	(92.9)*
Above 25	32	(27.6)	2	(7.1)
Marital Status				
Married	8	(7.8)	2	(7.4)
Other	95	(92.2)	25	(92.6)
Is Stalker A Student?				
Yes	27	(25.7)	9	(39,1)
No	78	(74.3)	14	(60.9)
Relationship of Stalker to Victim				
Ex-Spouse	4	(3.3)	0	
Ex-Boyfriend/Girlfriend	47	(38.5)	11	(40.7)
Friend	11	(9.0)	5	(18.5)
Personal Acquaintance	10	(8.2)	2	(7.4)
Business Acquaintance	2	(1.6)	1	(3.7)
Knew Stalker/No Prior				
Relationship	12	(9.8)	1	(3.7)
Stranger	22	(18.0)	3	(11.1)
Other	14	(11.5)	4	(14.8)
Average Length of Prior Relationship	2.30 Years		1.22 Years	
	(840 days)		(447 days)	
	1 day to 16 years		7 days to 4 years	
	(SD = 1011.86)		(SD = 421.12)	

*Chi-square significance at $p < .05$.

reported that their stalkers were students. Males and female victims were also similarly acquainted with their stalkers. In fact, 41.8% of the females and 40.7% of the males reported that their were either ex-boyfriends/girlfriends or ex-spouses. Interestingly, female victims knew their stalkers for approximately a year longer than male victims. An F-test, however, revealed that this difference was not statistically significant.

A Profile of Stalking Incidents

Table 6.3 examines the characteristics of the stalking event by the gender of the victim. Overall, the most frequent method of contact utilized by the stalkers for both male and female victims is phone calls, followed by face to face contacts. Over two-thirds of both the males

Table 6.3 Characteristics of the Stalking Event by Gender of the Victim

	Female Victims (N = 122)		Male Victims (N = 29)	
Ever Phoned	93	(76.2)	21	(72.4)
In Phone Call Stalker Expressed:				
Love for you	58	(63.7)	12	(57.1)
Desire to marry	32	(35.2)	4	(19.0)
Desire for sex	32	(35.2)	7	(33.3)
Desire for contact	63	(69.2)	7	(33.3)*
Average Number of Phone Calls		43.7		89.2
		(SD = 73.25)		(SD = 245.11)
Ever Sent Mail	34	(27.9%)	7	(24.1%)
Mail Contained				
Photographs	4	(11.8)	2	(28.6%)
Threatening drawings	3	(8.8)	0	
News/magazine clippings	2	(5.9)	1	(14.3)
In Mail Did Stalker Express:				
Love for you	28	(82.4)	4	(57.1)
Desire to marry you	15	(44.1)	4	(57.1)
Desire for sex	13	(39.2)	3	(42.9)
Desire for contact	23	(67.6)	4	(57.1)
Average Number of Letters		7.4		3.5
		(SD = 19.35)		(SD = 2.51)
Did Stalker Attempt Face-to-Face Contact	91	(74.6)	20	(69.0)
Stalker Was Successful in Contacting Victim	75	(82.4)	16	(84.2)
Face-to-Face Contact at:				
Home	54	(59.3)	13	(65.0)
Job	35	(38.5)	9	(45.0)
Friend's house	19	(20.9)	4	(20.0)
During Encounter Stalker Expressed:				
Love for you	45	(60.0)	9	(60.0)
Desire to marry	20	(26.7)	5	(33.3)
Desire for sex	18	(24.0)	5	(33.3)

*Chi-square significant at $p < .05$.

and females indicated that they had been called by their stalkers. The male victims, however, indicated that on average they received twice as many phone calls as the female victims, although this difference was not statistically significant. Among those who had been called by their stalkers, 69.2% of the female victims indicated that their stalkers expressed a desire to make personal contact. Only 33.3% of the male victims had their stalkers express this same desire. This difference is statistically significant (χ^2 = 9.38, df = 1, p = .002). The next most common response for the female victims was that their stalkers expressed love for them. This was also the most common response among the male victims(57.1%).

Male and female victims were almost equally likely to have received mail from their stalkers. Among those who did receive mail, both males and females report that photographs were the most common enclosures. Almost 9% of the females reported receiving threatening drawings and 6% stated that they had received newspaper or magazine clippings. Among the males who had received mail, 14.3% indicated that they received newspaper or magazine clippings and none of them indicated that they had received threatening drawing. The female victims stated that their stalkers were most likely to express love for them in the letters (82.4%), followed by a desire for face-to-face contact (67.6%). Equal proportions of the male victims indicated that their stalkers expressed their love for them, a desire to marry them and a desire for personal contact (57.1%). Females reported receiving twice as many letters as males. These differences, however, were not found to be statistically significant.

More than two-thirds of both the male and female victims reported that their stalkers attempted face-to-face contact. Of those who attempted contact, slightly over 80% were successful in making contact with the victim with almost no differences between male and female victims. Both male and female victims were most likely to be contacted at home, followed by contacts on their job and at a friend's house. Chi-squares revealed no significant differences between the male and female victims in terms of the location of the contact.

Stalkers who made face-to-face contact with their victims were most likely to express their love for both their male and female victims. One-third of those male victims' stalkers also expressed a desire to marry and for sex, while around one-fourth of the female victim's stalkers expressed these desires.

Threats and Fear of Victim

Table 6.4 describes the types of threats received by the victims and their levels of fear. Overall, very few victims reported being threatened by letter. Of those who received mail threats, both males and females were most likely to receive a threat of physical violence. Although 2.5% of the female victims, compared to none of the male victims, reported receiving a death threat or a threat to their family through the mail, this difference was not statistically significant.

Among those who had been phoned by their stalkers, 23.8% of the females and 13.8% of the males were threatened with physical vio-

Table 6.4 Types of Threats and Fear Levels by Gender of Victim

	Female Victims (N = 122)		Male Victims (N = 29)	
Threats				
Stalker Sent Letter That				
Threatened Physical Violence	7	(5.7%)	3	(10.3%)
Threatened to Kill	3	(2.5)	0	
Threatened Family	3	(2.5)	0	
Stalker Phoned and				
Threatened Physical Violence	29	(23.8)	4	(13.8)
Threatened to Kill	14	(11.5)	4	(13.8)
Threatened Family	10	(8.2)	0	
Stalker Contacted Face to Face and				
Threatened Physical Violence	23	(18.9)	3	(10.3)
Threatened to Kill	7	(5.7)	1	(3.4)
Threatened Family	6	(4.9)	0	
Stalker Threatened to Physically Harm Victim	43	(36.1)	6	(21.4)
Victim Felt Stalker Had Ability to Carry Out				
Threat	32	(82.1)	4	(66.7)
Fear Levels				
Fear of Physical Safety	69	(56.6)	6	(20.7)*
Fear for Life	28	(23.0)	3	(10.3)
Fear for Emotional Health	67	(54.9)	6	(20.7)*
Overall Level of Fear (1–10 scale)	6.3		3.2[a]	
	(SD = 2.48)		(SD = 2.64)	

*Chi-square significance at $p < .05$.

[a]F-test significant at $p < .05$.

lence by their stalkers. Again, this difference was not statistically significant. Males and females were equally likely to receive a death threat over the phone. Eleven percent of the females and 13.8% of the males reported receiving a death threat over the phone. Only the female victims, however, reported that their families were threatened over the phone.

Female victims who had been contacted face-to-face by their stalkers were almost twice as likely to be threatened with physical violence than the male victims, although this difference was not statistically significant. Almost one-fifth of the female victims reported being physically threatened during the encounter. Females were also slightly more likely than males to receive a death threat and to have their families threatened when approached by their stalkers.

In general, female victims were more likely than male victims to have been threatened by their stalker, although these differences were not statistically significant. Likewise, female victims were more likely to believe that their stalkers had the ability to carry out their threats. Over two-thirds of the victims, regardless of gender, believed in the validity of their stalker's threats.

In terms of the victim's fear, it is clear that females are more affected by the stalking incidents than males. Over half of the females expressed fear for their physical safety, while only 20.7% of the males reported these fears ($\chi^2 = 12.06$, $df = 1$, $p = .001$). While both males and females were less likely to report fearing for their lives, females were again twice as likely to have experienced this fear. This difference was not statistically significant. In rating their overall fear, females were significantly more fearful than males ($F = 35.27$, $df = 1, 149$, $p < .001$). However, it is important to note that neither males nor females reported exceedingly high levels of fear.

The Influence of Threats on Approaching Behaviors, Fear and Harm to Victim

Table 6.5 examines the relationships between the stalker's threats and approaching behaviors, fear and harm to the victim. Logically, being threatened in any fashion increases fear levels for both male and female victims. Female victims, however, are more likely to indicate higher levels of fear than the male victims, frequently almost twice the levels experienced by males. Females who were threatened with physical violence were significantly more fearful than the males who had likewise been threatened ($F = 14.92$, $df = 1,90$, $p < .001$). They were also significantly more fearful than female victims who had not been threatened ($F = 21.83$, $df = 1, 120$, $p < .001$). Likewise, females who had been threatened with death were significantly more fearful than males who had been threatened with death ($F = 13.28$, $df = 1, 19$, $p = .002$) and females who had not been threatened ($F = 17.91$, $df = 1, 120$, $p < .001$). Since only female victims reported having their families threatened, significance tests could not be run between the males and females. Females whose families had been threatened were significantly more fearful than females who had not been threatened ($F = 14.88$, $df = 1, 120$, p<.001). Even among those victims who had not received threats, females were significantly more fearful than males ($F = 20.15$, $df = 1, 90$, $p < .001$).

More important, stalkers who threatened their victims were more likely to approach their victims and ultimately to physically attack their victims. Ninety percent of the females who had been threatened with physical violence also had their stalkers attempt face-to-face contact and the stalkers were successful in 90% of those cases. This is significantly more than those females who had not been threatened ($\chi^2 = 6.36$, $df = 1$, $p = .012$). Females who had been threatened with death were also significantly more likely to have their stalkers attempt to make personal contact than females who had not received any threats ($\chi^2 = 3.97$, $df = 1$, $p = .046$). Stalkers with male victims attempted face-to-face contact in roughly 70% of the cases regardless of whether or not they had threatened their victims. Therefore, the presence of threats seems to increase the risk of approaching behaviors only for the females. The presence of any type of threat did not significantly increase the risk of the attempt being successful for either male or female victims.

Even more alarming, 39.4% of the female victims who had been threatened with physical violence were physically harmed by their stalkers. This is in contrast to only 2.8% of the females who received no threats ($\chi^2 = 13.73$, $df = 1$, $p < .001$). Females who had received a death threat were significantly more likely than both females who had not received a threat ($\chi^2 = 16.06$, $df = 1$, $p < .001$). Therefore, among the females, receiving a threat of violence significantly increases the chance of actual violence. Very few of the males (5%) reported being physically harmed by their stalkers and none of the males who were threatened was physically attacked.

The Influence of Approaching Behaviors on Fear and Harm to Victim

Table 6.6 examines the relationships between approaching behaviors, fear and violence by the gender of the victim. Again, females express close to twice the levels of fear that males express regardless of the stalkers' approaching behaviors. Female victims whose stalkers attempted face-to-face contact were not only more fearful than the male victims ($F = 20.69$, $df = 1$, 109, $p < .001$), but they were also significantly more fearful than females whose stalkers did not attempt personal contact ($F = 5.28$, $df = 1$, 120, $p = .023$). Likewise, females whose stalkers made contact were significantly more fearful than males whose stalkers had made contact ($F = 22.16$, $df = 1$, 89, $p < .001$).

Both male and female victims whose stalkers attempted or succeeded in making personal contact were also more likely to report being physically harmed. Again, females were much more likely to report being physically harmed by their stalkers, although this difference was not statistically significant. Almost 23 percent of the females whose stalkers made personal contact were physically harmed by their victims.

Victim Reactions

Table 6.7 assesses the reactions of the victims by gender. Female victims were significantly more likely to report having called the police in response to their stalking ($\chi^2 = 6.86$, $df = 1$, $p = .009$). Similarly, while nine percent of the female victims reported that they had actually gone to court as a result of the stalking, none of the male victims reported going to court. Interesting, only one female reported obtaining a restraining order against her stalker. Females are much more likely to report, turning to the criminal justice system for assistance. This is consistent with the findings from a study conducted by the Center for Policy Research (Tjaden, 1997, p. 2) which also found that substantially more women than men obtained temporary restraining orders. This may simply be the result of males perceiving their inability to deal with the situation or having to seek outside assistance for their problems a weakness. It could also be a reflection of the fact that males were less likely to be threatened or physically harmed by their stalkers.

Both males and females similarly report having had to change their phone numbers, jobs, and/or residents in response to the stalking. Females were more likely to report having sought counseling in re-

Table 6.5 Relationship Between Threats, and Fear, Approaching Behaviors and Violence by Gender

	Threatened With Physical Violence		Threatened With Death		Family Threatened		Not Threatened	
	Females (N = 33)	Males (N = 7)	Females (N = 17)	Males (N = 4)	Females (N = 13)	Males (N = 0)	Females (N = 72)	Males (N = 20)
Overall Level of Fear (1–10 Scale)	7.91[a] (SD = 2.04)	4.71* (SD = 1.70)	8.53[a] (SD = 1.84)	4.50* (SD = 2.65)	8.69[a] (SD = 1.38)	0	5.64 (SD = 2.38)	2.90* (SD = 2.85)
Stalker Attempted Face to Face Contact	30 (90.9%)[a]	5 (71.4%)[a]	16 (94.1%)[a]	3 (75.0%)[a]	12 (92.3%)	0	49 (68.1%)	14 (70.0%)
Stalker Made Face to Face Contact	27 (90.0%)	5 (100%)	15 (93.8%)	3 (100%)	12 (100%)	0	37 (75.5)	11 (84.6)
Stalker Physically Harmed Victim	13 (39.4%)[a]	0*	9 (52.9%)[a]	0*	6 (46.2%)	0	2 (2.8)	1 (5.0)

*Significant at $p < .05$ between genders—chi-square significance for percentages and F-test significance for means.
[a]Significant at $p < .05$ within genders—chi-square significance for percentages and F-test significance for means.

Table 6.6 Relationship Between Approaching Behaviors, Fear and Violence by Gender

	Attempted Face to Face Contact		Made Face to Face Contact		Did Not Attempt Face to Face Contact	
	Females (N = 91)	Males (N = 20)	Females (N = 75)	Males (N = 16)	Females (N = 3 1)	Males (N = 9)
Overall Level of Fear (1–10 Scale)	6.62[a] (SD = 2.49)	3.75* (SD = 2.81)	6.79 (SD = 2.44)	3.56* (SD = 2.71)	5.45 (SD = 2.25)	2.11* (SD = 1.90)
Stalker Physically Harmed Victim	18 (19.8%)	1 (5.0%)	17 (22.7%)	1 (6.3%)	4 (13.3%)	0

*Significant at $p < .05$ between genders—chi-square significance for percentages and F-test significance for means.
[a]Significant at $p < .05$ within genders—chi-square significance for percentages and F-test significance for means.

Table 6.7 Victim Reactions by Gender

	Female Victims (N = 122)		Male Victims (N = 29)	
Have You Ever:				
Called the police	43	(35.2%)	3	(10.3%)*
Gone to court	11	(9.0)	0	
Obtained a restraining order	1	(0.8)	0	
Installed a security system	8	(6.6)	0	
Bought a gun	4	(3.3)	1	(3.4)
Changed phone number	27	(22.1)	5	(17.2)
Changed jobs	10	(8.2)	2	(6.9)
Changed residences	27	(22.1)	2	(6.9)
Sought counseling	11	(9.0)	1	(3.4)
Specifically Requested Person Stop Behavior	95	(77.9)	16	(55.2)*
Person Stopped at Your Request	11	(12.4)	0	

*Chi-square test of significance $p < .05$.

sponse to the incident. Females were significantly more likely to report specifically asking their stalkers to stop their behavior and also more likely to have had their stalkers actually stop at their request (χ^2 = 6.20, df = 1, p = .013). It is troubling that only slightly more than half of the males reported requesting their stalkers stop their behavior. Interestingly, at the time of the survey, North Carolina required that the victim inform his or her stalker that the contact was unwanted. This means that almost half of the males and roughly 22% of the females would not have been classified legally as stalking victims.

Aside from calling the police, the most frequent response for both female and male victims was to change their phone number. This is logical considering the large number of victims that reported being stalked by phone. Females were also more likely to have moved or changed residents in response to the stalking. Similarly, females were also more likely to have sought counseling. This is consistent with the fact that significantly more females than males reported fearing for their emotional health during the stalking incident. Although fewer than half of the respondents indicated making these major changes, these findings still indicate that for a portion of victims the stalking incidents resulted in some type of major disruption to their lives.

DISCUSSION AND CONCLUSION

The purpose of this research was to empirically study stalking victimization. Utilizing a random sample of 788 college students, it was discovered that twenty-one percent of the sample (24.7% of the females and 10.9% of the males) had been stalked at one point in their lives and that six percent were currently being stalked. While it must be remembered that this study examined a very specific sample of college students, these results support the notion that stalking is clearly an important public issue affecting a significant number of individuals. It is not clear at this point whether these findings could be extrapolated to the general population, although these estimates are consistent with those found by other researchers.

Consistent with prior research, this study found that stalking is a crime that predominantly affects women. Likewise, the majority of stalkers are men who stalk female victims. No significant differences were found between male and female victims with regard to their race, age, marital status or household income. Likewise, no significant differences were found between males and females who had been stalked and those who had not been stalked. Most of the victims knew their stalkers, with the largest percentage of both males and females indicating that the stalker was an ex-boyfriend/girlfriend. Both male and female victims reported that the average stalker was of the opposite sex, White, single and age 18–25, although females were significantly more likely to be stalked by someone above 25. The age of the stalker may, however, be an artifact of this particular sample.

Males reported being stalked for slightly longer periods of time, although both males and females reported that on average the stalking incidents lasted several months. Both genders reported very similar profiles of their stalkers. The average stalker was white, 18–25 years of age and single.

Both males and females reported being contacted by a variety of methods with the most common method being phone contacts, followed by face-to-face contact. Both male and female victims experienced similar types of contacts by their victims. Stalkers of female victims, however, were more likely to express over the phone a desire to make personal contact with their victims. In addition, female victims were also more likely to report that their stalkers threatened them, regardless of their method of contact. As a result, females also reported higher levels of fear for their physical safety, their lives and their emotional health.

The female victims appear to be justified in their increased perceptions of fear. Those who had been threatened by their stalkers were more likely to be approached by their stalkers. More important, they were also more likely to have been physically harmed by their stalkers. As a result, female victims also reported a wider array of responses to their stalking incidents. Females were more likely to involve the criminal justice system and more likely to take drastic measures such as moving, installing a security system or buying a gun. These results indicate that we need to take these threats very seriously, especially among the female victims.

Although these findings are somewhat limited due to the nature of the sample, they are nevertheless important. Stalking is a problem affecting a significant number of people. Victims of this offense suffer fear and emotional distress. Victims who receive threats logically experience greater levels of fear and are placed in greater danger. They are many times forced to change their lifestyles and to engage in a variety of behaviors in response to the stalking. Although a large percentage of the females in this sample reported being harmed by their stalkers, it is still important to note that the majority were not so harmed. Perhaps the presence of a credible threat, since it appears to increase both the danger to the victim and the victim's fear, could be used to enhance the penalty for the offense rather than be utilized as a prerequisite of the offense. It might also help us narrow down the class of victims who are in the greatest amount of danger from their stalkers.

Overall, stalking is a serious problem that is being appropriately acknowledged by state legislatures. Although remedies are now in place to potentially address this issue, it is important to note that only a small percentage of victims, predominantly female, actually called the police. Future research should focus on examining this issue more in-depth and determining what facts influence a victim to involve the criminal justice system and their experiences once they do take action. It appears that the criminal justice system needs to develop additional methods of protecting these victims. Since it appears that the established legislation is only being utilized in a small percentage of stalking cases, it cannot be protecting the majority of stalking victims.

Comprehensive knowledge concerning the crime of stalking and its participants should help legislatures formulate solutions that will protect the largest possible class of victims. It is hoped that this research will provide a stepping stone in that direction.

ACKNOWLEDGMENTS

The author wishes to thank David Spinner, Paul Friday and the anonymous reviewers for their helpful comments on earlier drafts. The author would also like to thank Nicole Hendrix and Melissa Fenwick for their assistance collecting the data. This work was supported, in part, by funds provided by the University of North Carolina at Charlotte.

REFERENCES

Attinello, K. (1993). Anti-stalking legislation: A comparison of traditional remedies available for victims of harassment versus California penal code section 646. 9. *Pacific Law Journal, 24,* 1945–1980.

Biden, J. (1992). *Antistalking legislation: Hearing on S. 2922 before Senate Comm.* On the Judiciary 102d Cong., 2d Sess. 1992.

Bjerregaard, B. (1996). Stalking and the First Amendment: A constitutional analysis of state stalking laws. *Criminal Law Bulletin, 32*(4), 307–341.

Browne, A. (1987). *When battered women kill.* New York: Free Press.

California Penal Code § 646. 9 (1990 and Supp. 1993).

David, J. W. (1994). Is Pennsylvania's stalking law constitutional? *University of Pittsburgh Law Review, 56,* 205–244.

Dietz, P. E., Matthews, D. B., Van Duyne, C., Martell, D. A., Parry, C. D. H., Stewart, T., Warren, J., & Crowder, J. D. (1991a). Threatening and otherwise inappropriate letters to Hollywood celebrities. *Journal of Forensic Sciences, 36*(1), 185–209.

Dietz, P. E., Matthews, D. B., Martell, D. A., Stewart, T. M., Hrouda, D. R., & J. Warren, J. (1991b). Threatening and otherwise inappropriate letters to members of the United States Congress. *Journal of Forensic Science, 36*(5), 1445–1468.

Faulkner, R. P., & Hsiao, D. H. (1993). And where you go i'll follow: The constitutionality of antistalking laws and proposed model legislation. *Harvard Journal on Legislation, 31,* 1–62.

Federal Bureau of Investigation—Uniform Crime Report. (21 April 1998). College and University Crime Statistics (On line) Available: http://www.soconline.org/tb9.pdf.

Fremouw, W. J., Westrup, D., & Pennypacker, J. (1997). Stalking on campus: The prevalence and strategies for coping with stalking. *Journal of Forensic Sciences, 42,* 664–667.

Gerberth, V. J. (1992). Stalkers. *Law and Order, 40*(10), 138–143.

Goldstein, R. L. (1987). More forensic romances: De Dlerambault's Syndrome in men. *Bulletin of the American Academy of Psychiatry and the Law, 15,* 267–274.

Guy, R. A. (1993). The nature and constitutionality of stalking laws. *Vanderbilt Law Review, 46,* 991–1029.

Hall, D. M. (1998). The victims of stalking. In J. R. Meloy (ed.), *The psychology of stalking: Clinical and forensic perspectives.* San Diego: Academic Press.

Harmon, R. B., Rosner, R., & Owens, H. (1995). Obsessional harassment and erotomania in a criminal court population. *Journal of Forensic Sciences, 40*(1), 188–196.

Hays, J. R., Romans, J. S. C., & Ritchhart, M. K. (1995). Reducing stalking behaviors for college and university counseling services. *Journal of College Student Psychotherapy, 10*(1), 57–63. <refs>Holmes, R. M. (1993). Stalking in America: Types and methods of criminal stalkers. *Journal of Contemporary Criminal Justice, 9*(4), 317–327.

Kienlen, K. K. (1998). Developmental and social antecedents of stalking. In J. R. Meloy (ed.) *The psychology of stalking: Clinical and forensic perspectives (pp. 51–67).* San Diego, CA: Academic Press.

Kienlen, K. K., Birmingham, D. L., Solbert, K. B., O'Regan, J. T., & Meloy, J. R. (1997). A Comparative study of psychotic and non-psychotic stalking. *Journal of the American Academy of Psychiatry & the Law, 25,* 317–334.

Kurt, J. L. (1995). Stalking as a variant of domestic violence. *Bulletin of the American Academy of Psychiatry and Law, 23*(2), 219–230.

Leong, G. B. (1994). De Clerambault Syndrome (Erotomania) in the criminal justice system: Another look at this recurring problem. *Journal of Forensic Sciences, 39*(1), 378–385.

McAnaney, K., Curliss, L., & Abeyta-Price, C. (1993). From imprudence to crime: Anti-stalking laws. *Notre Dame Law Review, 68,* 819–909.

McCreedy, K. R., & Dennis, B. G. (1996). Sex-related offenses and fear of crime on campus. *Journal of Contemporary Criminal Justice, 12*(1), 69–79.

Meloy, J. R. (1996). Stalking (obsessional following): A review of some preliminary studies. *Aggression and Violent Behavior, 1*(2), 147–162.

Meloy, J. R. (1998). The psychology of stalking. In J. R. Meloy (ed.) *The psychology of stalking: Clinical and forensic perspectives (pp. 1–23).* San Diego, CA: Academic Press.

Meloy J. R., & Gothard, S. (1995). Demographic and clinical comparison of obsessional followers and offenders with mental disorders. *American Journal of Psychiatry, 152*(2), 258–263.

Morin, K. S. (1993). The phenomenon of stalking: Do existing state statutes provide adequate protection? *San Diego Justice Journal, 1,* 123–162

Mullen, P. E., & Pathe, M. (1994). The pathological extensions of love. *British Journal of Psychiatry, 165,* 614–623.

Mullen, P. E., Pathe, M. Purcell, R., & Stuart, G. W. (1999). Study of stalkers. *American Journal of Psychiatry, 156,* 1244–1249.

National Criminal Justice Association (1993). *Project to develop a model anti-stalking code for states.* Washington D.C.: National Institute of Justice.

Noone, J., & Cockhill, L. (1987). Erotomania: The delusion of being loved. *American Journal of Forensic Psychiatry, 8,* 23–31.

Pathe, M. & Mullen, P. E. (1997). The impact of stalkers on their victims. *British Journal of Psychiatry, 170,* 12–17.

Perez, C. (1993). Stalking: When does obsession become a crime. *American Journal of Criminal Law, 20,* 263–280.

Poling, B. E. (1994). Stalking: Is the law hiding in the shadow of constitutionality. *Capital University Law Review, 23,* 279–311.

Puente, M. (1992). Legislators tackling the terror of stalking: But some experts say measures are vague. *U.S.A. Today,* July 21, 9A.

Rudden, M., Sweeney, J., & Frances, A. (1990). Diagnosis and clinical course of erotomania and other delusional patients. *American Journal of Psychiatry, 47*(5), 625–628.

Schwartz-Watts, D., Morgan, D. W., & Barnes, C. J. (1997). Stalkers: The South Carolina experience. *Journal of American Academy of Psychiatry & Law, 25,* 541–545.

Spitzberg, B. H., Nicastro, A. M., & Cousins, A. V. (1998). Exploring the interactional phenomenon of stalking and obsessive relational intrusion. *Communication Reports, 11,* 33–47.

Strikis, S. (1993). Stopping stalking. *The Georgetown Law Journal, 81,* 2771–2813.

Taylor, P., Mahendra, B., & Gunn, J. (1983). Erotomania in male. *Psychological Medicine, 13,* 645–650.

Thomas, K. R. (1993). How to stop the stalking: State antistalking laws. *Criminal Law Bulletin, 29,* 124–136.

Tjaden, P. (1997). *The crime of stalking: How big is the problem?* Washington, D.C.: National Institute of Justice.

Tjaden, P., & Thoennes, N. (1998). *Stalking in America: findings from the national violence against women survey.* Denver, CO: Center for Policy Research.

Wallace, H. (1995). A prosecutor's guide to stalking. *The Prosecutor, 29*(1), 26–30.

Wallace, H., & Kelty, K. (1995). Stalking and restraining orders: A legal and psychological perspective. *Journal of Crime and Justice, 18*(2), 99–111.

Welch, J. M. (1995). Stalking and anti-stalking legislation: A guide to the literature of a new legal concept. *Reference Services Review, 23*(3), 53–68.

Wright, J. A., Burgess, A. G., Burgess, A. W., McCray, G. O., & Douglas, J. E. (1995). Investigating stalking crime. *Journal of Psychosocial Nursing, 33*(9), 38–43.

Zona, M. A. Sharma, K. K., & J. Lane, J. (1993). A comparative study of erotomanic and obsessional subjects in a forensic sample. *Journal of Forensic Sciences, 38*(2), 894–903.

7

Obsessive Relational Intrusion: Incidence, Perceived Severity, and Coping

William R. Cupach and Brian H. Spitzberg

The occurrence of various forms of relational harassment has received heightened media attention (Way, 1994). Excessive pursuit of personal relationships is the object of increasing scrutiny from social scientists (Meloy, 1998), policy-makers (Cohen, 1993), and threat management specialists (de Becker, 1997). The stalking of celebrities and the obsessive pursuit that attends cases of domestic violence are the types of harassment that receive the most attention. Focus on these highly publicized types of pursuit, however, may mask the full magnitude and diversity of obsessive relational intrusion activities (Pathé & Mullen, 1997). The investigations reported here attempt to identify the incidence of a broad range of relationally intrusive behaviors, to identify the ways in which objects of pursuit respond, and to assess the relative perceived severity of intrusion behaviors.

Defining Obsessive Relational Intrusion

Obsessive relational intrusion (ORI) is defined as the "repeated and unwanted pursuit and invasion of one's sense of physical or symbolic privacy by another person, either stranger or acquaintance, who desires and/or presumes an intimate relationship" (Cupach & Spitzberg,

1998, pp. 234–235). There are several implications of this definition. First, ORI involves individuals who disagree about relational goals. The pursuer presses his or her need for more connection, intimacy, and interdependence with the object of pursuit, whereas the victim simultaneously desires some degree of autonomy, distance, and independence with respect to the pursuer.

Second, ORI is not commonly associated with a single event. Rather, obsessive intrusion is repeated over several occasions. Isolated, individual acts of harassment or imposition are not by themselves obsessive. Obsessiveness is reflected in the fact that the intruder is fixated on the target of attention. The intruder's thoughts and behaviors are persistent, pre-occupying, and often morbid. Pursuit is persistent despite the absence of reciprocity by the obsessional object, and even in the face of resistance by the object. Consequently, episodes of intrusion often tend to escalate in intensity over time as the pursuer exerts greater and greater effort to capture the attention and affection of the object.

Third, intrusion can be psychological and symbolic as well as physical. Imposition on one's autonomy and invasion of one's privacy are meaningful manifestations of intrusion. Assaults on and threats to person and property are overt forms of harassment. However, unwanted intrusion into psychological or symbolic space can be accomplished without overt threat and can be just as debilitating for the victim of intrusion.

Obsessive relational intrusion is closely aligned with, but also distinct from, other phenomena such as stalking and obsessional following. Stalking is typically defined legalistically as the persistent pursuit or harassment of a person in a manner that a reasonable person would find threatening. Such a definition would technically include many political or for-hire assassins, serial killers, serial rapists, and others who harass leaders, administrators, and the like for the purpose of inflicting harm upon a victim. Although it is clearly important to understand such phenomena, these examples do not constitute attempts to establish intimate relationships. The phrase obsessional following reveals the same limitation. Given that most stalkers know their victim, and that most cases are likely to involve a person attempting to re-establish this relationship, or move it to a different level of intimacy (Tjaden & Thoennes, 1998), we employ the term "obsessive relational intrusion" to emphasize the relational aspect of the phenomenon.

Manifestations and Incidence of ORI

ORI is represented in the literature by such diverse labels as obsessional following (Meloy, 1996; Meloy & Gothard, 1995), obsessional harassment (Harmon, Rosner, & Owens, 1995), and stalking (Wright et al., 1996; Zona, Palarea, & Lane, 1998). Explanations for the occurrence of obsessional pursuit also are varied. Pursuers are described as suffering from erotomania (Leong, 1994; Zona, Sharma, & Lane, 1993), borderline erotomania (Meloy, 1989; Meloy & Gothard, 1995), love addiction (Peele, 1981; Timmreck, 1990), pathological narcissism (Meloy, 1996), or pathological love (Mullen & Pathé, 1994a, 1994b). ORI can be attributed to delusional beliefs about the object of pursuit (i.e., erotomania), jealousy (Dutton, van Ginkel, & Landolt, 1996), unrequited love (Baumesiter, Wotman, & Stillwell, 1993), general psychological disturbance or pathology (Spencer, 1998), and relational separation or termination. In the latter case, many scholars believe that ORI is a frequent concomitant of domestic violence (Kurt, 1995; Tjaden & Thoennes, 1998; Walker & Meloy, 1998).

Stalking, when in pursuit of a relationship, represents a particularly severe and menacing form of ORI. Stalking is commonly defined as "the willful, malicious, and repeated following and harassing of another person that threatens his or her safety" (Meloy & Gothard, 1995, p. 258). Stalking is a pattern of behavior that can stem from various underlying motives. When it is motivated by a desire on the part of the pursuer to increase intimacy with the object, it is a manifestation of ORI.

As the most blatant form of ORI, stalking has been evidenced in several studies of specific populations (e.g., Fremouw, Westrup & Pennypacker, 1997; Romans, Hays, & White, 1996). However, studies suggest a much broader array of actions representing unwanted attention that do not necessarily qualify as stalking. These actions include privacy invasion (Burgoon et al., 1989; Pathé & Mullen, 1997), lewd or threatening phone calls (Katz, 1994; Smith & Morra, 1994), harassing letters (Dietz et al., 1991; Dietz et al., 1991), intrusive e-mail messages (Lloyd-Goldstein, 1998; Ross, 1995), unexpected visits at home or work (Jason, Reichler, Easton, Neal, & Wilson, 1984; Pathé & Mullen, 1997), pestering for a date despite prior refusals (Jason et al., 1984; Leonard et al., 1993), clandestine surveillance (Jason et al., 1984; Pathé & Mullen, 1997; Tjaden & Thoennes, 1998), property damage (Pathé & Mullen, 1997; Tjaden & Thoennes, 1998), sexual harassment (Leonard et al., 1993; Roscoe, Strouse, & Goodwin, 1994), verbal or physical threats (Harmon et al., 1995; Pathé & Mullen, 1997; Zona et al., 1993), sexual coercion or assault (DiVasto et al., 1984; Spitzberg & Rhea, 1999), and physical abuse (Dutton, van Ginkel, & Landolt, 1996; Kurt, 1995). One purpose of the present study is to assess the incidence of a full range of such ORI behaviors.

Threat Management

Relatively little is currently known about how victims of ORI respond to intruders' unwanted overtures. The sexual harassment literature suggests that responses likely range from wholesale avoidance to direct and forceful confrontation (e.g., Clair, McGoun, & Spirek, 1993). In response to obscene phone calls specifically, people tend to respond with a neutral statement, simply hang up, insult the caller, continue listening but say nothing, call the police, or call the phone company (Savitz, 1986; Sheffield, 1989). In Jason et al.'s (1984) study of relational harassment, women reported that they tend to do nothing, try to be nice, indicate a preference not to see the harasser again, change their phone number, move, or seek civil protection. Coleman (1997) found that stalking victims were more likely to use reasoning rather than verbal or physical violence. Fremouw et al. (1997) found that victims of stalking most often ignored the stalker, confronted the stalker, or changed their schedule to avoid the stalker. Tjaden and Thoennes's (1998) study indicated that most victims of stalking contacted the police, took extra precautions, enlisted the help of family and friends, got a gun, or changed locations. Pathé and Mullen (1997) found that most victims of stalking seek help and advice from third parties (e.g., police, lawyers, family, friends, counselors, etc.), curtail their social and work activities, and a substantial percentage change their workplace, school or career. To date, there has been no systematic attempt to describe victim responses to the broader phenomenon of ORI. Such description is vital and preliminary to investigations of the efficacy of victim responses. Thus, one goal of the present research is to examine the occurrence of a wide range of victim responses to ORI.

STUDY 1: ORI INCIDENCE AND COPING

The first study reported here was designed to address three questions: (1) What is the perceived incidence of a broad range of ORI behaviors? (2) In what ways do victims of ORI respond? (3) What is the association between coping responses and ORI behaviors? To answer these questions, we sampled college students on two campuses—a large public university in Texas, and a large public university in southern California. The same items and instructions were presented to both samples.

Method

Participants. Participants in the Texas sample were 366 students (193 females, 173 males) from large lecture sections of the introductory psychology courses. Partcipants were assured that responses would be kept anonymous. The average age of participants was 21.72. The sample was predominantly White (79.6%), with small percentages of African American (8.4%), Mexican American (3.5%), and Asian American (2.7%) participants. More than one-third of the participants claimed to be currently in a steady dating relationship (35.4%), with smaller percentages claiming to be occasionally dating (25.5%), not dating (20.6%), married (19.2%), or engaged (8%).

The California sample consisted of 300 college students (164 females, 134 males) with a mean age of 20.67. Participants were assured that their responses would be kept anonymous. Approximately 60% were White, 13% Mexican American, 7% Asian American, and 5% African American. Participants reported that they were currently involved in a steady dating relationship (42%), an occasional dating situation (27%), engaged (3%), married (5%), or not currently dating (23%).

INSTRUMENTATION

We consulted literatures on stalking and relational harassment to derive a list of 50 obsessive relational intrusion items. The initial list of items was presented to several students and experts (i.e., a psychologist, a threat management expert, and a city attorney, all specializing in stalking) expressly for expanding the list. The resulting items were then screened for redundancy, clarity, and observability.

These procedures produced a list of 63 ORI behaviors. These items were presented to participants along with the definition of ORI. Specifically, the instructions read: The purpose of this survey is to assess how often people experience relational intrusion, and how they feel about various intrusion behaviors. The intruder may have been a former boyfriend or girlfriend, a classmate, or even a work acquaintance. But in some way or another, it should be someone who, in your own mind, you clearly did not want to share with the same kind of relationship that the intruder desired. In some cases, you may have to report on your suspicion rather than certainty (e.g., someone who calls you and hangs up immediately might be a random caller rather than someone with whom you were acquainted).

Participants were asked to rate the extent to which they had experienced each of the behaviors in this context since the age of 18. The response scale was as follows: 0 = never, 1 = once since the age of 18, 2 = rarely (i.e., 2 to 4 times since the age of 18), 3 = sometimes (i.e., 5 to 9 times since the age of 18), and 4 = frequently (i.e., more than 10 times since the age of 18).

Similar procedures as those just outlined were employed to produce a list of coping activities. The research on coping strategies (e.g., Burgoon et al., 1989; Meyer & Taylor, 1986) and victim responses to stalking (e.g., Meloy & Gothard, 1995; Mullen & Pathé, 1994a, 1994b) were examined, and presented to experts for review. The resulting list of 50 coping responses was presented to participants using the following scale: 0 = never engaged in this response, 1 = I engaged in this response once, 2 = I engaged in this response two to three times, and 3 = I engaged in this response frequently.

Results

Table 7.1 reports the percentage of participants who reported experiencing each ORI behavior at least once. All 63 ORI behaviors were perceived by some participants in each sample to have occurred at least once. The most commonly cited behaviors, identified as occurring at least once by 63–75% of participants, were: "would call and hang up without answering," "called and argued with you," "asked if you were seeing someone," "made exaggerated claims of affection for you," "constantly asked for another chance," "watched you from a distance," and "gossiped or bragged about your relationship to others." The behaviors that were cited by the fewest participants (6–11%) included "recorded conversations without your knowledge," "broke into your home or apartment," and "sent you offensive photographs."

Table 7.1 Percentage of Participants Reporting Being the Target of ORI Behaviors

	Study 1		Study 2
	CA	TX	IL
Pursuit			
Drove by your house or work	57	64	51
Visited you at work	50	51	42
Showed up before or after work	50	52	38
Left notes on your car windshield	42	59	35
Called you while you were working	44	47	33
Waited in a car near where you were	37	43	26
Waited outside your place	38	45	26
Left you written messages in or at your residence	43	47	25
Violation			
Took photos of you without your knowledge or consent	15	13	6
Recorded conversations without your knowledge	10	9	4
Broke into your home or apartment	10	11	4
Sent you offensive photographs	6	7	3
Threat			
Called and argued with you	73	78	68
Tried to argue with you in public places	48	56	45
Used profanity and/or obscenities in reference to you	46	49	45
Accused you of sleeping around	49	46	38
Made vague warnings that bad things will happen to you	36	41	26
Physically shoved, slapped, or hit you	33	37	25
Warned that bad things would or might happen to you	29	34	25
Threatened you with physical harm	33	36	22
Damaged property or possessions of yours	30	29	19
Hyperintimacy			
Asked if you were seeing someone	74	45	67
Made exaggerated claims about his/her affection for you	65	54	54
Refused to take hints that he or she wasn't welcome	61	67	54
Gossiped or bragged about your relationship to others	63	67	53
Constantly apologized for past wrongs or transgressions	58	62	50
Spread false rumors about you to your friends	51	47	49
Engaged in excessive self-disclosure	49	70	44
Told others you were more intimate than you currently were	52	61	40
Made up things about your past relationship	46	48	34
Joined you uninvited while you were conversing with others	44	48	33
Inappropriately touched you in an intimate way	37	42	27
Described acts of sex to you	41	43	25
Claimed to still be in a relationship with you	39	42	22
ORI Items Not Loading on a Specific Factor			
Would call and hang up without answering	73	75	63

Table 7.1 *(Continued)*

	Study 1		Study 2
	CA	TX	IL
Constantly asked for another chance	63	70	58
Watched or stared at you from a distance	63	68	55
Argued with you about your relationships with other people	55	58	53
Told you to stop doing certain things	58	59	51
Accused you of being unfaithful	55	54	50
Checked up on you through mutual acquaintances	60	63	50
Used third parties to "spy" or keep tabs on you	60	59	46
Called at all times of the day to check up on you	50	58	41
Performed large favors for you without your permission	58	60	38
Spied on you	47	54	36
Sent you unwanted cards or letters	44	46	35
Complained to you how you ruined his/her life	45	48	32
Left frequent messages on your answering machine	52	50	32
Sent you unwanted gifts	34	37	31
Waited around near your conversation with another person	43	46	30
Made obscene phone calls to you	31	28	30
Went through your private things in your room	35	39	28
Increased contact w/ your family members to stay involved	41	44	27
Showed up before or after classes	38	40	23
Followed you in a walking conversation	36	35	19
Knocked on your window unexpectedly	31	28	16
Followed you from place to place	31	36	15
Exposed him/herself to you	30	34	14
Called radio station and devoted songs to you	17	15	14
Mailed or left gifts you previously gave	19	17	13
Sent threatening notes/letters/messages to you	18	19	12
Forced sexual behavior	18	20	11
Cluttered your e-mail with messages	13	13	5

Note. Items are grouped according to ORI factor structure. California (CA) N = 300; Texas (TX) N = 367; Illinois (IL) N = 209.

The Texas and California samples were combined (N = 675) in order to conduct exploratory principal components factor analysis on the ORI items. Factor extraction was based on factors with eigenvalues greater than one, and leveling of the scree. Factor definition required that a minimum of three items load (Velicer & Fava, 1998) with primary loadings of .50 or greater, and no secondary loadings greater than .30. There were eight factors with eigenvalues greater than one, and the scree plot indicated leveling at the fifth factor. The four-factor solution was the first to produce a successful definition, accounting for 52% of the common variance.[1] The KMO measure of sampling adequacy was .96.

The first factor loaded eight items (e.g., showed up before or after work, left notes on car windshield, etc.), and was labeled pursuit (α = .91). The second factor loaded four items (e.g., sent offensive photographs, recorded your conversations, etc.),[2] and was labeled violation (α = .75). The third factor loaded nine items, such as threatened with physical harm and made vague warnings, and was labeled threat (α = .89). The final factor loaded 13 items (e.g., described acts of sex to you, touched you inappropriately, made things up regarding your relationship, etc.), and was labeled hyperintimacy (α = .92).

The combined samples were also used to examine the dimensional structure of the coping items, employing the same procedures and criteria as for the ORI items. There were eight factors with eigenvalues over one, and the scree plot indicated leveling after five factors, and the four-factor model was the first successful structure, accounting for 52% of the common variance.[3] The KMO was .96. The first factor loaded 10 items (e.g., yelled at the person, had a serious talk with the person, etc.), and was labeled interaction (α = .94). The second factor loaded 12 items (e.g., pursued trespass laws, called the police, obtained restraining order, etc.), and was labeled protection (α = .84). The third factor loaded four items (e.g., threatened physical harm, belittled or shamed person, etc.), and was labeled retaliation (α = .80). The final factor loaded eight items (e.g., avoided eye contact, pretended to be preoccupied, ignored them, etc.), and was labeled evasion (α = .89).

The factor definitions were used to create averaged variables for each factor. The intercorrelations among these factors are shown in Table 7.2. Large intercorrelations are revealed among the ORI factors, with large to moderate intercorrelations between ORI and coping factors. ORI pursuit, threat, and hyperintimacy are strongly related to coping through interaction, suggesting that direct conversations with the pursuer are highly likely to co-occur with most forms of pursuit. It is interesting to note that violation forms of ORI (e.g., took photographs of you, broke into your home or apartment) are more strongly related to coping through protective measures (e.g., called police, obtained restraining order, etc.), perhaps because of the level of deviance, and perhaps danger implicit in such violations. Although the use of

Table 7.2 Intercorrelations and Coefficient Alpha Reliabilities for ORI and Coping Variables

	1	2	3	4	5	6	7	8
1. ORI Pursuit	.91							
2. ORI Violation	.69	.75						
3. ORI Threat	.69	.64	.89					
4. ORI Hyperintimacy	.76	.58	.74	.92				
5. Coping Interaction	.63	.45	.71	.71	.94			
6. Coping Protection	.49	.69	.56	.48	.46	.84		
7. Coping Retaliation	.42	.44	.54	.50	.60	.44	.80	
8. Coping Evasion	.55	.35	.50	.70	.65	.35	.43	.89

Note. All correlations are significant at $p < .001$. Coefficients in the diagonal represent the factor reliability.

threats and evasion to cope were significantly related to types of ORI victimization, the interrelationships are more moderate than the use of direct interaction.

Sex differences were explored across ORI and coping factors, but revealed neither consistently significant nor meaningful differences. First, we performed a 2 (male, female) x 2 (Texas, California) x 4 (pursuit, violation, threat, hyperintimacy) repeated measures MANOVA, with sex and sample as between-subject factors and ORI as a within-subject factor. The only significant multivariate effect was for ORI ($\Lambda = .408$, Exact $F = 306.31$, $p < .001$, $\eta^2 = .592$). Univariate ANOVA ($F = 363.62$, $p < .001$, $\eta^2 = .361$) with post hoc comparisons (with Bonferroni correction) indicated that hyperintimacy ($M = 1.21$) was reported more frequently than pursuit ($M = 1.04$), which was reported more frequently than threat ($M = .92$), which in turn was reported more frequently than violation ($M = .33$). All effects involving sex and sample were not significant.

We also conducted a 2 (male, female) x 2 (Texas, California) x 4 (protection, interaction, retaliation, evasion) repeated measures MANOVA, with sex and sample as between-subject factors and coping as a within-subject factor. Significant multivariate effects were obtained for coping ($\Lambda = .301$, Exact $F = 495.37$, $p < .001$, $\eta^2 = .699$) and coping x sex ($\Lambda = .935$, Exact $F = 14.92$, $p < .001$, $\eta^2 = .065$) only. Univariate follow-ups with Bonferroni correction ($F = 704.87$, $p < .001$, $\eta^2 = .524$) showed that evasion ($M = 1.47$) was reported more frequently than interaction (M = 1.16), which was reported more frequently than retaliation (M = .51), which was reported more frequently than protection (M = .25). Women reported slightly higher tendencies to use interaction (M^f = 1.27, M^m = 1.05, F = 9.09, p = .003, η^2 = .014) and protection (M^f = .29, M^m = .21, F = 5.02, p = .025, η^2 = .008), and less retaliation (M^f = .44, M^m = .57, F = 7.02, p < .008, η^2 = .011) modes of coping than men reported using, although the effect sizes are so small as to make such a conclusion relatively moot. For all practical purposes, in these samples of college students there were no meaningful sex differences in the reported victimization or modes of coping with obsessive relational intrusion.

STUDY 2: SEVERITY OF ORI BEHAVIORS

We contend that ORI behaviors differ in their relative perceived severity. Some behaviors seem mildly intrusive, some moderately so, and some intensely invasive. Mildly intrusive behaviors amount to pestering and importunity; they are annoying but not particularly threatening. Receiving unwanted gifts or favors, being pestered for a date, being begged for forgiveness, or getting numerous non-threatening calls or messages are inconveniencing and intrusive to a degree, but they are not likely to be threatening or highly upsetting.

Behaviors that invade privacy but pose little intrinsic threat, such as being spied on or having false rumors spread about you to your friends, are relatively more aggravating. They are more than merely annoying; they are moderately severe. Most upsetting of all are behaviors that are perceived to be threatening, such as being the victim of stalking, home invasion, verbal threats, physical assault, or property damage. Thus, we argue that ORI behaviors are perceived by victims as being more or less intrusive, more or less invasive of privacy, and more or less threatening. In an attempt to distinguish empirically less severe from more severe ORI behaviors, Study 2 is designed to answer the following question: What is the perceived severity of ORI behaviors?

The question of perceived threat and invasiveness of ORI tactics should be of interest to law enforcement and the judiciary. Currently, a key test of stalking prosecution is whether "a reasonable person" would find a course of conduct threatening. Relatively little is known, however, about what constitutes threatening conduct in any normative sense.

Method

Participants. A convenience sample of 209 students was drawn from large lecture classes at a public university in Illinois. Volunteers were solicited during regular class time and assured that their responses would be kept anonymous. The average age of respondents was 20.5 (range = 18–36). Females comprised 62% of the sample, males 38%. Approximately 89% of respondents reported that they were Caucasian; 7.7% indicated they were African American.

Instrumentation. The survey contained the same introductory description of obsessive pursuit as in Study 1. These directions were followed by the 63 items designed to depict potential relational intrusion behaviors. For each item, respondents were asked to circle YES or NO to indicate whether or not they actually had experienced the behavior from a relational intruder. Also for each item respondents were asked to indicate the extent to which they felt (if they marked YES) or would feel (if they marked NO): annoyed, upset, threatened, and violated. Ratings for each of the four concepts were made using an 11–point scale accompanied by the following anchors: 0 = Not at All, 5 = Moderately, 10 = Extremely.

Results

Table 7.1 shows the percentage of respondents who reported being the target of each of the 63 ORI behaviors. Between 3% and 68% of respondents reported experiencing each of the ORI behaviors. The most frequently reported behaviors included: "called and argued with you," "asked if you were seeing someone," "would call and hang up without answering," "constantly asked for another chance," and "watched or stared at you from a distance." The least frequently reported behaviors were: "took photos of you without your knowledge or consent," "cluttered your e-mail with messages," "recorded conversations without your knowledge," "broke into your home or apartment," and "sent you offensive photographs." These findings parallel those of Study 1.

Using the factor structure obtained in Study 1, we created four measures of severity (i.e., annoyance, upset, threatened, and privacy violated) for each of the four ORI behavior categories (i.e., pursuit, violation, threat, and hyperintimacy). Participants' judgments of severity were averaged across the items comprising each ORI behavior cat-

Table 7.3 Reliability Coefficients for Severity Ratings for Each ORI Factor

ORI Behaviors	Severity Ratings			
	Annoyed	Upset	Threatened	Privacy Violated
Pursuit	.87	.89	.91	.89
Violation	.73	.73	.78	.61
Threat	.83	.87	.87	.85
Hyperintimacy	.88	.89	.93	.90

egory (as defined in Study 1). Reliability coefficients for the resulting 16 measures are shown in Table 7.3.

In order to assess whether actual experience of ORI behaviors affected severity ratings, the sample was split into two groups for each ORI behavior category—those respondents who never experienced any of the behaviors comprising the ORI factor, and those respondents who experienced at least one of the behaviors comprising the ORI factor. This was done for each of the four ORI factors (pursuit, violation, threat, and hyperintimacy), thus creating four pairs of groups. Mean scores on each of the four severity ratings were compared for each pair of groups. For example, those never experiencing pursuit were compared to those who had experienced at least some pursuit in terms of ratings of annoyance, upset, threat, and violation. Only one of the 16 F-tests was significant at the .05 probability level. Respondents who never experienced violation perceived such intrusion to be more upsetting than those individuals who had experienced some form of violation ($F = 3.89$, $p = .05$, $\eta^2 = .019$). In all other comparisons, those who never experienced a type of ORI behavior did not rate the severity of such behavior any differently than their more experienced counterparts. We therefore performed subsequent analyses on the entire sample.

In order to assess differences in mean ratings of severity across ORI behavior categories, and to discern sex differences in ratings of severity, we performed repeated measures MANOVA with severity (i.e., annoy, upset, threat, violated) and ORI (i.e., pursuit, violation, threat, hyperintimacy) as within-subject factors and sex as a between-subject factor. Significant multivariate effects were obtained for severity ($\Lambda = .365$, Exact $F = 113.59$, $p < .001$, $\eta^2 = .635$), ORI ($\Lambda = .651$, Exact $F = 121.63$, $p < .001$, $\eta^2 = .651$), severity x sex ($\Lambda = .873$, Exact $F = 9.50$, $p < .001$, $\eta^2 = .127$), severity x ORI ($\Lambda = .371$, Exact $F = 35.74$, $p < .001$, $\eta^2 = .629$), and severity x ORI x sex ($\Lambda = .814$, Exact $F =$

Table 7.4 Mean Severity Ratings for ORI Behaviors

ORI Behaviors	Severity Ratings			
	Annoyed	Upset	Threatened	Privacy Violated
Pursuit	7.41_c	5.94_a	4.65_a	5.40_b
Violation	8.40_a	8.05_b	6.71_b	7.71_a
Threat	7.74_{bc}	7.76_c	6.05_c	5.26_b
Hyperintimacy	7.93_b	6.69_d	4.18_d	5.33_b

Note. Column means with uncommon subscripts are significantly different, $p < .05$, with Bonferroni correction for multiple comparisons. All ratings were made on scales ranging from 0 (not at all) to 10 (extremely).

4.84, $p < .001$, $\eta^2 = .186$).[4] The multivariate effect for ORI x sex was not significant.

Table 7.4 presents the mean ratings of severity for each of the ORI behavior categories. Virtually all categories of ORI are considered rather annoying, with all means exceeding 7 on the 0–10 scale. Violation was considered more annoying than other forms of ORI ($F = 29.05$, $p < .001$, $\eta^2 = .126$). Similarly, all forms of ORI are at least moderately upsetting, with violation being the most upsetting of all ($F = 165.56$, $p < .001$, $\eta^2 = .450$). As expected, pursuit and hyperintimacy are relatively less threatening than violation and threat ($F = 281.71$, $p < .001$, $\eta^2 = .482$). Also, violation is seen as more privacy invasive than are the other forms of ORI ($F = 169.20$, $p < .001$, $\eta^2 = .456$), although all ORI categories are seen as at least moderately privacy invasive.
Univariate F-tests were performed to identify sex differences in severity ratings (see Table 7.5). The pattern of results is remarkably consistent. For all ORI behavior categories (i.e., pursuit, violation, threat, and hyperintimacy) females perceived the behaviors to be more upsetting, more threatening, and more privacy-violating than did males. Females also perceived violation, threat, and hyperintimacy to be more annoying than did males. The only severity rating on which males and females did not differ was for the perceived annoyance of pursuit.

DISCUSSION

The evidence presented here suggests that obsessive relational intrusion manifests itself in a wide range of pursuer actions. ORI is a

Table 7.5 Sex Differences in ORI Mean Severity Ratings

	Males		Females		F	η2
Pursuit						
Annoyance	7.24	(2.21)	7.39	(2.16)	0.22	.001
Upset	5.31	(2.39)	6.22	(2.31)	7.15**	.034
Threatened	3.25	(2.55)	5.36	(2.45)	34.40***	.145
Privacy Violated	4.87	(2.49)	5.61	(2.64)	3.92*	.019
Violation						
Annoyance	7.89	(2.11)	8.73	(1.68)	9.72**	.047
Upset	7.23	(2.29)	8.60	(1.68)	23.64***	.107
Threatened	5.22	(2.75)	7.64	(2.12)	48.90***	.198
Privacy Violated	6.96	(2.26)	8.22	(1.78)	19.02***	.088
Threat						
Annoyance	7.43	(1.66)	7.97	(1.61)	5.23*	.025
Upset	6.78	(2.10)	8.37	(1.28)	45.10***	.182
Threatened	4.78	(2.41)	6.81	(1.63)	51.24***	.202
Privacy Violated	4.22	(2.26)	5.82	(2.17)	25.43***	.111
Hyperintimacy						
Annoyance	7.50	(1.76)	8.18	(1.41)	9.47**	.044
Upset	5.97	(2.10)	7.12	(1.67)	18.90***	.085
Threatened	3.14	(2.36)	4.75	(2.29)	23.24***	.102
Privacy Violated	4.65	(2.24)	5.70	(2.22)	10.63***	.050

Note. Standard deviations in parentheses.

$*p < .05; **p < .01; ***p < .001$

common experience and its less threatening forms are ubiquitous. The percentage of respondents reporting specific ORI behaviors was remarkably consistent across all three samples. Although more serious forms of intrusion—the forms that could be considered stalking (e.g., following from place to place, waiting outside your place, etc.)—are not universal, they are experienced by more than one-third of the college students we surveyed. The more threatening actions (e.g., threatening notes, property damage, etc.) were experienced by 20%–30% of students.

With the aid of factor analysis we were able to identify four general types of ORI behavior: pursuit, violation, threat, and hyperintimacy. While violation and threat are escalated and are more threatening forms of ORI, pursuit and hyperintimacy represent activities that are quite common in normal courtship. Pursuit involves making contact and hyperintimacy entails the fabrication of relationship closeness.

Although such behaviors can be harassing, they are often not considered threatening and thus would not qualify technically as stalking. Indeed, as Emerson, Ferris, and Gardner (1998) point out, individuals "who become the focus of such attention may initially frame these activities as romantic pursuit or friendship-building, only later reinterpreting them as stalking" (p. 292).

Factor analysis of coping items in college students reveal a coherent four-factor structure to ORI responses: interaction, protection, retaliation, and evasion. Future investigations will need to discern the conditions under which these particular responses aggravate or mitigate obsessive intrusion (Aldwin & Revenson, 1987). In addition, research should investigate the context generality of such responses, given that this factor structure displays both overlap with, and difference from, taxonomies of coping responses in other contexts of trauma (e.g., Burgoon et al., 1989; Meyer & Taylor, 1986). Furthermore, there may be more conceptual bases for identifying taxonomies of coping. For example, technology can serve the role of evasion (e.g., home security), retaliation (e.g., stun gun) or protection (e.g., caller ID). Intervention of law enforcement can serve both a protection function as well as a retaliation function. Further research and theoretical consideration are needed to identify the most coherent and practical taxonomies of coping responses to obsessive pursuit, as well as their relative efficacy.

The finding that frequency of victimization is positively related to frequency of coping responses suggests that the more victimized a person is, the more that person resorts to various attempts to manage the intrusion (Spitzberg et al., 1998). It would have been preferable to find a negative relationship between some coping responses and ORI, which might suggest a type of threat management that could effectively diminish pursuit and intrusion. Such a finding may require a methodology more sensitive to the sequential nature of obsessive pursuit and intrusion. It may be, for example, that it is not which coping response so much as the timing of the response that determines the efficacy of the management effort.

Evidence from the current study supports the view that ORI behaviors can be arrayed on a continuum of severity. Virtually all ORI behaviors were perceived by recipients to be rather annoying and at least moderately upsetting. Not all behaviors, however, were perceived to be particularly threatening. Highly threatening behaviors were reported less frequently than merely annoying behaviors, although the incidence of threatening behaviors is remarkable. Consistent with the fact that pursuit and hyperintimacy are common in normal relationship development, they are clearly less upsetting than violation and threat.

The current legal definitions of stalking are predicated on pursuit being "threatening". What constitutes threat is based on a "reasonable person" standard (NIJ, 1993); that is, would a reasonable person find such behavior threatening, or behavior that places person, valued others, or property at risk. The results of this study suggest that there are empirically normative variations in the perception of threat. Further research may uncover the factors upon which such perceptions of threat depend.

An examination of sex differences revealed that men and women did not differ in the reported indicence of either ORI behaviors or coping responses. However, women perceived most types of intrusion to be more distressing than did men. This is consistent with the qualitative data reported by Emerson et al. (1998). They concluded that "When women followed and pursued men, the latter rarely expressed deep concern or upset, did not appear to be particularly threatened by the knowledge of their pursuit, and took few countermeasures in reaction" (p. 300). Although men may feel less vulnerable than women to the risks associated with ORI victimization, it may also be the case that there are subtle differences in manifestations of pursuit behaviors that account for this pattern. More fine-grained analysis of serial episodes of ORI is needed to shed further light on this issue.

Current theory on stalking (e.g., Kienlen, 1998; Meloy, 1998; Zona, Palarea & Lane, 1998) and obsessive relational intrusion (e.g., Spitzberg, 1998) has taken largely psychological approaches to the phenomenon. A psychological approach places the locus of explanation in the disturbance of an individual's developmental background and current, typically pathological, traits. However, some approaches are beginning to conceptualize stalking and obsessive relational intrusion more as disturbed versions of relatively normal relational processes (Cupach & Spitzberg, 1998; Emerson et al., 1998). Westrup and Fremouw (1998) view stalking as a product of reinforcement contingencies in which the pursuit serves to fulfill an arousal function for the pursuer. Mustaine and Tewksbury (1999) have studied stalking as a product of routine activities that increase the likelihood that people will come into contact with pursuers. Cupach, Spitzberg, and Carson (2000) conceptualize stalking as a product of goal-linking, and rumination that paradoxically reinforces obsessive fixation as a target of pursuit increasingly demonstrates disinterest or rejection. Such approaches emphasize the behavioral complexity of stalking, pursuit and intrusion, and therefore place a premium on the importance of assessing a broad range of pursuit, harassment, and coping behaviors. The research presented here utilized a more extensive range of such behaviors than has been previously reported in the literature, and suggests the true breadth and scope with which people can experience unwanted and persistent intrusion. The fact that many of these behaviors are common, and often even normative, in the pursuit of intimate relationships suggests that theory should begin to integrate stalking and obsessive relational intrusion into models of relatively normal relationships gone awry.

Numerous methodological limitations qualify inferences from the present data. The large number of items completed by respondents could have produced undesirable response sets. In addition, the focus on individual behaviors may have led some respondents to report being the recipient of a behavior, even if it was not in the context of an ongoing intrusion.

Abstracting the individual behaviors out of serial episodes of intrusion, as in the present study, renders a static picture of ORI. Intrusive behavior occurs in a relational or perhaps sometimes "quasi-relational" context. ORI has a serial quality, consisting of sequential and cumulative actions and reactions involving both pursuers and targets. Furthermore, the behaviors of both pursuers and targets are likely to be mutually contingent. At present, our knowledge about ORI is primarily at the level of particular actions and events that are construed as intrusive. A more complete understanding of the dynamics of ORI will require investigations into the temporal and interactive aspects of pursuer and target behaviors. Such investigations will be helpful in ultimately identifying the sequelae of ORI, and in assessing the efficacy of strategies for managing it.

NOTES

1. Factor loadings available from the authors upon request.

2. One item was allowed to define on this factor that had a secondary loading of $-.367$ on the third factor due to the substantial increase in reliability it afforded the violation factor.

3. There were strong loadings of two items on the use of technology

(i.e., caller ID, ordered callback phone feature), but no third item loaded on this factor, and the reliability was below .70 for the two items. These results suggest that more items on technological forms of coping should be added to the coping measure in future research.

4. We were not interested in exploring interaction effects involving both within-subjects factors. Thus, the ORI x severity and ORI x severity x sex effects were regarded as unwanted effects partitioned from the design in order to maximize statistical power.

ACKNOWLEDGMENT

The authors gratefully acknowledge feedback on previous versions of this manuscript provided by Keith Davis, Irene Frieze, and an anonymous reviewer.

REFERENCES

Aldwin, C. M., & Revenson, T. A. (1987). Does coping help? A reexamination of the relation between coping and mental health. *Journal of Personality and Social Psychology, 53,* 337–348.

Baumeister, R. F., Wotman, S. R., & Stillwell, A. M. (1993). Unrequited love: On heartbreak, anger, guilt, scriptlessness, and humiliation. *Journal of Personality and Social Psychology, 64,* 377–394.

Burgoon, J. K., Parrott, R., LePoire, B. A., Kelley, D. L., Walther, J. B., & Parry, D. (1989). Maintaining and restoring privacy through communication in different types of relationships. *Journal of Social and Personal Relationships, 6,* 131–158.

Clair, R. P., McGoun, M. J., & Spirek, M. M. (1993). Sexual harassment responses of working women: An assessment of current communication-oriented typologies and perceived effectiveness of the response. In G. L. Kreps (Ed.), *Sexual harassment: communication implications* (pp. 209–233). Cresskill, NJ: Hampton Press.

Cohen, W. S. (1993). *Antistalking proposals. Hearing before the Committee on the Judiciary, United States Senate (J-103-5).* Washington, DC: U.S. Government Printing Office.

Cupach, W. R., & Spitzberg, B. H. (1998). Obsessive relational intrusion and stalking. In B. H. Spitzberg & W. R. Cupach (Eds.), *The dark side of close relationships* (pp. 233–263). Mahwah, NJ: Lawrence Erlbaum Associates.

Cupach, W. R., Spitzberg, B. H., & Carson, C. L. (2000). Toward a theory of obsessive relational intrusion and stalking. In K. Dindia & S. Duck (Eds.), *Communication and personal relationships* (pp. 131–146). New York: Wiley.

de Becker, G. (1997). *The gift of fear.* Boston: Little, Brown and Company.

Dietz, P., Matthews, D., Van Duyne, C., Martell, D., Parry, C., Stewart, T., Warren, J., & Crowder, J. (1991). Threatening and otherwise inappropriate letters to Hollywood celebrities. *Journal of Forensic Sciences, 36,* 185–209.

Dietz, P., Matthews, D., Martell, D., Stewart, T., Hrouda, D., & Warren, J. (1991). Threatening and otherwise inappropriate letters to members of the United States Congress. *Journal of Forensic Sciences, 36,* 1445–1468.

DiVasto, P. V., Kaufman, A., Rosner, L., Jackson, R., Christy, L., Pearson, S., & Burgett, T. (1984). The prevalence of sexually stressful events among females in the general population. *Archives of Sexual Behavior, 13,* 59–67.

Dutton, D. G., van Ginkel, C., & Landolt, M. A. (1996). Jealousy, intimate abusiveness, and intrusiveness. *Journal of Family Violence, 11,* 411–423.

Emerson, R. M., Ferris, K. O., & Gardner, C. B. (1998). On being stalked. *Social Problems, 45,* 289–314.

Fremouw, W. J., Westrup, D., & Pennypacker, J. (1997). Stalking on campus: The prevalence and strategies for coping with stalking. *Journal of Forensic Sciences, 42,* 664–667.

Harmon, R. B., Rosner, R., & Owens, H. (1995). Obsessional harassment and erotomania in a criminal court population. *Journal of Forensic Sciences, 40,* 188–196.

Jason, L. A., Reichler, A., Easton, J., Neal, A., & Wilson, M. (1984). Female harassment after ending a relationship: A preliminary study. *Alternative Lifestyles, 6,* 259–269.

Katz, J. E. (1994). Empirical and theoretical dimensions of obscene phone calls to women in the United States. *Human Communication Research, 21,* 155–182.

Kienlen, K. K. (1998). Developmental and social antecedents of stalking. In J. R. Meloy (Ed.), *The psychology of stalking: Clinical and forensic perspectives* (pp. 51–67). San Diego, CA: Academic Press.

Kurt, J. L. (1995). Stalking as a variant of domestic violence. *Bulletin of the Academy of Psychiatry and the Law, 23,* 219–223.

Leonard, R., Ling, L. C., Hankins, G. A., Maidon, C. H., Potorti, P. F., & Rogers, J. M. (1993). Sexual harassment at North Carolina State University. In G. L. Kreps (Ed.), *Sexual harassment: Communication implications* (pp. 170–194). Cresskill, NJ: Hampton Press.

Leong, G. B. (1994). De Cérambault syndrome (erotomania) in the criminal justice system: Another look at this recurring problem. *Journal of Forensic Sciences, 39,* 378–385.

Lloyd-Goldstein, R. (1998). De Cérambault on-line: A survey of erotomania and stalking from the old world to the world wide web. In J. R. Meloy (Ed.), *The psychology of stalking: Clinical and forensic perspectives* (pp. 193–212). San Diego, CA: Academic Press.

Meloy, J. R. (1989). Unrequited love and the wish to kill: Diagnosis and treatment of borderline erotomania. *Bulletin of the Menninger Clinic, 53,* 477–492.

Meloy, J. R. (1996). Stalking (obsessional following): A review of some preliminary studies. *Aggression and Violent Behavior, 1,* 147–162.

Meloy, J. R. (1998). The psychology of stalking. In J. R. Meloy (Ed.), *The psychology of stalking: Clinical and forensic perspectives* (pp. 1–23). San Diego, CA: Academic Press.

Meloy, J. R., & Gothard, S. (1995). Demographic and clinical comparison of obsessional followers and offenders with mental disorders. *American Journal of Psychiatry, 152,* 258.

Meyer, C. B., & Taylor, S. E. (1986). Adjustment to rape. *Journal of Personality and Social Psychology, 50,* 1226–1234.

Mullen, P. E., & Pathé, M. (1994a). The pathological extensions of love. *British Journal of Psychiatry, 165,* 614–623.

Mullen, P. E., & Pathé, M. (1994b). Stalking and the pathologies of love. *Australian and New Zealand Journal of Psychiatry, 28,* 469–477.

Mustaine, E. E., & Tewksbury, R. (1999). A routine activity theory explanation for women's stalking victimizations. *Violence Against Women, 5,* 43–62.

National Institute of Justice. (1993). *Project to develop a model anti-stalking code for states.* Washington, DC: U.S. Department of Justice.

Pathé, M., & Mullen, P. E. (1997). The impact of stalkers on their victims. *British Journal of Psychiatry, 170,* 12–17.

Peele, S. (1981). *Love and addiction.* New York: Signet Books.

Romans, J. S. C., Hays, J. R., & White, T. K. (1996). Stalking and related behaviors experienced by counseling staff members from current or former clients. *Professional Psychology: Research and Practice, 27,* 595–599.

Roscoe, B., Strouse, J. S., & Goodwin, M. P. (1994). Sexual harassment: Early adolescent self-reports of experiences and acceptance. *Adolescence, 29,* 515–523.

Ross, E. S. (1995). E-mail stalking: Is adequate legal protection available? *Journal of Computer and Information Law, 13,* 405–432.

Savitz, L. (1986). Obscene phone calls. In T. F. Hartnagel & R. A. Silver-mamn (Eds.), *Critique and explanation: Essays in honor of Gwynne Nettler* (pp. 149–158). New Brunswick, NJ: Transaction.

Sheffield, C. J. (1989). The invisible intruder: Women's experiences of obscene phone calls. *Gender and Society, 3*, 483–488.

Smith, M. D., & Morra, N. N. (1994). Obscene and threatening telephone calls to women: Data from a Canadian national survey. *Gender and Society, 8*, 584–596.

Spencer, A. C. (1998). *Stalking and the MMPI-2 in a forensic population.* PhD dissertation, University of Detroit Mercy, Detroit, MI.

Spitzberg, B. H. (1998, February). *Toward a propositional model of obsessive relational intrusion and stalking.* Paper presented to the Western States Communication Association Conference, Denver, CO.

Spitzberg, B. H., Nicastro, A. M., & Cousins, A. V. (1998). Exploring the interactional phenomenon of stalking and obsessive relational intrusion. *Communication Reports, 11*, 33–48.Spitzberg, B. H., & Rhea, J. (1999). Obsessive relational intrusion and sexual coercion victimization. *Journal of Interpersonal Violence, 14*, 3–20.

Timmreck, T. C. (1990). Overcoming the loss of a love: Preventing love addiction and promoting positive emotional health. *Psychological Reports, 66*, 515–528.

Tjaden, P., & Thoennes, N. (1998). *Stalking in America: Findings from the National Violence Against Women Survey.* Washington, DC: National Institute of Justice and Centers for Disease Control and Prevention (NCJ 169592).

Velicer, W. F., & Fava, J. L. (1998). Effects of variable and subject sampling on factor pattern recovery. *Psychological Methods, 3*, 231–251.

Walker, L. E., & Meloy, J. R. (1998). Stalking and domestic violence. In J. R. Meloy (Ed.), *The psychology of stalking: Clinical and forensic perspectives* (pp. 139–161). San Diego, CA: Academic Press.

Way, R. C. (1994). The criminalization of stalking: An exercise in media manipulation and political opportunism. *McGill Law Journal, 39*, 379–400.

Westrup, D., & Fremouw, W. J. (1998). Stalking behavior: A literature review and suggested functional analytic assessment technology. *Aggression and Violent Behavior: A Review Journal, 3*, 255–274.

Wright, J. A., Burgess, A. G., Burgess, A. W., Laszlo, A. T., McCrary, G. O., & Douglas, J. E. (1996). A typology of interpersonal stalking. *Journal of Interpersonal Violence, 11*, 487–502.

Zona, M. A., Palarea, R. E., & Lane, J. C. (1998). Psychiatric diagnosis and the offender-victim typology of stalking. In J. R. Meloy (Ed.), *The psychology of stalking: Clinical and forensic perspectives* (pp. 69–84). San Diego, CA: Academic Press.

Zona, M. A., Sharma, K. K., & Lane, J. (1993). A comparative study of erotomanic and obsessional subjects in a forensic sample. *Journal of Forensic Sciences, 38,* 894–903.

II

Perpetrator Issues

8

An Integrative Contextual Developmental Model of Male Stalking

Jacquelyn White, Robin M. Kowalski, Amy Lyndon, and
Sherri Valentine

The purpose of the present article is to contribute to the emerging
scholarly discussion of stalking, as legally defined, by considering it
within the context of violence against women. We first discuss definitional issues concerning stalking. This is followed by our rationale for
focusing specifically on men stalking women. We then present a theoretical model of violence against women that we suggest is a useful
framework for studying stalking.

DEFINITIONAL ISSUES

There has been considerable effort to clarify the nature of stalking and
to distinguish it from other forms of stalking-like behavior, as evidenced by the numerous attempts to develop a typology of stalking
(see Holmes, 1998; McCann, 1998; Wright et al., 1996). This is even
more important now that researchers are showing increased interest in
examining courtship persistence and stalking-like behaviors in college
students. We contribute to this effort by suggesting that research based
on operational definitions that distinguish stalking from other stalking-like behaviors is essential.

Although the legal definition of stalking varies by state, generally it is defined as "the willful, malicious, and repeated following and harassing of another person that threatens his or her safety" (Meloy & Gothard, 1995, p. 258). The model antistalking law proposed by the National Criminal Justice Association Project (1993) defines stalking as "a course of conduct directed at a specific person that involves repeated visual or physical proximity, nonconsensual communication, or verbal, written, or implied threats, or a combination thereof, that would cause a reasonable person fear" (p. 43–44). The important concepts here *are repeated* behaviors that that would cause *a reasonable person* fear.

In contrast to stalking as legally defined, obsessive relational intrusions (ORI) have been defined as "repeated and unwanted pursuit and invasion of one's sense of physical or symbolic privacy by another person, either stranger or acquaintance, who desires and/or presumes an intimate relationship" (Cupach & Spitzberg, 1998, pp. 234–235). Missing from the definition of ORI are elements of maliciousness, threat, and fear.

We argue that the dimensions of frequency and fear are critical. The restriction that the behavior occurs more than once is necessary to distinguish stalking and ORI from other behaviors that are unwanted, harassing, threatening or harmful, such as occur in courtship violence or domestic violence cases. Similarly, to distinguish stalking from these other forms of violence that occurs in intimate relationships, it is useful to consider as stalking only behaviors ocurring in the context of relationships in which there is a discrepancy in the level of contact desired by the two parties, when one desires more contact than the other. Additionally, the presence of fear has been used to determine whether from a legal perspective a behavior is stalking or not. The arguments developed in the present are based on the legal definition of stalking: It occurs more than once, induces fear, and occurs in an undesired relationship.

WHY IS STALKING A FORM OF VIOLENCE AGAINST WOMEN?

We argue that stalking as defined in the present article is a form of violence against women for three reasons: More men than women engage in stalking; stalking co-occurs with several other forms of violence against women; and women suffer more fear and other serious consequences as victims of stalking than do men.

Men Stalk More Than Women

Research data from community samples indicate that men stalk more than women. The National Violence Against Women survey of 8,000 women and 8,000 men in the United States asked respondents about being followed or harassed "on more than one occasion by strangers, friends, relatives or even husbands and partners." Specific behaviors by these persons included spying, sending unsolicited letters, making unsolicited phone calls, standing outside one's home, school or workplace, showing up at places at where one had no business being, leaving unwanted items, communicating in other unwanted ways, vandalizing property or destroying something. Results revealed that 78% of the victims of stalking were female and 87% of the perpetrators were male (Tjaden & Thoennes, 1998). According to the National Institute of Justice (1996) as many as 80% of stalking incidents, as legally defined, occur within the context of intimate relationships.

Additionally, clinical samples of stalkers have consisted primarily of court-referred male perpetrators (Burgess et al., 1997; Harmon, Rosner, & Owens, 1995; Kienlen, Birmingham, Solberg, O'Regan, & Meloy, 1997; Meloy & Gothard, 1995; Zona, Sharma, & Lane, 1993). These studies found that most stalkers were older men with some psychiatric diagnosis, engaged in a higher percentage of stranger than acquaintance stalking, and displaying high levels of violence toward the victim. Although these men represent convenience samples, the fact that women are rarely seen in an adjudicated group supports the argument that more men than women engage in stalking as legally defined.

Co-occurrence of Stalking with Other Forms of Violence Against Women

Evidence of co-occurrence can be found in the data from the National Violence Against Women Survey (Tjaden & Thoennes, 1998). Eighty-one percent of the women who were stalked by a current or former intimate partner also had been physically abused by that partner. Thirty-one percent had been sexually assaulted by that partner. Other researchers have also reported the co-occurrence of stalking with verbal and physical aggression (Coleman, 1997), as well as psychological abuse[1], and with sexual coercion (Spitzberg & Rhea, 1999). The Coleman (1997) sample obtained data from male and female participants, but they only analyzed the female data for this particular study. They divided up their sample via a factor analysis into one of three groups: A control group (did not report experiencing any ORI or stalking behaviors), harassed group (mostly calls, following, leaving messages, letters-surveillance items), and a stalked group (break-ins, threats, attempted and completed harm, damage). Coleman found that stalking victims were more likely to have been the victims of verbal and physical abuse in the relationship, with the stalker prior to the end of the formal relationship and prior to the stalking. Some have also suggested that stalking may be a part of the "cycle of violence" that characterizes domestic abuse (Beck et al., 1992; Burgess et al., 1997; Coleman, 1997; Kurt, 1995; Walker & Meloy, 1998).

More Fear and Severe Consequences for Women Than Men

The same kind of stalking behavior from a man to a woman elicits more fear and concern than that behavior does when engaged in by women toward men. Men are more dangerous to women than women are to men (Schwartz-Watts & Morgan, 1998). Hall (1998) found that 83% of the stalking victims in her study reported that their personality had changed as a result of the stalking: They considered themselves as less outgoing, more frightened, more paranoid, and /or more aggressive. Jason, Reichler, Easton, Neal and Wilson (1984) found female victims of stalking suffered from anorexia, depression, loss of trust, and anxiety. They also found that the more assertive women's attempts to end a relationship, the more months they were subjected to harassment. Also, the more assertive the steps taken to end the harassment, the more times per week women were subjected to harassment and the more threatening and disrupting the effects. This sample appeared to have fairly severe and long-standing stalking: The majority of the women perceived the harassment as threatening and disturbing and over half have reported psychological or physical problems. About half of the women were visited at work or home and about one-fourth were threatened, followed, and sent things. On average, harassment lasted for about a year and episodes occurred almost daily.

Pathé and Mullen (1997) found consequences of stalking victimization to include heightened anxiety, panic attacks, and an exaggerated startle response. One woman developed severe bruxism because she ground her teeth at night. They also found evidence of chronic sleep disturbance, appetite disturbance, weight fluctuations, persistent nausea, increased alcohol and/or cigarette consumption, excessive tiredness or weakness, increased frequency and severity of headaches. Most victims reported PTSD symptoms, 37% meeting all of the criteria. Of those meeting all of the criteria, the majority were female.

THE GENDERED NATURE OF STALKING

We argue that stalking is a gendered phenomenon. By gendered we mean that the meaning, motives, behavioral manifestations and consequences of stalking, as well as it developmental precursors, are different for women and men.

The earliest historical accounts of stalking and obsessive love invoked gendered constructs. Although both women and men could be afflicted, the manifestation of the obsession supposedly was different for each (Rather, 1965). For example, gendered language is apparent in Bartholomy Pardoux's (1545–1611) (from Rather) discussion of the pathology of love in which he distinguished uterine furor (*nymphomania*) from insane love (*amor insanus*). Stalking was identified explicitly as a female behavior in the early part of the 20th century. De Clérambault (cited in Lloyd-Goldstein, 1998) and Kraepelin (1921) characterized erotomania as an affliction of lovesick women "of a certain age" who were delusional in their belief that older, high status men (sometimes public figures) were in love with them. More recently, stalking was reconceptualized as a predominantly male behavior, when women gained the power to leave relationships.

Research on partner violence suggests that even when reported frequencies of violence are similar for men and women, there are very different psychological and social profiles. The levels of violence and the consequences of those violent acts differ greatly according to gender (Archer, 2000; White, Smith, Koss, & Figueredo, 2000). It is important to distinguish the number of violent acts from the severity of those acts.

The gendering of violence begins early in life and continues across the life span (White, Donat, & Bondurant, 2001). The perception and evaluation of violence is an essential element. Men see anger expression as a means of reasserting control over a situation, whereas women see anger expression as a loss of control; men perceive women's aggression as expressive and women judge men's aggression to be instrumental. Apparently, women and men share the belief that his aggression is a means of control and hers is a sign of loss of control (Campbell, Muncer, Guy, & Banim, 1996). A man who hits is risking serious harm to his partner; he is typically stronger and more likely to have experience with weapons. Women who hit do not expect to really harm or injure their partners but rather want to let them know how upset they are about something. There is a good reason for this: Men who either lose control or who deliberately use violence are typically more dangerous than women (Magdol et al., 1997). Thus, there is an important gender story, but it does not have to do with frequencies of violence or stalking, but with how any specific behavior is seen or evaluated and with the real consequences of violent behavior for damage to physical and mental health.

Therefore, the goal of the present analysis is to tell part of this story by examining male stalking in the context of ongoing and recently terminated relationships. The remainder of this paper evaluates theory and data on stalking as part of a larger picture of male violence against women. Specifically, we examine the degree to which stalking fits within an integrative contextual developmental model created by White and Kowalski (1998) to evaluate various forms of male violence against women. This model suggests that "an individual's behavior can be best understood by considering the impact of historical, sociocultural, and social factors across time on cognitive and motivational processes that result in aggression and violence against women" (p. 204). In designing the model, White and Kowalski were guided by Koss et al.'s (1994) working definition of male violence against women:

> Male violence toward women encompasses physical, visual, verbal, or sexual acts that are experienced by a woman or girl as a threat, invasion, or assault and that have the effect of hurting her or degrading her and/or taking away her ability to control contact (intimate or otherwise) with another individual (p. xvi).

An Integrative Contextual Developmental Model

The integrative contextual developmental model integrates a wide range of factors across various forms of violence against women.[2] The model provides a meta-theoretical framework within which to think about the commonalities among various forms of violence against women.

The model is intended to guide researchers in the generation of substantive hypotheses derived from various theoretical perspectives. The model assumes an embedded or hierarchical perspective. Five levels of interacting factors are proposed: Sociocultural (including historical and cultural values), interpersonal (social networks), dyadic (the relationship between the perpetrator and his victim), situational, and intrapersonal. This perspective examines individual behavior in context. A core assumption is that patriarchy operating at the historical/sociocultural level affects the power dynamics of all social networks. These power dynamics become enacted at the dyadic level and affect personality and behaviors. Historical and sociocultural factors create an environment in which the developing child learns rules and expectations, first in the family network, and later in peer, intimate, and work relationships. Early experiences define the context for later experiences (Huesmann & Eron, 1995; Olweus, 1993; White & Bondurant, 1995).

Using this model as a framework, White and Kowalski (1998) identified key factors that distinguish various types of violence against women: The nature of the relationship, the ages of the perpetrator and victim, and the form the violence takes. For example, forcible sexual intercourse between a father and daughter is labeled incest, whereas forced sexual intercourse between a non-related man and woman is labeled rape. Similarly, beating up one's wife is called spouse abuse, whereas beating up one's dating partner is called dating violence. In a work relationship, coerced sexual intercourse in exchange for job security is called sexual harassment, but in a dating relationship it is called acquaintance rape. In all cases the violence varies on a severity continuum and may be psychological, verbal, or physical and may be episodic or continuous. From this perspective, stalking is a form of violence against women that can occur in a variety of relationships. For the purposes of the present analysis, factors associated with stalking have been catalogued under one of the five levels identified by the model. These levels are presented in Table 8.1, along with a representative sample of studies examining variables at each level.

Sociocultural Level

The sociocultural level of analysis examines historical, cultural, social, community, and neighborhood influences on behavior. Factors examined include sexual inequalities, gender role prescriptions (including dating and sexual scripts), and cultural norms and myths about wom-

Table 8.1 Variables Associated with Stalking at Each Level of Analysis

Sociocultural	Social Networks	Dyadic	Situational	Perpetrator Characteristics
• Media influences • Dating scripts • Gender role expectations (no empirical studies)	• violent family background (Hall, 1998) • Unsuccessful relationship history (Meloy & Gothard, 1995) • Some type of loss in the previous 7 months (Kienlen et al., 1997) • Attachment (Dutton et al.; • Lifestyle (Mustaine & Tewksbury, 1999)	• Intimate relationships (Cupach & Spitzberg, 1998; Hall, 1998) • Rejection by desired love object (Tjaden & Thoennes, 1998) • Relationship characteristics: -type of love experienced -degree of dependence -relationship satisfaction -sexual satisfaction -history of abuse (Langhinrichsen-Rohling et al., this vol.)	• Use of alcohol and/or drugs just prior to the offense (Mustaine & Tewksbury, 1999) • If under the influence, violence is more likely to occur (Kienlen et al., 1997)	• Mostly male (national sample—Tjaden, Thonnes, & Allison, this vol., college sample—Fremouw et al., 1997; no sex differences in college samples—Spitzberg et al., 1998) • Average age is 35–40, but can range from 20–66 years of age (Harmon et al., 1995) • Lives alone (Burgess et al., 1997) • Under or unemployed (Kienlen et al., 1997) • Above average IQ (Meloy & Gothard, 1995 • Axis I and Axis II diagnoses (Meloy & Gothard, 1995) • Most are not erotomaniacs (Meloy, 1996) • Reported motivations: hostility, anger (Meloy, 1996) jealousy, sensitivity to rejection (Langhinrichsen-Rohling et al., this vol.) • Prior criminal histories (Kienlen et al., 1997) • History of alcohol abuse (Kienlen et al., 1997) • More accepting of rape myths (Sinclair & Frieze, this vol.) • Impaired self-esteem (Emerson et al., 1998)

en, men, children, family, sex and violence, as well as scripts for enacting relationships. Expectations about the appropriate roles for men and women are communicated through various institutionalized practices of a society, including those of the legal system, the church, schools, media, politics, and the military. All set the stage for the evolution of cultural myths that perpetuate male violence against women. Cultural norms governing aggression as a tool of the powerful to subdue the weak interact with gender inequalities to create a context conducive to violence against women. A common theme involves male dominance and female submissiveness.

MEDIA PORTRAYALS

Although empirical investigations have not focused explicitly on socio-cultural influences as they relate to stalking, cultural images of stalking have existed since at least the 16th century, as we noted earlier. Images of stalking can be seen as well in contemporary media. Media, in the form of movies, songs, and books, are powerful purveyors of gender roles and attitudes that shape cultural myths about obsessive love. Outright stalking and more subtle behaviors and attitudes that encourage stalking are commonly portrayed in popular movies and songs. These forms of entertainment often express the sentiment that persistence in the face of rejection is admirable, love conquers all, and that it is possible to make someone fall in love with you if you try hard enough.

Movies such as *The Piano*, *Only You*, and *Addicted to Love* utilize themes of persistence and harassment as romantic strategies to make someone fall in love. In the movie *Only You*, both the romantic leads engage in stalking behaviors. The female lead character follows a man across several continents because she is convinced that they are meant to be together. The male lead character falls in love with her while she is chasing this elusive man. Continually rejected by his love interest, the hero follows her and eventually his persistence pays off and they fall in love. *Addicted to Love* shows the lengths that people will go to win back their former partners. The two lead characters cause mayhem, chaos, and destruction in the lives of their love interests in their attempts to reunite with their boyfriend and girlfriend, all in the name of love. Some of these tactics begin to work on one partner, and the movie is labeled a "romantic comedy." Other popular movies show stalking in a negative light: *Sleeping With the Enemy* combines both stalking and domestic violence. After years of abuse, a woman leaves her husband, only to be pursued and threatened by him.

The song, "Every Breath You Take" by The Police (1983) is the quintessential example of stalking: "Every breath you take/Every move you make/Every bond you break/Every step you take/I'll be watching you." Sarah McLachlin's (1993) song, "Possession" is unique for the fact that she used as lyrics segments from letters sent to her by a stalker: "The night is my companion and /Solitude my guide/Would I spend forever here/And not be satisfied?/And I would be the one to hold you down/Kiss you so hard/I'll take your breath away and/After I'd wipe away the tears/Just close your eyes dear." The lyrics represent the stalker's rape fantasy of "holding her down," after which he would "wipe away her tears" and she would begin to love him. The stalker in fact sued her for the use of his letters before committing suicide (Silberger, 1998).

Social Network Level

Even though members of a given culture are typically exposed to similar sociocultural pressures to behave in accordance with their assigned gender roles (i.e., male aggressiveness, female submissiveness), not all men commit violent acts against women. Embedded within one's culture are other influences that may either increase the likelihood of or mitigate against stalking. The social network level of analysis focuses on one's history of personal experiences within various social institutions (family, peers, school, church, and work settings). The gendered norms and expectations that contribute to male violence against women are transmitted through these institutions. For example, family and friends can affect the likelihood that crime victims will actually see themselves as victims (Bourque, 1989). Similarly, witnessing and experiencing violence in the family of origin alters the likelihood of later involvement in violent episodes. Men who either witnessed or experienced violence as a child show a higher likelihood of being sexually aggressive than men who were not exposed to violence (Koss & Dinero, 1989), and of perpetrating courtship or domestic violence (Kalmuss, 1984; Straus et al., 1980). The model we present suggests that stalkers may learn interactional styles from various social networks.

Childhood relationships with care-givers shape the way future relationships are viewed (Bartholomew, 1990; Bowlby, 1973; Cashdan, 1988; Meloy, 1992, 1996). For example, insecure attachment relationships in childhood are related to later dysfunctional relationship styles for stalkers (Dutton, Saunders, Starzomiski, & Bartholomew, 1994). Although not empirically tested, Kienlen et al. (1997) has suggested that stalkers' attachment patterns may be an extreme version of the preoccupied category. Consistent with this preoccupied pattern, Kienlen (1998) suggested that when an intimate bond is threatened, a potential stalker may escalate attention-seeking behaviors, much as a neglected child might, to reestablish the bond. Kienlen et al. (1997)

found that 63% of the stalkers that they interviewed had experienced disrupted relationships with their primary caregiver during childhood. For some of the stalkers, this disruption consisted of divorce, death, or some type of emotional, physical, or sexual abuse. Hall (1998) found that 31% of stalkers had a violent family background as opposed to only 13% of nonstalkers. Kienlen et al. (1997) also reported that over half of stalkers in their sample came from an abusive household. Over half of these abused men went on to become abusers as well as stalkers.

Although stalking occurs in the context of intimate relationships, stalkers do not appear to have successful relationships (Harmon et al., 1995; Kienlen et al., 1997; Meloy & Gothard, 1995; Zona, Sharma, & Lane, 1993). Many (80%) experienced some type of relational disruption (e.g., relationship breakup, unemployment, custody loss, or death) in the 7 months preceding the initiation of the stalking behavior (Kienlen et al., 1997). They also tend to live alone (Burgess et al., 1997). The majority of stalkers in clinical samples have been found to be either never married, divorced, or separated when the stalking began, and they tended not to have children (Kienlen et al., 1997).

As with the family social unit, other networks, such as peers, may promote a system of values that reflect sociocultural understandings of gender inequality. Within these networks, adversarial sexual relationships and the acceptance of interpersonal violence may be encouraged and rewarded. Although the role of the peer group has been implicated in sexual assault (Ageton, 1983), virtually nothing is known about the peer relationships of stalkers. Sev'er's (1997) adaptation of social learning theory reflects the social network level, when he talks about the influence of family and peers. Sev'er has suggested that at least the milder forms of stalking behaviors are actually taught and reinforced by the family, peers and the media. That is, efforts to re-establish a relationship are seen as acceptable, and individuals are encouraged to pursue the target of their affection in spite of rejection.

Dyadic Level

Whereas social networks focus attention on a stalker's history of interpersonal relationships, particularly within the family and peer groups, the dyadic level focuses on the nature of one specific relationship, the one between the perpetrator and victim. This approach recognizes that personal characteristics of the stalker or the victim are not enough to account for stalking. "It is partly in the relationship that the dynamics of unwanted intrusion are found, as much as in the recesses of individual psychopathology" (Cupach & Spitzberg, 1998, p. 235). Dyadic, or interpersonal, theories of stalking focus on relationship dynamics (Cupach & Spitzberg, 1998).

Stalking most frequently occurs within the context of an interpersonal relationship, typically an interpersonal relationship that has ended recently. The few empirical studies conducted on stalking all agree that stalking is most common, and most dangerous, when the perpetrator and the victim are or have been in an intimate relationship with one another (Hall, 1998; Kienlen et al., 1997; Pathé & Mullen, 1997; Tjaden & Thoennes, 1998). The most prevalent time for stalking to begin is after the termination of the relationship (Tjaden & Thoennes, 1998), when the stalker is rejected by his desired love object. Bachman and Saltzman (1995) found that women separated from their husbands were three times more likely to be victimized by spouses than divorced women and 25 times more likely to be victimized by spouses than married women.

Some researchers have suggested that stalking represents the extreme end of a continuum of behaviors at the benign end of which are people's everyday feelings of hurt and anger at being rejected by a sought-after partner. One person's attempt to establish or maintain a relationship with another individual always involves the possibility that relational overtures will be met with rejection (Baumeister & Wotman, 1992; Baumeister, Wotman, & Stillwell, 1993; Bratslavsky, Baumeister, & Sommer, 1998). The feelings and behaviors of the initiator and of the target are interdependent. For example, in response to the would-be-suitor's romantic overtures, the target can respond either positively by accepting the overtures or negatively by turning the suitor down. If the latter choice is made, the would-be-suitor can choose to leave well enough alone or he may choose to continue his pursuit of the target in hopes that she will eventually change her mind (Baumeister et al., 1993; Bratslavsky et al., 1998). According to Emerson, Ferris, and Gardner (1998), "the dynamic characteristic of most cases of what ultimately come to be recognized as stalking involve efforts to establish (or reestablish) a relationship in the face of the other's resistance" (p. 289). Davis, Ace, and Andra (2000) also support this conclusion.

Langhinrichsen-Rohling et al (2000) report that the degree of dependence, history of abuse, type of love experiences, and degree of relationship and sexual satisfaction are all related to stalking. However, nothing is known about other dyadic features, either descriptive, such as social class differences, or interactive, such as communication patterns or conflict resolution strategies.

Situational Level

This level of analysis focuses on situational variables that increase or decrease the likelihood of interpersonal violence. Mustaine and Tewksbury (1999) have used the principles of routine activities theory to account for stalking. They argue that women's social interactions and substance use increase exposure to potential stalkers.

Although a number of situational variables influencing interpersonal violence have been examined, including time of day, location, and the presence of social inhibitors or disinhibitors, including alcohol and drugs (White & Koss, 1991), very little is known about the influence of situational factors on stalking behavior specifically. However, it is reasonable to assume that a stalker's behavior is influenced by the time of day and the location in which the behaviors might be perpetrated. The only research currently available at the situational level shows a positive relationship between stalking and the use of alcohol and drugs (Kienlen et al. 1997; Lasley, 1989; Mustaine & Tewksbury, 1999). Violence is also more likely to result when alcohol is involved (Kienlen et al., 1997).

Intrapersonal Level

The most developed theories of stalking occur at the intrapersonal level. For example, we found examples of sociobiological (Luke, 1997), psychodynamic (Meloy, 1998) and attachment (Kielan, 1998) theories being applied to stalking. These theories focus on individual motives, characteristics or experiences. Whereas Luke (1998) draws parallels between men pursuing women and the hunting of animals, arguing that hunting is a basic instinct, Meloy (1998) argues that rage is the primary motive underlying stalking. A psychodynamic approach to stalking suggests that there is something inherent to the stalker (i.e., personality characteristics, attitudinal variables) that precipitates the behavior.

The focus at the intrapersonal level is on attitudinal, motivational, and characterological features of the individual. However, it is recognized that individual attributes typically emerge as the result of experiences in various social networks. Thus, there is a dynamic interplay between factors operating at these various levels. For example, attachment style reflects an intrapsychic characteristic that results from earlier interpersonal interactions. Similarly, the attitudinal underpinnings of male violence against women, in particular the endorsement of traditional sex-role stereotypes and cultural myths about violence, often stem from having been reared in households where violence was considered normative.

Little is known about stalkers' gender-related attitudes. Only recently have Frieze and colleagues begun to explore the relationship between stalking and gender-related attitudes. However, research has established connections between gender-related attitudes and other forms of violence against women. A consistent pattern emerges from this work. Men who are violent toward intimate partners tend to be traditional in their gender role attitudes and have hostile attitudes toward women. They endorse conservative family values, believe in the subordination of women, and adhere to tenets of traditional sexual and dating scripts (White & Kowalski, 1998).

Motivations for stalking include feelings of hostility and anger toward their victim (Davis et al., 2000; Meloy, 1996), as well as jealousy, sensitivity to rejection, (Langhinrichsen-Rohling et al., 2000), obsession, feelings of possession (Wright et al., 1996), and revenge (Emerson et al., 1998; Kurt, 1995; National Institute of Justice, 1996). A need for power and dominance may be aroused when one is threatened by a loss of control, such as by being rejected. The motives for stalking highlight two different perceptions that stalkers may have toward their victims (Cupach & Spitzberg, 1998). On one hand, some stalkers may view the victim favorably and try, albeit in a maladaptive way, to establish or reestablish a relationship with that individual. On the other hand, some stalkers view their victims negatively, believing that the victims have mistreated or unjustly rejected them. As his repeated attempts to facilitate this relationship are met with rejection, the stalker's feelings of affection may change to feelings of anger and hatred of the victim (Harmon et al., 1995).

Certain personality and behavioral variables also predict violence against women. These include antisocial tendencies (Malamuth, 1986), nonconformity (Rapaport & Burkhart, 1987), impulsivity (Calhoun, 1990), low socialization and responsibility (Barnett & Hamberger, 1992; Rapaport & Burkhart, 1984), hypermasculinity, delinquent behavior, affective dysregulation (Hall & Hirschman, 1991; Murphy, Meyer, & O'Leary, 1991) and self-centeredness, coupled with insensitivity to others

(Dean & Malamuth, 1997). Whether these same characteristics describe stalkers remains to be determined empirically.

However, given the co-occurrence of stalking with physical and sexual assault, a relationship is likely. Research on clinical populations of stalkers shows that many have been diagnosed with Axis I and Axis II disorders (Meloy & Gothard, 1995). Most clinically identified stalkers have some type of Axis I diagnosis, most commonly mood disorders, adjustment disorders, or substance abuse, as well as Axis II personality disorders, most frequently narcissism and borderline personality disorder (Meloy, 1997; Zona, Palarea, & Lane, 1998). In their sample of obsessional followers, Meloy and Gothard (1995) found that 60% of the sample had undergone either inpatient or outpatient treatment before the study. Eighty-five percent of the obsessional followers had some type of Axis I disorder at the time of the clinical interview and 70% had a history of substance abuse or dependence and a mood disorder. Whether such personality disorders are generalizable to a general population of stalkers remains to be determined.

If the individual perceives that he has been rejected because his potential lover sees him as undesirable and unworthy, then the rejection strikes a blow to the man's identity and self-esteem (Baumeister et al., 1993). To the degree that a person feels excluded by others with concomitant changes in self-esteem, he will experience shame, inadequacy, and awkwardness. To bolster their damaged self-esteem and to reestablish their inclusionary status, some individuals might persist in their efforts to win the hearts of the very individuals who have rejected them. The sociometer theory of self-esteem suggests that self-esteem is a subjective indicator of the degree to which one feels included (i.e., high self-esteem) or excluded (i.e., low self-esteem) by others (Leary, Tambor, Terdal, & Downs, 1995).

Critique of Theories of Stalking

Our analysis of current theories of stalking in terms of the integrative developmental model suggests that they focus on variables that fall primarily at the intrapersonal and dyadic levels of analysis. Furthermore, these theories tend to rely on evidence based primarily on clinical samples of stalkers. To date there is little research at the sociocultural, social network, and situational levels. Furthermore, there have been few attempts to integrate across levels of analysis. Emerson et al.'s (1998) use of the sociometer theory of self-esteem is an example of a theory that integrates across the intrapersonal and the dyadic, in that certain characteristics of dyadic interaction interact with intrapersonal characteristics to increase the risk of stalking. The work of Baumeister and his colleagues also reflects this integrative perspective (Baumeister et al., 1998).

Although theories of stalking have provided information about the personality characteristics of stalkers and their relationships, these theories fall short on at least three dimensions (White & Kowalski, 1998).

First, gender is not a core construct, nor is the gendered nature of aggression and violence acknowledged. Aggression and violence cannot be fully understood without considering the central role gender plays in their social construction. In a male-dominated society, men are expected to protect "their" women as a form of chivalry, but are also expected to be dominant and to control those women (Griffin, 1971). In a patriarchal system, women have been viewed as property of men. As with any other property, men have the right to do anything they want with women. This flip side of patriarchy/chivalry is the fact that, because women are considered property, men can shape them into whatever and however they want them to be. If a woman doesn't recognize her place, it is acceptable to forcibly show it to her through rape or other forms of abuse. The word rape itself comes from the Latin word rapere which means, "to seize property" (Blum, 1997). Therefore, under certain circumstances, it is acceptable to be violent toward women in order to "teach" the women a "lesson."

Second, although some theories recognize sociocultural influences, the research focus is at the level of the individual. For example, the individual's perspective, usually obtained via self-report, is used to obtain information about dyadic factors and sociocultural variables.

Third, little attention has been paid to the co-occurrence of stalking and other forms of violence, in spite of the fact that theories of stalking resemble those that have been proposed for other forms of violence against women.

All of these factors collectively point to the need for a multi-faceted theory. Hints that a multi-faceted theory of stalking is needed can be found in the literature. For example, Kurt (1995, p. 229) stated that "stalking . . . is a complex behavior with social and cultural underpinnings as well as psychological determinants." However, such a theory has yet to be applied to stalking. We suggest that the integrative contextual developmental model provides a step in the direction of examining stalking from a multi-faceted perspective.

CONCLUSIONS

A levels-of-analysis approach to male violence against women is the basis of the integrative contextual developmental model (White & Kowalski, 1998). The model acknowledges the gendered nature of social relationships, including family, work, and peer relationships. It also recognizes the interconnectedness of various forms of violence against women. Our analysis is that current theories of stalking are in their infancy and have yet to examine multiple sources of influence acting on the stalker. The integrative contextual developmental model encourages one to think about multiple sources of influence on stalking at various levels and cautions against focusing on only one level of analysis. Stalking is conceived of as a dynamic interpersonal behavior rooted in the framework of culture, the family, and other social contexts. Developmental factors alter attitudes, beliefs and personality of the potential stalker and his victim. Stalking occurs in a dyadic relationship with specific features that include not only the victim's characteristics but also interactional processes. Various situational factors affect the likelihood of the behaviors actually being carried out. Because of the gendered nature of stalking it is imperative to understand the contribution of patriarchy and its resultant gender-related beliefs and motives in any analysis of violence against women.

The model is useful in providing conceptual and empirical guidance. The model provides a meta-theoretical framework for developing substantive hypotheses concerning the development of risk factors for stalking, its initiation, maintenance, and cessation. The model suggests that theories that account for the multiple levels of interacting factors will be most useful.

At the empirical level, the model suggests a host of variables at each level of analysis that should be investigated. The model also suggests testing for interactions between factors that at first glance might not be obvious. For example, how does media exposure interact with alcohol use to affect perceptions of rejection? Or, how does one's peer group's attitudes toward male control in relationships affect acceptance or rejection?

An examination of Table 8.1 indicates that very little is known about the social networks of stalkers or about the situational context of the stalking episodes. The research has not examined what kinds of media messages or peer messages these men have received that might influence the initiation and persistence of stalking. What influence does their history of both familial and dating relationships have on their behavior? There are some data on dysfunctional attachment styles among these men, yet we actually know very little about the nature of their relationships prior to the stalking incidents. We also know nothing about the immediate situational influences on a stalker's behavior. As with instances of sexual assault, are there certain seasons or times of day when stalking is more likely? We know that many stalkers have a history of substance abuse, but are they using alcohol or drugs at the time they engage in the stalking behavior? How does stalking as a form of violence against women relate to other forms, such as verbal, non-sexual physical and sexual assault, as well as harassment? What is the relationship between obsessional relational intrusions and stalking; does ORI precede stalking? Importantly, we know little about the attitudes and beliefs of men who stalk. Do they endorse adversarial sexual beliefs and are they high in their acceptance of interpersonal violence? How do perpetrators perceive the stalking incidences? Most of the literature that we have on stalking and on other forms of violence against women focuses on victim as opposed to perpetrator perceptions. For the purposes of intervention and prevention, are there certain strategies victims might use to deter or at least reduce the likelihood and/or severity of stalking?

To date most studies of stalking have focused on clinical samples and victim perceptions of the perpetrator. Although the victim's perceptions are invaluable, more research on perpetrators in nonclinical samples is needed. Stalking research is still in its infancy, with more questions raised than answers found at this time. We suggest that the integrative contextual developmental model will provide guidance in generating hypotheses for further research.

NOTES

1. Analyses were based on items indicative of ORI as well as stalking based on the definitions used in the present article. Fear was not explicitly specified.

2. Although the focus of this article is on male violence against women, we suggest that the model can be extended to account for female violence as well.

REFERENCES

Archer, J. (2000). Sex differences in aggression between heterosexual partners: A meta-analytic review. *Psychological Bulletin, 126,* 651–680.

Bachman, R., & Saltzman, L. (1995). *Violence against women: Estimates from the redesigned survey.* NCJ-154348. Washington, DC: Bureau of Justice Statistics, U. S. Department of Justice.

Barnett, O., & Hamberger, L. K. (1992). The assessment of maritally violent men on the California Psychological Inventory. *Violence and Victims, 7,* 15–22.

Bartholomew, K. (1990). Avoidance of intimacy: An attachment perspective. *Journal of Social and Personal Relationships, 7,* 147–178.

Baumeister, R. F., & Wotman, S. R. (1992). *Breaking hearts: The two sides of unrequited love.* New York: Guilford.

Baumeister, R. F., Wotman, S. R., & Stillwell, A. M. (1993). Unrequited love: On heartbreak, anger, guilt, scriptlessness, and humiliation. *Journal of Personality and Social Psychology, 64,* 377–394.

Beck, M., Rosenberg, D., Chideya, F., Miller, S., Foote, D., Manly, H., & Katel, P. (1992). Murderous obsession. *Newsweek, 120*(2), 60–62.

Blum, H. (1997). *Sex on the brain: The biological differences between men and women.* Middlesex, New England: Penguin Books, Ltd.

Bourque, L. (1989). *Defining rape.* Durham, NC: Duke University Press.

Bowlby, J. (1973). *Attachment and loss: Vol. II. Separation, anxiety, and anger.* New York: Basic Books.

Bratslavsky, E., Baumeister, R. F., & Sommer, K. L. (1998). To love or be loved in vain: The trials and tribulations of unrequited love. In B. H. Spitzberg & W. R. Cupach (Eds.), *The dark side of interpersonal relationships* (pp. 307–326). Mahwah, NJ: Lawrence Erlbaum.

Burgess, A. W., Baker, T., Greening, D., Hartman, C. R., Burgess, A. G., Douglas, J. E., & Halloran, R. (1997). Stalking behaviors within domestic violence. *Journal of Family Violence, 12,* 389–403.

Calhoun, K. (1990, March). *Lies, sex, and videotapes: Studies in sexual aggression.* Presidential address, presented at the Southeastern Psychological Association, Atlanta, GA.

Campbell, A., Muncer, S., Guy, A., & Banim, M. (1996). Social representations of aggression: Crossing the sex barrier. *European Journal of Social Psychology, 26,* 135–147.

Cashdan, S. (1988). *Object relations therapy.* New York: W. W. Norton & Company.

Coleman, F. L. (1997). Stalking behavior and the cycle of domestic violence. *Journal of Interpersonal Violence, 12,* 420–432.

Cupach, W. R., & Spitzberg, B. H. (1998). Obsessional relational intrusions and stalking. In B. H. Spitzberg & W. R. Cupach (Eds.), *The dark side of close relationships* (pp. 233–263). Mahwah, NJ: Lawrence Erlbaum.

Dean, K. E., & Malamuth, N. (1997). Characteristics of men who aggress sexually and of me who imagine aggressing: Risk and moderating variables. *Journal of Personality and Social Psychology, 72,* 449–455.

Dutton, D. G., Saunders, K., Starzomiski, A., & Bartholomew, K. (1994). Intimacy-anger and insecure attachment as precursors of abuse in intimate relationships. *Journal of Applied Social Psychology, 24,* 1367–1386.

Emerson, R. M., Ferris, K. O., & Gardner, C. B. (1998). On being stalked. *Social Problems, 45,* 289–314.

Griffin, S. (1971). Rape: The all-American crime. *Ramparts, 10,* 26–35.

Hall, D. M. (1998). The victims of stalking. In J. R. Meloy (Ed.) *The psychology of stalking: Clinical and forensic perspectives* (pp. 113–137). San Diego, CA: Academic Press.

Hall, G. C. N., & Hirschman, R. (1991). Toward a theory of sexual aggression: A quadripartite model. *Journal of Consulting and Clinical Psychology, 59,* 662–669.

Harmon, R. B., Rosner, R., & Owens, H. (1995). Obsessional harassment and erotomania in a criminal court population. *Journal of Forensic Sciences, 40,* 188–196.

Holmes, R. M. (1998). Stalking in America: Types and methods of criminal stalkers. In R. M. Holmes & S. T. Holmes (Eds.). *Contemporary perspectives on serial murder.* Thousand Oaks, CA: Sage Publications, Inc. pp. 137–148.

Huesmann, L. R., & Eron, L. (1992). Childhood aggression and adult criminality. In J. McCord (Ed.), *Facts, frameworks, and forecasts: Advances in criminological theory. Vol. 3.* New Brunswik, NJ: Transaction Publishers.

Jason, L. A., Reichler, A., Easton, J., Neal, A., & Wilson, M. (1984). Female harassment after ending a relationship: A preliminary study. *Alternative Lifestyles, 6,* 259–269.

Kalmuss, D. S. (1984). The intergenerational transmission of marital aggression. *Journal of Marriage and the Family, 46,* 11–19.

Kienlen, K. K. (1998). Developmental and social antecedents of stalking. In J. R. Meloy (Ed.), *The psychology of stalking* (pp. 51–67). New York: Academic Press.

Kienlen, K. K., Birmingham, D. L., Solberg, K. B., O'Regan, J. T., & Meloy, J. R. (1997). A comparative study of psychotic and non-psychotic stalking. *Journal of the American Academy of Psychiatry and the Law, 25,* 317–334.

Koss, M. P., & Dinero, T. E. (1989). Discriminant analysis of risk factors for sexual victimization among a national sample of college women. *Journal of Consulting and Clinical Psychology, 57,* 242–250.

Koss, M. P., Goodman, L. A., Browne, A., Fitzgerald, L. F., Keita, G. P., & Russo, N. F. (1994). *No safe haven: Male violence against women at home, at work, and in the community.* Washington, DC: American Psychological Association.

Kraepelin, E. (1921). *Manic-depressive insanity and paranoia.* Edinburgh: E & S Livingstone.

Kurt, J. L. (1995). Stalking as a variant of domestic violence. *Bulletin of the American Academy of Psychiatry and the Law, 23,* 219–230.

Lasley, J. (1989). Drinking routines/lifestyles and predatory victimization: A causal analysis. *Justice Quarterly, 6,* 529–542.

Leary, M. R., Tambor, E. S., Terdal, S. K., & Downs, D. L. (1995). Self-esteem as an interpersonal monitor: The sociometer hypothesis. *Journal of Personality and Social Psychology, 68,* 518–530.

Luke, B. (1998). Violent love: Hunting, heterosexuality and erotics of men's predation. *Feminist Studies, 24,* 627–656.

Lloyd-Goldstein, R. (1998). DeClerambault on-line. In J. R. Meloy (Ed.), *The psychology of stalking* (pp. 193–212). New York: Academic Press.

Magdol, L., Moffitt, T., Caspi, A., Newman, D., Fagan, J., & Silva, P. (1997). Gender differences in partner violence in a birth cohort of 21–year-olds: Bridging the gap between clinical and epidemiological approaches. *Journal of Consulting & Clinical Psychology, 65,* 68–78.

Malamuth, N. M. (1986). Predictors of naturalistic aggression. *Journal of Personality and Social Psychology, 50,* 953–962.

Malamuth, N. M., Sockloskie, R. J., Koss, M. P., & Tanaka, J. S. (1991). Characteristics of aggressors against women: Testing a model using a national sample of college students. *Journal of Consulting and Clinical Psychology, 59,* 670–681.

McCann, J. T. (1998). Subtypes of stalking (obsessonal following) in adolescents. *Journal of Adolescence, 21,* 667–675.

McLachlan, S., (1993). Possession, on *Fumbling Towards Ecstasy* [CD]. Arista Records.

Meloy, J. R. (1992). *Violent attachments.* Northvale, NJ: Jason Aronson.

Meloy, J. R. (1996). Stalking (obsessional following): A review of some preliminary studies. *Aggression and Violent Behavior, 1,* 147–162.

Meloy, J. R. (1997). The clinical risk management of stalking: "Someone is watching over me . . . " *American Journal of Psychotherapy, 51,* 174–184.

Meloy, J. R. (1998). The psychology of stalking. In J. R. Meloy (Ed.), *The psychology of stalking: Clinical and forensic perspectives* (pp. 1–23). San Diego, CA: Academic Press.

Meloy, J. R., & Gothard, S. (1995). A demographic and clinical comparison of obsessional followers and offenders with mental disorders. *American Journal of Psychiatry, 152,* 258–263.

Murphy, C. M., Myers, S., & O'Leary, K. D. (1991). *Emotional vulnerability, psychopathology, and family of origin violence in men who assault female partners.* Unpublished manuscript, State University of New York, Stony Brook.

Mustaine, E. & Tewksbury, R. (1999). A routine activities theory explanation for women's stalking victimization. *Violence Against Women, 5,* 43–62.

National Criminal Justice Association. (1993). *Project to develop a model anti-stalking code for states.* Washington, DC: U.S. Department of Justice, National Institute of Justice, October.

National Institute of Justice. (1996, April). *Domestic violence, stalking, and antistalking legislation: An annual report to Congress under the Violence Against Women Act.* Washington, DC: Author.

Olweus, D. (1993). Victimization by peers: Antecedents and long-term outcomes. In K. H. Rubin & J. B. Asendorpf (Eds.), *Social withdrawal, inhibition, and shyness in childhood.* Hillsdale, NJ: Erlbaum.

Pathé, M., & Mullen, P. E. (1997). The impact of stalkers on their victims. *British Journal of Psychiatry, 170,* 12–17.

Rapaport, K. R., & Burkhart, B. R. (1984). Personality and attitudinal characteristics of sexually coercive college males. *Journal of Abnormal Psychology, 93,* 216–221.

Rather, L. J. (1965). *Mind and body in eighteenth century medicine.* London: The Wellcome Historical Medical Library.

Schwartz-Watts, D., & Morgan, D. W. (1998). Violent versus nonviolent stalkers. *Journal of the American Academy of Psychiatry and the Law, 26,* 241–245.

Se'ver, A. (1997). Recent or imminent separation and intimate violence against women. *Violence Against Women, 97,* 566–590.

Silberger, K. (1998, Jan. 8). Q & A: Sarah McLachlan, *Rolling Stone.*

Spitzberg, B. H., & Rhea, J. (1999). Obsessive relational intrusion and sexual coercion victimization. *Journal of Interpersonal Violence, 14,* 3–20.

Tjaden, P., & Thoennes, N. (1998). *Stalking in America: Findings from the national violence against women survey.* Denver, CO: Center for Policy Research.

The Police (1983). Every Breath You Take. *On Synchronicity* [CD]. New York: A & M Records.

Walker, L. E., & Meloy, R. (1998). Stalking and domestic violence. In J. R. Meloy (Ed.), *The psychology of stalking* (pp. 139–161). New York: Academic Press.

White, J. W., & Bondurant, B. (1996) Gendered violence. In J. T. Wood (Ed), *Gendered relationships* (pp. 197–210). Mountain View, CA: Mayfield Press.

White, J. W., Donat, P. L. N., & Bondurant, B. (2001). A developmental examination of violence against girls and women. In R. Unger (Ed.), *Handbook of the psychology of women and gender.* (pp. 343–357). New York: John Wiley & Sons.

White, J. W., & Koss, M. P. (1991). Adolescent sexual aggression within heterosexual relationships: Prevalence, characteristics, and causes. In H. E. Barbarbee, W. L. Marshall, & D. R. Laws (Eds.), *The juvenile sexual offender* (pp. 182–202). New York: Guilford Press.

White, J. W., & Kowalski, R. M. (1998). Violence against women: An integrative perspective. In R. G. Geen & E. Donnerstein (Eds.), *Perspectives on human aggression* (pp. 205–229). New York: Academic Press.

White, J. W., Smith, P. H., Koss, M. P., & Figueredo, A. J. (2000). Intimate Partner Aggression: What Have We Learned? Commentary of Archer's Meta-Analysis. *Psychological Bulletin, 126,* 690–696.

Wright, J. A., Burgess, A. G., Burgess, A. W., Laslo, A. T., et al. (1996). A typology of interpersonal stalking. *Journal of Interpersonal Violence, 11,* 487–502.

Zona, M. A., Palarea, R. E., & Lane, J. C. (1998). Psychiatric diagnosis and the offender-victim typology of stalking. In J. R. Meloy (Ed.), *The psychology of stalking* (pp. 69–84). New York: Academic Press.

Zona, M. A., Sharma, K. K., & Lane, J. (1993). A comparative study of erotomanic and obsessional subjects in a forensic sample. *Journal of Forensic Sciences, 38,* 894–903.

9

Initial Courtship Behavior and Stalking: How Should We Draw the Line?

H. Colleen Sinclair and Irene Hanson Frieze

In 1992, Leidig proposed a "continuum of violence against women" that included a range of threatening behaviors from street hassling to incest. Missing from this spectrum of behaviors was mention of the crime of stalking. Stalking affects approximately 1% of women annually, as well as .4% of men in the United States (Tjaden & Thoennes, 1997). The omission of stalking from the list of crimes of violence against women is perhaps due to stalking being a somewhat amorphous phenomenon that encompasses a broad scope of severity. The term "stalking" can include anything from benign courtship attempts to assault and murder. As Mullen, Pathé, Purcell, and Stuart (1999) suggest, "stalking . . . is part of a spectrum of activities that merge into normal behavior, often around such aspirations as initiating or reestablishing a relationship" (p. 1244). In this study, we seek to empirically examine the question of whether there is a continuum of stalking behaviors from very mild to more severe. In addition, this study investigates some possible motivations for certain stalking-related behaviors, within the context of individuals attempting to initiate a romantic relationship.

Generally defined as a pattern of harassing or threatening behavior, stalking, while not a new crime, is a new term—one that has been receiving increasing research attention since the first stalking law was passed in California in 1990. The majority of work to date focuses on the perspective of the victim (e.g., Dziegielewski & Roberts, 1995; Hall, 1998; Pathé & Mullen, 1997), clinical assessments of psychopathological stalkers (e.g., Meloy, 1989; Meloy, 1997; Wallace & Kelly, 1995; Zona, Palarea, & Lane, 1998; Zona, Sharma & Lane, 1993) or legal debates about aspects of stalking statutes (e.g., Anderson, 1993; Lingg, 1993; Patton, 1994; Saunders, 1998). More recent research, as represented by many of the papers in this special issue, has begun to focus on stalking both in ongoing or recently ended interpersonal relationships, particularly within battering relationships, and on attempts to construct a typology of stalkers (see, for example, interpersonal: Emerson, Ferris, & Gardner, 1998; typology: Mullen et al., 1999; Wright et al., 1996; battering: Coleman, 1997; Kurt, 1995; Walker & Meloy, 1998).

Although the public stereotype of the stalker may be the crazed fan of a celebrity, the majority of stalking victims are stalked by an intimate partner or someone they know (Tjaden & Thoennes, 1997), often as a relationship is breaking up (Langhinrichsen-Rohling, Palarea, Cohen, & Rohling, this volume; Logan, Lenkefeld, & Walker, this volume; Mechanic, Weaver, & Resick, this volume). Because data regarding the relationship status between the individuals in the Tjaden & Thoennes study were limited, we do not know whether any of the stalkers in this national study had been in the process of seeking a relationship rather than hoping to avoid a breakup. There is evidence that such prerelationship stalking does exist. In one sample of self-defined stalking victims recruited via the media to participate in a study on stalking (Hall, 1998), 23% of stalkers were perceived as persons who were seeking a relationship. In Mullen, Pathé, Purcell, and Stuart's (1999) clinical sample of stalkers, 49% were classified as attempting to seek some form of intimacy with a love object.

The relationship status of interest to us is one that encompasses both the initial pursuit of a romantic relationship as well as the rejection of that pursuit. In this unrequited love scenario, one individual is attracted to another, and those feelings of attraction are not reciprocated. Bratslavsky, Baumeister and Sommer (1998) describe three scenarios in which unrequited love may occur. Two extend from individuals having an existing relationship (either as friends or romantic partners), where one member seeks to change the status of the relationship (either to elevate it to a romantic relationship or to terminate it), and the other is resistant to this change. The third type involves "falling upward." This is when an individual falls for a love interest that is more desirable in the "dating marketplace" and is thus "out of his/her league." This last type is not unlike one of the criteria for a diagnosis of De Cherambault's syndrome, known more commonly today as erotomania—a delusional disorder often found in celebrity stalkers (Lloyd-Goldstein, 1998; Seeman, 1978 as cited in Anderson, 1993). Specifically, the erotomanic patient typically had an obsession with an individual of a higher status. However, we would argue that it is possible for unrequited love to occur between strangers or acquaintances without falling upward. In any case, when either falling upward or unrequited love between acquaintances otherwise occurs, the pursuer often does not know a great deal about the love object and would most likely be classified as experiencing Sternberg's (1986) "fatuous love" or simply "infatuation." Interestingly, "infatuation" was a term used to describe stalking behaviors prior to 1990 when the label of "stalking" emerged (Lowney & Best, 1995).

According to Baumeister, Wotman, and Stillwell (1993), the options for the pursuer are somewhat limited when s/he is confronted with unreciprocated love. Essentially, s/he can give up upon realizing that his/her affection is unwanted, or s/he can persist. S/he can persist by either choosing not to take "no" for an answer or by just being oblivious to the fact of rejection. In either case, the person continues to try and court his/her love interest despite rejection. Persistence is hardly disapproved of in our society. In fact, common sayings such as "if at first you don't succeed, try, try again" are present in our culture and may be seen as providing a model for persistent behavior. Further, a number of theorists argue that courtship persistence in particular is portrayed via media as the script for pursuits, especially unrequited pursuits (Anderson & Accomando, 1999; Baumeister et al., 1993; de Becker, 1997; Emerson et al., 1998; Meloy, 1998). The persistence script often proves successful for media heroes and heroines. This can be seen in the 1999 summer movie blockbuster, *There's Something About Mary*, for example, or the classic Dustin Hoffman film, *The Graduate*. However, it was in this situation (when an individual received a rejection but continued to persist in pursuit of the relationship despite that rejection) that participants in Emerson and associates (1998) sample felt they were being stalked. Others have also equated persistence with stalking. For example, de Becker (1997) implies that courtship persistence blurs the line between acceptable courtship behavior and stalking. Similarly, Schaum and Parrish (1995) argue that it is stalking that obscures the line between normal persistence and obsessive behavior.

In this study, we hope to examine whether there is a continuum of stalking behaviors in courtship that ranges from "normal" courtship to persistent to obsessive forms of behavior. Following rejection from a love interest, other pursuit behaviors might fall into what Emerson and colleagues' (1998) refer to as "pre-stalking." Such behavior may be perceived by a rejecter as a nuisance (Dziegelewski & Roberts, 1995), but has not yet reached a level of "stalking." Not unlike Baumeister and colleagues (1993) approach, in this research we asked individuals to share with us their experiences with unrequited love. Participants were asked to recall an instance when they loved someone who did not love them in return. They were encouraged to focus on a pursuit of an individual with whom they had felt strongly, but where no more than one or two, if any, dates had ensued. Grote and Frieze's (1994) "Love Styles" survey and Hatfield and Rapson's "Passionate Love" scale (see Hatfield & Sprecher, 1986) were utilized to measure the degree and type of love a participant reported feeling for the love interest. Participants were then asked how they felt about being rejected, what pursuit behaviors they employed, and what impact they felt their actions had upon their love interest's feelings. It was hoped that not only would we discover the various behaviors participants used in their pursuits, but also that we would find out their feelings regarding their love interest's response. Their feelings, whether jealousy, anger, or vengeance, or whether they were only positive, might shed light on their individual motivations for continuing a pursuit and using aggressive tactics. Further, inquiring about their perceptions of their love interest's feelings is meant to highlight the degree to which rejecter reactions might predict aggressive persistence or obsessive behavior as some theorists argue they might (de Becker, 1997). In addition, we attempted to determine how aware the pursuer was of the feelings of the rejecting love interest. De Becker (1997) argues that some courtship pursuers become "naive" stalkers, because they are oblivious of the fact that their pursuit is both unwanted and uncomfortable for the love interest. Inquiring about the perceptions of the love interest will indicate whether the pursuer was or was not oblivious, as purported by the "naive" stalker model.

Asking the pursuer about his/her behavior and perceptions is a relatively unique approach in the existing stalking literature. State stalking statutes often require that stalking behavior be of such a degree that it causes the victim to fear for his or her personal safety, thereby placing the duty of defining what is threatening or harassing squarely on the shoulders of the victim (Tjaden & Thoennes, 1997; Tjaden, Thoennes, & Allison, this volume). Thus, much of research has focused on the victim's perspective and the victim's definition of stalking. In this examination, pursuers reflected upon their past experiences and assessed whether their behaviors crossed a line between what could be considered acceptable courtship behaviors and what might be viewed as "obsessional relational intrusion" (Cupach & Spitzberg, 1998).

Based on what is known in the stalking literature as well as in courtship and dating literature, we can make some initial predictions. First, it is important to acknowledge the role of gender when dealing with both courtship and interpersonal violence. Although some research has shown men are primarily the stalkers (Tjaden & Thoennes, 1997) and the suitors (Baumeister, Wotman, & Stillwell, 1993), this does not exclude women taking either role. In fact, Baumeister and colleagues (1993) and Simpson and coworkers (1999) report little difference between male and female courtship patterns. Certainly, both genders hold socially sanctioned scripts about the way that pursuers and the pursued should act during a courtship (Baumeister et al., 1993). Some of these beliefs appear to highlight an adversarial courtship relationship between men and women. Some men, for example, might believe that their love interest doesn't want to appear "easy" and thus any initial rejection is not to be heeded, because she doesn't really mean it. Malamuth and Brown (1994) call this a "suspicion schema" that "women's communications about romantic or sexual interest cannot be trusted as veridical" (p. 701). Alternately, women may believe that they should be pursued by men, but that ultimately "men are out for only one thing." This belief implies that women do not trust men's communications about their romantic intentions either. These attitudes are well captured in Burt's (1980) "Adversarial Sexual Beliefs" scale. In the present study, this scale was expanded to include items oriented specifically toward the initial courtship process as opposed to interactions in an established interpersonal relationship. For instance, using the previous example of a man who does not believe a woman's rejection, he might be expected to agree that "many times a woman will pretend she doesn't want to date you, but really she just wants to be pursued more." Our goal in including this courtship-version of the Burt scale is to test for any correlates between adversarial sexual beliefs and a likelihood of utilizing more extreme types of courtship behaviors.

Whereas both genders are likely to utilize the suspicion schema, we also believed that all pursuers dealing with unrequited love will reveal an apparent disregard to the reactions of their beloved, what Malamuth and Brown (1994) refer to as "negativeness blindness." To some extent, this lack of empathy may be related to the suspicion schema that leads pursuers to suspect that their love interest is not being truthful about their lack of interest. Doubt about the veracity of rejections could lead a pursuer to just not take 'no' for an answer, and choose to persist in pursuits because at least persistence provides a chance for success. Nearly half (41%) of Baumeister and associates' sample were cited as deceiving themselves in this way. To highlight any ways in which these aspects of "negativeness blindness" items predict certain types of stalking-related behavior, statements such as "I felt led on" and "I would not take 'no' for an answer" were included in the survey.

It is expected that there will be some difference between men and women in their courtship tactics. For instance, de Weerth and Kalma (1995) noted that women were more likely to report using eye contact and body language to signal their interest in another individual, whereas men felt that they made the first move by approaching their love interest. Thus, in this study it is likely that more assertive direct approach tactics might be used by men, whereas women may prefer tactics that place them in the "right place at the right time." Further, men are more likely than women to use "strong tactics," such as coercion or manipulation, to try and influence a partner's decision (Bui, Raven, & Schwarzwald, 1994). This finding once again signals the use of more aggressive behaviors by men. Also, Baumeister and associates (1993) reported that men were more unwilling to give up on an unrequited love and thus were more likely to persist. Accordingly, it is to be expected that men might have longer pursuits. Finally, men and women might differ in how far they are willing to go in a courtship. As de Becker (1997) suggests, "some invisible line exists between what is all right and what is too far—and men and women don't always agree on where to place that line." (p.195)

However, where to draw the line is a problem with the concept of stalking in general. As noted by Emerson and coworkers (1998), it is difficult to draw the line between what is courtship and what is stalking behavior. One of the primary goals of this article is to try to address the question: What is going too far? Where do individuals draw the line between what is acceptable courtship behavior and what is not? In the Baumeister and colleagues (1993) study, none of the pursuers perceived their acts as unacceptable, whereas 21.7% of the rejecters reported use of "unscrupulous tactics" by the would-be-lover. Obviously, physically violent behavior would be unacceptable. However, things like the "strong tactics" mentioned by Bui and associates (1994) blur the line between courtship and stalking and might fall into the category of what Emerson and associates (1998) term "pre-stalking." Consequently, the label of stalking is interpretative (Emerson et al., 1998). As reflected in the legal statutes, stalking is often judged by the level of fear experienced by a "reasonable" person (Tjaden & Thoennes, 1997). What one person feels frightened by may be different from the level of threat experienced by another in a similar situation. These differences might depend upon whether the individual is a woman or a man. And, of course, differences between victim accounts and perpetrator definitions of going too far in courtship have been noted to exist and are expected to show up in our research (Baumeister et al., 1993). However, research thus far has focused primarily on the efficacy of legal definitions and victims' accounts. This study asks what we can learn from pursuer accounts.

METHOD

Participants

Study participants were 241 volunteers from students enrolled in an Introduction to Psychology course at the University of Pittsburgh who needed study participation credit as a course requirement. There were 197 women[1] and 44 men in the final sample, after nonheterosexuals and those over 26 were excluded.[2] The sample was 87% Caucasian, with a modal age of 18–19 (82% of the sample). There were 6% African Americans, 3% Asian, 2% mixed race, and 2% other.

Procedures

Students were recruited for a study of "Loving when your partner does not love back." Study participants had to have agreed that there was at least one person "whom you had a crush on, had a love interest in, or were otherwise interested in who was less interested in you than you were in him or her" or to have been the love interest of an unwanted pursuer. Those included in this analysis were from the former group. Students were surveyed anonymously in mixed gender groups ranging from 5 to 20. The experimenter was a college-aged White female student. All participants were invited to ask questions and not to answer any items that made them uncomfortable. After completing the survey, participants were given oral and written feedback about the purpose of the study, and advised of resources for further information or counseling.

MEASUREMENT

Seeking to clarify the range of stalking-related behavior, we developed a list of possible stalking behaviors from sources such as Tjaden and Thoennes' "Violence and Threats of Violence Against Women" survey. We also examined personal accounts of stalking and courtship found in popular and largely nonempirical books such as de Becker (1997) and Schaum and Parrish (1996). The list of 52 specific behaviors included nonviolent, potentially psychologically and physically violent courtship tactics that range from the sending of notes to extreme forms of assault. Participants were asked to report on crushes, love interests or passionate love they felt for another that was not reciprocated.

The stalking-related behaviors scale asked participants what acts they used to "express their interest." Participants responded along a frequency scale to indicate how often (1 = never, 2 = rarely [once or twice], 3 = occasionally [more than twice], 4 = repeatedly [more than 5 times], and 5 = frequently [more than 10 times]). In order to simplify the data, these 52 items were factored into 6 subscales (see Table 9.1 for details of factor analysis).

To assess pursuer response when their affection was not returned, participants indicated on a scale from 1 (not at all) to 5 (very much) "how much a given statement pertain[ed] to [their] feelings about [the love interest] at the time [their] feelings were not reciprocated." Examples of more positive reactions include: "I felt it had been worth trying" and "I learned something positive from the experience." Negative responses include: "I felt vengeful," "I felt I had been led on," and "I felt angry." More neutral reactions include: "I found someone else" or

"I focused my energy elsewhere." The complete list of 22 items is available from the authors.

The final 29 items of the survey tapped participant perceptions of their love interests' feelings and reactions. Specifically, they were asked: "During the time you were interested in this person how did s/he react to your attempts to get his/her attention?" Using a scale of 1 (never) to 5 (frequently, more than 10 times), possible responses included different forms of rejection such as passivity ("Says s/he just wants to be friends"), explicit ("Says s/he was definitely not interested") and humiliating ("Makes jokes or laughs at you"). The scale also allowed for positive reactions to the participant ("Says s/he was interested"), responses that indicate blame on behalf of the love interest ("Plays hard to get"), and emotive reactions ("S/he seemed afraid").

Several standard scales were included in the survey. All items for these scales were answered on a 1 to 5 Likert scale. Scale scores were computed as average item scores. The 9–item "Adversarial Sexual Beliefs" scale (Burt, 1980) was included. Two items from Burt's (1980) "Acceptance of Interpersonal Violence" scale were added ("Being roughed up is sexually stimulating to many women" and "Sometimes the only way a man can get a woman turned on is to use force."). An additional seven items were constructed to more specifically address any adversarial tendencies in heterosexual courtship. These items were added to Burt's scales to further illuminate any sexist beliefs or suspicion schema. They are "Many times a woman will pretend she doesn't want to date you, but really she just wants to be pursued more"; "In courtship, the man should pursue the woman"; "Women play games with men's affections"; "Even if a woman says no, she really just needs to be convinced"; "A woman will pretend she doesn't want to have intercourse because she doesn't want to seem loose, but she's really hoping a man will force her"; "Men can be nice during the courtship period, but once they are in a relationship they act like a different person" and "A woman can say one thing, but mean something entirely different." The combined scale consisting of 18 items yielded an alpha of .82. The predictive power of the original Adversarial Sexual Beliefs and Acceptance of Interpersonal Violence scales alone did not differ from the original scales when combined with the seven new items.

Items from the "Love Styles" scale (Grote & Frieze, 1994) and the Hatfield and Rapson "Passionate Love" scale (Hatfield & Sprecher, 1986) were used to assess the type of love felt for the other person.

One love style measured was eros, or passionate love (Lee, 1973). This scale had 8 items, with an alpha of .86. Items were: "I was physically attracted to my love interest"; "I felt we had the right physical chemistry between us"; "Just seeing my love interest excited me"; "I felt that I knew and really understood my love interest"; "I yearned to know all about my love interest"; "For me, my love interest was the perfect romantic partner"; "I wanted my love interest to know me— my thoughts, my fears, and my hopes"; "I possessed a powerful attraction for my love interest." Mania was measured with a 13–item scale, with an alpha of .91. Items were: "When things didn't go right between my love interest and me, it affected me physically"; "I became jealous to the point of conflict, if I suspected my love interest was with someone else"; "My thoughts were constantly on my love interest; I tried to get my love interest to show more feeling for me"; "I would have done almost anything to get my love interest to love me"; "When my love interest didn't make time for me, I felt sick all over"; "I felt despair when my love interest did not go out with me"; "I couldn't control my thoughts; they were obsessively on my love interest"; "I would have rather been with my love interest than anyone else"; "I'd get jealous if I thought my love interest were in love with someone else"; "I had an endless appetite for affection from my love interest"; "My love interest always seemed to be on my mind"; "I eagerly looked for signs indicating my love interest's desire for me."

RESULTS

Unrequited Love

To be included in the sample, the study participants had to have had at least one experience of loving someone who did not reciprocate those feelings. The large majority of women and men in the sample reported more than one instance of unrequited love. Thirty-four percent said this had happened twice and 44% reported this happening 3 or more times. In these situations, they were asked to complete the survey in reference to "the one person you liked the most."

In describing this person, study participants were asked a series of yes-no questions about the characteristics of this person. Only 11% said the person was a stranger. Some of the more common responses were that the person was an acquaintance (66%), a friend (74%), a classmate (59%), a friend of a friend (49%), and a date (35%). When asked if this was an e-mail correspondent, 5% said "yes." When asked whether this person was a current love interest, 32% said "yes." In general, these "relationships" were described as lasting a few months (40%). Twenty-nine percent said the relationship had lasted from a few days to a few weeks, and 15% reported it lasting a year. Sixteen percent said it had lasted 2 or more years. There were no significant gender differences for length, although contrary to our expectation, women reported slightly longer pursuits.

TYPES OF STALKING-RELATED BEHAVIORS

As described earlier, study participants were asked to rate how often (from 1 = Never to 5 = Frequently—more than 10 times) they had engaged in a series of behaviors to "express their interest." We first examined percentages of female and male students who reported doing any of these behaviors at least once. These percentages are shown in Table 9.1.

As can be seen, nearly all of our respondents attempted to communicate with the person with whom they were in love. Other very common responses were asking friends about the person, trying to show up at social events where the person would be, sending the person notes, doing unrequested favors, and finding out information about the person. By themselves, none of these behaviors would typically be labeled as "stalking."

A number of behaviors that might more commonly be classified as stalking were also reported. For example, more than half of our sample reported waiting for the person outside class or work, driving by their home or work, and more than 20% of the sample reported calling on the phone and hanging up, following the person or making sexual overtures. More extreme acts of aggression were much less common, but none of the behaviors listed in the survey received a zero response.

To further examine the various stalking-related behaviors, the individual items were factor analyzed. Because of sample size limitations, we could not do all the items at one time, so they were done in groups in order to form stronger, clearer factors. The first grouping contained the less violent items. A principal components analysis was done with

Table 9.1 Courtship Behavior Items With Percentages (organized by highest to lowest frequency)

Approach Items (a = .77) Percentages doing at least once:	Male	Female
99. Send or give him/her notes, letters, e-mail or other written communication?	79	71
116. Ask him/her out as friends?	77	58
101. Do unrequested favors for him/her?	74	72
117. Ask him/her out on a date?	72	39
100. Send or give him/her gifts?	67	51

Surveillance Items (a = .80) Percentages doing at least once:	Male	Female
114. Ask friends about him/her?	86	92
109. Try to show up at social or recreational events where you'd knew s/he be?	79	85
111. Find out information about him/her (phone number, address, hobbies, plans, love interests, etc.) by means other than asking him/her for it?	70	74
108. Drive, ride or walk purposefully by residence, work or school?	63	75
107. Wait or stand outside of his/her class, school, home, or work?	58	60
110. Follow him/her?	26	24
113. Change classes, offices, or otherwise take up an activity to be closer to him/her?	26	23
125. Spy on him/her?	12	23

Intimidation Items (a = .76) Percentages doing at least once:	Male	Female
119. Try to manipulate or coerce him/her into dating me?	28	17
122. Try to scare him/her?	9	10
123. Leave unwanted items for him/her to find?	9	9
112. Secretly take his/her belongings?	7	8
124. Give him/her unusual parcels?	5	6

Harm-Self Items (a = .87) Percentages doing at least once:	Male	Female
140. Attempt to hurt yourself?	9	8
147. Physically hurt yourself?	7	4
134. Threaten to hurt yourself?	2	8

Verbal Abuse & Mild

Aggression Items (a = .82) Percentages doing at least once:	Male	Female
143. Verbally abuse him/her?	14	13
136. Attempt to verbally abuse him/her (i.e., use sexually explicit or obscene language)?	7	15
126. Harass him/her?	5	10
130. Threaten to hurt him/her emotionally (i.e., ruin reputation, verbally abuse, etc.)?	5	5

Table 9.1 *(Continued)*

Aggression Items (a = .77) Percentages doing at least once:	Male	Female
141. Attempt to physically harm him/her slightly (slap, single punch, grab, push or shove)?	2	16
148. Physically harm him/her slightly?	2	9
129. Trespass on his/her property?	2	6

Extreme Harm Items (a = .92) Percentages doing at least once:	Male	Female
133. Threaten to physically hurt someone s/he knew?	9	4
139. Attempt to physically harm someone s/he knew?	7	4
150. Force sexual contact?	5	3
131. Threaten to damage belongings (i.e., threaten to vandalize, steal, break, etc. . . .)?	2	4
137. Attempt to damage his/her belongings?	2	4
135. Threaten to physically hurt him/her?	2	3
132. Threaten to vandalize home or car (i.e., break in, fix locks, use graffiti, cut brakes . . .)?	2	2
138. Attempt to vandalize home or car?	2	2
142. Attempt to physically harm him/her more than slightly?	2	2
144. Damage his/her property?	2	2
145. Vandalize his/her car or home?	2	2
146. Physically harm someone s/he knew?	2	2
149. Physically harm him/her more than slightly?	0	1

a varimax rotation. Only factors yielding a minimum eigenvalue of 1.5 were retained. This conservative eigenvalue was used because of the relatively small sample size and so that larger factors would be formed. The first three factors (accounting for 41% of the variance) were meaningful and were used to create scales. The scales were Approach behavior (alpha = .77), Surveillance (alpha = .80), and Intimidation (alpha = .76). Items within each scale are shown in Table 9.1.

A second factor analysis for the more violent behaviors, again using the same procedures, yielded three factors, accounting for 62% of the variance. Based on the factor loadings, three scales were formed. These were Hurting the Self (alpha = .87), Verbal and Mild Aggression (alpha = .84), and Physical Violence (alpha = .92). These second three scales were all relatively low-frequency behaviors and all were highly skewed. For this reason, we dichotomized each of these so that if the person had ever done any of the behaviors in this scale, this person received a score of 2. If they had done none of these, the score was 1.

Table 9.2 Gender Differences in Courtship Behaviors

			Courtship Behaviors			
	Approach	Surveillance	Intimidation	Hurting Self*	Verbal/Mild Aggression*	Physically Violent*
FOR MALES (n = 43)						
M	2.49	2.27	1.25	1.09	1.11	1.12
SD	.89	.70	.66	.29	.39	.32
Ever Did	100%	100%	30%	9%	19%	12%
FOR FEMALES (n = 197)						
M	2.1	2.46	1.15	1.11	1.25	1.14
SD	.84	.74	.37	.31	.44	.35
Ever Did	89%	99%	28%	11%	25%	14%
p-value for means	.01	.14	.18	.79	.35	.66

Note. Scales from 1 = Never to 5 = Frequently. *Scales dichotomized with 2 = Yes, 1 = No.

A MANOVA was done using the six behavioral scales as dependent variables and gender as the independent variable. The overall F was significant for gender ($F[6, 233] = 2.87$, $p < .01$). Men were found to do more of the approach behaviors, as shown in Table 9.2. In general, none of the behaviors was done at a high frequency level. On average, across all the different behaviors listed, approach behavior was done from once or twice to occasionally (for males), as was surveillance. For women, surveillance was more common than normal courtship approach behavior. Other "stalking" behaviors were rarely reported, with means of only slightly over "never." Intimidating behavior was relatively common, with 28% of women and 30% of men reporting doing one of these items at least once. Trying to manipulate or coerce the other was the most common behavior within this group of intimidation items. Verbal aggression was reported by 25% of women and 19% of men. Physically violent behavior directed at the target or third party was reported by 12% of men and 14% of women.

These data suggest that college students of both sexes do engage in a wide range of stalking-related behaviors, when responding to unrequited love. Their behaviors do not range from low level to high level, but instead form clusters of related behaviors, some of which are more violent than others.

In attempting to decide which of these 6 sets of stalking-related behaviors might be labeled as stalking, we first looked at self-definitions of "going too far." Affirmative responses (answering "2" or "yes" instead of "1" or "no") to this item would indicate that participants drew a line as to what behavior was inappropriate or which individuals were able to recognize that their acts were too aggressive. This was examined by using 2 x 2 MANOVAS on self-reports of going too far by gender as the independent variables, with the six stalking behavior scales as the dependent variables. There were no gender by "going too far" rating interactions for perceptions of going too far. There was a significant main effect for the "too far" rating [Multivariate $F(6, 229) = 4.99$, $p < .001$]. Significant univariate effects indicated that those who answered "yes" to having gone too far were more likely to have engaged in "normal courtship" approach behaviors, to have used surveillance, to have used intimidating behaviors, and to have used verbal aggression. There were no significant differences for the more violent measures of harming the self or severe violence, perhaps because these were such low-frequency behaviors. Thus, self-ratings of going too far do not differentiate among different forms of stalking-related behaviors.

Another way of assessing "stalking" is in terms of victim reactions. When were the targets of these behaviors seen as fearful? We did not directly survey victims in these data, but we did ask our study participants to rate a number of potential reactions of the other person as they reacted to the attempts of the study participant to get his or her attention. Looking at Table 9.3, it can be seen that men reporting intimidation and surveillance were most likely to see their "victims" as expressing fear. Men using mild or severe violence perceived their "victims" as being more annoyed. Ignoring was most associated with mild aggression. Approach and surveillance were received with flattery, while saying "maybe" was associated with the use of intimidation.

For women, as shown in Table 9.4, only intimidation was associated with perceived fear in their male victims. The male victims were seen as annoyed in response to all six types of behaviors as displayed by women. When the victims failed to exhibit that they were flattered, their female pursuers were more likely to engage in intimidation and hurting the self. These data suggest that fear may be associated with even mild forms of male "stalking," but that female "stalkers" may not generate fear, even for more extreme behaviors. However, these data could also be interpreted as indicating that those engaging in stalking-related behaviors are simply insensitive to the feelings of the targets of their affection.

Table 9.3 Courtship Behaviors and Attitudinal Correlates for Men

	Courtship Behaviors					
	Approach	Surveillance	Intimidation	Hurting Self*	Mild Aggression*	Violent*
Love Styles						
Eros	.41**	.36*	.31*	.00	.12	.03
Mania	.37**	.38*	.31*	.22	.50**	.33*
Revised Burt scale	.33*	.42**	.33*	.17	.25	.04
Rejection Reactions						
Frustrated	.23	.28	.31*	.23	.35*	.07
Hurt	.20	.33*	.31*	.18	.21	.15
Angry	.21	.30*	.34*	.34*	.46**	.29
Depressed	.12	.22	.39*	.37*	.40**	.26
Found new interest	–.20	–.10	–.28	–.35*	–.09	.00
Vengeful	.38*	.46**	.58**	.09	.45**	.42**
Deceived	.46**	.44**	.58**	–.01	.22	.44**
Not take no	.42**	.23	.42**	.07	.06	–.00
Want to hurt	.27	.43**	.55**	–.07	.43*	.12
Reactions of Other						
Ignore you	.10	.11	.10	.11	.35*	.16
Flattered	.51**	.46**	.27	.16	.09	.26
Afraid	.44**	.54**	.68**	.13	.10	.20
Lead you on	.19	.12	.06	–.14	.10	.33*
Annoyed	.07	.06	.03	.11	.76**	.42**
Say maybe	.24	.28	.55**	–.13	.19	.15

*$p < .05$; **$p < .01$.

CORRELATES OF STALKING-RELATED BEHAVIORS

The six stalking-related behaviors were correlated with other variables in the study as shown in Tables 9.3 and 9.4. Looking at the study participants' self-reported reactions to being rejected, it can be seen that for men, feeling vengeful, deceived, or wanting to hurt the person were most correlated with intimidation. These reactions were also significantly correlated with approach behavior, surveillance, and mild and more severe aggression. Not wanting to take "no" for an answer was equally correlated with approach and intimidation. Anger and depression were most correlated with mild aggression, intimidation, and hurting the self. Similar patterns were seen for women.

Table 9.4 Courtship Behaviors and Attitudinal Correlates for Women

			Courtship Behaviors			
	Approach	Surveillance	Intimidation	Hurting Self*	Mild Aggression*	Violent*
Love Styles						
Eros	.30**	.31**	.21**	.17*	.16*	.20**
Mania	.33**	.34**	.34**	.27**	.34**	.32**
Revised Burt Scale	.09	.11	.18*	.05	.11	.05
Rejection Reactions						
Frustrated	.26**	.30**	.17*	.17*	.18*	.13
Hurt	.26**	.21**	.26**	.22**	.18*	.14*
Angry	.24**	.19**	.31**	.28**	.31**	.26**
Depressed	.24**	.29**	.39**	.35**	.28**	.28**
Found new interest	−.17*	−.17*	−.08	−.19**	−.04	−.02
Vengeful	.21**	.32**	.42**	.31**	.31**	.41**
Deceived	.19**	.12	.30**	.20**	.30**	.27**
Not take no	.24**	.21**	.29**	.15*	.24**	.23**
Want to hurt	.13	.17*	.40**	.36**	.37**	.34**
Reactions of Other						
Ignore you	.00	.22**	.16*	.10	.11	.06
Flattered	.15*	−.01	−.22**	−.15*	−.08	−.08
Afraid	.06	.02	.20**	.06	.03	.10
Lead you on	.19**	−.01	.24**	.06	.21**	.21**
Annoyed	.21**	.16*	.36**	.20**	.29**	.26**
Say maybe	.14	−.01	.02	.06	.10	−.01

*$p < .05$; **$p < .01$.

We had predicted that stalking-type behaviors would be more common in those with either a mania ($\alpha = .91$) or an eros ($\alpha = .86$) love style. This was tested by computing correlates between the love styles and the six types of "stalking" behaviors separately for each gender, as shown in Tables 9.3 and 9.4. Results indicated that for women, both love styles were significantly correlated with all six of the stalking measures. For men, those higher in eros and mania were significantly more likely to engage in approach behaviors, surveillance, and intimidation. Mania was also significantly correlated with verbal coercion and physical aggression.

Finally, we had expected that the scores on Burt's scale (with the additional seven items) that tapped the belief that relations between men and women are adversarial would correlate with the various "stalking" behaviors. Correlations indicated that revised Burt's scale scores were positively correlated with all six scales for men, although the effects were statistically significant only for approach, surveillance, and intimidation. For women, significant positive correlates were found with revised Burt scales' scores only for intimidation. (See Tables 9.3 and 9.4.)

DISCUSSION

It is clear that the extreme forms of stalking that are discussed in popular media are only the most extreme of a potentially more general phenomenon. The large majority of our sample described engaging in behaviors that might be interpreted as stalking or prestalking when responding to a situation of loving someone who did not love them back. This makes stalking similar to other forms of interpersonal violence that also range from quite mild to very severe (e.g., Ryan, Frieze, & Sinclair, 1999). To make a clear distinction for what behavior should properly be labeled as stalking is not possible. Perceptions will vary depending upon who the victim is (Tjaden et al., this issue), as well as upon who is doing the behavior, with male perpetrators generating more fear than female, even when doing the same things. Asking the perpetrators about when they themselves think they have gone too far is also not a reliable indicator. In order to further examine this issue, we briefly review the types of behaviors reported by males and females in this study.

As in previous studies, this survey revealed that unrequited love is far from an uncommon occurrence in college students (Aron, Aron, & Allen, 1998; Baumeister, Wotman, & Stillwell, 1993). The majority of participants in this study identified more than one unrequited love. Further, this study, replicating findings on courtship and dating tactics, revealed that men were more likely than women to utilize overt approach behaviors (de Weerth & Kalma, 1995). There is also some evidence that women use slightly more covert behaviors than men to attract the attention of their love interest as found in de Weerth and Kalma (1995), while men were found to be marginally more likely to use more manipulative tactics as mentioned in Bui and colleagues (1994). Aside from the fact that Baumeister and associates (1993) found that men were more likely to persist in a romantic pursuit than women, no significant gender difference was found in the length of the pursuits. However, this might largely be a function of the types of courtship behaviors used. While men may be more likely to persist after a rejection, women, using less obvious courtship maneuvers, may be less likely to receive a rejection as early in the courtship as their male counterparts. Thus, women's pursuits may last longer simply because their love interest takes longer to realize that not only is he an object of a pursuit but this pursuit may also be unwanted.

Some theorists believe that the responses of the rejecter to unwanted advances can be suggestive of the perpetuation of courtship persistence, and in some cases may even serve as a catalyst (de Becker, 1997). However, in this study the perceived reactions of the love interest to the pursuer were not as predictive of stalking or stalking-related behaviors as the pursuer's own reactions to rejection. For female pursuers, only one rejecter reaction (expressed annoyance) yielded a correlation of over .25. For male pursuers, the rejecter's reactions predicted more. Notably, perceptions that the love interest had been flattered by the advances yielded the most correlates exceeding .25, with reactions of fear being second. Yet neither of these reactions are strong predictors of violent behavior. This could be a function of the pursuers being oblivious to their love interests' feelings, as proposed by the "naive" stalker model (de Becker, 1997), or it could be that victim reactions do not predict aggressor actions as much as the aggressor's feelings do. Accordingly, it is perhaps more valuable to focus on the pursuer's reactions for insight into motivation and intent, although replication of these data from the victim's perspective would provide a much clearer picture of these dynamics.

Examining the correlational data reveals some potentially interesting patterns. Most apparent is that the intimidation factor (a category that includes attempting to manipulate or coerce the other, trying to scare the other, and leaving or taking objects from the other) yielded the highest frequency of consistently significant and strong correlates with all predictors. However, other bivariate relationships also prove interesting. It could be construed that feelings such as hurt and frustration are milder expressions of feelings like depression and anger, respectively. Meanwhile, anger and depression seem to have a stronger affect associated with them. Accordingly, one might anticipate that fewer negative reactions would be correlated with milder behaviors, while stronger reactions would be correlated with more aggressive behaviors. For both men and women, it appears that once intimidation tactics are utilized, strong reactions such as anger and depression prove to be stronger correlates of aggression than frustration or hurt.

Similar patterns occur for the responses to the love styles measures. Eros correlates more strongly with approach and surveillance tactics, while mania has equivalent or smaller predictive abilities for those behaviors. When the behaviors become intimidating or violent, though, mania becomes a stronger predictor for both men and women. This indicates that individuals experiencing unrequited love are likely to both idealize and obsess over their love interest. For example, s/he may be thinking about him/her constantly (e.g., answer affirmatively to mania item; "My thoughts were constantly on my love interest") in the best of lights (e.g., answer affirmatively to the eros item; "For me, my love interest was the perfect romantic partner"). When behaviors turn violent, however, only the obsession remains. Gone is the rose-colored view and attraction to an exciting new love interest, remaining is the despair, desperation, jealousy, and loss of control that characterize the mania scale.

Meanwhile, men and women appear to differ when examining other patterns of predictors of more aggressive tactics. For women, expressions of vengeance (e.g., answering positively to items such as "I feel vengeful," "I feel spiteful," or "I want to hurt him/her like he/she had hurt me"), feelings that one had been deceived, and exhibiting negativeness (e.g., "I would not take 'no' for an answer," see Malamuth & Brown, 1994) correlate moderately to strongly with intimidation, harming self, mild aggression, and violent behaviors. For men, these feelings are less correlated with more obviously aggressive tactics, and curiously prove to be correlated with approach, surveillance, and intimidation tactics. Perhaps men are successful at utilizing these apparently less aggressive behaviors to cause fear in their love interests and get revenge for the rejection and perceived deception, while not having to resort to overtly violent tactics to achieve the desired result. While women may utilize these more extreme "courtship" tactics to express vengeance, even that doesn't result in their perceiving that their male rejecter fears them. Failing to perceive fear on the part of her male love interest may be due to a man not feeling threatened by a woman, no matter what she does. Alternately, she may not believe that she could cause fear in a male target. Whatever the case, it appears that men use overt courtship tactics when pursuing a love interest, and covert aggression when trying to get back at their love interest. Yet, women are more likely to utilize less obvious courtship tactics when seeking a relationship, but use blatant violence when seeking revenge.

Different results for men and women were also revealed with regard to the Burt (1980) Adversarial Sexual Beliefs scale. The Burt scale (with and without the revised items) did not predict much for women. Although, as might be expected, women had a lower rate of endorsement of the beliefs overall. For men, however, these items correlated with approach, surveillance, and intimidation tactics. While endorsement of these adversarial beliefs was expected to be associated with more extreme tactics, it failed to correlate with physically violent behavior. Recall that it was believed that the Burt scale was similar to the construct of the suspicion schema which states that men question the validity of women's claims that they are uninterested in a relationship. This may enable men to ignore a rejection as invalid, and continue to convince themselves that the relationship may still have a chance. While under this impression, the pursuer will continue to try what he perceives as his nonviolent courtship tactics. Violent behavior, meanwhile, seems reserved for vengeance and a desire to hurt the love interest for the rejection. Correlations with romantic aspirations (as indicated by the eros scale) are absent, as are correlations with the statement "I just wouldn't take no for an answer." When physical violence comes into play, the pursuer seems no longer interested in establishing a relationship—rather he has most likely been forced to acknowledge the rejection, thus can no longer wear the blinders provided by the endorsement of beliefs that women are not truthful about their romantic interests. The Burt scale, believed to be related to this concept, is thus no longer correlated with behavior that involves an acknowledgment of rejection.

One of the questions targeted by this article was when does courtship go too far? The answer that many legal statutes provide is that pursuit behaviors cross a line whenever the target of the pursuit begins to feel fear for his or her physical safety (Tjaden & Thoennes, 1997). However, the majority of states do not depend on this definition, and as revealed by Tjaden, Thoennes, and Allison (this volume), even this victim-dependent definition fails to encompass all persons who feel they have been subjected to stalking. It could be that these individuals are experiencing behaviors that fall short of "true stalking" such as prestalking (Emerson et al., 1998) or obsessional relational intrusion

(Cupach & Spitzberg, 1998), but there is no terminology other than "stalking" to use. Or it could be that stalking has other defining variables aside from the level of victim fear. Asking the perpetrators when they believe they went too far doesn't reveal a great deal. As Baumeister and coworkers (1993) found, few pursuers admitted to the use of unscrupulous tactics in their courtship that might identify them as having gone over the line in seeking a relationship. Similarly, in our study, those who utilized more violent tactics were significantly less likely than individuals who had used more "normal" maneuvers, such as approach or surveillance, to report they had "gone too far." Accordingly, self-reported assessments of having gone too far are not likely to be informative of what was really going too far, as those individuals most likely to have stalked their love interests are those least likely to recognize that these tactics are unacceptable.

If using victim or perpetrator perspectives to determine what is stalking and what is courtship, the remaining option is to examine the types of behaviors and assess their severity and intent. Early in the introduction the theory of a possible continuum of stalking behaviors was raised. Factor analyses revealed a clustering of types of behaviors. These types of behaviors could form a continuum ranging from approach tactics to violent behaviors. However, one does not necessarily proceed from approach to surveillance to intimidation and so forth. In fact, women appear more likely to use surveillance tactics, thus may use surveillance first, and may not ever use approach behaviors. Further, it is quite conceivable that men may use surveillance behaviors before approaching a love interest so that they might find out information about her. Consequently, it might be better to view these behaviors as a typology of stalking-related behaviors rather than a continuum that implies a progression.

At this time, surveillance-type behaviors are included in the majority of state stalking statutes. Only three states include intimidation. However, of all the behavioral factors, intimidating behaviors show the highest number of predictors and the strongest correlations with all of the scales included. It is also here that more benign and common reactions to rejection appear to become noticeably more negative. Further, it is at this point that fear, as expressed by the love interest, has the strongest correlation with intimidation for both men and women. Finally, simply by examining the frequencies of the different behaviors, some (28%-30%) use intimidation, but behavioral frequencies quickly decrease after that for the more obviously violent behaviors. Thus, the majority of individuals draw the line before using intimidating tactics, before courtship becomes fear-inducing (prestalking). After that, others stop with intimidation (stalking behavior). A few move on to extreme violence that while having elements of stalking, takes on a different view in the eyes of the law (e.g., individuals committing these behaviors are more likely to be charged with assault).

The interpretations provided here would be better supported with further research, preferably with a larger sample of men and in an experimental, nonself-report context. Moving beyond a convenience sample of University of Pittsburgh students would also be critical. Do similar patterns exist for older adults and for those not in college? Further study is needed to examine the potential generalizability of these findings. In general, more research is needed on the topics of courtship and unrequited love to further develop our understanding of interpersonal aggression. Examining violence and correlates of violence at the courtship level is beneficial in that it might provide the knowledge to prevent violence before the relationship attains advanced levels of intimacy. Further, while research examining victim perceptions is important, future research should also address the aggressor. Certainly, it is likely that the reports of the pursuers are not going to accurately reflect the degree to which the targets of the pursuers felt violated by the pursuit. However, it is with the pursuer that perceptions of acceptable and unacceptable behavior needs to be delineated and changed, because it is the pursuer who should be prevented from crossing the line in a romantic pursuit.

NOTES

1. The large number of female participants is merely reflective of the present enrollment in Introduction to Psychology, which is predominantly female.

2. Same-sex relationships were excluded because there were far too few ($n = 6$) of them to effectively examine possible stalking behaviors within homosexual courtship. Similarly, persons over the age of 26 were few in number. They were omitted because we felt their experiences might differ from the majority of the group.

ACKNOWLEDGMENTS

The authors would like to thank Kristin Anderson at Antioch College, Keith Davis at the University of South Carolina and Eugene Borgida and Marti Gonzales at the University of Minnesota for their helpful suggestions on an earlier version of this article.

REFERENCES

Anderson, K. J., & Accomando, C. (1999). Madcap misogyny and romanticized victim-blaming: Discourses of stalking in a summer blockbuster. *Women & Language, 22,* 24–28.

Anderson, S. C. (1993). Anti-stalking laws: Will they curb the erotomaniac's obsessive pursuit? *Law & Psychology Review, 17,* 171–191.

Aron, A., Aron., E. N., & Allen, J. (1998). Motivations for unreciprocated love. *Personality and Social Psychology Bulletin, 24,* 787–796.

Baumeister, R. F., Wotman, S. R., & Stillwell, A. M. (1993). Unrequited love: On heartbreak, anger, guilt, scriptlessness and humiliation. *Journal of Personality and Social Psychology, 64,* 377–94.

Bratslavsky, E., Baumeister, R. F., & Sommer, K. L. (1998). To love or be loved in vain: The trials and tribulations of unrequited love. In B. H. Spitzberg & W. R. Cupach (Eds.), *The dark side of close relationships* (pp. 307–326). Mahwah, NJ: Lawrence Erlbaum.

Bui, K. V. T., Raven, B. H., & Schwarzwald, J. (1994). Influence strategies in dating relationships: The effects of relationship satisfaction, gender and perspective. *Journal of Social Behavior and Personality, 9,* 429–442.

Burt, M. R. (1980). Cultural myths and supports for rape. *Journal of Personality and Social Psychology, 38,* 217–30.

Coleman, F. L. (1997). Stalking behavior and the cycle of domestic violence. *Journal of Interpersonal Violence, 12,* 420–432.

Cupach W. R., & Spitzberg, B. H. (1998). Obsessive relational intrusion and stalking. In B. H. Spitzberg & W. R. Cupach (Eds.), *The dark side of close relationships* (pp. 307–326). Mahwah, NJ: Lawrence Erlbaum.

de Becker, G. (1997). *The gift of fear.* Boston: Little, Brown & Company.

de Weerth, C., & Kalma, A. (1995). Gender differences in awareness of courtship initiation tactics. *Sex Roles, 32*(11–12), 717–734.

Dziegielewski, S. F., & Roberts, A. R. (1995). Stalking victims and survivors. In A. R. Roberts (Ed.), *Crisis intervention & time-limited cognitive treatment* (pp. 73–90). Thousand Oaks, CA: Sage Publications.

Emerson, R. M., Ferris, K. O., & Gardner, C. B. (1998). On being stalked. *Social Problems, 45,* 289–314.

Grote, N. K., & Frieze, I. H. (1994). The measurement of friendship-based love in intimate relationships. *Personal Relationships, 1,* 275–300.

Hall, D. M. (1998). The victims of stalking. In J. R. Meloy (Ed.), *The psychology of stalking* (pp. 115–136). San Diego, CA: Academic Press.

Hatfield, E. & Sprecher, S. (1986). Measuring passionate love. *Journal of Adolescence, 9,* 383–410.

Kurt, J. L. (1995). Stalking as a variant of domestic violence. *Bulletin of the Academy of Psychiatry and the Law, 23,* 219–223.

Lee, J. A. (1973). *The colors of Love.* Don Mills, Ontario, Canada: New Press.

Lingg, R. A. (1993). Stopping stalkers: A critical examination of anti-stalking statutes. *St. John's Law Review, 67,* 347–381.

Lloyd-Goldstein, R. (1998). De Clerambault on-line: A survey of erotomania and stalking from the old world to the world wide web. In J. R. Meloy (Ed.), *The psychology of stalking* (pp. 193–212). San Diego, CA: Academic Press.

Lowney, K. S., & Best, J. (1995). Stalking strangers and lovers: Changing media typifications of a new crime problem. In J. Best (Ed.), *Images of issues* (pp. 33–55). New York: Walter de Gruyte, Inc.

Malamuth, N. M., & Brown, L. M. (1994). Sexually aggressive men's perceptions of women's communications: Testing three explanations. *Journal of Personality and Social Psychology, 67,* 699–712.

Meloy, J. R. (1989). Unrequited love and the wish to kill: Diagnosis and treatment of borderline erotomania. *Bulletin of the Menninger Clinic, 53,* 477–492.

Meloy, J. R. (1997). A Rorschach case study of stalking: "All I wanted was to love you. . . . " In J. R. Meloy, M. W. Acklin, C. B. Gacono, & J. F. Murray (Eds.), *Contemporary Rorschach interpretation* (177–189). Mahwah, NJ: Lawrence Erlbaum Associates, Inc.

Meloy, J. R. (1998). *The psychology of stalking.* San Diego, CA: Academic Press.

Mullen, P. E., Pathé, M, Purcell, R., & Stuart, G. W. (1999). Study of stalkers. *The American Journal of Psychiatry, 156,* 1244–1249.

Pathé, M., & Mullen, P. E. (1997). The impact of stalkers on their victims. *British Journal of Psychiatry, 170,* 12–17.

Patton, E. A. (1994). Stalking laws: In pursuit of a remedy. *Rutgers Law Journal, 25,* 465–515.

Ryan, K. M., Frieze, I. H., & Sinclair, H. C. (1999). Physical violence in dating relationships. In M. A. Paludi (Ed.), *The psychology of sexual victimization: A handbook* (pp. 33–54). Westport, CT: Greenwood Publishing.

Saunders, R. (1998). The legal perspective on stalking. In L. E. Walker & J. R. Meloy (Eds.), *The psychology of stalking* (pp. 25–49). San Diego, CA: Academic Press.

Schaum, M., & Parrish, K. (1995). *Stalked: Breaking the silence on the crime of stalking in America.* New York: Pocket Books.

Simpson, J. A., Gangestad, S. W., Christensen, P. N., & Leck, K. (1999). Fluctuating asymmetry, sociosexualtiy and intrasexual competitive tactics. *Journal of Personality and Social Psychology, 76,* 159–172.

Sternberg, R. L. (1986). A triangle theory of love. *Psychological Review, 93,* 119–135.

Tjaden, P., & Thoennes, N. (1997, July). *Stalking in America: Findings from the National Violence Against Women survey.* Washington, DC: National Institute for Justice and the Center for Policy Research report.

Walker, L. E., & Meloy, J. R. (1998). Stalking and domestic violence. In J. R. Meloy (Ed.), *The psychology of stalking* (pp. 140–164). San Diego, CA: Academic Press.

Wallace, H., & Kelly, K. (1995). Stalking and restraining orders: A legal and psychological perspective. *Journal of Crime and Justice, 18,* 99–111.

Wright, J. A., Burgess, A. G., Burgess, A. W., Laszlo, A. T., McCrary, G. O., & Douglas, J. E. (1996). A typology of interpersonal stalking. *Journal of Interpersonal Violence, 11,* 487–502.

Zona, M. A., Palarea, R. E., & Lane, J. C. (1998). Psychiatric diagnosis and the offender-victim typology of stalking. In J. R. Meloy (Ed.), *The psychology of stalking* (pp. 70–84). San Diego, CA: Academic Press.

Zona, M. A., Sharma, K. K., & Lane, J. (1993). A comparative study of erotomanic and obsessional subjects in a forensic sample. *Journal of Forensic Sciences, 38,* 894–903.

10

Breaking Up is Hard To Do: Unwanted Pursuit Behaviors Following the Dissolution of a Romantic Relationship

Jennifer Langhinrichsen-Rohling, Russell E. Palarea, Jennifer Cohen, and Martin L. Rohling

Unwanted pursuit behaviors (UPB), broadly defined, include activities that constitute ongoing and unwanted pursuit of a romantic relationship between individuals who are not currently involved in a consensual romantic relationship with each other. Theoretically, UPBs are thought to be most likely to occur at two different points in the developmental trajectory of a romantic relationship (i.e., prior to starting a consensual romantic relationship and after a consensual relationship has been terminated). Unwanted pursuit behaviors that occur prior to a consensual relationship can be conducted by strangers or acquaintances to the victim. UPBs that occur after the breakup of a romantic relationship are, by definition, perpetrated by individuals who previously had a consensual romantic relationship with the victim.

Unwanted pursuit behaviors are expected to vary in severity (e.g., from a hang-up call to threatening behavior and stalking). They are also expected to vary in frequency and in impact. In fact, a priori, it is expected that some unwanted pursuit behaviors will be viewed as having a positive impact. For example, they may serve as precursors to a consensual romantic relationship, they may function to restore a romantic relationship in which a breakup has occurred, or they may help move a relationship that has been romantic back to a platonic relationship. Psychologically, these behaviors may also help some individuals resolve their feelings of loss and grief after an important romantic relationship has ended.

Unwanted pursuit behaviors are conceptually similar to obsessive relational intrusion (ORI) behaviors as described by Cupach and Spitzberg (1998). ORIs were defined as repeated and unwanted pursuit and invasion of one's sense of physical and symbolic privacy by another person, either stranger or acquaintance, who desires and/or presumes an intimate relationship with the victim. ORIs typically constitute a violation of the victim's privacy and right to autonomy. Like unwanted pursuit behaviors, obsessive relational intrusion acts are thought to vary in severity from frequent calls for a date to surreptitious observation, stalking, and/or assault (Spitzberg & Rhea, 1999). Also similarly, the most severe end of the ORI continuum was defined as repeated acts of serious unwanted pursuit that are perceived as threatening and cause the victim to fear for her or his safety (i.e., intimate relationship stalking).

Cupach and Spitzberg (1998) did not as clearly articulate the other end of the ORI continuum. In passing, they suggested that it might be erroneous to assume that milder activities such as unwanted phone calls and unwanted letters/notes comprise this pole, because even these relatively "mild" forms of intrusion can result in annoyance, fear, stress, depression, and anxiety on the part of the victim. Consistent with this line of reasoning, it may not be the severity of a specific act that is important, but rather the impact that the act has on the victim. Consequently, it is currently proposed that the other end of the unwanted pursuit behavior continuum comprise any unwanted pursuit behaviors that occur out of the victim's awareness. Next are unwanted pursuit behaviors that are noticed but perceived as non-threatening and non-coercive by the victim. The furthest end of the UPB continuum would be unwanted pursuit behaviors that have a positive impact on the recipient (e.g., they helped ex-partners to reunite).

Although unwanted pursuit behaviors can occur both at the beginning and after the end of a romantic relationship, focusing on UPBs that occur after an intimate relationship has terminated seems particularly important because of the potential for two quite different outcomes for the perpetrator:

1. relationship reconciliation, or
2. stalking.

Consequently, it is proposed that researching the occurrence, frequency, and perceived impact of the full range of unwanted pursuit behaviors that occur postrelationship dissolution will be important. This research is likely to facilitate our understanding of potential relationship repair mechanisms, while also aiding prevention and intervention efforts for such coercive relationship behaviors as stalking.

Since literature on stalking and unwanted pursuit is still relatively new, there are few studies that compare reports obtained by individuals who are perpetrators of unwanted pursuit behaviors with reports obtained by individuals who are victims of unwanted pursuit behaviors (as an exception, see Fremouw, Westrup, & Pennypacker, 1997). These comparisons will be important because previous research on related topics (e.g., relationship violence) substantiates that rates of negative relationship behaviors vary by informant (Kaufman, Jones, Stieglitz, Vitulano, & Mannarino, 1994). For example, social desirability may explain the low rates of stalking reported by perpetrators in comparison to rates reported by victims (Fremouw et al., 1997). To further our understanding of unwanted pursuit behaviors, the current study was designed to obtain reports from both victims and perpetrators of unwanted pursuit behaviors. Specifically, individuals who may have been pursued by an ex-partner after they had initiated the breakup of their romantic relationship (relationship dissolvers) were compared with reports from individuals who may have pursued an ex-partner after they had broken up (breakup sufferers).

Because researchers are still arguing the parameters, definitions, and best nomenclature to use with this phenomenon, and the literature has only recently advanced from anecdotal to empirically descriptive (Spitzberg, Nicastro, & Cousins, 1998), few studies have been conducted to identify predictors of unwanted pursuit behaviors. In regard to the most severe unwanted pursuit behavior (i.e., stalking), existing research highlights the importance of both individual (gender, presence of mental disturbance, violent tendencies) and relationship factors (history of relationship violence, history of consensual involvement). Relationship factors clearly take on increased importance when a consensual intimate relationship has previously existed. In fact, theorists have proposed that intimate relationship stalkers may be more motivated by their need to continue or reestablish their faltering relationship rather than by their overall level of psychopathology (Dziegielewski & Roberts, 1995; Hendricks & Spillane, 1993).

Consistent with this supposition, Cupach and Spitzberg (1998) postulated that many types of unwanted pursuit behaviors directed toward a former intimate partner might be rooted in the darker aspects of the relationship, such as the need to control or manipulate one's partner. The available research supports their assertion. For example, Coleman (1997) recruited 141 female subjects from undergraduate psychology classes. Each was given a relationship questionnaire about the last person with whom they had had an intimate relationship. As hypothesized, Coleman found that victims reported an association between extreme unwanted pursuit behaviors, such as stalking, and a history of verbal and physical violence in the preexisting dating relationship. The association between a history of domestic violence and stalking in marital relationships has also been demonstrated empirically (Burgess et al., 1997).

The primary purpose of the current study was to determine the prevalence and predictors of unwanted pursuit behaviors in the dating relationships of college students. Consistent with previous work, participating individuals in the current study were required to have been involved in an intimate relationship that had terminated, as this was expected to be a time when a larger number of unwanted pursuit behaviors would occur. In contrast to some previous work (e.g., Coleman, 1997), data were gathered from both male and female participants. Previous work with similar populations has indicated that men may be more likely to stalk than women (Fremouw et al., 1997). However, related research that has described the prevalence and predictors of relationship violence has found equivalent prevalence rates of dating violence perpetration in both men and women (e.g., Arias, Samios, & O'Leary, 1987). Studies of stalking and obsessive relational intrusion in college students also reported that males and females were not differentially victimized (Spitzberg et al., 1998). Moreover, although few gender differences in the prevalence of stalking behaviors were reported in the National Violence Against Women survey, women were found to be more afraid and distressed by these behaviors than men (Tjaden & Thoennes, 1998).

Thus, the initial goal of this study was to describe and compare male and female rates of engagement in unwanted pursuit behaviors, following the dissolution of an intimate relationship, and their effect on the victim. A priori, men were expected to engage in more frequent and more severe acts of unwanted pursuit than were women, and women were expected to report a more negative impact from these behaviors than men.

Second, data were collected from self-reported perpetrators and victims of unwanted pursuit by an ex-partner. Although these individuals were not reporting on the same relationships, comparisons were made to determine if there were differences in frequency, assessments of impact, and predictors as a function of the participant's role in the relationship breakup and in the unwanted pursuit. At the outset, it was hypothesized that victims would report significantly more acts of unwanted pursuit than would perpetrators. Victims were also expected to view the impact of these unwanted behaviors as more negative. It was further hypothesized that victims of unwanted pursuit would relate their pursuit more to their ex-partner's psychopathology than to characteristics of themselves or their relationship. In contrast, it was expected that perpetrators of unwanted pursuits would ascribe their behavior more to characteristics of their failed relationship than to their own psychopathology or tendencies toward violence and jealousy.

Finally, three groups of variables were proposed as potential predictors of unwanted pursuit postrelationship dissolution. First, the nature of the attachment between the ex-partners was expected to predict the level of unwanted pursuit that would occur after the relationship had ended. Attachment refers to the ability to make emotional bonds with others (Bowlby, 1977). Variations on how many types of attachment disturbances exist have been noted in the literature, however, there is general agreement that there is an anxious, insecure (i.e., seeks contact yet manifests anger and resentment about the separation) and an avoidant (i.e., refuses to acknowledge the attachment figure after a separation) attachment style. Attachment disturbances and the degree of emotional engagement have been shown to relate to levels of postrelationship distress (Fine & Sacher, 1997; Simpson, 1990). Similar work conducted with marital batterers has demonstrated that an anxious and insecure and/or preoccupied attachment style is related to the perpetration of violence and jealousy, a negative affect during conflict, following, surveillance, and separation behaviors (Dutton, Saunders, Starzomski, & Bartholomew, 1994; Guerrero, 1998; Holtzworth-Munroe, Stuart, & Hutchinson, 1997). While individual differences in attachment style are thought to be relatively stable, attachment styles are also thought to be somewhat relationship-specific. This is consistent with Bowlby's assertion, that in healthy individuals, attachment schema's are modified with experience (Berscheid, 1994). Thus, both an overall attachment style measure and a partner-specific attachment measure will be utilized as predictors of unwanted pursuit behavior in the current study.

Unwanted pursuit behaviors were also expected to relate to the degree of jealousy, abusiveness, and physical violence that had preexisted in the relationship. In general, jealousy has been shown to motivate individuals to engage in proximity-seeking behavior with their partners (Sharpsteen, 1995). Theoretically, pathological jealousy may predict the occurrence of continuous and unwanted proximity-seeking behaviors and intrusiveness (Dutton, van Ginkel, & Landolt, 1996). Some have even described domestic violence as the "violence of jealousy" (White & Mullen, 1989). Furthermore, relationships that included control, violence, and abusiveness prior to their dissolution may be the most difficult and potentially risky from which to disentangle (Palarea, Zona, Lane, & Langhinrichsen-Rohling, 1999). In keeping with this reasoning, some have suggested that there is a domestic violence subtype of stalker. These individuals may want to reestablish their romantic connection in order to maintain control over their victim and as a continued expression of their ambivalent, jealous, love-hate relationship (Burgess et al., 1997; Dziegielewski & Roberts, 1995).

Finally, it was expected that the type of love style exhibited in the relationship would be a significant predictor of unwanted pursuit. Relationships have been shown to differ in their nature of the expression of love between partners (Hendrick, Hendrick, & Dicke, 1998). In the current study, it was hypothesized that relationship breakups at risk for unwanted pursuit would have had higher levels of possessive and dependent love, more erotic love, higher levels of game-playing love, and lower levels of friendship love than relationship breakups not at risk.

METHOD

Participants

The sample consisted of 282 college students (43.6% male and 56.4% female) who were enrolled in introductory psychology courses at a large public midwestern university. All students participated in this study in partial fulfillment of a research requirement. Prior to the study, all participating students indicated that they had experienced the termination of an important intimate relationship. This relationship must have lasted at least one month to be eligible. The sample consisted of 162 individuals (39.5% males and 60.5% females) who reported that they had initiated the relationship breakup (i.e., relationship dissolvers). These students reported about themselves, their perspective of the relationship, and their ex-partner's behavior following the breakup. The remaining students (n = 120; 49.2% male and 50.8% female) indicated that they had been broken up with (i.e., breakup sufferers). These students reported on themselves, their perspective of their relationship, and their own behavior following the breakup. Relationship dissolvers and breakup sufferers were not reporting on the same relationship. The gender difference in designation as a relationship dissolver or a breakup sufferer was not significant, χ^2 = 2.62, p > .10.

Overall, the sample was predominantly Caucasian (91.8%). The remaining students were Asian American (3.5%), African American (1.4%), Hispanic (1.1%), Native American (.7%) and other (1.4%). There were no significant differences between relationship dissolvers and breakup sufferers on this variable, χ^2 < 1. The mean age at time of breakup was 18.6 years (18.6 years for relationship dissolvers; 18.5 years for breakup sufferers). The modal student was reporting on a relationship that had broken up within the past 12 months. The mean duration of the intimate relationship being reported on was 17.0 months (SD = 14.9 months, ranging from 2 to 72 months). Duration had a multi-modal distribution with peaks at 4, 6, 18, 24, and 36 months. The majority were dating relationships (95.4%) and 3.9% had been engaged. The two married individuals were dropped from all subsequent data analysis. Just over 5% of the sample indicated that they had lived together and 2.5% had a child with their ex-partner. More than 40% of the sample had broken up at least once previous to the breakup they were describing. Relationship dissolvers and breakup sufferers were not found to differ significantly on any of the above demographic variables (p > .10).

Procedure

Informed consent was obtained from all participants. Each consenting participant was then given a two-page questionnaire that consisted of 22 items. These items assessed demographics (e.g., age, gender, ethnicity), as well as relationship characteristics (e.g., the duration of the relationship, the extent of involvement, and how much time had elapsed since the breakup had occurred). Some open-ended questions about their perceptions of how and why the breakup occurred were also included. When participants had completed their responses to this packet, they were instructed to raise their hand. The research coordinator then came to collect the first packet. While picking it up, the coordinator glanced at the participant's response to question 5: "Who initiated the breakup?" A participant's response to this question was used to determine whether the person perceived him-or herself as the initiator or sufferer of the breakup process. Those who indicated that the breakup was mostly or completely initiated by their ex-partner were classified as "breakup sufferers." Those who answered that the breakup was mostly or completely initiated by themselves were classified as "relationship dissolvers." Separate second packets were given to relationship dissolvers and breakup sufferers. The two packets were very similar. For example, each contained the following identical measures (Love Attitudes Scale, Conflict Tactics Scale, and the Attachment measure). All other measures in the packet, described below, differed in one way. In the relationship dissolvers' packet, participants were reporting on their ex-partner's behavior in the relationship; in the breakup sufferers' packet, participants reported on their own behavior. All participants were given 60 minutes to complete the self-report surveys. Only identification numbers were used to link information from packet 1 to packet 2. At the conclusion of the study, all participants were given a debriefing sheet that included a list of available mental health resources for their consideration.

MEASURES

Determining the Occurrence of Stalking and Pursuit Behaviors

UNWANTED PURSUIT BEHAVIOR INVENTORY

The Unwanted Pursuit Behavior Inventory (UPBI; Palarea & Langhinrichsen-Rohling, 1998) is a 26–item instrument that assesses the presence, frequency, impact, and motivations underlying a full range of unwanted pursuit behaviors. Items from the UPBI are shown in Table 10.1. A priori, mild acts were defined as items 1–13. Severe acts included items 14–26. All items on the UPBI were generated via a review of the empirical liter-

Table 10.1 Percent of Breakup Relationship Dissolvers ($n = 160$) and Breakup Sufferers ($n = 120$) Experiencing or Perpetrating Pursuit Behaviors

	Occurrence			Perceived Response		
	Relationship Dissolvers	Breakup Sufferers		Relationship Dissolvers	Breakup Sufferers	
Pursuit Behavior	%	%	χ^2	% Neg	% Neg	χ^2
1. Unwanted Phone Message	25.0	55.0	26.2***	83.9	18.0	37.1***
2. Unwanted Letters/Gifts	18.8	44.2	21.2***	62.5	15.6	15.9***
3. Unwanted Phone Calls	36.3	77.5	47.0***	69.1	9.4	53.9***
4. Unwanted E-mail/Chat	0.0	2.5	4.0$^{p=.08}$	00.0	33.3	1.3*
5. In Person Conversation	30.6	73.3	50.0***	48.8	8.9	25.2***
6. In Person Gifts	13.1	30.0	12.0***	63.2	6.1	20.0***
7. Ask Friends About You	56.3	53.8	< 1	60.0	42.2	3.1$^{p=.08}$
8. Family Contact	19.4	19.2	< 1	70.0	16.7	10.9***
9. Show Up at Places	39.6	33.3	1.2	56.3	26.9	5.8*
10. Efforts to Run Into You	20.1	25.0	< 1	64.0	0.0	16.0***
11. Home Visits	29.4	22.5	1.7	29.3	21.8	< 1
12. School/Work Visits	20.8	13.3	2.6	36.7	0.0	6.4*
13. Wait Outside School	13.1	7.5	2.3	44.4	0.0	4.0*
14. Following	6.9	2.5	2.8$^{p=.09}$	—	—	
15. Making Vague Threats	8.8	.8	8.5**	—	—	
16. Threaten Info Release	1.9	2.5	< 1	—	—	
17. Threaten to Harm Ex	1.3	0.0	1.5	—	—	
18. Threaten Pets/Family	1.9	0.8	< 1	—	—	
19. Threaten With a Weapon	0.0	0.0	< 1	—	—	
20. Release Harmful Info	1.9	0.8	< 1	—	—	
21. Steal Items	3.1	0.0	3.8*	—	—	
22. Damage Property	3.1	0.8	1.7	—	—	
23. Harm Family/Pet	0.0	0.0	< 1	—	—	
24. Injure	2.5	0.0	3.0$^{p=.08}$	—	—	
25. Kidnap/Hold Against Will	1.3	0.0	1.5	—	—	
26. Force Sex After Breakup	1.9	0.0	< 1	—	—	
1. Physical Protection Sought	3.2	4.2	< 1			
2. Sought Help From Police	1.3	0.0	1.5			
3. Current Contact Occurring	51.3	35.6	6.6**			
4. Mean # of UPB Acts	3.57	4.69	$F(1, 278) = 9.68$**			
5. Mean UPB Severity Index	3.88	1.73	$F(1, 274) = 8.89$**			

Note. Negative response was not assessed for the most severe pursuit behaviors.
*$p < .05$. **$p < .01$. ***$p < .001$.

ature and an assessment of the behaviors engaged in by stalkers who had been investigated by the Los Angeles Police Department's Threat Management Unit. The coefficient alpha for this scale in the current sample was .81. Relationship dissolvers filled out the UPBI about their victimization from their ex-partner. In contrast, breakup sufferers reported about their perpetration of unwanted pursuit behavior after their breakup. Unwanted pursuit behavior total scores were then created by summing the number of different acts endorsed by each individual.

A second total score was also created: the Unwanted Pursuit Behavior Severity Index. To compute this index, only unwanted pursuit behaviors that were reported to have a negative impact on the recipient were included. Negative-impact UPBs were then weighted by reports of frequency. In addition, all the acts that were severe (items 14–26) were double-weighted. The coefficient alpha for the severity index was .82 in the current sample.

Predictors

INDIVIDUAL ATTACHMENT

Participants' general attachment style was measured with the 36–item measure entitled Experiences in Close Relationships (Brennan, Clark, & Shaver, 1998). Previous factor analysis had revealed that the measure is composed of two 18–item subscales, Avoidance and Anxiety. Both of these subscales have been shown to have good internal consistency; both had coefficient alphas of .90 in the current sample. Relationship dissolvers and breakup sufferers reported on their own anxious and avoidant attachment style in relationships. Breakup sufferers' attachment anxiety was expected to predict unwanted pursuit behavior perpetration, while relationship dissolvers' attachment avoidance was expected to predict pursuit victimization.

SPOUSE-SPECIFIC DEPENDENCY

The spouse-specific dependency scale (SSDS; Rathus & O'Leary, 1997) is a 24–item measure that was designed to measure attachment in reference to a particular partner and relationship. The measure consists of three 8–item subscales. In the current study, the SSDS was adapted to address ex-partners rather than spouses. The three subscales represent anxious attachment, exclusive dependency, and emotional dependency. Relationship dissolvers reported on their ex-partners' dependency. Breakup sufferers reported on their own dependency. Coefficient alphas for the three subscales ranged from .84 to .89 in a college student sample.

Relationship Characteristics

TYPE OF LOVE

The relationship-specific, 42–item, Love Attitudes Scale-Short Form (LAS; Hendrick, Hendrick, & Dicke, 1998) was used to measure the degree to which several different types of love styles were present in the terminated relationship. The love styles, originally described by Lee (1973), that were included in the current study are: Eros (passionate love), Ludus (game-playing love), Storge (friendship love), and Mania (possessive, dependent love). Each style is assessed with 7 items. The alpha coefficients for the love styles ranged from .74 to .84, indicating reasonable internal consistency (Hendrick & Hendrick, 1990). Both relationship dissolvers and breakup sufferers reported on the love styles that were present in their failed relationship.

THE REVISED CONFLICT TACTICS SCALE (CTS2)

The CTS2 was used to assess the occurrence of physical and emotional abuse in the intimate relationship. Preliminary psychometric studies of the CTS2 have been conducted on college students. Internal consistency of the CTS2 scales was shown to range from .79 to .95 in this population (Straus, Hamby, Boney-McCoy, & Sugarman, 1996). In the current sample, the coefficient alpha for the victimization items was .88. The coefficient alpha for the perpetration items was .78. Both relationship dissolvers and breakup sufferers reported on their perpetration and victimization of psychological and physical abuse in their relationships. Consistent with previous research, individuals were assigned to categories based on the highest level of abuse reported. Thus, scores on the abuse indices were 0 (no abuse), 1 (psychological abuse only), 2 (at least one act of mild physical abuse), to 3 (at least one act of severe physical abuse).

JEALOUSY

Jealousy was assessed with the Interpersonal Jealousy Scale (IJS; Mathes, 1992; Mathes, Phillips, Skowran, & Dick, 1982; Mathes & Severa, 1981).

This scale consists of 26 items that follow a hypothetical format. Relationship dissolvers reported on their ex-partners' jealousy. Breakup sufferers reported on their own experience of jealousy in the relationship. The coefficient alpha for this scale was .91 in the current sample.

RESULTS

Prevalence of Pursuit Behaviors

The obtained results revealed that unwanted pursuit behaviors are common following the termination of college student's dating relationships. For example, 119 of 120 breakup sufferers (99.2%) indicated perpetrating at least one unwanted activity assessed by the Unwanted Pursuit Behavior Inventory. As presented in Table 10.1, the most frequently reported unwanted pursuit activities were engaging in unwanted phone calls (77.5%) and unsolicited in-person conversations (73.3%). Six of the breakup sufferers (5%) reported perpetrating at least one unwanted pursuit act that included following, threatening, and/or injuring their ex-partner and/or their ex-partners' friends, pets, or family members. However, when only unwanted pursuit behaviors that were thought to result in a negative response from the ex-partner were considered, just 27.5% of breakup sufferers indicated engagement in unwanted pursuit behavior.

Contrary to expectation, there were no gender differences in the total Unwanted Pursuit Behavior scores of breakup sufferers ($F < 1$). Furthermore, item-analysis of the UPBI revealed that there were few gender differences in breakup sufferers' endorsements of UPBI items. Specifically, males were more likely than females to indicate that they had made in-person contacts (32.2% versus 13.1%), such as unwanted home visits to their ex-partner, χ^2 (1) = 6.27, $p < .05$, and waiting for their ex-partner after school (males: 13.6% versus females: 1.6%), χ^2 (1) = 6.14, $p < .05$. In contrast, there was a trend for females to report leaving more unwanted phone messages than males, χ^2 (1) = 2.67, $p = .07$.

When considering the reports of relationship dissolvers, 88.9% reported that their ex-partner had engaged in at least one unwanted pursuit behavior. As shown in Table 10.1, the most common acts experienced were having your ex-partner show up at places unexpectedly (39.6%), receiving an unwanted phone call (36.3%) and having an ex-partner ask friends about you (56.3%).

Contrary to expectation, there were no gender differences in the mean number of unwanted pursuit behaviors experienced by relationship dissolvers, $t(155) = -1.16$, $p > .10$. Furthermore, chi-square analyses revealed only one significant gender difference in relationship dissolvers' reports of unwanted pursuit behavior experiences. Consistent with expectation, females (12.5%) were more likely than males (3.1%) to report that their ex-partner had threatened them, $\chi^2 (1) = 4.23$, $p < .05$.

Overall, significant differences emerged in the occurrence reports of breakup sufferers compared to relationship dissolvers, as shown in Table 10.1. By self-report, breakup sufferers made significantly more unwanted phone calls, left more unwanted phone messages and hang-up calls, and dropped off more unwanted gifts and letters than relationship dissolvers indicated that they had experienced from their ex-partners. Breakup sufferers also indicated that they had more unwanted in-person conversations with their ex-partners and gave more in-person gifts than did relationship dissolvers. However, as the unwanted pursuit behaviors increased in severity, the reporting differences between groups changed. Specifically, there were trends for relationship dissolvers to report experiencing more threats, stolen items, following, and physical injury from their ex-partners than breakup sufferers admitted to perpetrating.

Relationship dissolvers and breakup sufferers also differed in their reports of their response to the unwanted pursuit behavior. In general, as shown in Table 10.1, relationship dissolvers experienced contact by their ex-partner as substantially more negative than breakup sufferers perceived their contact to be. For example, 83.9% of the relationship dissolvers who were left an unwanted phone message indicated that their response was negative; whereas only 18.0% of breakup sufferers perceived their unwanted phone messages as having a negative impact. Likewise, 62.5% of relationship dissolvers indicated that receiving an unwanted letter or gift from their ex-partner was negative; while only 15.6% of the breakup sufferers reported that their gift giving elicited a negative response from their ex-partner. Some gender differences in impact ratings were not assessed because of the small sample size for many of these analyses.

For both groups, two different summary scores were derived from the UPBI. The UPBI total score was a count of the number of different unwanted pursuit behaviors that were reported. Contrary to hypothesis, breakup sufferers reported perpetrating more total UPBI acts ($M = 4.69$) than relationship dissolvers reported experiencing ($M = 3.57$),

$F(1, 278) = 9.68$, $p < .01$. The second summary score was a derived severity index that included only acts with a perceived negative response. These acts were then weighted by frequency of occurrence. Furthermore, UPBI acts 15–26 were double-weighted to reflect the severity of the unwanted behavior being reported. When mean UPBI severity indices were compared between relationship dissolvers and breakup sufferers, as anticipated, relationship dissolvers reported significantly more victimization ($M = 3.88$) than breakup sufferers reported perpetrating ($M = 1.73$), $F(1, 274) = 8.89$, $p < .01$. Correlations between the UPBI total score and the UPBI derived index were ascertained for relationship dissolvers and breakup sufferers. For relationship dissolvers, the two victimization scores were very similar, $r = .79$, $p < .001$, $n = 156$. In contrast, breakup sufferers revealed a smaller correlation between the indices, $r = .26$, $p < .01$, $n = 120$.

Correlations Among the Predictors Variables

For both relationship dissolvers and breakup sufferers, the correlations among the predictor variables are shown in Table 10.2. For both

Table 10.2 Correlations Among the Predictor Variables for Relationship Dissolvers and Breakup Sufferers

Relationship Dissolvers ($n = 160$) Breakup Sufferers ($n = 120$) Variables	1	2	3	4	5	6	7	8	9	10	11
1. SSDS-Narrow	—	.46*	.49*	−.14	.04	.26*	−.17	−.11	.14	.19	.42*
2. SSIDS-Nuture	.30*	—	.38*	−.14	.09	.12	−.04	.01	.10	.23*	.41*
3. SSIDS-Insecure	.16	.25*	—	.11	−.10	.32*	−.18*	.04	.11	.24*	.61*
4. ECR-Attach	.11	.29*	.51*	—	.09	−.07	.05	.50*	.12	.10	−.07
5. Passionate	.23	.38*	−.15	.08	—	−.22*	.15	.31	.10	.05	−.06
6. Game-Playing	−.06	−.19	−.00	.04	−.16	—	−.17	−.26	−.07	−.03	.22*
7. Friendship	.01	.06	−.30*	−.24	.20	−.00	—	.04	−.06	−.17	−.30
8. Possessive	.26*	.53*	.34*	.21	.34*	−.13	.10	—	.26*	.25*	.07
9. Level of Perp	.12	.31*	.07	.17	.16	.03	.01	.10	—	.58*	.12
10. Level of Victim	.19	.34*	.19	.17	.19	.06	−.14	.21	.67*	—	.34*
11. Jealousy	.32*	.41	.59*	.53*	.18	.02	−.22	.42	.11	.18	—

Note. *Denotes correlations that are significant at the $p < .01$ level. N's vary slightly across analyses due to missing data. Correlations for Relationship Dissolvers ($n = 160$) are above the diagnoal and correlations for Breakup Sufferers ($n = 120$) are below the diagonal.

relationship dissolvers and breakup sufferers, generally low to moderate correlations were obtained between the predictor variables. Therefore, on the basis of theory and empirical data, three groups of predictor variables were retained for the regression analyses. The first group consisted of the four attachment measures. The second group included the four love types. The third group consisted of the level of violence measures and the jealousy scale.

Predicting Relationship Dissolvers' Reports of Pursuit-Behavior Victimization

Three separate regression analyses were conducted with data obtained from relationship dissolvers. In the first regression analysis, the attachment measures were used to predict total unwanted pursuit behavior victimization scores. In the second analysis, the love styles were used to predict UPBI total victimization scores. In the third analysis, the relationship violence victimization and perpetration indices and the jealousy measure were used to predict UPBI total victimization scores. In all three regression analyses, all predictors were entered simultaneously into the regression equation.

As shown in Table 10.3, as hypothesized, the attachment measures

Table 10.3 Summary of Regression Analyses to Predict Unwanted Pursuit Behaviors Experienced by Relationship Dissolvers ($N = 160$)

Variable	B	SE B	Beta	t	R	R^2	F	df	Sig.
Predicted: Total # Unwanted, Pursuit Behaviors					.37	.14	5.98	4,150	***
Ex's Narrow Focus	.00	.04	.02	< 1					
Ex's Support Seek	.00	.04	.12	1.41					
Ex's Insecure Attach	.12	.04	.28	3.11					
Dissolver's Avoidance	.00	.01	.04	< 1					
Predicted: Total # Unwanted Pursuit Behaviors					.26	.07	2.69	4,153	*
Passionate Love	.00	.05	–.05	< 1					
Game-Playing Love	.00	.05	–.02	< 1					
Friendship Love	.00	.04	–.19	–2.42*					
Possessive Love	.00	.05	.18	2.09*					
Predicted: Total # Unwanted Pursuit Behaviors					.56	.32	23.45	3,150	***
Perpetration Level	.70	.28	.21	2.46*					
Victimization Level	.83	.28	.26	2.95**					
Jealousy	.00	.01	.28	3.86***					

*$p < .05$. **$p < .01$. ***$p < .001$.

significantly predicted the total number of unwanted pursuit behaviors experienced, $F(4, 150) = 5.98$, $p < .001$, accounting for 14% of the variance. Specifically, more pursuit behaviors were experienced by dissolvers who described their ex-partner as insecurely and anxiously attached in the relationship, $\beta = .28$, $t(1, 150) = 3.11$, $p < .01$.

In the second analysis, type of love style also significantly predicted UPBI total scores, $F(4, 153) = 2.69$, $p < .05$. Seven percent of score variance was accounted for in this analysis. In particular, relationship dissolvers who experienced higher levels of unwanted pursuit were more likely to describe their relationships as characterized by a possessive and dependent love, $\beta = .18$, $t(1, 153) = 2.09$, $p < .05$. Lack of friendship love in the relationship was also significantly related to levels of unwanted pursuit, $\beta = -.19$, $t(1,153) = -2.42$, $p < .05$.

In the third regression analysis, jealousy and abusiveness were also shown to be significant predictors of unwanted pursuit, after the relationship had ended, $F(3, 150) = 23.45$, $p < .001$. All three variables (i.e., dissolver's level of abuse victimization, dissolver's level of abuse perpetration, and reports of ex-partner's jealousy) were retained as independent predictors.

Predicting Breakup Sufferers' Reports of Pursuit Behavior Perpetration

Three same analyses were conducted with self-reports of perpetration obtained from breakup sufferers. As shown in Table 10.4, as hypothesized, the attachment measures significantly predicted the total number of unwanted pursuit behaviors perpetrated, $F(4, 113) = 2.93$, $p < .05$. As a whole, these variables accounted for 9% of the variance in UBPI total scores. Specifically, more unwanted pursuit behaviors were perpetrated by breakup sufferers who described themselves as high on the nuturance-and-support-seeking subscale of the SSDS, $\beta = .23$, $t(1, 113) = 2,39$, $p < .05$.

In the second analysis, types of love style were also significant predictors of UPBI total scores, $F(4, 103) = 4.04$, $p < .05$. Fourteen percent of score variance was accounted for by the four love style predictors. In particular, breakup sufferers who perpetrated unwanted pursuit characterized their ex-relationships as high in possessive and dependent love [$\beta = .31$, $t(1, 103) = 3.18$, $p < .01$] and low in sexual passion [$\beta = -.20$, $t(1, 103) = -2.00$, $p < .05$]. Contrary to expectation, high levels of friendship love was a predictor of unwanted pursuit for breakup sufferers, $\beta = .18$, $t(1, 103) = 1.94$, $p < .05$.

Table 10.4 Summary of Regression Analyses to Predict Unwanted Pursuit Behaviors Perpetrated by Breakup Sufferers ($N = 120$)

Variable	B	SE B	Beta	t	R	R²	F	df	Sig.
Predicted: Total # Unwanted Pursuit Behaviors					.31	.09	2.93	4,113	*
Narrow Focus	.00	.04	.06	< 1					
Support Seek	.00	.04	.23	2.39*					
Insecure/Anx	.00	.04	.15	1.40					
ECR-Anxiety	.00	.02	−.06	< 1					
Predicted: Total # Unwanted Pursuit Behaviors					.37	.14	4.04	4,103	**
Passionate	−.10	.05	−.20	−2.00*					
Game-playing	.00	.05	−.09	< 1					
Friendship	.00	.04	.18	1.94*					
Possessive	.16	.05	.31	3.18**					
Predicted: Total # Unwanted Pursuit Behaviors					.16	.03	1.01	3,110	$p=.39$
Perpetration	−.26	.41	−.08	< 1					
Victimization	.45	.36	.17	1.27					
Jealousy	.00	.01	.09	< 1					

*p <.05. **p < .01. ***p < .001.

The third regression analysis found no relationship between level of violence perpetrated, level of violence experienced, self-reports of jealousy, and levels of unwanted pursuit behavior perpetration.

Predicting Breakup Sufferers' Unwanted Pursuit Behavior Severity Index

Because of the relatively low correlation ($r = .26$) between UPB total scores and UPB severity index scores for breakup sufferers, both scores were retained for data analysis. Thus, the same three regression analyses were conducted a second time with the UPB severity perpetration index as the dependent measure. Once again, all predictors were entered simultaneously into the regression equation.

As shown in Table 10.5, and as hypothesized, the attachment measures were also significant predictors of the UPB severity perpetration indices, $F(4, 113) = 4.16$, $p < .01$. As a whole, these four variables accounted for 13% of the variance in severity perpetration scores. Specifically, frequent unwanted pursuit behaviors with negative impact were perpetrated by breakup sufferers who were high on the SSDS nurturance-and-support-seeking subscale and who described themselves as anxious and insecurely attached to the relationship. UPB severity

Table 10.5 Summary of Regression Analyses to Predict Unwanted Pursuit Behaviors Perpetrated by Breakup Sufferers (N = 120)

Variable	B	SE B	Beta	t	R	R²	F	df	Sig.
Predicted: Total # Unwanted Pursuit Behaviors					.36	.13	4.16	4,113	**
Narrow Focus	.00	.06	.05	< 1					
Support Seek	.12	.06	.20	2.04*					
Insecure/Anx	.15	.05	.30	2.94**					
ECR—Anxiety	.00	.02	−.28	−2.64**					
Predicted: Unwanted Pursuit Severity Index					.36	.13	3.83	4,103	
Passionate	−.22	.08	−.29	−2.92**					
Game-playing	.00	.08	−.06	< 1					
Friendship	.00	.06	−.05	<1					
Possessive	.25	.08	.31	3.82**					
Predicted: Unwanted Pursuit Severity Index					.16	.03	< 1	3,110	p=.42
Perpetration	.00	.50	.01	< 1					
Victimization	.00	.57	.02	< 1					
Jealousy	.00	.01	.15	1.58					

*p < .05. **p < .01. ***p < .001.

perpetration indices were also predicted by the ECR attachment anxiety subscale, β = -.28, $t(1, 113)$ = -2.64, $p < .01$.

In the second analysis, type of love style also significantly predicted UPBI severity indices, $F(4, 103)$ = 3.83, $p < .01$. Thirteen percent of score variance was accounted for in this analysis. Significant predictors of severe perpetration included a possessive and dependent love style [β = .31, $t(1, 103)$ = 3.82, $p < .01$] and the absence of a passionate love style [β = -.29, $t(1,103)$ = -2.92, $p < .01$]. Consistent with hypothesis, in the third regression analysis, level of violence perpetrated, level of violence experienced, and jealousy did not emerge as significant predictors of the unwanted pursuit behavior severity index for breakup sufferers.

All the above reported analyses were rerun with gender as a predictor variable. Gender did not emerge as a significant predictor in any of the analyses.

DISCUSSION

The findings indicate that unwanted pursuit behaviors are common after the termination of college students' dating relationships, as 99%

of breakup sufferers indicated that they had engaged in at least one act of unwanted pursuit behavior. According to breakup sufferers, the most common pursuit behaviors they engaged in were unwanted phone messages, phone calls, and unwanted in-person conversations with their ex-partner. According to relationship dissolvers, the most common behaviors they experienced from their ex-partners were unwanted phone calls and having their ex-partner ask friends about them.

Prevalence data from this study provides additional support for the notion that unwanted pursuit behaviors fall along a continuum of typicality and severity as has been described by Coleman (1997), Cupach and Spitzberg (1998), and others. Assessing for the full continuum of unwanted pursuit behaviors, as is common in Guttman-like scales, may help to gauge the difficulty of the breakup as well as to identify individuals who may be at risk for intimate relationship stalking.

It was hypothesized that the frequency of unwanted pursuit behaviors would differ as a function of gender. However, consistent with data reported by Cupach and Spitzberg (1998), only a few gender differences in rates of pursuit behaviors were obtained in this sample. The obtained differences suggest that women may be more likely to leave unwanted phone messages, whereas men may be more likely to seek in-person contact with their ex-partners. Gender also did not emerge as a predictor in any of the regression equations, suggesting few gender-specific associations for unwanted pursuit. As a whole, these results suggest that unwanted pursuit behaviors may occur in a relatively gender-neutral manner. These findings are consistent with dating violence prevalence studies conducted with college students (e.g., Arias et al., 1987). It is also possible, however, that there may be gender-specific motivations underlying similar behavior (e.g., men may be more likely to continue pursuing in order to intimidate and control; women may be more likely to continue pursuing in order to cope with depression and fear of loss). There may also be some gender-specific risk factors for particular acts of violent and/or for dangerous pursuit behavior, which has been found in the dating violence literature (e.g., Bookwala, Frieze, Smith, & Ryan, 1992). Moreover, some acts with similar descriptions may evoke quite different responses from men and women. Further research will be needed to examine these hypotheses.

As expected, reports of the frequency of unwanted pursuit behaviors did differ on the basis of informant (i.e., breakup sufferer or relationship dissolver). Breakup sufferers reported engaging in milder types of unwanted pursuit behaviors, such as leaving unwanted phone messages and/or hang-up calls, than relationship dissolvers reported receiving after their breakups. One interpretation of these findings might be that breakup sufferers were disclosing information about their actions, about which relationship dissolvers were unaware (e.g., the dissolvers didn't know that the hang-up message was from their ex-partner). It is also possible that these behaviors may have been more salient, and consequently more memorable, for the breakup sufferer. Finally, if the behavior had a positive response by the receiver, it might not have been coded as an "unwanted" pursuit behavior by relationship dissolvers and thus may not have been reported.

There were trends, however, for these reporting differences to reverse as the reported behaviors became more serious. In general, breakup sufferers were less likely than relationship dissolvers to report severe pursuit behaviors (e.g., following, threatening, injuring the ex-partner). These findings are likely to reflect social desirability concerns on the part of perpetrators (Fremouw et al., 1997).

Relationship dissolvers and breakup sufferers also differed in their assessment of the impact of the unwanted pursuit behaviors. In general, breakup sufferers indicated more positive impact for the pursuit behaviors that they perpetrated than relationship dissolvers reported experiencing. This suggests that perpetrators may be unaware of the negative effects of their postbreakup pursuit behavior, which would make it harder for them to self-correct their behavior. However, caution is recommended when interpreting these findings, as this study utilized relationship dissolvers and breakup sufferers from different relationships. Future research is needed that will replicate these findings with relationship dissolvers and breakup sufferers who are reporting on the same failed relationship.

Furthermore, a surprising number of both relationship dissolvers and breakup sufferers indicated a positive response to the unwanted pursuit behavior. If unwanted pursuit behaviors occur frequently at the end of intimate relationships and if these behaviors sometimes have positive consequences for the pursuer (e.g., they are received positively or they restart the relationship), then it is likely to be more difficult to prevent many types of unwanted pursuit and to determine when unwanted pursuit clearly warrants intervention. Furthermore, identification of potential stalkers will be particularly difficult if only perpetrators' perspectives of their unwanted pursuit behaviors are available for consideration, as these individuals may be most likely to minimize the severity and impact of their unwanted pursuit behaviors.

In the current study, relationship dissolvers' and breakup sufferers' reports of attachment style, love types, jealousy, and abusiveness were used to predict pursuit behavior total scores. Separate models were constructed for relationship dissolvers and breakup sufferers. For relationship dissolvers, total UPBI victimization scores were predicted by their perceptions that their ex-partner was jealous and physically abusive. These variables accounted for 32% of the variance in total scores. Unwanted pursuit behavior total scores were also significantly predicted by reports of an ex-partner who was anxiously and insecurely attached in the relationship. Finally, relationships that ended with unwanted pursuit behaviors were more likely to be characterized as low in friendship love and high in possessive-dependent love, according to relationship dissolvers.

By comparison, breakup sufferers revealed no predictive relationships between the level of physical violence in the relationship, their jealousy, and their UPB total perpetration scores. Instead, they related higher levels of unwanted pursuit behaviors to high levels of nuturance and support-seeking behaviors in the relationship and more friendship love. High levels of possessive, dependent love and low levels of passionate love also emerged as predictors of total UPB perpetration scores for breakup sufferers. These findings support the contention that some breakup sufferers may perceive their unwanted pursuit behaviors as legitimate efforts to restore their intimate relationship, continue to seek nuturance and support from their ex-partner, or as an attempt to maintain a friendship with their ex-partner after the love affair has ended.

A second set of regression analyses was conducted to determine predictors of the unwanted pursuit behavior perpetration severity index, as the two summary scores were found to be only moderately correlated for breakup sufferers. The UPBI severity index included only unwanted pursuit behaviors that were judged by the perpetrator to have had a negative impact on the receiver. The included negative impact UPBI items were then weighted by their frequency of occurrence and their item-type severity. A priori, this index was designed to be more closely related to behaviors which could be considered stalking (i.e., repeated, fear inducing, unwanted). For breakup sufferers, partner-specific dependency and attachment emerged as significant predictors of the UPBI perpetration severity index. Breakup sufferers engaging in UPB perpetration were more insecurely and anxiously attached to their ex-partner. They also reported engaging in more nuturance and support seeking. UPB severity indices were also predicted by higher levels of possessive and dependent love. These results suggest that those who lack the skills to successfully meet their relationship needs while they are dating, may also lack the skills to endure relationship termination successfully. Prevention of unwanted pursuit behavior and intimate relationship stalking may be enhanced by helping individuals form more secure attachments, with less dependent and possessive love between dating partners. Prevention and intervention efforts may also be enhanced by furthering our understanding of the role of friendship in the production of unwanted pursuit behaviors, as breakup sufferers indicated more unwanted pursuit in relationships that had been characterized as high in friendship, while relationship dissolvers indicated lower levels of friendship were associated with experiencing unwanted pursuit from their ex-partner.

Several limitations to this study should be noted. First, the sample was drawn exclusively from college students. Care should be used when generalizing these findings to samples who have chosen not to attend college. Second, relationship reports were obtained retrospectively. Different results may be obtained with prospective studies on the dissolution of dating relationships. Also, the nature of these relationships might be further clarified by considering unwanted pursuit behaviors that occur before, during, and after the intimate relationship. Third, this sample was predominantly Caucasian. Further research will be needed to determine the extent to which the obtained results hold for other ethnic and/or socioeconomic groups. Finally, these results apply primarily to individuals whose dating relationships have terminated. The predictors of unwanted pursuit behaviors after the termination of a marital relationship may be different.

Overall, however, these results support the importance of considering a range of unwanted pursuit behaviors that may lead to and include stalking. The findings also support the importance of obtaining reports from multiple sources. Both perpetrators and victims in this study indicated that attachment processes and love styles are important predictors of unwanted pursuit behaviors, but the role of psychological and physical abuse in the production of unwanted pursuit behaviors deserves further edification. Furthermore, understanding how friendship works after the dissolution of a consensual romantic relationship may be important. It seems likely, however, that identification of these predictors of unwanted pursuit behaviors may facilitate efforts to intervene when breaking up is hard to do.

ACKNOWLEDGMENT

We would like to acknowledge the research assistance provided by Melissa Fredenberg.

REFERENCES

Arias, I., Samios, M., & O'Leary, K. D. (1987). Prevalence and correlates of physical aggression during courtship. *Journal of Interpersonal Violence, 2,* 82–90.

Berscheid, E. (1994). Interpersonal relationships. *Annual Review of Psychology, 45,* 79–129.

Bookwala, J., Frieze, I. H., Smith, C., & Ryan, K. (1992). Predictors of dating violence: A multivariate analysis. *Violence and Victims, 7,* 297–310.

Bowlby, J. (1977). The making and breaking of affectional bonds. *British Journal of Psychiatry, 130,* 201–210.

Brennan, K. A., Clark, C. L., & Shaver, P. R. (1998). Self report measure of adult attachment: An integrative overview. In J. Simpson & W. Rholes (Eds.), *Attachment theory and close relationships* (pp. 46–76). New York: Guilford.

Burgess, A. W., Baker, T., Greening, D., Hartman, C. R., Burgess, A. G., Douglas, J. E., & Halloran, R. (1997). Stalking behaviors within domestic violence. *Journal of Family Violence, 12,* 389–403.

Coleman, F. (1997). Stalking behavior and the cycle of domestic violence. *Journal of Interpersonal Violence, 12,* 420–432.

Cupach, W. R., & Spitzberg, B. H. (1998). Obsessive relational intrusion and stalking. In B. H. Spitzberg & W. R. Cupach (Eds.), *The dark side of close relationships* (pp. 233–263). Hillsdale, NJ: Lawrence Erlbaum Associates.

Dutton, D. G., Saunders, K., Starzomski, A., & Bartholomew, K. (1994). Intimacy-anger and insecure attachment as precursors of abuse in intimate relationships. *Journal of Applied Social Psychology, 24,* 1367–1386.

Dutton, D. G., van Ginkel, C., & Landolt, M. A. (1996). Jealousy, intimate abusiveness, and intrusiveness. *Journal of Family Violence, 11,* 411–423.

Dziegielewski, S. F., & Roberts, A. R. (1995). Stalking victims and survivors. In A. R. Roberts (Ed.), *Crisis intervention and time-limited cognitive treatment* (pp. 73–90). Thousand Oaks, CA: Sage.

Fine, M. A., & Sacher, J. A. (1997). Predictors of relationship distress following relationship termination among college students. *Journal of Social and Clinical Psychology, 16,* 381–388.

Fremouw, W. J., Westrup, D., & Pennypacker, J. (1997). Stalking on campus: The prevalence and strategies for coping with stalking. *Journal of Forensic Science, 42,* 666–669.

Guerrero, L. K. (1998). Attachment-style differences in the experience and expression of romantic jealousy. *Personal Relationships, 5,* 273–291.

Hendrick, C., & Hendrick, S. S. (1990). A relationship-specific version of the Love Attitudes Scale. *Journal of Social Behavior and Personality, 5,* 239–254.

Hendrick, C., Hendrick, S. S., & Dicke, A. (1998). The Love Attitudes Scale: Short Form. *Journal of Social and Personal Relationships, 15,* 147–159.

Hendricks, J. E., & Spillane, L. (1993, December). Stalking: What can we do to forestall tragedy? *The Police Chief,* 68–70.

Holtzworth-Munroe, A., Stuart, G. L., & Hutchinson, G. (1997). Violent versus nonviolent husbands: Differences in attachment patterns, dependency, and jealousy. *Journal of Family Psychology, 11,* 314–331.

Kaufman, J., Jones, B., Stieglitz, E., Vitulano, L., & Mannarino, A. P. (1994). The use of multiple informants to assess children's maltreatment experiences. *Journal of Family Violence, 9,* 227–248.

Lee, J. A. (1973). *The colors of love: An exploration of ways of loving.* Don Mills, Ontario: New Press.

Mathes, E. W. (1992). *Jealousy: The psychological data.* Lanham, MD: University Press of America.

Mathes, E. W., Phillips, J. T., Skowran, J., & Dick, W. E., III (1982). Behavioral correlates of the interpersonal scale. *Educational and Psychological Measurement, 42,* 1227–1231.

Mathes, E. W., & Severa, N. (1981). Jealousy, romantic love, and liking: Theoretical considerations and preliminary scale development. *Psychological Reports, 49,* 23–31.

Molidor, C., & Tolman, R. M. (1998). Gender and contextual factors in adolescent dating violence. *Violence Against Women, 4,* 180–194.

Palarea, R. E., & Langhinrichsen-Rohling, J. (1998). *Unwanted Pursuit Behavior Inventory.* Unpublished measure.

Palarea, R. E., Zona, M. A., Lane, J., & Langhinrichsen-Rohling, J. (in press). Stalking in intimate relationships. *Law and Human Behavior.*

Rathus, J., & O'Leary, K. D. (1997). Spouse-specific dependency scale: Scale development. *Journal of Family Violence, 12,* 159–168.

Sharpsteen, D. (1995). The effects of relationship and self-esteem threats on the likelihood of romantic jealousy. *Journal of Social and Personal Relationships, 12,* 89–101.

Simpson, J. (1990). Influence of attachment styles on romantic relationships. *Journal of Personality and Social Psychology, 59,* 971–980.

Spitzberg, B. H., Nicastro, A. M., & Cousins, A. V. (1998). Exploring the interactional phenomenon of stalking and obsessive relational intrusion. *Communication Reports, 11,* 33–47.

Spitzberg, B. H., & Rhea, J. (1999). Obsessive relational intrusion and sexual coercion victimization. *Journal of Interpersonal Violence, 14,* 3–20.

Straus, M., Hamby, S. L., Boney-McCoy, S., & Sugarman, D. B. (1996). The Revised Conflict Tactics Scales (CTS2): Development and preliminary psychometric data. *Journal of Family Issues, 17,* 283–316.

Tjaden, P., & Thoennes, N. (1998). *Stalking in America: Findings for the National Violence Against Women Survey (Report No. NCJ 169592).* Washington, DC: National Institute of Justice and Centers for Disease Control and Prevention.

White, G. L., & Mullen, P. E. (1989). *Jealousy: Theory, research, and clinical strategies.* New York: Guilford.

11

Stalking Perpetrators and Psychological Maltreatment of Partners: Anger-Jealousy, Attachment Insecurity, Need for Control, and Break-Up Context

Keith E. Davis, April Ace, and Michelle Andra

> "She would tear the strings from an archangel's harp to tie up parcels: she has done that with my very heart strings."
> —George Bernard Shaw to his former lover, Stella Campbell

In this article, we report two studies of the correlates of self-reported stalking-like behaviors among college samples. Our major contributions are threefold: (a) we show that the level of courtship persistence and stalking following a relationship break-up are quite substantial when an anonymous self-report is provided; (b) we show that psychological maltreatment of partners and stalking are correlated with each other and predicted by attachment anxiety and need for control; and (c) we show that several features of the nature of break-ups are relevant to degree of stalking. Among these are emotional reactions to break-ups such as anger, jealousy, and obsessiveness, who initiates the break-up, and the number of break-ups.

In 1990, California was the first state to pass an antistalking statute, defining stalking as the "willful, malicious and repeated following or harassing" of another person (National Institute of Justice, 1993, p.

13). The common thread among the legal definitions is usually that the stalking must involve behavior that causes fear, actual danger, or credible threats of danger. In contrast with legal definitions, behavioral scientists have sought to identify a continuum of behaviors that could be seen as stalking, but which provided a broader basis for the identification of the motivational bases of stalking (Cupach & Spitzberg, 1998; Langhinrichsen-Rohling, Palarea, Cohen, & Rohling, this volume). The major national survey of victimization found a much larger prevalence of stalking than even experts had anticipated. That survey (Tjaden and Thoennes, 1998) indicated that between 8% and 12% of adult women had been stalked at some time in their life and that approximately 1 million women were stalked each year within the United States. Furthermore, being stalked created a very high level of distress among victims, such that as many as 1/3 of the victims sought psychological counseling, 56% took some precautionary action (which included such things as getting a gun [17%], or moving their residences [11%]) to avoid the stalker. The Tjaden & Thoennes (1998) survey showed that, contrary to the media impression, most cases of stalking occurred in the context of previous intimate relationships rather than being cases of being stalked by a stranger. At the time we began these studies, the systematic study of stalking perpetrators had been restricted to the clinical examination of forensic cases (Meloy, 1998; Pathé & Mullen, 1997; Zona, Palarea, & Lane, 1998).

The current studies make three contributions to the fast-growing literature on stalking. First, we have developed measures of emotional reactions to breakups and behavioral responses to breakups designed to allow participants to acknowledge, anonymously, a broad range of motivational bases for courtship persistence and harassing behavior following the breakup (see Coleman, 1997, for the first attempt to measure perpetration; Langhinrichsen-Rohling, Palarea, Cohen, & Rohling, this volume, and Sinclair & Frieze, this volume, have also developed alternative measures that accomplish the same goal). On both clinical and theoretical grounds, there should be a variety of bases for persistent and harassing behavior of an ex-partner, ranging from the desire to re-establish a romantic relationship to a desire for revenge on an ex-partner who has misled and mistreated them (Baumeister, Wotman, & Stillwell, 1993; Meloy, 1998).

The second contribution of the article is the further development and testing of the thesis, first stated by Kurt (1995), that stalking is a form of coercion that is an extension of psychological and physical coercion in relationships. A crucial implication of this thesis is that stalking after a breakup should be predicted by psychological mal-treatment of partners prior to the breakup and by some of the same emotional and personal dispositions as intimate partner psychological and physical violence. We present a framework that integrates aspects of breakup contextual and personal characteristic variables to predict a range of stalking-like behaviors and psychological violence. Third, we take advantage of having two studies to present a replicated path model among the key predictors of psychological maltreatment of partners and stalking.

BREAKUP CONTEXT, EMOTIONAL REACTIONS, AND STALKING

Three aspects of breakup context seemed to us worthy of examination in developing a theory of stalking perpetration. First is the issue of who initiated the breakup. That the conditions under which a relation-ship ends are associated with the nature and degree of subsequent distress has been known since the classic study of Hill, Rubin, and Peplau (1976). Most breakups are not mutual and the partner who initiates the breakup tends to feel a mixture of guilt, relief, and (some-times) ambivalence (Davis & O'Hearn, 1989; Frazier & Cook, 1993; & Sprecher, 1994), but generally experiences less emotional distress than the partner who has been left. The partners who are left (receiv-ers) tend to experience some mixture of anger, sadness, depression, anxiety, and feelings of distress (Davis & O'Hearn, 1989; Hill et al., 1976; & Sprecher, 1994). The differences in emotional reactions and degree of distress have been interpreted in terms of the initiator having more control over his/her outcomes than does the receiver (Sprecher, Felmlee, Metts, Fehr, & Vanni, 1998). Because stalking is hypothesized to represent an attempt to gain control over an ex-partner, *we antici-pate that those respondents who were rejected (recipients of the break-up) are more likely to stalk than those who initiate or participate in mutual breakups.*

While the initiator versus recipient distinction is important, we wanted to examine the emotional reactions to the breakup as a second factor that may transcend these distinctions. Specifically, we anticipat-ed that some respondents who classified the breakup as mutual or personally initiated would nonetheless be subject to the core of emotional reactions that has been shown to be connected to relationship violence—anger, jealousy, and obsessiveness (Dutton, Saunders, Starzomski, & Bartholomew, 1994; Holtzworth-Munroe, Stuart, & Hutchinson, 1997). This core set of feelings is often mentioned in the clinical-forensic literature and in recently published research on stalking (Meloy, 1998). From the victim's perspective, the National Violence Against Women Survey data are particularly revealing. Tjaden and Thoennes (1998) reported that victims thought that their stalkers wanted to control them (21%), to keep them in the relationship (20%), or to scare them (18%). Among ex-husbands who stalked, there was a strong connection with control, emotional abuse, and jealousy (Tjaden & Thoennes, 1998). When Langhinrichsen-Rohling and colleagues (this volume) asked their respondents who had initiated breakups about the kinds of things the stalkers did and their characteristics, a similar cluster appeared. Degree of pursuit behavior was related to the perception of the partner as jealous, controlling, and emotionally abusive prior to the breakup. Sinclair and Frieze (this volume) likewise report that feelings of anger and vengefulness were two of the strongest emotional correlates of stalking behaviors.

Because some initiators of breakups might have taken the step of breaking-up because of being betrayed or mistreated, it is particularly important to assess the meaning of the breakup for all types of breakups. *If feelings of anger and jealousy are central to stalking, then these feelings will be predictive of stalking regardless of the respondents' self-classification of their breakups. Thus, while we anticipate greater levels of anger, upset, jealousy, and obsessiveness among those who were rejected than those who initiate or engage in mutual breakups, the degree of anger, upset, jealousy, and obsessiveness will be predictive of stalking across conditions.*

The third contextual variable that we identified as important is the number of breakups and reunions that had occurred previously. In reading the narratives of the relationship histories provided by individuals in our pilot work, we noticed that many couples had what we called a "Velcro" pattern. They would breakup and get back together several times before eventually settling down or breaking up. Theoretically, this pattern of relating may reinforce the view that if one tries hard enough one may get back together (Westrup, 1998). Alternatively, it may be seen from an attachment perspective as an indication of a dynamic to be found among mutually insecure individuals with significant anxiety about abandonment (Kirkpatrick & Davis, 1994; Kirk-patrick & Hazan, 1994). These studies indicate that despite being relatively unhappy in relationships, participants high in anxious at-tachment are both less likely to breakup permanently, more likely to show strong ambivalence, and to engage in significant relationship conflict. Whatever theoretical perspective is taken, such *a history should be associated with a greater likelihood of stalking-like behaviors after a recent breakup. Ours is the first empirical evaluation of this propo-sition.*

PERPETRATORS OF STALKING

Self-Reported Incidents of Stalking

There is no national probability sample dealing with the perpetration of stalking to parallel the National Violence Against Women Survey of victimization (Tjaden & Thoennes, 1998). At the time we began this work, we were aware of only one other research program on college student perpetrators. Fremouw, Westrup, and Pennypacker (1997) re-ported that only 3 males (2.3%) and no females acknowledged engag-ing in stalking defined as "knowingly and repeatedly following, harassing, or threatening someone (p. 667)." It seemed to us that, by breaking down the report of perpetration into several specific behav-iors paralleling the victimization reports, we would be able to obtain a more realistic reporting. Sixteen specific behaviors were identified, covering a range of behaviors from mild harassment to threats and vandalism to form an overall assessment of stalking behavior. The items were derived from the clinical and forensic literature and the NVAW survey. By mild harassment, we mean behaviors that could be, from the perpetrator's point of view, attempts to reestablish a relation-ship, but which from the victim's point of view, could be irritating intrusions into his or her life. A specific example is "Wrote, called, or emailed after s/he told me not to." The next level, which if repeated would move closer to legally defined stalking, is the category of threats. We identified 7 possible threats, such as "Tried to scare him/her into coming back to me." The essential element in the threats category is the willingness to use coercion to attain the goal of reunion. The vandalism category involves the actual damage of property, or breaking and entering, or taking the person some place against his/her will. We intentionally did not include items that could reasonably be classified as psychological abuse, such as put-downs, swearing at, calling names, or physical abuse or forced sexual contact. If these are included in the measure of stalking, then one has contaminated the measure.

Expressions of Love

One implication of the analysis of cultural patterns of courtship enshrined in myth, song, and the mass media is that persistence in the pursuit of a love-object is rewarded (see Sinclair & Frieze, this volume; White, Kowalski, Lyndon, & Valentine, this volume, for a development of this analysis). Maxims such as "Faint heart never won fair maid," and the numerous stories and songs in which persistence in wooing is rewarded by winning the loved one's heart attest to the power of this cultural theme. Given this cultural pattern, it is possible for stalkers to be engaging in what they see as persistence when the recipient finds their behaviors harassing, unpleasant, and even threatening (see Cupach & Spitzberg, this volume, for relevant data). We wanted to develop a brief measure of the degree to which the stalking perpetrator saw himself as doing what he did as an expression of love and thus to have an opportunity to see just how strongly associated were expressions of love (or courtship persistence, in Sinclair & Frieze's phrase) and the more harassing and threatening forms of stalking.

Psychological Maltreatment

Kurt (1995) has advanced the hypothesis that stalking is a form of coercion that is an extension of psychological and physical violence. Victims of stalking certainly see it as a means of control through fear (Tjaden & Thoennes, 1998). If Kurt is correct, then stalking ought to be correlated with psychological maltreatment in the relationship prior to the breakup and also psychological maltreatment should be predicted by some of the same relationship context and dispositional variables as stalking. Fortunately, Tolman (1989, 1999) has developed a well-validated measure of psychological maltreatment that O'Hearn and Davis (1997) adapted to self-report perpetration as well as victimization.

PERSONAL CHARACTERISTICS PREDICTIVE OF STALKING

Control

A persistent theme in the research on intimate partner violence is that the need to control the partner is a central motivation. Stets (1988; Stets & Pirog-Good, 1987) has developed a control theory model of this process. When one's control in a relationship falls below the desired level, then one will engage in behavior designed to reassert one's desired level of control. Consistent with her analysis, she found that, when individuals in dating relationships experienced a loss of control due to conflict, they tended to compensate by engaging in controlling behaviors such as setting rules for the relationship or keeping tabs on their partners. Follingstad, Rutledge, McNeill-Harkins, and Polek (1988) and Follingstad, Bradley, Laughlin, and Burke (1999) have developed a self-report Control Scale. The components of this scale were (a) controlling out of jealousy, (b) controlling with verbal criticism, (c) controlling of free time, (d) controlling a partner's appearance and duties, (e) controlling with verbal and physical coercion, and (f) controlling by insisting on knowledge of prior sexual history. Follingstad and associates (1999) have shown that the short form of the Control Scale is a particularly sensitive discriminator of the severity of physical aggression in dating couples and of the frequency of physical violence as indexed by the Conflict Tactics Scale (Straus & Gelles, 1990). Given the preceding information on the perceptions (attributions) of victims and several sources that point to control motivation as central to psychological and physical violence in relationships, *control should also be predictive of both the degree of stalking-like behaviors and the psychological maltreatment engaged in by men and women.*

Attachment Insecurity

At the adult level, the initial model of attachment styles was based on a direct extension of Ainsworth's observations of children's responses to separation and reunion with attachment figures to adult romantic behaviors (Hazan & Shaver, 1987). Bartholomew and Horowitz (1991) subsequently provided persuasive evidence for four attachment styles that could be described by two dimensions. These two dimensions have been conceptualized by Brennan, Clark, and Shaver (1998) as attachment anxiety (model of self) and attachment avoidance (model of other). Recently, attachment insecurity has been implicated as a predictor of intimate partner violence—both physical and psychological. As this line of research is relatively new, we shall examine both the theoretical rationale and several studies that provide the empirical basis for taking insecure attachment, particularly anxious attachment, seriously as a predictor of partner violence. Conceptually, relationship abuse can be seen as an exaggerated form of protest behavior designed to hold onto or reunite with the attachment figure (partner) (Bartholomew, Henderson, & Dutton, 2001; Bowlby, 1980). In attachment theory, fears of abandonment typify the highly anxious dimension of attachment insecurity. Fears of abandonment and threats to an established relationship thus can trigger rage, attacks, and, when the partner has left, stalking to reestablish contact.

Dutton and his associates (Dutton et al., 1994; Dutton, van Ginkel, & Landolt, 1996) have established several empirical connections between attachment styles and both psychological and physical aggression. In the Dutton and colleagues (1994) and Holtzworth-Munroe, Stuart, and Hutchinson (1997) studies of violent marital partners, degree of anxious attachment separated the violent from the nonviolent males. Roberts and Noller (1998) have examined the three-way relationship among communication patterns, attachment dimensions, and couple violence. Either partner's anxiety over abandonment predicted their psychological violence toward the other, but the effect was conditioned by the attachment characteristics of the partner. Anxiety over abandonment was related much more strongly to violence when the partner was avoidant of intimacy than not. This finding suggests that a "person's fear of abandonment may be exacerbated by a partner's fear of intimacy, and violence may consequently be used by the [anxious] partner to control the emotional distance" with the avoidant partner (Roberts & Noller, 1998, p. 340).

Guerrero (1998) has explored the relationship between attachment styles and the experience and expressions of jealousy. Those with a preoccupied attachment style (high on attachment anxiety) reported both more fear/distress and more sadness in response to jealousy-arousing situations and reported more spying and checking on the partner. These findings connect the attachment anxiety directly to stalking-like behavior. Brennan and Shaver (1995) have shown that anxious attachment is associated with anger toward the partner, jealousy, and disappointments with the partner.

Thus, we expect that *the degree of anxious attachment will be linked to all four areas of concern: Anxious attachment will be associated with (a) greater anger, jealousy, and obsessiveness, (b) greater expressions of love following the breakup, (c) more stalking-like behaviors after couple breakups and (d) greater psychological maltreatment of the partner prior to breakup* (Davis & Boudreaux-Kraft, 1997).

METHOD

Participants: Study 1 and Study 2

For Study 1, 180 students participated in the completion of an anonymous survey on relationship history for course credit. Nine had never had a breakup and thus were not relevant for the analyses planned, and two had enough missing data to warrant exclusion from the analysis. The resulting sample was 169 (123 women & 46 men), all of whom had had at least one serious romantic relationship that had broken up. For Study 2, 212 students participated, 203 of whom met the criterion of one significant romantic relationship that had broken up. One hundred and ten were women and 93 men. The procedures and measures for Study 1 and 2 were the same except for (a) more elaborate questioning concerning the number of breakups and reunions in Study 2 and (b) instructions in Study 2 that made it clear that one could report on breakups in which the partners had got back together. (See below for the exact language.)

Procedure

After completing the informed consent, participants completed a single Relationship History Survey which consisted of several parts, including a relationship demographics section (current relationship status; dating/marital history; duration of current relationship; age of first dating; first sexual intercourse; number of dating partners; and sexual orientation). Age of participants was between 19 and 24, with the modal age being 19. The data reported herein deal exclusively with emotional reactions to the breakup, behaviors within the relationship and subsequent to it. No data are reported on stalking victimization.

The questions concerning the breakup of their most recent relationships were introduced in the following manner:

These questions concern the history of your breakups with romantic partners. While some persons go with the same partner in high school and whom they ultimately marry and live happily, others have several partners before they settle down—if they ever do. In these questions we will be asking about who initiated the separations, when they occurred, how you felt about them, and what you tended to do after a separation/breakup. [Added for Study 2: A breakup need not be permanent. It may have seemed permanent at the time but you may have gotten back together.]

In your most recent breakup who wanted to breakup and insisted on it? (Circle the most appropriate alternative): (a) I did; (b) S/he did; (c) It was more or less mutual.

The response to this question provided the measure of the key variable, *initiator status*. Multiple breakups were indexed by responses to the question, "Were there multiple breakups?" followed by another question, "How many times?"

Instruments

ATTACHMENT

Brennan and associates' (1998) 36–item self-report of Experiences in Close Relationships (ECR) was based on a factor analytic investigation of 323 items from all previous self-report measures of attachment styles. As anticipated, the results showed that a two-factor solution was best at representing the data, and the 18 items that were most highly correlated with each factor were selected and unit weighted to create scales for avoidance (average alphas for these samples = .92) and anxiety (average alpha = .90). Brennan and colleagues (1998) have shown good predictive validity to criteria such as comfort with interpersonal touch and preference for forms of sexual experience.

CONTROL SCALE (FOLLINGSTAD ET AL., 1988; FOLLINGSTAD ET AL., 1999)

This scale was developed empirically based on reports of spouses and partners in abusive relationships. A rational analysis of the content of the original 52 items indicated that perhaps 6 subcomponents could be identified. However, the subcomponents were so highly intercorrelated with each other that a shortened (25-item) version was created without the attempt to subdivide the types of controlling expressed. Alpha in these samples was .90 and .92 for the 25-item version. Follingstad and colleagues (1999) have shown that the short form of the Control Scale is a particularly sensitive discriminator of the severity of physical aggression in dating couples and of frequency of physical violence as indexed by the CTS.

Sample items included on the short form are: "How often have you tried to point out a dating partner's faults when you were alone together?" "How often have you tried to plan how your dating partner generally spends his/her time?" "How often have you tried to keep your dating partner from looking at members of the opposite sex when you were together?" "How often have you tried to get a dating partner to inform you of where s/he was going and what s/he was going to do so you would know that you could trust him/her?"

Responses to Breakups: Emotional Reactions, Expressions of Love, and Stalking-Like Behaviors

EMOTIONAL REACTIONS: THE ANGER-JEALOUSY CLUSTER

Five items reflecting these emotional reactions were included among a longer list of negative, neutral, or positive reactions to the breakup. The adjectives included were "Angry," "Upset at being left," and "Jealous," which the respondent selected in answer to the question, "How did you feel about the breakup? Check all that are applicable." Also included were items designed to measure obsessiveness which were worded, "Couldn't get him/her off my mind" and "Thought about him/her a lot." The items were derived from and validated in a study by Davis and O'Hearn (1989). Internal consistencies for these two samples were .65 and .74.

EXPRESSIONS OF LOVE

Four items were used: "Told him/her how much I loved him/her," "Tried to demonstrate love by always being around," "Sent gifts as expressions of love" and "Tried to get back together." The mean alpha was .69 in the two studies.

COMPOSITE STALKING MEASURE

All 16 items for the three stalking behavior subscales are treated as a single index, and the internal consistencies were quite substantial (average inter-item correlations of .47 and .53 and alphas of .74 and

.82). The response scale for stalking items was a 3-point scale: "No," "Did it once," and "Did it more than once." Because the distribution of responses was quite skewed, we explored alternative scoring of the scale by collapsing the range from the theoretical range of 1.00 to 3.00 into three groups based on frequency. These groups were defined as nonstalkers, those with one to five stalking behaviors, and those with more than six behaviors. All but one significant difference obtained with the continuous scale also held for the three-category scale. In a separate sample of 47 students, the test-retest stability was $r = .79$.

STALKING SUBSCALES: MILD HARASSMENT

Six items were used covering much of the same ground as the NVAW measure of stalking harassment victimization. The mean alpha was .67. Examples are "Went by his/her house/dorm to see what s/he was doing," "Wrote, called, or e-mailed after s/he told me not to," "Made a point of talking with friends or co-workers," and "Stood close to him/her and touched him/her without being asked." From the perpetrator's point of view, these behaviors could represent attempts to reestablish a relationship, but from the victim's point of view, they could be irritating intrusions into his or her life.

THREATS

Seven items reflecting a range of threats that have been identified as realistic for stalkers were included. The mean alpha was .71. If repeated, these behaviors would move closer to legally defined stalking. Sample items are "Tried to scare him/her into coming back to me," "Made specific threats to hurt others if s/he did not come back to me," "Made specific threats to harm her pet, if s/he did not come back to me," "Made threats to damage her property, if s/he did not come back to me." The essential element in the threats category is the willingness to use coercion to attain the goal of reunion.

VANDALISM

Three items were used for this aspect of stalking. The alpha for these items in response to the most recent breakups was .54 in both studies. The vandalism category involves the actual damage of property, or breaking and entering, or taking the person some place against her/his will.

PSYCHOLOGICAL MALTREATMENT OF PARTNER (PMP)

The five items from Tolman's (1989) original long form of his Psychological Maltreatment of Women Inventory with the highest loading on his emotional/verbal abuse subscale were selected and reworded so that they could be asked for perpetration of maltreatment as well as being the victim of such treatment. The effectiveness of this rewording was validated in O'Hearn and Davis (1997). These five items were included in his recently published short form (Tolman, 1999), as items number 10–13, and 45. The internal consistency of these as a single scale was .75 and .81 in our two samples.

RESULTS

Descriptive Analyses of Stalking Behaviors

HOW MUCH STALKING EXISTS IN COLLEGE SAMPLES AFTER RELATIONSHIP BREAKUPS?

Are the levels of stalking-like behaviors high enough to qualify as legal stalking or harassment? Although the exact legal requirements vary from state to state, two features are common: A requirement of repeated harassment and stalking and a threat to harm. In Table 11.1, we present both the means for the stalking and psychological maltreatment of partner scales, and also an index of the percent of the sample that would qualify as having engaged in the behaviors repeatedly. For the overall summary scale of all stalking items, in Study 1, 61.5% engaged in no stalking, 30.1% engaged in one to five acts, and 10.7% engaged in six to 23 acts. In Study 2, 55.4% engaged in no stalking, 36.4% engaged in one to five acts, and 7.6% engaged in six to 33 acts. For the subscales, by using a mean of 2.0 for the criterion of severe stalking behaviors in Table 11.1, we included only persons who acknowledged engaging in all of the items within the scale at least once or who have engaged in some of the items at least a few times. For the Threat scale, they are admitting to threatening their ex-partner in several different ways, and for the Vandalism scale, they are admitting to physically restraining the ex-partner, breaking into their apartment or home, or damaging something loved by the partner. With respect to the mild harassment scale, 13% to 22% ($M = 17.2\%$) of the two

Table 11.1 Means and Percentages Severe/Serious for All Dependent
Variables by Gender

	Study One				Study Two			
	Meen (n = 46)		Women (n = 123)		Men (n = 93)		Women (n = 110)	
	M	% Severe	M	% Severe	M	% Severe	M	% Severe
Expressions of								
love	1.26	10.9	1.25	8.9	1.57	17.4	1.61	22.9
Mild harassment	1.47	17.4	1.45	16.3	1.41	13.0	1.54+	22.0
Threats	1.04	2.2	1.03	0.0	1.06	2.2	1.09	3.8
Vandalism	1.13	4.3	1.15	2.4	1.12	1.1	1.24*	10.3
Stalking								
Composite	1.08	9.1	1.10	11.8	1.07	6.4	1.15	8.9

Note. + = $p < .10$. *= $p < .05$ or less for gender mean differences within the same study. Percent severe is defined as at least 2 behaviors in each category. For the composite stalking measure, 6 or more behaviors were used to categorize a person as severe. The response range for all scales was 1 to 3.

samples admitted engaging in these behaviors at a high level. For both the threats ($M = 1.9\%$) and vandalism ($M = 4.6\%$) scales, the levels reported ranged from 0% to 10.9%. The levels were substantial enough to support the promise of anonymous self-reports as a technique that can be useful in detecting stalking and to indicate how serious a problem stalking can be on campuses after breakups.

Tests of Major Hypotheses

A multivariate analysis of variance was conducted in each study with breakup status (I vs. S/he vs. Mutual) and gender as the independent variables and the anger-jealousy cluster, expressions of love, the composite stalking measure, and psychological maltreatment of partner as the dependent variables. For each study, the overall MANOVA was significant [Study 1: $F(df\ 4, 161) = 5.16$, $p < .001$; Study 2: $F(df\ 4, 188) = 3.86$, $p < .01$] for breakup status, but not for either gender or the Gender x Breakup Status interaction. In Table 11.2, the means, standard deviations, and F-ratios are reported for the univariate ANOVAs for the breakup status effects.

Table 11.2 Means and Standard Deviations for Emotional Reactions, Expressions of Love, Stalking, and Psychological Maltreatment of Partner Scales in Study 1 and 2.

	Breakup Status				
	I did	S/he Did	Mutual	Univariate F-ratio	p-value
Study 1					
Anger-Jealousy	0.52$_a$ (0.32)	1.03$_b$ (0.38)	0.61$_a$ (0.33)	34.30	.001
Ex. Of Love	1.17$_a$ (0.29)	1.41$_b$ (0.40)	1.24$_b$ (0.43)	6.60	.002
PMP	0.81 (0.80)	1.04 (1.11)	1.01 (0.70)	1.12	.33
Stalking	1.07$_a$ (0.15)	1.15$_b$ (0.24)	1.08$_a$ (0.13)	4.82	.009
Study 2					
Anger-Jealousy	0.59$_a$ (0.32)	0.97$_b$ (0.40)	0.68$_a$ (0.34)	20.67	.001
Ex. of Love	1.44$_a$ (0.30)	1.82$_b$ (0.49)	1.53$_a$ (0.49)	16.87	.001
PMP	1.13 (0.60)	1.70 (0.70)	1.56 (0.66)	1.34	.46
Stalking	1.07$_a$ (0.14)	1.13$_b$ (0.20)	1.09$_a$ (0.16)	3.38	.05

Note. PMP = Psychological maltreatment of partner. Means in the same row with different letters are significantly different from each other by Tukey LSD. There were no significant gender main effects or gender by breakup status interactions. For anger-jealousy, the range is from 0 to 1.25. For the other scales the range is from 1 to 3.

ANGER-JEALOUSY

As predicted, the anger-jealousy cluster was strongly related to break-up status, with those on the receiving end of the breakup endorsing much higher levels of anger-jealousy than either the initiator or mutual breakup conditions. But some of the respondents in the initiator and mutual conditions had feelings of anger-jealousy that corresponded to those in the receiving condition. Sixteen percent of the initiators in Study 1 and 17% in Study 2 endorsed four of the five items in the scale. In the mutual condition, 20% in Study 1 and 37% in Study 2 endorsed four items. This distribution of anger-jealousy is relevant to the correlational analysis presented below.

EXPRESSIONS OF LOVE

As expected, those on the receiving end of the breakup were also more likely to continue, for a while, trying to reunite and in letting the ex-partners know that they still loved them.

COMPOSITE STALKING

The effect of breakup status on stalking was less dramatic, but statistically significant in each study. Receivers were more likely to stalk than either initiators or mutuals. This result supported a critical expectation for the formulation given above.

PSYCHOLOGICAL MALTREATMENT OF PARTNER

In neither study was PMP related to breakup status. This result is not particularly surprising since the maltreatment occurred before the breakup.

NUMBER OF BREAKUPS AS A FACTOR IN STALKING

In Study 2, we had detailed questions concerning the number of breakups and reunions. It turned out that the number of breakups, which ranged from only 1 (62%) to 4 or more (9%), was not correlated with breakup status, so that we were able to treat these as two separate factors in an ANOVA. We obtained similar results when number of breakups was categorized into only 1, 2, 3, and 4 or more, as we did when we simply distinguished one from two or more. In the latter case the F-ratio for number of breakups (in a gender [2] x breakup status [3] x number of breakups [2] ANOVA) with the overall stalking measure as the criterion was 11.37, $df = 1, 188, p < .001$. This finding supported our hypothesis that number of breakups would contribute to stalking.

Correlational Analysis of Stalking and Psychological Maltreatment of Partners

In Table 11.3, the correlational patterns for Study 1 and Study 2 are presented with the data from Study 2 presented above the diagonal and Study 1 below. The findings from the two studies are quite consistent. Stalking perpetration and the perpetration of psychological maltreatment of the partner before breakup are modestly but significantly correlated in both studies. These findings hold if one transforms the stalking measure into a three-category measure to control for the skewed distribution. The anger-jealousy cluster consistently predicted the degree of stalking, and this pattern held if one looked at the relationship

Table 11.3 Intercorrelations Among Predictors of Expressions of Love, Composite Stalking, and Psychological Maltreatment of Partner (PMP).

Study 1	Study 2						
	Anger-Jealousy	Need for control	Anxious Attach.	Avoidant Attach.	Express of Love	Stalking	PMP
Anger-Jealous		.08	.28**	−.16*	.50**	.28**	.09
Need for control	.17*		.30**	.15*	.19**	.51**	.24*
Anxious attach	.30**	.32**		.06	.36**	.35**	.22*
Avoidant attach	.17*	.19*	.32*		−.10	−.01	−.01
Express of love	.49**	.21**	.25**	.13		.55**	.25*
Stalking	.44**	.22**	.21**	.13	.54**		.21*
PMP	.20**	.39**	.25**	.11	.16*	.21**	

Note. Study 1 below the diagonal (df = 167); Study 2 above (df =201).

In neither study were the correlations significantly different from each other as a function of gender, so the data above combine both men and women.

$*p < .05.$ $**p < .01.$

within each of the three breakup status conditions. We had expected that anger-jealousy would be positively related to the degree of anxious attachment, but not necessarily to avoidant attachment, and that held. In fact avoidant attachment was inconsistently related, being slightly positive in Study 1 and slightly negative in Study 2. Need for control was only modestly related to anger-jealousy, but it was consistently related to stalking—dramatically so in Study 2—and to PMP. As expected, anxious attachment was consistently related to expressions of love, stalking, and PMP, and avoidant attachment was not. Expressions of love were highly related to the composite stalking measure in both studies and modestly but significantly related to PMP. Among the predictors, anger-jealousy and anxious attachment were somewhat more strongly connected to expressions of love than was need for control, but the latter was nonetheless a significant, although modest, predictor of expressions of love—not just of stalking and PMP. The correlational patterns were quite consistent for both men and women so that the results in Table 11.3 have been combined. The results were similar enough that we were able to examine a path model implied in our collective hypotheses. That model is contained in Figure 11.1, with the standardized path weights.

Two questions were examined. Were the hypothesized paths significant when controlling for the effects of other variables in the model?

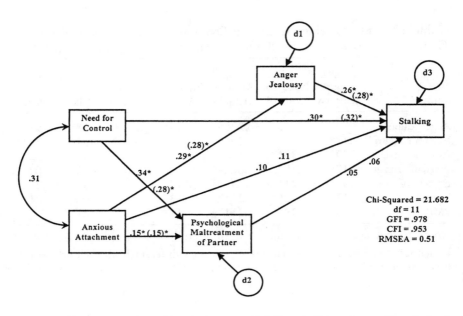

Figure 11.1. A structural equations model for stalking in studies 1 & 2 with the standardized path coefficients. Path coefficients were derived from maximum likelihood estimates and those for Study 2 are in parentheses. The signficance values are based on the critical ratios derived from dividing the covariances by their standard errors (Arbuckle & Wothe, 1999, pp. 151–156).

Specifically, (a) did anxious attachment have a significant direct effect or was it mediated largely by the association of anxious attachment and anger-jealousy? (b) can the contribution of Psychological Maltreatment of Partner be considered a causal influence on stalking or is it better conceived of as a correlate that reflects other potential causes. In both Studies 1 and 2, the proposed SEM model was a good fit, and all of the proposed paths were statistically significant except 2. The direct path for anxious attachment to stalking was not significant in either sample—but the indirect paths through anger-jealousy to stalking were both highly significant. The degree of PMP prior to breakup did not remain a significant contributor to the level of stalking. Because all of the other proposed paths were significant in each sample, we tested the hypothesis that the same model had replicated in the two samples. The test of that is shown in Figure 11.1 (where the path weights for Study 2 are in parentheses), and it shows good fit, as indicated by four different goodness of fit indices. Need for control was predictive of both PMP and stalking. Anxious attachment was predictive of PMP. Thus the major hypotheses of the study were supported, with the exception of the expectation that a behavioral pattern of psychological abuse prior to breakup would have a potentially causal role in stalking after breakup. Rather, both stalking and psychological abuse were reflections of various combinations of need for control, anxious attachment, and the degree of anger-jealousy over the breakup.

DISCUSSION

What Have We Learned About Stalking Perpetration on College Campuses?

Reports from victims of stalking suggest that between 60% and 80% of stalking occurs in the context of intimate relationships that are being terminated or not progressing as one partner wishes (Palarea, Zona, Lane, & Langhinrichsen-Rohling, 1999; Tjaden & Thoennes, 1998). Estimates of the prevalence of stalking victimization on college campuses have been marred by a failure to get clear evidence about the degree to which the person felt genuinely afraid when faced with the variety of harassing and stalking behaviors. Several different samples have provided estimates of being stalked that range from 14%-27% (Coleman, 1997; Cupach & Spitzberg, this volume; Langhinrichsen-Rohling et al., this volume; Sinclair & Frieze, this volume). One major goal of this study was to develop a procedure for securing estimates of stalking perpetration in an anonymous context that might reduce the inhibitions on self-reporting stalking. We chose to ask about stalking-like behaviors in the context of relationship breakups, and we provided an opportunity to describe their emotional reactions to the breakup, their attempts to reunite and convince the ex of their feelings of love before we asked about behaviors that became progressively more obvious as instances of stalking such as threats and vandalism. The data from two separate studies indicate that this approach elicits self-reports of fairly high levels of stalking following breakups—particularly those in which the respondent is a receiver of the breakup, where 23.8% (Study 1) and 14.1% (Study 2) admitted to six or more incidents of stalking their ex-partner. Across all breakup contexts, 38.5% (Study 1) and 44.6% (Study 2) engaged in at least one stalking behavior following a breakup. In the Sinclair and Frieze (this volume) study, 18% of the perpetrators admitted going too far in their persistence, 12%-14% admitted engaging in one act of physical aggression, and 19%-25% engaged in one act of mild aggression or verbal abuse. In the Langhinrichsen-Rohling and colleagues' study (this volume), 27.5% of those receiving the breakup engaged in an act that they recognized as having a negative impact on the victim. Even though each of these research groups indexes stalking perpetration in different ways, we can see that it occurs more frequently than would have appeared to be the case and poses a more serious problem for its victims than might have been estimated.

The Anatomy of Stalking

Taken together, the findings from these two studies suggest that stalking is most likely to occur in the context of relationship breakups in which the person is on the receiving end of the breakup. Part of the explanation for the power of this condition is that it elicits high levels of anger, jealousy, and obsessive thoughts about the ex-partner, and these are consistently related to stalking. A pattern of multiple breaking up and getting back together is also a contributing factor. The multiple breakups are a context in which each partner may learn that it is not really over, and thus learn that persistence and some stalking behaviors will be rewarded by reuniting. Finally, even when participants indicated that the breakup was mutual or personally initiated, the degree of anger-jealousy was strongly predictive of stalking. Overall, then, multiple aspects of the context of a breakup must be considered to understand the likelihood of stalking.

WHAT DO STALKERS THINK THEY ARE DOING?

Our approach to assessment has allowed us to obtain data on the stalker's perspective. The high level of correlation ($r = .54$ and $.55$) between the expressions of love scale and stalking is one indication that, to stalkers, much of what they have done is directed toward reunion and a continued expression of their feelings of love. Part of these effects may well be method effects due to the assessment of both expressions of love and stalking behaviors in the same format and in closely related questions, but expressions of love were significantly correlated with PMP in both studies. Another interesting pattern is that levels of anger-jealousy-obsessiveness were strongly correlated with expressions of love. Nothing prevents a person from both wanting a partner back very badly and also being very angry with him or her for leaving.

PERSONAL CHARACTERISTICS OF STALKERS

Not everyone who experiences all of the triggers for stalking does in fact stalk or engage in relationship abuse prior to the breakup. Our premise in selecting individual difference variables is that those implicated in relationship violence would be highly predictive of stalking. It seemed to us that Kurt (1995) had identified an important continuity between coercion in relationships and the continuation of coercion through stalking after a breakup. Furthermore, the attachment theory analysis of relationship violence may be seen as an exaggerated form of protest behavior over the potential loss of an attachment figure (namely, the partner) (Bowlby, 1980). Bartholomew et al. (2001) have shown that those attachment types high in anxiety (preoccupied and fearful) engaged in more psychological maltreatment of partners, both heterosexual and gay, and more physical abuse also. In both the Dutton and colleagues (1994) and Holtzworth, Munroe and associates (1997) studies of abusive male spouses, degree of fearful attachment was strongly related to abuse. One of the potential mediators of the connection between anxious attachment and stalking is the connection of both to anger-jealousy. Our findings in these two studies replicate the research of Brennan and Shaver (1995), showing that preoccupied attachment style is connected to jealousy, dissatisfaction with partners, and high levels of anger-frustration. In their powerful birth-cohort study of partner abuse, Magdol, Moffitt, Caspi, and Silva (1998) have shown that disturbances of parental-adolescent attachment relationships at age 15 provide significant predictions of the perpetuation of partner abuse at age 21. Our major contribution is to suggest that we will understand the attachment anxiety and stalking relationship more fully by examining potential mediators of this relationship. Negative attributions, negative emotional reactions of an angry, jealous, and obsessive sort seem the most promising candidates for elucidating the connection.

NEED FOR CONTROL

The literature on perpetrators of domestic abuse has implicated feelings of personal control and threat to control as a central theme (Hamberger & Hastings, 1986; Stets, 1988). Follingstad and associates (1988, 1999) have shown that a self-report scale reflecting the need to control a partner in intimate relationships is highly predictive of physical abuse in dating relationships. The studies reported here develop the theme by showing that need for control is predictive of psychological maltreatment of partners prior to breakups, and highly predictive of stalking—particularly in Study 2. Although need for control and anxious attachment was significantly related in both samples, regression analyses—not reported in detail here—showed that each contributed a significant unique variance to the prediction of stalking. Their pattern of correlations with other predictors and outcome variables was somewhat different. Attachment was more strongly connected to the anger-jealousy cluster and to expressions of love whereas need for control was more strongly connected to the threats subscale of the stalking measure. The pattern is consistent with theoretical expectations. Because the need for a control measure is relatively new, additional research will be required to flesh out its implications.

How consistent are these findings with those of other studies of college samples and with the clinical and forensic studies of adjudicated stalkers? The manic love style measured by Sinclair and Frieze (2000) has previously been shown to load on the same factor as the anxious attachment style (Davis, Kirkpatrick, Levy, & O'Hearn, 1994; Hendrick & Hendrick, 1989). Mania and anxious attachment (in its general and relationship-specific forms) seem to be promising as components of a theory of who stalks (Langhinrichsen-Rohling et al., this volume). The control scale brings in a somewhat novel dimension in stalking research. It might be redescribed as the need for control in the context of intimate relationships. It embodies feelings of not being able to trust the partner, which may explain some of its association with anxious attachment. It also touches on power/dominance feelings identified as important in the general relationship violence literature by Ronfeldt, Kimerling, and Arias (1998) and by Stets (1988).

The complexity of the considerations that seem necessary to predict stalking is consistent with White and colleagues' (this volume) developmental contextual framework. But we do not find that stalking or its predictors at the college campus level are a highly gendered phenomenon.

LIMITATIONS OF THE STUDIES

First, the measures of stalking are in an early stage of development and admittedly crude. Now that we have at least four separate measures—Cupach and Spitzberg's (this volume), Langhinrichsen-Rohling and associates (this volume), Sinclair and Frieze's (this volume) and ours in the research literature—it is time for comparative work on their merits and a movement toward a smaller number of instruments. We currently have such work under way. In college samples the number of respondents who would qualify as stalking following a breakup in a legal sense is low—perhaps lower than 10%. Nonetheless, the level of harassing behaviors that can be rather distressful to victims is quite substantial by whichever estimate one uses. For theory testing, we must move beyond the pickup college sample to samples with more older adults who are undergoing the loss of established relationships and a greater loss of standing in the community when that happens than are college students. Schwartz-Watts and Morgan (1998) have shown that stalkers are older, better educated, more likely to be White, and more likely to have a military or police background than other criminal groups. Finally, all of our current data are cross-sectional. To understand the development of stalking, we need to create a longitudinal data set, having life history data at different points in time, so that we can distinguish among theoretically viable interpretations. Now we cannot really tell if need for control is a preexisting personality characteristic or a product of conflicted and unsatisfying relationship experiences. Attachment theory allows that a change of attachment style may come about due to changes in the quality of the ongoing relationship experiences. To what extent are the observed relationships among anxious attachment, jealousy, anger, and mild harassment a product of attachment as a causal influence or as outcomes of relationship difficulties and breakups? At least now we have some promising places to look.

CONCLUSION

Our major contributions are fourfold. (a) From the stalker's perspective, we have shown that the degree of stalking is highly connected to expressions of love and the level of anger, jealousy, and obsessiveness. (b) We have shown that the level of courtship persistence and stalking following a relationship breakup are quite substantial when an anonymous self-report is provided. (c) We have shown that several features of the nature of breakups are relevant to degree of stalking. Among these are who initiates the breakup, the number of breakups, and the emotional reactions to breakups such as anger, jealousy, and obsessiveness. (d) We have provided a replicated path model of the relationships among need for control, anxious attachment, and anger-jealousy that shows the role they play in psychological maltreatment of partners and stalking. A framework that includes both breakup context factors and personal dispositions relevant to relationship violence appears to be essential to the understanding of stalking perpetration.

ACKNOWLEDGMENTS

We would like to acknowledge the comments and suggestions of Kelly Brennan, R. Chris Fraley, Irene Hanson Frieze, Jenny Langhinrichsen-Rohling , and Robin Kowalski on previous drafts of this article. We are indebted to Tim Keith for his consultation on our SEM models and expertise in the AMOS software system. We owe a significant debt of gratitude to graduate students and undergraduates who have, over the 3–year period from the fall of 1996 through this fall (1999), administered surveys, scored data, pretested the early versions of the Relationship History Survey, and helped in the analysis of the two studies reported herein. Among the graduate students are Diane Boudreaux-Kraft, Meredith Cato, Melanie Dye, James Hartell, Lisa Johnson, Colleen Reardon, and Mags Runge. Among the undergraduates are Sherry Brabham, Kevin Byrd, Will Gettis, Krystal Heyward, Katherine Johnson, Matthew King, Marsha Platt, Christine Ross, David Smith, David Usher, Todd Wagoner, and Forrest Wicks.

REFERENCES

Arbuckle, J. L., & Wothe, W. (1999). *Amos 4.0 user's guide*. Chicago: SmallWaters Corporation.

Bartholomew, K., Henderson, A. J. Z., & Dutton, D. G. (2001). Insecure attachment and abusive intimate relationships. In C. Clulow (Ed.), *Adult attachment and couple work: Applying the "secure base" concept in research and practice* (pp. 43–61). London: Routledge.

Bartholomew, K., & Horowitz, L. M. (1991). Attachment styles among young adults: A test of a four-category model. *Journal of Personality and Social Psychology, 61,* 226–244.

Baumeister, R. F., Wotman, S. R., & Stillwell, A. M. (1993). Unrequited love: On heartbreak, anger, guilt, scriptlessness, and humiliation. *Journal of Personality and Social Psychology, 64,* 377–394.

Bowlby, J. (1980). *A secure base.* New York: Basic Books.

Brennan, K. A., Clark, C. L., & Shaver, P. R. (1998). Self-report measure of adult attachment: An integrative overview. In J. Simpson & W. Rholes (Eds.), *Attachment theory and close relationships* (pp. 46–76). New York: Guilford.

Brennan, K. A., & Shaver, P. R. (1995). Dimensions of adult attachment, affect regulation, and romantic relationship functioning. *Personality and Social Psychology Bulletin, 21,* 267–283.

Coleman, J. R. (1997). Stalking behavior and the cycle of domestic violence. *Journal of Interpersonal Violence, 12,* 420–432.

Cupach, W. R., & Spitzberg, B. H. (1998). Obsessional relational intrusion and stalking. In B. H. Spitzburg, & W. R. Cupach (Eds.), *The dark side of close relationships* (pp. 233–263). Mahwah, NJ: Lawrence Erlbaum Associates.

Davis, K. E., & Boudreaux-Kraft, D. (1997, July 1). *Stalking, erotomania, and pathologies of romantic love.* Presented at the International Network on Personal Relationship Conference, Athens, Ohio.

Davis, K. E., Kirkpatrick, L., Levy, M., & O'Hearn, R. E. (1994). Stalking the elusive love style: Attachment styles, love styles, and the prediction of romantic relationship outcomes. In R. Erber & R. Gilmour (Eds.), *Theoretical frameworks for personal relationships* (pp. 179–210). Hillsdale, NJ: LEA.

Davis, K. E., & O'Hearn, R. (1989, May 12). *Doing and being done to: Attachment style and the degree of post-breakup distress among formerly dating couples.* Presented as part of the Symposium, "New developments in Attachment Theory" at the Iowa Network on Personal Relationships, Iowa City, Iowa.

Dutton, D. G., Saunders, K., Starzomski, A., & Bartholomew, K. (1994). Intimacy-anger and insecure attachment as precursors of abuse in intimate relationships. *Journal of Applied Social Psychology, 24,* 1367–1386.

Dutton, D. G., van Ginkel, C., & Landolt, M. A. (1996). Jealousy, intimate abusiveness, and intrusiveness. *Journal of Family Violence, 11,* 411–423.

Follingstad, D. R., Bradley, R. G., Laughlin, J. E., & Burke, L. (1999). Risk factors and correlates of dating violence: The relevance of examining frequency and severity levels in a college sample. *Violence & Victims, 14,* 365–380.

Follingstad, D. R., Rutledge, L., McNeill-Harkins, K., & Polek, D. (1988). Factors related to physical violence in dating relationships. *Journal of Family Violence, 3,* 169–182.

Frazier, P. A., & Cook, S. W. (1993). Correlates of distress following heterosexual relationship dissolution. *Journal of Social & Personal Relationships, 10,* 55–67.

Fremouw, W. J., Westrup, D., & Pennypacker, J. (1997). Stalking on campus: The prevalence and strategies for coping with stalking. *Journal of Forensic Sciences, 42,* 664–667.

Guerreo, L. K. (1998). Attachment-style differences in the experience and expression of romantic jealousy. *Personal Relationships, 5,* 273–291.

Hall, D. M. (1998). The victims of stalking. In J. R. Meloy (Ed.), *The psychology of stalking* (pp. 113–137). San Diego, CA: Academic Press.

Hamberger, L. K., & Hastings, J. E. (1986). Personality correlates of men who abuse their partners: A cross-validation study. *Journal of Family Violence, 1,* 323–346.

Hazan, C., & Shaver, P. R. (1987). Romantic love conceptualized as an attachment process. *Journal of Personality and Social Psychology, 52,* 511–524.

Hendrick, C., & Hendrick, S. S. (1989). Research on love: Does it measure up? *Journal of Personality and Social Psychology, 56,* 784–794.

Hill, C. T., Rubin, Z., & Peplau, L. A. (1976). Breakups before marriage: The end of 103 affairs. *Journal of Social Issues, 32,* 147–168.

Holtzworth-Munroe, A., Stuart, G. L., & Hutchinson, G. (1997). Violent vs. nonviolent husbands: Differences in attachment patterns, dependency, and jealousy. *Journal of Family Psychology, 11,* 314–331.

Kienlen, K. K., Brimingham, D. L., Solberg, K. B., O'Regan, J. T., & Meloy, J. R. (1997). A comparative study of psychotic and nonpsychotic stalking. *Journal of the American Academy of Psychiatry and Law, 25,* 317–334.

Kirkpatrick, L. A., & Davis, K. E. (1994). Attachment style, gender, and relationship stability: A longitudinal study. *Journal of Personality and Social Psychology, 66,* 602–612.

Kirkpatrick, L. A., & Hazan, C. (1994). Attachment styles and close relationships: A four-year prospective study. *Personal Relationships, 1,* 123–142.

Kurt, J. L. (1995). Stalking as a variant of domestic violence. *Bulletin of the Academy of Psychiatry and the Law, 23,* 219–223.

Magdol, L., Moffitt, T. E., Caspi, A., & Silva, P. (1998). Developmental antecedents of partner abuse: A prospective-longitudinal study. *Journal of Abnormal Psychology, 107,* 375–389.

Meloy, J. R. (1998). The psychology of stalking. In J. R. Meloy (Ed.), *The psychology of stalking* (pp. 1–27). San Diego, CA: Academic Press.

National Institute of Justice. (1993). *Project to develop a model anti-stalking code states* (Publication No. NCJ 144477). Washington, DC: U.S. Department of Justice.

O'Hearn, R., & Davis, K. E. (1997). Women's experience of giving and receiving emotional abuse. *Journal of Interpersonal Violence, 12,* 375–391.

Palarea, R. E., Zona, M. A., Lane, J. C., & Langhinrichsen-Rohling, J. (1999). The dangerous nature of intimate relationship stalking: Threats, violence, and associated risk factors. *Behavioral Sciences and the Law , 17,* 269–283.

Pathé, M., & Mullen, P. E. (1997). The impact of stalkers on their victims. *British Journal of Psychiatry, 170,* 12–17.

Roberts, N., & Noller, P. (1998). The association between adult attachment and couple violence. In J. A. Simpson & W. S. Rhodes (Eds.), *Attachment theory and close relationships* (pp. 317–350). New York: Guilford.

Ronfeldt, H. M., Kimerling, R. K., & Arias, I. (1998). Satisfaction with relationship power and the perpetuation of relationship violence. *Journal of Marriage and the Family, 60,* 70–78.

Schwartz-Watts, D., & Morgan, D. W. (1998). Violent versus nonviolent stalkers. *Journal of the American Academy of Psychiatry & Law, 26,* 241–245.

Sprecher, S. (1994). Two sides to the breakup of romantic relationships. *Personal Relationships, 1,* 199–222.

Sprecher, S., Felmlee, D., Metts, S., Fehr, B., & Vanni, D. (1998). Factors associated with distress following the breakup of a close relationship. *Journal of Social & Personal Relationships, 15,* 791–809.

Straus, M. A., & Gelles, R. J. (1990). *Physical violence in American families.* New Brunswick, NJ: Transaction Publishers.

Stets, J. E. (1988). *Domestic violence and control.* New York: Springer-Verlag.

Stets, J. E., & Pirog-Good, M. A. (1987). Violence in dating relationships. *Social Psychology Quarterly, 50,* 237–246.

Tjaden, P., & Thoennes, N. (1998). *Stalking in America: Findings from the national violence against women survey.* Denver, CO: Center for Policy Research.

Tolman, R. M. (1989). The development of a measure of psychological maltreatment of women by their male partners. *Violence and Victims, 4,* 159–177.

Tolman, R. M. (1999). The validation of the Psychological Maltreatment of Women Inventory. *Violence and Victims, 14*, 25–37.

Westrup, D. (1998). Applying functional analysis to stalking behavior. In J. R. Meloy (Ed.), *The psychology of stalking: Clinical and forensic perspectives* (pp. 275–297). New York: Academic Press.

Zona, M., Palarea, R. E., & Lane, J. C. (1998). Psychiatric diagnosis and the offender-victim typology of stalking. In J. R. Meloy (Ed.), *The psychology of stalking: Clinical and forensic perspectives* (pp. 69–84). New York: Academic Press.

12

Stalking as a Variant of Intimate Violence: Implications From a Young Adult Sample

TK Logan, Carl Leukefeld, and Bob Walker

The primary focus on stalking in the research literature has been on obsessional followers and erotomanic stalkers from a clinical perspective (e.g., Meloy & Gothard, 1995; Mullen & Pathé, 1994; Zona, Sharma, & Lane, 1993). Recently, several studies have taken a different perspective on stalking. For example, Wright and colleagues (1996) and Roberts and Dziegielewski (1996) discuss a typology of interpersonal stalking while other recent articles suggest that stalking is a variant or extension of intimate violence (Burgess et al., 1997; Coleman, 1997; Kurt, 1995). In support of the thesis that stalking is a variant of intimate violence, national data indicate that 1 in 12 women and 1 in 45 men will be stalked sometime in their lifetime and that most stalking victims are female (4 out of 5 stalking victims are women), while most stalking perpetrators are male. Further, the majority of women who were stalked (59%) were stalked by an intimate partner (e.g., a current or former spouse, cohabitant, or boyfriend) while approximately 30% of the male victims were stalked by an intimate partner (Tjaden & Thoennes, 1998). A large majority of women (80%), being stalked by an intimate partner, reported the stalking either started or continued after the woman left the relationship. In addition, 81% of women who were stalked by a current or former husband or cohabiting partner were also physically assaulted by that partner and 31% had been sexually assaulted. Thus, husbands or cohabiting partners who stalked their partners were four times more likely than husbands or cohabiting partners in the general population to have physically assaulted their partners, and they were six times more likely than husbands and cohabiting partners in the general population to have sexually assaulted their partners. Also, ex-husbands who stalked (either before or after the relationship ended) were significantly more likely than ex-husbands who did not stalk to have engaged in emotionally abusive and controlling behavior (Tjaden & Thoennes, 1998).

Kurt (1995) notes that ". . . common wisdom suggests that stalking behavior is generally employed following a separation or the dissolution of a relationship, but there is little empirical data about its incidence, course, or resolution in the absence of a disastrous denouement" (p. 221). It is during the separation period when abused women are potentially at high risk of being the focus of repeated, unwanted attention and harassment from their partner either as an attempt to maintain the relationship and/or out of anger (Burgess et al., 1997; Buzawa & Buzawa, 1996; Dutton, van Ginkel, & Landolt, 1996; Edelson, Eiskovitz, Guttman, & Sela-Amit, 1991; Hall, 1998; Walker, 1991). Further, separation from an abusive relationship for women can be a dangerous time. Research has found that separation or divorce increases the risk of serious intimate violence. For example, women separated from their husbands were three times more likely to be victimized by spouses than divorced women and 25 times more likely to be victimized by spouses than married women (Bachman & Saltzman, 1995). Consistent with these data, Klein (1996) found that 49% of abusers re-abused their victims within two years of the protective order, although most of the revictimization occurred within the first three months. Another study found that of a sample of women applying for a restraining order, 23% were stalked, while 60% of women reported acts of abuse and 30% reported severe violence after filing a restraining order (Harrell & Smith, 1996).

Thus, current data suggest that:

1. stalking is something a number of women experience;
2. stalking is related to intimate violence;
3. stalking either begins or continues after separation from a relationship; and,

4. the separation period is a potentially dangerous time for women leaving an abusive relationship.

However, many of these conclusions have been drawn from research with married or cohabiting couples. Recent research indicates that intimate violence, however, is not restricted to married or cohabiting couples and exists in dating relationships among couples on college campuses and among adolescents (e.g., Aizenman & Kelley, 1988; Arias, Samios, & O'Leary, 1987; Carlson, 1996). Marshall and Rose (1988) found that as many as three-quarters of all college students may have experienced intimate violence in a current or past dating relationship. Moreover, it has been reported that physical aggression occurs in more than 20% of students' ongoing relationships (Arias, Samios, & O'Leary, 1987; Riggs, O'Leary, & Breslin, 1990). Physical aggression and abuse can include anything from slapping, pushing, and shoving an intimate partner to beating an intimate partner up, threatening and/or using a weapon on an intimate partner (Straus & Gelles, 1990). Further, psychological or emotional abuse frequently occurs with physical violence in intimate relationships (Browne, 1987; Crowell & Burgess, 1996; Dobash & Dobash, 1979; Dutton, Goodman, & Bennett, 1999; Follingstad, Rutledge, Berg, Hause, & Polek, 1990; Hart & Brassard, 1991; Margolin, John, & Gleberman, 1988; O'Leary & Curley, 1986; Sabourin, Infante, & Rudd, 1993; Walker, 1979, 1984).

Consistent with the research indicating that physical and psychological abuse frequently co-occur in intimate relationships, there have also been several studies documenting a high prevalence of psychological abuse using undergraduate student samples (Neufeld, McNamara, & Ertl, 1999; Tolman, 1992; White & Koss, 1991). Further, Follingstad and associates (1990) found that 98% of the women who experienced physical abuse also experienced psychological abuse. Psychological abuse has been found to be as harmful or more harmful than physical abuse (Follingstead et al., 1990; Tolman & Bhosley, 1991) and psychological abuse in early stages of a relationship has been found to be predictive of physical aggression (Leonard & Senchak, 1996; Murphy & O'Leary, 1989; O'Leary, Malone, & Tyree, 1994). Psychological abuse includes verbal attacks such as ridicule, verbal harassment, and name calling—degradation in order to keep a woman under the control of the abuser; isolation that separates her from social support networks or denies her access to finances and other resources, thus, increasing her dependence on the abuser; extreme jealousy or possessiveness including monitoring her behavior and repeated accusations of infidelity; verbal threats of abuse, harm, or torture directed at the woman or at her family, children, friends, or pets; repeated threats of abandonment, divorce, or of initiating an affair; and damage or destruction of the women's personal property or harming or killing her pets (Marshall, 1996, 1999; O'Leary, 1999; Sackett & Saunders, 1999). Thus, given the rates of physical and psychological abuse among college dating samples and the hypothesis that stalking is a variant or extension of intimate violence, it is logical to examine stalking among college dating samples.

In fact, stalking among college students has recently become a popular research topic (Coleman, 1997; Cupach & Spitzberg, 1998; Elliott & Brantley, 1997; Fremouw, Westrup, & Penny-Packer, 1996; Gallagher, Harmon, & Lingenfelter, 1994; Levitt, Silver, & Franco, 1996; McCreedy & Dennis, 1996; Roscoe, Strouse, & Goodwin, 1994; Spitzberg & Rhea, 1999). For example, Spitzberg, Nicastro, and Cousins (1998) found that 28% of their sample of college males and females self-reported being stalked and that there were no gender differences in victimization rates. Fremouw and colleagues (1996) found that 27% of women and 19% of the men had been stalked and only 3 of 294 in the sample admitted to stalking someone. In another study of college males and females, Spitzberg and Rhea (1999) found a significant association between stalking victimization and sexual coercion. Coleman (1997) examined stalking prevalence in a sample of college-aged females and found 27% had experienced stalking/harassment (less violent stalking behaviors such as being watched and/or getting multiple phone calls) and 9% had experienced violent stalking. Also, Coleman found that being stalked was related to verbal and physical abuse victimization.

There are also studies indicating there is mutual violence among some dating couples with from 45% to 68% of students involved in violent relationships reporting both sustaining and initiating psychological and physical violence (Billingham, 1987; Bookwala, Frieze, Smith, & Ryan, 1992; Cate et al., 1982; Gray & Foshee, 1997; O'Keeffe, Brockopp, & Chew, 1986; Pederson & Thomas, 1992). Gray and Foshee (1997) found that individuals in mutually violent relationships experienced and perpetrated more violence, including severe violence, and received more injuries than adolescents in one-sided violent relationships. In order to understand more clearly the context in which stalking behavior occurs, examining both victimization and perpetration of intimate violence among males and females is critical.

Another important factor to consider in intimate violence victimization is alcohol (Brewer, Fleming, Haggerty, & Catalano, 1998; Hoteling & Sugarman, 1986; Kaufman Kanter & Asdigian, 1997; Kilpatrick et al., 1997; Miller, 1990; Miller & Downs, 1993; Stewart, 1996). A review of the literature shows that while, in general, there is a strong association between alcohol use and intimate violence, estimates of the strength of the relationship vary widely (Maiden, 1997). For example, several studies have shown that between 25% to 80% of intimate violence perpetrators abuse alcohol (Flanzer, 1982; 1990; Klein, 1996; Pernanen, 1991; Roizen, 1997). Intimate violence victimization is also associated with alcohol and other drug use (Brewer et al., 1998; Hoteling & Sugarman, 1986; Kaufman Kanter & Asdigian, 1997; Kilpatrick et al., 1997). Research studies indicate that 25%-58% of victims report using alcohol (Kaufman Kantor & Asdigian, 1997; Murdoch, Phil, & Ross, 1990; Plichta, 1996) and that alcohol use by victims is associated with more frequent and severe violence (Kaufman Kantor & Asdigian, 1997).

The findings from college and adult studies on psychological and physical abuse as well as stalking suggest it is important to consider the context in which violence occurs. The context could include both the interrelationship of psychological and physical violence and stalking, as well as examining perpetration rates for each of these types of violence and abuse. However, few studies to date have examined physical abuse, psychological abuse, stalking victimization, and perpetration among males and females. It is important to examine physical and psychological abuse in relationship history when stalking occurs in order to examine whether stalking is an extension or a variant of intimate violence. The hypothesis would be that victims of stalking by a former partner would be more likely to report physical and psychological abuse during their relationship with the intimate partner who stalked them. In addition, alcohol use is a critical factor to examine with regard to the context of intimate violence. This information may be critical to prevent intimate violence as well as to assess the risk for violent behavior in relationships. Within this context, this study had two main purposes:

1. to examine differences among males and females who had been stalked after a breakup and those who did not report being

stalked after a breakup and psychological abuse and physical abuse victimization while that relationship was intact;

2. to examine perpetration of physical abuse, psychological abuse, and stalking among stalking victimization groups by gender; and

3. to examine alcohol use among males and females who report being stalked after a breakup and those who do not report being stalked after a breakup.

METHOD

Participants

The overall sample was 147 males and 190 females with an average age of 20 who volunteered to participate in the study for research credit in their Introductory Communications class at a medium-sized southeastern university. These students were invited to participate in research in exchange for class credit. There were no other selection criteria imposed. Participants were selected for the current study if they answered all of the victimization and perpetration questions about the same relationship. In addition, two participants were 30 years old or older and were dropped from the analysis. This resulted in a sample of 130 (46 males and 84 females); 87% were White and with an average age of 20 (18-24 years old). Also, 96% of the sample indicated they were heterosexual, 3% reported they were bisexual, and 1% reported they were homosexual. There is no evidence to suggest that intimate violence is restricted only to heterosexuals, so all of these participants were included in the subsequent analysis.

Measures

The questionnaire included the following measures:

1. demographic information;
2. alcohol use;
3. psychological abuse victimization;
4. psychological abuse perpetration;
5. physical abuse victimization;
6. physical abuse perpetration;
7. stalking victimization; and
8. stalking perpetration.

Demographic Information included age, gender, race, and sexual orientation. *Alcohol use* was adapted from Harrington and associates (1999) and consisted of 4 items. The first question asked how many drinks they typically have when they drink alcohol (1 = 1-3 drinks at a time; 2 = 4-6 drinks at a time; 3 = 7-12 drinks at a time; 4 = 13 or more drinks at a time). The second question asked how many days in the past month they drank the amount of alcohol they reported in the first question (0 = did not drink in the past 30 days; 1 = on 1 to 4 days; 2 = on 5 to 9 days; 3 = on 10-19 days; 4 = on 20+ days). The third question asked how many times in the past month they got very drunk (0 = drank but did not get drunk in the past 30 days; 1 = daily, 2 = just one or two times in the past month, 3 = 1 or 2 days a week, 4 = almost daily). The fourth question asked at what age they were when they began drinking alcoholic beverages once a month or more often (0 = don't drink once a month or more, 1 = under 16, 2 = 16, 3 = 17, 4 = 18 or older).

The *Psychological Abuse Scale* was developed to assess the prevalence of psychological abuse and was adapted from Tolman's Psychological Maltreatment of Women Inventory (1989, 1999). There were 26 Likert-type items with the following response scale to record how often the behavior occurred in the relationship: 0-never, 1-once or twice, 2-more than twice, 3-once a day, 4-more than once a day. The alpha coefficient of internal consistency for the victimization scale was .95 and for the perpetration scale the alpha was .90. Examples of items include how often did your partner: Try to keep you from seeing or talking to your family? Threaten to have an affair with someone else? Blame you for causing his/her violent behavior? Try to make you feel like you were crazy? Change mood radically, from very calm to very angry or vice versa? For the current study, participants were asked to answer the questions using a time frame reference of the last relationship they were involved in that was one year or longer, or to answer the questions regarding their longest relationship.

The *Conflict Tactics Scale* (Straus, 1990) was developed to assess physical abuse victimization and perpetration by asking whether or how often a specific behavior occurred. For the current study, 10 items from the Conflict Tactics Scale (CTS) were included in the questionnaire with the following response format: 0—never, 1—once or twice, 2—more than twice, 3—once a day, 4—more than once a day. The items focused on behaviors including: Your partner threw something at you; Your partner pushed, grabbed, or shoved you; Your partner beat you up; and, Your partner threatened you with a knife or gun.

Table 12.1 Stalking Items

Once a Day or More	Males (N = 46)	Females (N = 84)
1. Called you at home	54.5	62.5
2. Called you at work	27.3	f8.7
3. Came to your home	36.4	12.5
4. Came to your work or school	36.4	16.7
5. Talked to others to get information about you	27.3	29.2
6. Followed you	18.2	16.7
7. Made hang up calls	18.2	12.5
8. Sent you letters	18.2	16.7
9. Sent you gifts	18.2	8.3
10. Drove by your house	9.1	20.8
11. Watched you	27.3	16.7
12. Left messages on your machine	18.2	16.7
13. Sent you photos	9.1	0
More Than Twice		
14. Made threats to your new partner	9.1	4.2
15. Attempted to break into your car	9.1	4.2
16. Attempted to break into your home	0	4.2
17. Broke into your home	0	0
18. Broke into your car	0	0
19. Violated a restraining order	9.1	0
20. Threatened to cause self-harm	9.1	12.5
21. Threatened to harm you	0	8.3
22. Stole/read mail	9.1	0
23. Attempted to harm you	9.1	4.2
24. Damaged property of new partner	20.0	0
25. Physically harmed him/herself	9.1	4.2
26. Harmed your new partner	0	0
27. Physically harmed you	0	0

Consistent with the psychological abuse scale, participants were asked to answer the questions regarding the last relationship they were involved in that was one year or longer, or to answer the questions using their longest relationship. The alpha coefficient of internal consistency for the victimization scale was .72, and for the perpetration scale was .66. Violence scores were computed by calculating a total violence score, weighting each of the items according to the procedure described by Straus (1990).

The *Stalking Behavior Checklist* was adapted from Coleman's (1997) stalking behavior checklist. Respondents indicated on a 5-point Likert-type scale how often each behavior occurred following a difficult break-up: 0 - never, 1 - once or twice, 2 - more than twice, 3 - once a day, 4 - more than once a day. The reliability coefficient for the victimization scale was .92 and was .93 for the perpetration scale in the current study (see Table 12.1 for items).

Procedure

After the study was described, participants were asked to read, sign, and date an informed consent form if they wished to participate in the study. After the consent forms were returned, the questionnaires were distributed. After each person completed their questionnaire, he/she was given a debriefing sheet and a referral sheet listing various professional organizations to contact for more information or support if needed. All questionnaires were administered in a group setting. However, because of the sensitive nature of the questions, participants were asked to sit at least one seat apart from their neighbors. Also, two forms of the questionnaire were used in order to assure privacy.

When answering the psychological and physical abuse questions, participants were asked to refer to the last relationship they had which lasted at least 1 year. If they had not had a relationship that lasted for 1 year or longer, they were asked to think back to the relationship that lasted the longest. When participants responded to the stalking behavior checklist, they were asked to refer to each of the items regarding the situation following a difficult breakup with an intimate partner. After answering the stalking questions participants were then asked if they answered all of the abuse victimization and perpetration questions about the same partner. Participants who answered all of the questions referring to the same partner were included in this study.

Overview of Analysis

The analysis was completed using two main procedures: Correlations and MANOVAs. Correlations were first computed for males and females separately. A series of multivariate analyses of variance (MANOVAs) were used to examine group differences among those stalked and those not stalked. Stalking scores for groups were computed by first imposing the criteria on each item described in Table 12.1. If participants indicated that the stalking items 1 through 13 occurred once a day or more and/or if participants indicated that the stalking behavior items 14 through 27 occurred more than twice, they were assigned a score of 1 for that item. If the participants did not meet the criteria described above, they were assigned a score of zero for that item. Then, scores were summed. Those with a score of 0 were classified into the no stalking victimization group and those with a score 1 or more were classified into the stalking victimization group. The criteria that the behavior must have occurred more than once was used for each item because most definitions of stalking require that the behavior be repeated (see Tjaden & Thoennes, 1998).

Table 12.1 presents the specific items experienced by males and females who were classified into the stalking victimization groups. The mean stalking victimization scale score for the two groups was 5 for those classified into the no stalking victimization group and 20 for those classified into the stalking victimization group. Thus, by sorting participants into two separate groups as described above, and then examining the scores for each item summed together using the original response format (frequency of item occurrence), the no stalking victimization group did experience some of the behaviors, just not at the intensity level to be classified into the stalking victimization group. This summed scale, using the original response format was also used for the correlation analysis. However, all other analysis used the dichotomous group classification.

RESULTS

Correlations

Table 12.2 reports the correlations for physical, psychological, and stalking victimization and perpetration scales, and alcohol use were computed by gender. For males, stalking victimization was significantly and strongly correlated with self-reported psychological abuse victimization, psychological abuse perpetration, and stalking perpetration. Interestingly, alcohol use was significantly related to psychological abuse perpetration and stalking perpetration (both the number of times drunk in the past month and the number of times they used drug or alcohol before or during sex). Also, the number of days they drank alcohol in the past month was significantly associated with stalking perpetration.

Table 12.2 Correlations for Males and Females

MALES (N = 46)	1	2	3	4	5	6	7	8
1. Stalking Victimization (M = 9.3, SD = 12.5)								
2. Physical Victimization (M = 2.5, SD = 3.6)	.12							
3. Psychological Victimization (M = 12.6, SD = 13.6)	.78**	.29						
4. Physical Abuse Perpetration (M = 1.6, SD = 2.9)	.08	.49**	.18					
5. Psychological Abuse Perpetration (M = 9.6, SD = 10.8)	.63**	.41**	.88**	.42**				
6. Stalking Perpetration (M = 4.5, SD = 10.6)	.84**	−.08	.74**	−.06	.56**			
7. Times drunk past 30 days (M = 1.0, SD = .96)	.53**	.09	.59**	−.10	.45**	.57**		
8. Days drank alcohol past month (M = 1.6, SD = 1.1)	.22	−.14	.29	−.05	.15	.42**	.70**	
9. Use drugs and/or alcohol during sex (M = 2.1, SD 1.1)	.42*	.15	.46*	.06	.44*	.53**	.65**	.56**

FEMALES (N = 84)								
1. Stalking Victimization (M = 8.9, SD = 9.5)								
2. Physical Victimization (M = 1.8, SD = 2.4)	.24*							
3. Psychological Victimization (M = 10.4, SD = 12.2)	.37**	.75**						
4. Physical Abuse Perpetration (M = 1.8, SD = 2.3)	−.01	.47**	.37**					
5. Psychological Abuse Perpetration (M = 7.8, SD = 6.7)	.21	.25*	.45**	.57**				
6. Stalking Perpetration (M = 3.0, SD = 2.9)	.23*	−.005	.27**	−.15	.13			
7. Times drunk past 30 days (M = .5, SD = .7)	.10	.11	.10	−.03	.05	−.17		
8. Days drank alcohol past month (M = 1.0, SD =.7)	−.03	.10	−.03	.04	.05	−.17	.70**	
9. Use drugs and/or alcohol during sex (M = 1.7, SD = 1.0)	.22	.05	.25	−.09	.11	.32*	.19	.29*

*p <.05. **p < .01.

For females, stalking victimization was significantly related to psychological abuse and physical abuse. Stalking victimization was also moderately correlated with stalking perpetration. Contrary to the males, alcohol use had no association with victimization or perpetration, with the exception of using drugs or alcohol before and during sex which was moderately associated with stalking perpetration.

The stalking victimization and stalking perpetration correlation for males (.84) and females (.23) was significantly different (z = 5.81, p < .001) as was the correlation for psychological abuse victimization and perpetration for males (.88) compared to females (.45, z = 5.23, p < .001). These results indicate more of a reciprocal relationship between stalking and psychological abuse victimization and perpetration for males than for females.

GROUP ANALYSIS

Stalking Prevalence

Overall, 27% of the sample were classified into the stalking victimization group. Approximately 1 in 4 males (24%) and almost 1 in 3 females (29%) reported being stalked after a difficult breakup. Also, of those in the stalking victimization group 42% of the males and 63% of the females reported at least one of the threatening behaviors listed in the lower half of Table 12.1 and 18% of the males and 29% of the females in the stalking victimization group reported that at least one of the threatening behaviors occurred more than twice (items 14-27 on Table 12.1).

Alcohol Use

The MANOVA for alcohol use for the 30 days preceding the interview—frequency used drugs and/or alcohol before or during sex, the number of days drunk, average number of drinks, number of days drank alcohol, and age of first full alcoholic drink. The MANOVA was not significant.

Victimization Experiences

There were no significant main effects of gender or of the gender by stalking victimization group interaction for victimization. However, the overall MANOVA for stalking victimization group was significant ($F(2, 125)$ = 9.8, p = .000, Wilks's lambda = .87). Univariate F values for the victimization variables by stalking victimization groups are reported in Table 12.3. The main effects for the stalking victimization group were then examined using univariate F tests and were significant for physical victimization (1.8 for the no stalking victimization group and 3.2 for the stalking victimization group, $F(1, 126) = 5.7$, $p < .05$, eta^2 = .04) and psychological victimization (8.6 for the no stalking victimization group and 19.7 for the stalking victimization group, $F(1, 126) = 19.7$, $p < .01$, eta^2 = .14). Those who reported stalking victimization after breaking up experienced significantly more physical and psychological victimization during the relationship than those who reported no stalking victimization.

Perpetration

Table 12.3 also shows means for the perpetration scales. The overall MANOVA for the stalking victimization group by gender interaction was significant for abuse perpetration ($F(3, 124) = 2.8$, Wilks's lambda = .94, $p < .05$). Males who reported being stalked reported perpetrating significantly more psychological abuse than females who reported

Table 12.3 Physical and Psychological Victimization by Stalking Victimization Group and Perpetration of Forms of Violence by Stalking Victimization Group and Gender

	Males		Females	
	No stalking victimization (N = 35)	Stalking victimization (N = 11)	No stalking victimization (N = 60)	Stalking victimization (N = 24)
Victimization				
Physical abuse victimization	2.0	4.1	1.5	2.3[a]
Scale scores ranged from 0 to 16	(SE = .48)	(SE = .86)	(SE = .37)	(SE = .58)
Psychological abuse victimization	9.5	22.5	7.7	17.0[a]
Scale scores ranged from 0 to 78	(SE = 2–0)	(SE = 3.6)	(SE = 1–5)	(SE = 2–4)
Perpetration				
Physical abuse perpetration	1.4	2.0	1.8	1.9
Scale scores ranged from 0 to 17	(SE = .43)	(SE = .78)	(SE = .33)	(SE = .52)
Psychological abuse perpetration	7.0	17.9	6.4	9.8[b]
Scale scores ranged from 0 to 48	(SE = 1.3)	(SE = 2.4)	(SE = 1.0)	(SE = 1.6)
Stalking perpetration	3.0	11.3	2.6	4.0[b]
Scale scores ranged from 0 to 70	(SE = 1.1)	(SE = 1.9)	(SE = .83)	(SE = 1.3)

[a]$p < .05$ for the main effect of stalking victimization group; [b]$p < .05$ for the interaction of stalking victimization group x gender.

stalking victimization, and males and females who did not report stalking ($F(1, 126) = 5.2$, $p < .04$, eta^2 = .04), see Figure 12.1. Also, there was a similar trend for stalking behavior perpetration, with males who reported stalking victimization also reporting more stalking perpetration than females who were stalked and both males and females who were not stalked ($F(1, 126) = 6.6$, $p < .05$, eta^2 = .05), see Figure 12.2.

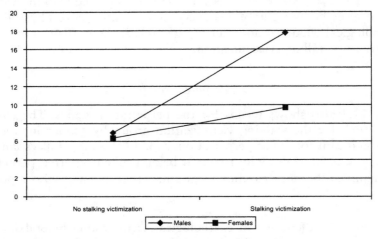

Figure 12.1. Psychological abuse perpetration

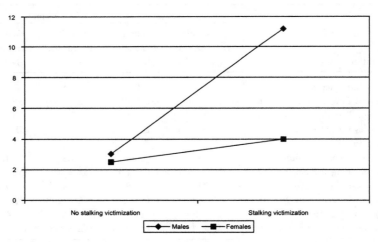

Figure 12.2. Stalking perpetration

DISCUSSION

Overall, 27% of the sample in this study was classified into the stalking victimization group, which is consistent with other stalking prevalence rates among college samples (Coleman, 1997; Fremouw et al., 1996; Spitzberg et al., 1998). Stalking victimization was significantly associated with physical and psychological abuse victimization for women, and was significantly associated with psychological abuse for men. Thus, the data from this study contribute to the hypothesis that stalking is a variant of or extension of intimate violence. In other words, the data from this study support the notion that stalking is a continuation of intimate violence toward a partner after the relationship ends. This study only focused on stalking after a difficult breakup, limiting generalizability of results to all stalking behavior. Examining differences in relationships in which stalking begins before the relationship ends, and relationships where stalking begins after the relationship is terminated is critical for understanding and clarifying the role stalking plays in relationships. This study asked whether stalking behavior occurred after a difficult breakup, but did not clarify whether the stalking actually began before the relationship ended, while the end of the relationship was being contemplated, or if the stalking began after the relationship broke up. In fact, it could be possible that the breakup occurred because of the stalking behavior. The National Crime Victimization survey reported that 43% of stalking began after the relationship ended for female stalking victims, and 36% of women indicated that stalking occurred both before and after the relationship ended (Tjaden & Thoennes, 1998).

It is also interesting to note that the stalking victimization in this study did not differ by gender. These results have several implications. One implication is for future research to focus on clarifying and understanding the consequences of stalking for male victims. There has been very limited focus on male victims in the research literature. Hall (1998) discussed male victims of stalking and suggests that male victims have fewer options available to them than women and that the psychological consequences for males are unclear. For males, in this study, stalking victimization was also related to psychological abuse victimization. Simonelli and Ingram (1998) examined male victims of psychological and physical abuse and found that males who experienced more abuse also reported greater levels of overall psychological distress and depression.

However, it is also important to note that there were significant gender by stalking victimization group interactions for perpetration of stalking and psychological abuse perpetration, suggesting a reciprocal relationship of victimization and perpetration for both psychological abuse and for stalking behavior especially for males. It is possible that the reciprocal relationship of stalking victimization and perpetration is characteristic of certain kinds of relationships, as has been reported previously for psychological and physical abuse (Bookwala et al., 1992; Breslin, Riggs, O'Leary, & Arias, 1990; Fiebert & Gonzalez, 1997; O'Keefe, 1997; Vivian & Langhinrichsen-Rohling, 1994). Research suggests that antecedents of intimate violence perpetration, for both males and females, include level of delinquency in adolescence (Giordano et al., 1999; Magdol, Moffit, Caspi, & Silva, 1998). In addition, Giordano and associates (1999) found that intimate violence perpetration for females was also related to a more angry self-concept and a perception of being labeled a troublemaker when they were adolescents. Krueger and colleagues (1998) takes this extension of problem behaviors into adulthood one step further by suggesting that not only is intimate violence an extension of antisocial behavior for both males and females, but that those who engage in antisocial actions are more likely to associate with others engaging in antisocial actions including intimate partners. Thus, mutually physically and psychologically violent couples characterize some relationships, and stalking may be an extension of the mutually violent relationship after a breakup.

Interestingly, alcohol use was more related to stalking and psychological abuse victimization and perpetration for males than for females, and the reciprocal relationship of stalking and psychological abuse victimization and perpetration was much stronger for males than for females. This may suggest that the males in this study were more likely to report victimization in order to justify their perpetration behaviors, and that perpetration of intimate violence is part of a constellation of problem behaviors for these males. Studies have linked intimate violence with alcohol use, drug use, delinquency and other criminal activities (Fagan, Stewart, & Hansen, 1983; Holtzworth-Monroe, Smutzler, & Bates, 1997; Magdol, Moffit, Caspi, & Silva, 1998; Moffit & Caspi, 1998; Simons, Lin, Johnson, & Conger, 1995; Simons, Lin, & Gordon, 1998; Stacy & Shupe, 1983). The role-stalking perpetration plays within the constellation of problem behaviors needs further clarification—especially given a developing literature which suggests intimate violence on campus is increasing (Gallagher, Harmon, & Lingenfelter, 1994). This self-justification hypothesis for males is consistent with other data suggesting that although there is a small percentage of males identified from national data who report being abused, it is clear that women are more often victims of intimate violence and are more likely to be injured from intimate violence (Tjaden & Thoennes, 1998).

For females, the reciprocal relationship of stalking and psychological abuse victimization and perpetration was more moderate than the relationship for the males. One hypothesis for the reciprocal relationship of physical and psychological abuse victimization and perpetration among women from other studies is that women are defending themselves from abuse or responding to previous violence out of hopeless desperation (Hamberger, 1997). Another explanation for this relationship is offered by Fiebert and Gonzalez (1997) who asked women who reported assaulting their intimate partners, why they did so. They found that women expressed aggression toward their male partners in part because they wished to engage their partner's attention, particularly emotionally, and that they did not believe that their male victims would be seriously injured or would retaliate. How these explanations extend to stalking perpetration and victimization is still unclear.

Thus, data indicate understanding the reciprocal relationships of victimization and perpetration and the interrelationships of different types of abuse, including stalking, are critical issues on which to focus future research. Furthermore, understanding the role that stalking plays in relationships and how stalking differs in married, cohabiting, and dating relationships will also be important. Magdol, Moffitt, Caspi, and Silva (1998) found that among young adults, intimate violence was more prevalent for cohabiting couples compared to dating couples. This study did not ask about marital or cohabiting status or history, but examining stalking prevalence among young adults who are and are not cohabiting or have never lived together will be critical in facilitating research on intimate violence.

Another critical area for future research consideration is what are the consequences for a woman who experiences stalking? The impact of physical, sexual, and psychological abuse on women has been fairly well documented and suggests that intimate violence has been linked to physical injury, chronic health problems, increased stress, emotional and cognitive distress, chronic pain, miscarriage, irritable bowel syndrome, psychosomatic and somatic complaints, depression, anxiety, PTSD, alcoholism, and use of prescription drugs (Domino & Haber,

1987; Drossmon, Leserman, & Nachman, 1990; Dutton, Haywood, & El-Bayoumi, 1997; Eby, Campbell, Sullivan, & Davidson, 1995; Goodstein & Page, 1981; Haber & Roos, 1985; Koss, 1990; Kurz & Stark, 1988; McFarlane, 1989; Plichta, 1996; Resnick, Acierno, & Kilpatrick, 1997; Stark, Flitcraft, & Frazer, 1979; Stark & Flitcraft, 1996; Walker, 1984; Wokenstein & Sterman, 1998). There have also been several studies which link stalking victimization to mental health consequences such as nightmares, sleeplessness, anxiety attacks, anger, and stress (Hall, 1998; Pathé & Mullen, 1997; Spitzberg & Rhea, 1999; Spitzberg et al., 1998). However, there has been a limited focus on understanding the cumulative effect stalking has on women who may have also endured other types of abuse, or in trying to understand the separate effects of each type of abuse. This understanding may be critical in helping a woman recover from trauma.

Other limitations of this study include the small number of participants and a sample which was limited to young adults in college. This may limit the generalization of the results to all college students and/ or young adults. Nevertheless, conclusions from this study and others highlight the importance of examining stalking victimization for both research and prevention education.

Another limitation of this study is the measurement of stalking. The current study included a list of behaviors that may be typical in stalking situations. However, the actual threat to the victim or whether the victim perceived himself/herself as a stalking victim was not included. By contrast, the National Violence Against Women survey asked about stalking behavior and classified respondents as stalking victims if they subsequently reported that the stalking behavior made them feel very frightened or if they feared bodily harm. The current study measured stalking victimization similarly as a way psychological abuse has been measured. Very few data have been reported in the literature regarding whether individuals perceive themselves as being psychologically abused, or the threat or fear that specific psychological abuse acts have on the victim. Pipes and LeBov-Keeler (1997) did examine the relationship between the perception of those who believed they were psychologically abused and psychological abuse using behavioral statements and found a significant overlap between the two. One area for further examination would be to determine the differences between stalking victims that are afraid, or threatened, or who perceive themselves as being stalked and those who do not. Another possibility is to examine the actual stalking behavior and whether it differs in situations where the victim does or does not feel threatened. In other words, what is it about a stalking situation that makes the victim feel afraid? Is it something about the victim? Something about the perpetrator? Or something about the situation? Does a woman, especially a young woman, always know when she should be afraid? Further, for those victims who don't necessarily feel afraid or threatened at the time of a survey or a research inquiry, are there some positive features about being pursued obsessively? For example, does a woman feel flattered by the repeated pursuit and attention? And what impact does stalking have on a person who is being pursued obsessively—but does not feel afraid? Does this experience make the victim more susceptible to and/or more accepting of later intimate violence? Attitudes and perceptions are important to consider primarily because research has shown that a main force in behavior is normative social influence, not informational influence (Zimbardo & Leippe, 1991). Norms and values of different subpopulations clearly influence behavior. When addressing violence between partners at any level—verbal, psychological, or physical—it is critical to understand the underlying attitudes and perceptions. Thus, an intermediate step in preventing and changing violent behavior among college students, is to understand the underlying attitudes and perceptions toward a behavior in order to ultimately change societal or subgroup norms (Zimbardo & Leippe, 1991). Given the potential link of stalking and intimate violence and the impact that stalking can have on victims, stalking may be an important behavior to include in violence prevention programs.

In summary, stalking is a complex and developing area of science. Although this study and other studies have linked stalking with psychological abuse and physical abuse (Burgess et al., 1997; Coleman, 1997; Kurt, 1995) and sexual coercion (Spitzberg & Rhea, 1999), there are still many questions about the nature of the interrelationships between different kinds of intimate violence. Understanding the role of stalking as a variant of intimate violence is important for further research and important for practitioners who should be aware of the interrelationships of these behaviors. The data from this and other studies, and the questions posed have major implications for assessing the risk of dangerousness in a stalking situation as well as coping for the victim. Stalking should be addressed in violence prevention programs, as well as counseling. It is possible that young males and females are not even aware of stalking and how it might be dangerous. Further, and most important, this study suggests along with other research that victimization should be examined with the full spectrum of victimization experiences in order to more clearly understand intimate violence.

ACKNOWLEDGMENTS

The authors thank the anonymous reviewers and the issue editors for their comments which improved the manuscript substantially. The authors also wish to thank Jennifer Lambert and Michele Staton for helping with the data collection.

REFERENCES

Aizenmann, M., & Kelley, G. (1988). The incidence of violence and acquaintance rape in dating relationships among college men and women. *Journal of College Student Development, 29,* 305-311.

Arias, I., Samios, M., & O'Leary, K. D. (1987). Prevalence and correlates of physical aggression during courtship. *Journal of Interpersonal Violence, 2,* 82-90.

Bachman, R., & Saltzman, L. (1995). *Violence against women: Estimates from the redesigned survey* (Special Report No. NCJ-154348). Washington, DC: Bureau of Justice Statistics, U.S. Department of Justice.

Billingham, R. (1987). Courtship violence: The patterns of conflict resolution strategies across seven levels of emotional commitment. *Family Relations, 36,* 283-289.

Bookwala, J., Frieze, I., Smith, C., & Ryan, K. (1992). Predictors of dating violence: A multivariate analysis. *Violence and Victims, 7,* 297-311.

Breslin, F., Riggs, D., O'Leary, D., & Arias, I. (1990). Expected and actual consequences of dating aggression. *Journal of Interpersonal Violence, 5,* 247-258.

Brewer, D., Fleming, C., Haggerty, K., & Catalano, R. (1998). Drug use predictors of partner violence in opiate-dependant women. *Violence and Victims, 13*(2), 107-115.

Browne, A. (1987). *When battered women kill.* New York: Free Press.

Burgess, A., Baker, T., Greening, D., Hartman, C., Burgess, A., Douglas, J., & Halloran, R. (1997). Stalking behaviors within domestic violence. *Journal of Family Violence, 12,* 389-403.

Buzawa, E. S., & Buzawa, C. G. (1996). *Domestic violence: The criminal justice response* (2nd ed.). Thousand Oaks, CA: Sage Publications.

Carlson, B. E. (1996). Dating violence: Students beliefs about consequences. *Journal of Interpersonal Violence, 11*(1), 3-18.

Cate, R., Henton, L., Koval, J., Christopher, S., & Lloyd, S. (1982). Premarital abuse: A social psychological perspective. *Journal of Family Issues, 3,* 79-90.

Coleman, F. L. (1997). Stalking behavior and the cycle of domestic violence. *Journal of Interpersonal Violence, 12,* 420-432.

Crowell, N., & Burgess, A. (Eds.). (1996). *Understanding violence against women.* Washington, DC: National Academy Press.

Cupach, W., & Spitzberg, B. (1998). Obsessive relational intrusion and stalking. In B. Spitzberg & W. Cupach (Eds.), *The dark side of close relationships* (pp. 233-263). Hillsdale, NJ: Lawrence Erlbaum Associates.

Dobash, R., & Dobash, R. (1979). *Violence against wives.* New York: Free Press.

Domino, J., & Haber, J. (1987). Prior physical and sexual abuse in women with chronic headache and clinical correlates. *Headache, 27,* 310-314.

Drossman, D., Leserman, J., & Nachman, G. (1990). Sexual and physical abuse in women with functional or organic gastrointestinal disorders. *Annals of Internal Medicine, 113,* 828-833.

Dutton, D. G., van Ginkel, C., & Landolt, M. A. (1996). Jealousy, intimate abusiveness, and intrusiveness. *Journal of Family Violence, 11,* 411-423.

Dutton, M., Goodman, L., & Bennett, L. (1999). Court-involved battered women's responses to violence: The role of psychological, physical, and sexual abuse. *Violence and Victims, 14*(1), 89-104.

Dutton, M., Haywood, Y., & El-Bayoumi, G. (1997). Impact of violence on women's health. In S. Gallant, G. Puryear Keita, & R. Royak-Schaler (Eds.), *Health care for women: Psychological, social, and behavioral influences* (pp. 41-56). Washington, DC: American Psychological Association.

Eby, K., Campbell, J., Sullivan, C., & Davidson, W. (1995). Health effects of experiences of sexual violence for women with abusive partners. *Health Care for Women International, 16,* 563-576.

Edelson, J. L., Eiskovits, Z. C., Guttman, E., & Sela-Amit, M. (1991). Cognitive and interpersonal factors in woman abuse. *Journal of Family Violence, 6,* 167-182.

Elliott, L., & Brantley, C. (1997). *Sex on campus: The naked truth about the real sex lives of college students.* New York: Random House.

Fagan, J., Stewart, D., & Hansen, K. (1983). Violent men or violent husbands? Background factors and situational correlates. In D. Finkelhor, R. Gelles, G. Hoteling, & M. Straus (Eds.), *The dark side of families: Current family violence research* (pp. 49-67). Beverly Hills, CA: Sage.

Fiebert, M. S., & Gonzalez, D. M. (1997). College women who initiate assaults on their male partners and the reasons offered for such behavior. *Psychological Reports, 80,* 583-590.

Flanzer, J. (1982). *The many faces of family violence.* Springfield, IL: Charles C Thomas.

Flanzer, J. (1990). Alcohol and family violence: Then and now—who owns the problem. In R. Potter-Efron, & P. Potter-Efron (Eds.), *Aggression, family violence, and chemical dependency* (pp. 61-80). New York: The Haworth Press, Inc.

Follingstad, D., Rutledge, B., Berg, E., Hause, E., & Polek, D. (1990). The role of emotional abuse in physically abusive relationships. *Journal of Family Violence, 5*(2), 107-120.

Fremouw, B., Westrup, D., & Pennypacker, J. (1996). Stalking on campus: The prevalence and strategies for coping with stalking. *Journal of Forensic Sciences, 42,* 666-669.

Gallagher, R. P., Harmon, W. W., & Lingenfelter, C. O. (1994). CSAO's perceptions of changing incidence of problematic college student behavior. *National association of School Personnel Administrator Journal, 32*(1), 37-45.

Giordano, P., Millhollin, T., Cernkovich, S., Pugh, M., & Rudolph, J. (1999). Delinquency, identity, and women's involvement in relationship violence. *Criminology, 37,* 17-40.

Goodstein, R., & Page, A. (1981). The battered wife syndrome: Overview of dynamics and treatment. *American Journal of Psychiatry, 138,* 1036-1044.

Gray, H. M., & Foshee, V. (1997). Adolescent dating violence. *Journal of Interpersonal Violence, 12,* 126-141.

Haber, J., & Roos, C. (1985). Effects of spouse abuse and/or sexual abuse in the development and maintenance of chronic pain in women. *Advances in Pain Research and Therapy, 9,* 889-895.

Hall, D. (1998). The victims of stalking. In J. Meloy (Ed.), *The psychology of stalking* (pp. 113-137). San Diego, CA: Academic Press.

Hamberger, L. K. (1997). Female offenders in domestic violence: A look at actions in their context. *Journal of Aggression, Maltreatment, & Trauma, 1*(1), 117-129.

Harrell, A., & Smith, B. (1996). Effects of restraining orders on domestic violence victims. In E. Buzawa & C. Buzawa (Eds.), *Do arrests and restraining orders work?* (pp. 214-242). Thousand Oaks, CA: Sage.

Harrington, N., Brigham, N., & Clayton, R. (1999). Alcohol risk reduction for fraternity and sorority members. *Journal of Studies on Alcohol, 60,* 521-527.

Hart, S., & Brassard, M. (1991). Psychological maltreatment: Progress achieved. *Development and Psychopathology, 3,* 61-70.

Holtzworth-Munroe, A. Smutzler, N., & Bates, L. (1997). A brief review of the research on husband violence part III: Sociodemographic factors, relationship factors, and differing consequences of husband and wife violence. *Aggression and Violent Behavior, 2,* 285-307.

Hoteling, G., & Sugarman, D. (1986). An analysis of risk markers in husband to wife violence: The current state of knowledge. *Violence and Victims, 1,* 101-124.

Kaufman Kantor, G., & Asdigian, N. (1997). When women are under the influence does drinking or drug use by women provoke beatings by men? In M. Galanter (Ed.), *Recent developments in alcoholism.* New York: Plenum Press.

Kilpatrick, D., Acierno, R., Resnick, H., Saunders, B., & Best, C. (1997). A 2-year longitudinal analysis of the relationship between violent assault and substance use in women. *Journal of Consulting and Clinical Psychology, 65,* 834-837.

Klein, A. (1996). Re-Abuse in a population of court-restrained male batterers: Why restraining orders don't work. In E. Buzawa & C. Buzawa (Eds.), *Do arrests and restraining orders work?* (pp. 192-213). Thousand Oaks, CA: Sage.

Koss, M. (1990). The women's mental health research agenda: Violence against women. *American Psychologist, 45,* 374-380.

Krueger, R., Moffitt, T., Caspi, A., Beske, A., & Siva, P. (1998). Assortive mating for antisocial behavior: Developmental and methodological implications. *Behavior Genetics, 28,* 3.

Kurt, J. L. (1995). Stalking as a variant of domestic violence. *Bulletin of the American Academy of Psychiatry and the Law, 23,* 219-230.

Kurz, D., & Stark, E. (1988). Not so benign neglect: The medical response to battering. In K Yllo & M. Bograd (Eds.), *Feminist perspectives on wife abuse* (pp. 249-266). Newbury Park, CA: Sage.

Leonard, K., & Senchak, M. (1996). Prospective prediction of husband marital aggression within newlywed couples. *Journal of Abnormal Psychology, 105,* 368-380.

Levitt, M., Silver, M., & Franco, N. (1996). Troublesome relationships: A part of human experience. *Journal of Social and Personal Relationships, 13,* 523-536.

Magdol, L., Moffit, T. E., Caspi, A., & Silva, P. A. (1998). Developmental antecedents of partner abuse: A prospective-longitudinal study. *Journal of Abnormal Psychology, 107,* 375-389.

Maiden, P. (1997). Alcohol dependence and domestic violence: Incidence and treatment implications. *Alcoholism Treatment Quarterly, 15*(2), 31-50.

Margolin, L., John, R., & Gleberman, L. (1988). Affective responses to conflictual discussions in violent and non-violent couples. *Journal of Consulting and Clinical Psychology, 56,* 24-33.

Marshall, L. (1996). The Psychological abuse of women: Six distinct clusters. *Journal of Family Violence, 11,* 369-399.

Marshall, L. (1999). Effects of men's subtle and overt psychological abuse on low-income women. *Violence and Victims, 11*(1), 69-88.

Marshall, L. L., & Rose, P. (1988). Family of origin violence and courtship abuse. *Journal of Counseling and Development, 66,* 414-418.

McCreedy, K., & Dennis, B. (1996). Sex Related offenses and fear of crime on campus. *Journal of Contemporary Criminal Justice, 12,* 69-80.

McFarlane, J. (1989). Battering during pregnancy: Tip of an iceberg revealed. *Womens Health, 15,* 69-84.

Meloy, J. R., & Gothard, S. (1995). Demographic and clinical comparison of obsessional followers and offenders with mental disorders. *American Journal of Psychiatry, 152,* 258-263.

Miller, B. (1990). The interrelationship between alcohol and drugs and family violence. In M. De La Rosa, E. Lambert, & B. Gropper (Eds.), *Drugs and violence: Causes, correlates, and consequences* (NIDA Research Monograph Series, 103, pp. 177-207). National Institute on Drug Abuse.

Miller, B. & Downs, W. (1993). The impact of family violence on the use of alcohol by women. *Alcohol Health Research World, 17*(2), 137-143.

Moffit, T. E., Caspi, A. (1998). Annotation: Implications of violence between intimate partners for child psychologists and psychiatrists. *Journal of Child Psychology and Psychiatry, 39*(2), 137-144.

Mullen, P. E., & Pathé, M. (1994). Stalking and the pathologies of love. *Australian and New Zealand Journal of Psychiatry, 28,* 469-477.

Murdoch, D., Phil, R. & Ross, D. (1990). Alcohol and crimes of violence: Present issues. *International Journal of the Addictions, 25,* 1065-1081.

Murphy, C., & O'Leary, K. (1989). Psychological aggression predicts physical aggression in early marriage. *Journal of Consulting and Clinical Psychology, 57,* 579-582.

Neufeld, J., McNamara, J. R., & Ertl, M. (1999). Incidence and prevalence of dating partner abuse and its relationship to dating practices. *Journal of Interpersonal Violence, 14*(2), 125-135.

O'Keefe, M. (1997). Predictors of dating violence among high school students. *Journal of Interpersonal Violence, 12,* 546-569.

O'Keeffe, N., Brockopp, K., & Chew, E. (1986). Teen dating violence. *Social Work, 31,* 456-468.

O'Leary, K., & Curley, A. (1986). Assertion and family violence: Correlates of spouse abuse. *Journal of Marital and Family Therapy, 12,* 281-289.

O'Leary, K. D. (1999). Psychological abuse: A variable deserving critical attention in domestic violence. *Violence and Victims, 14,* 3-24.

O'Leary, K., Malone, J., & Tyree, A. (1994). Physical aggression in early marriage: Prerelationship and relationship effects. *Journal of Consulting and Clinical Psychology, 62,* 594-602.

Pathé, M., & Mullen, P. (1997). The impact of stalkers on their victims. *British Journal of Psychiatry, 170,* 12-17.

Pederson, P., & Thomas, C. (1992). Prevalence and correlates of dating violence in a Canadian university sample. *Canadian Journal of Behavioral Science, 24,* 490-501.

Pernanen, K. (1991). *Alcohol in human violence.* New York: Guilford Press.

Pipes, R. B., & Lebov-Keeler, K. (1997). Psychological abuse among college women in exclusive heterosexual dating relationships. *Sex Roles: A Journal of Research, 36,* 585-599.

Plichta, S. (1996). Violence and abuse: Implications for women's health. In M. Falik & K. Scott Collins (Eds.), *Women's health: The Commonwealth Fund survey* (pp. 237-270). Baltimore, MD: Johns Hopkins University Press.

Resnick, H., Acierno, R., & Kilpatrick, D. (1997). Health impact of interpersonal violence 2: Medical and mental health outcomes. *Behavioral Medicine, 23,* 65-78.

Riggs, D. S., O'Leary, K. D., & Breslin, F. C. (1990). Multiple correlates of physical aggression in dating couples. *Journal of Interpersonal Violence, 5,* 530-548.

Roberts, A. R., & Dziegielewski, S. F. (1996). Assessment typology and intervention with the survivors of stalking. *Aggression and Violent Behavior, 1,* 359-368.

Roizen, J. (1997). Epidemiological issues in alcohol-related violence. In M. Galanter (Ed.), *Recent developments in alcoholism, Volume 13: Alcoholism and violence.* New York: Plenum Press.

Roscoe, B., Strouse, J., & Goodwin, M. (1994). Sexual harassment: Early adolescent self-reports of experiences and acceptance. *Adolescence, 29,* 515-523.

Sabourin, T., Infante, D., & Rudd, J. (1993). Verbal aggression in marriages: A comparison of violent, distressed but nonviolent, and nondistressed couples. *Human Communication Research, 20,* 245-267.

Sackett, L., & Saunders, D. (1999). The impact of different forms of psychological abuse on battered women. *Violence and Victims, 11,* 105-117.

Simonelli, C. J., & Ingram, K. M. (1998). Psychological distress among men experiencing physical and emotional abuse in heterosexual dating relationships. *Journal of Interpersonal Violence, 13,* 667-681.

Simons, R., Wu, C., Johnson, C., & Conger, R. (1995). A test of various perspectives on the intergenerational transmission of domestic violence. *Criminology, 33,* 141-172.

Simons, R. L., Lin, K.-H., & Gordon, L. C. (1998). Socialization in the family of origin and male dating violence: A prospective study. *Journal of Marriage and Family, 60,* 467-478.

Spitzberg, B., Nicastro, A., & Cousins, A. (1998). Exploring the interactional phenomenon of stalking and obsessive relational intrusion. *Communication Reports, 11,* 33-47.

Spitzberg, B., & Rhea, J. (1999). Obsessive relational intrusion and sexual coercion victimization. *Journal of Interpersonal Violence, 14,* 3-20.

Stacy, W., & Shupe, A. (1983). *The family secret: Domestic violence in America.* Boston: Beacon Press.

Stark, E., & Flitcraft, A. (1996). *Women at risk: Domestic violence and women's health.* Thousand Oaks, CA: Sage.

Stark, E., Flitcraft, A., & Frazer, W. (1979). Medicine and patriarchal violence: The social construction of a private event. *International Journal of Health and Science, 9,* 461-493.

Stewart, S. (1996). Alcohol abuse in individuals exposed to trauma: A critical review. *Psychological Bulletin, 120*(1), 83-112.

Straus, M., & Gelles, R. (Eds.). (1990). *Physical violence in American families: Risk factors and adaptation to violence in 8,145 families.* New Brunswick, NJ: Transaction Publications.

Straus, M. A. (1990). Measuring intrafamilly conflict and violence: The Conflict Tactics Scale. In M. A. Straus & R. J. Gelles (Eds.), *Physical violence in American families: Risk factors and adaptation to violence in 8,145 families* (pp. 29-48). New Brunswick, NJ: Transaction Publications.

Tjaden, P., & Thoennes, N. (1998). *Stalking in America: Findings from the national violence against women survey* (Special Report No. NCJ-1669592). National Institute of Justice, Centers for Disease Control and Prevention. Washington, DC: Bureau of Justice Statistics, U.S. Department of Justice.

Tolman, R. (1992). Psychological abuse of women. In R. Ammerman & M. Hersen (Eds.), *Assessment of family violence: A clinical and legal sourcebook.* New York: Wiley.

Tolman, R., & Bhosley, G. (1991). The outcome of participation in a shelter-sponsored program for men who batter. In D. Knudsen & J.

Miller (Eds.), *Abused and battered: Social and legal response to family violence.* Hawthorne, NY: Adline, De Gruyter.

Tolman, R. M. (1989). The development of a measure of psychological maltreatment of women by their male partners. *Violence and Victims, 4,* 159-177.

Tolman, R. M. (1999). The validation of the psychological maltreatment of women inventory. *Violence & Victims, 14,* 25-35.

Ulrich, Y. (1991). Women's reasons for leaving abusive spouses. *Health Care for Women International, 12,* 465-473.

Vivian, D., & Langhinrichsen-Rohling, J. (1994). Are bi-directionally violent couples mutually victimized? A gender-sensitive comparison. *Violence and Victims, 9,* 107-124.

Walker, L. (1979). *The battered woman.* New York: Harper and Row.

Walker, L. (1984). *The battered woman syndrome.* New York: Springer Publishing Co.

Walker, L. E. (1991). Post-traumatic stress disorder in women: Diagnosis and treatment of battered woman syndrome. *Psychotherapy, 28,* 21-29.

Way, R. C. (1994). The criminalization of stalking: An exercise in media manipulation and political opportunism. *McGill Law Journal, 39,* 379-400.

White, J., & Koss, M. (1991). Courtship violence: Incidence in a national sample of higher education students. *Violence and Victims, 6,* 247-256.

Wokenstein, B., & Sterman, L. (1998). Unmet needs of older women in a clinic population: The discovery of possible long-term sequelae of domestic violence. *Professional Psychology: Research and Practice, 29,* 341-348.

Wright, J. A., Burgess, A. G., Burgess, A. W., Laszlo, A. T., McCrary, G. O., & Douglas, J. E. (1996). A typology of interpersonal stalking. *Journal of Interpersonal Violence, 11,* 487-502.

Zimbardo, P. G., & Leippe, M. R. (1991). *The psychology of attitude change and social influence.* New York: McGraw-Hill.

Zona, M. A., Sharma, K. K., & Lane, J. L. (1993). A comparative study of erotomania and obsessional subjects in a forensic sample. *Journal of Forensic Sciences, 65,* 894-903.

13

Stalking by Former Intimates: Verbal Threats and Other Predictors of Physical Violence

Mary P. Brewster

Violence against women has received unprecedented attention in recent years. Based on the National Crime Victimization Survey (NCVS), Bachman and Saltzman (1995, p. 2) estimate that women experience 3.8 million assaults annually. The survey data also lead to estimates that as many as three-quarters of victims of "lone-offender" violence knew their offenders, and 29% were intimates or former intimates of the violent offender. About 9 in 1,000 women are victims of violence by intimates or former intimates (Bachman & Saltzman, 1995, p. 3), and females are 10 times as likely as men to experience violence at the hands of someone with whom they are, or have been, intimate (U.S. Department of Justice, 1995, p. 2). Results of the NCVS also revealed that young women with low incomes were the most likely victims of violence by intimates, but race was not a determinant of violence by an intimate partner. Those women who were separated from their husbands were most likely to be victims of their former intimate partners, followed by those who were divorced. Women who were still married were the least likely victims of violence perpetrated by intimate partners (Bachman & Saltzman, 1995, p. 4). Similarly, Wilson and Daly (1993), in a study of homicide risk, found that wives who were separated from their husbands were at greater risk than those who were still living together.

While Bachman and Saltzman have combined intimates and former intimates in their results, it is important to explore current intimates and former intimates as separate groups.[1] Current intimates tend to have more frequent and consensual contact with each other, either through cohabitation or dating. Former intimate situations more often will involve the possibility of stalking types of behavior. That is, the women in this subsample may be victims of violence in a setting or situation that is much different from that of living together or currently dating. Therefore, regardless of any apparent similarities, the distinction between current and former intimates requires researchers to examine the victimization experiences of each group separately. The focus here is on the victimization of women by former intimates (i.e., ex-husbands, ex-boyfriends, ex-fiancés, etc.).

FORMER INTIMATE STALKING

The problem of stalking has only recently been recognized after the media coverage of a few "high-profile" cases involving celebrities such as actresses Teresa Saldana, Rebecca Schaffer, and Jodie Foster, talk-show host David Letterman (see Perez 1993, pp. 268–270), and, most recently, Nicole Simpson, the murdered ex-wife of O. J. Simpson. The result of increased public awareness of this type of behavior has resulted in the passage of antistalking laws during the past seven years in nearly every state, beginning with California in 1990 (Cal. Penal Code, Section 646.9).[2] Although laws vary from one jurisdiction to another, stalking is typically defined to include a pattern of behaviors toward another person with the intent to cause "substantial emotional distress" or "reasonable fear of bodily harm" (see e.g., PA Code Section 18: 2709, rev. 1994). Among the behaviors that might occur during stalking are following, watching, harassing by telephone and/or letter, causing property damage, threatening harm, and violence. In an exploratory study of stalking behavior, Burgess and associates (1997) found an escalation in the types of behaviors by stalkers as the stalking period progressed. They also suggest that the escalation "from clandestine [e.g., anonymous hang-up phone calls] to open behavior [e.g., breaking into the victim's residence] . . . may be predictive of lethal actions (p. 402)."

Researchers have identified various types of stalkers (e.g., erotomanic, psychopathic, former intimate), but the former intimate is believed to be the most common (Roberts & Dziegielewski, 1996; Thomas,

1993). Not surprisingly, stalking by former partners has been found to be correlated with jealousy (Dutton, vanGinkel, & Landolt, 1996). Threats toward an intimate or former intimate may be an attempt to control her, and ultimately coerce her to remain in, or return to, the relationship. If the threats are not successful in accomplishing that end, violence may be utilized either for instrumental purposes (i.e., to exert greater control over the woman) or merely as an expression of the perpetrator's anger. Men whose partners have attempted to terminate the relationship likely experience a greater loss of control than those whose partners remain in the relationship. Therefore, one would expect a greater use of threats and violence in situations where the wife or girlfriend has left the relationship (see e.g., Daly & Wilson, 1997; Wilson & Daly, 1993).

THREATS AND VIOLENCE

"To threaten someone is to declare one's intention to punish or hurt, or inflict injury to reputation or property which may restrain a person's freedom of action" (Hough, 1990, p. 169). Threats can include explicit verbal threats, conditional threats or blackmail, or even implied verbal and/or nonverbal threats. Few researchers have investigated the prevalence of verbal and nonverbal threats, and fewer still have considered the link between threats and violence.[3] In his review of nearly 20 years of research on obsessional following, Meloy (1996, p. 158) found that "much speculation and little research" existed with respect to the threats and violence relationship. Two conclusions drawn by Meloy based on the sparse body of research were that 75% of those obsessional followers who made threats did not carry out violent acts, and that violence did not usually occur when the obsessional follower did not make threats. Alternately, Ryan (1995), who conducted a study that included an examination of the relationship between threats and violence in intimate relationships, found that threats were predictive of intimate violence.

OTHER PREDICTORS OF VIOLENCE BY INTIMATES

Many researchers have identified predictors and correlates of various types of violence. Based on the National Crime Victimization Survey, the Bureau of Justice Statistics highlights victim characteristics associated with intimate and former intimate violence (U.S. Department of Justice, 1995, p. 2). Age, education, and income were all reported to have an inverse relationship to violence. Marital status was also related to the rate of intimate violence; the highest rates were among divorced/separated women, followed by those who never married. Married women had the lowest rate of intimate violence. Victims' race, ethnicity, and location of residence (i.e., urban, suburban, rural areas) were not correlated with the rate of intimate violence.

Other researchers have noted offender characteristics associated with intimate violence. Factors such as marital conflict, socioeconomic status, a history of observing family violence, verbal abuse, sudden mood swings, quick temper, dependency, psychological aggression, perceived power imbalance, male sexual proprietariness, and the use of alcohol and drugs have all been found to be correlated with violence in one or more empirical research studies (e.g., Aldarondo & Sugarman, 1996; Brookoff, 1997; Daly & Wilson, 1997; Leonard & Senchak, 1996; Murphy & O'Leary, 1989; Ryan, 1995; Sugarman & Hotaling, 1989).

THE PRESENT STUDY

This study focuses on the experiences of female former intimate stalking victims, or women who were stalked by someone with whom they once had a relationship (e.g., through marriage, cohabitation, serious or casual dating). Although there are other types of stalking relationships, including women who are stalked by psychopathic strangers or mentally ill acquaintances, it is commonly believed that "former intimate" is the most prevalent type of stalking relationship (e.g., Thomas, 1993, p. 126). It has also been stated that nearly all (possibly 90% of) men who kill their wives or girlfriends stalked them first (Sohn, 1994, p. 205). Typically, the former intimate stalker is seeking revenge or reconciliation through stalking. While the intimate violence literature has dealt with a combination of current and former intimates, only the former intimates are included in this study. According to McAnaney, Curliss, and Abeyta-Price (1993, pp. 839–840), former intimate stalkers "are intensely emotionally dependent on their partner" and "may be jealous of real or imagined infidelities and exhibit a need to control their former partner."[4]

The purpose of this analysis is to examine the correlates of violence within stalking situations and, more specifically, to assess the relationship between verbal threats and physical violence toward former inti-mate stalking victims. The research builds upon the extant literature by broadening our understanding of stalking behavior. Additionally, it will enable policymakers to understand the importance of threats in deter-mining appropriate courses of actions in handling stalking incidents.

RESEARCH METHODS

Sample

One-hundred-eighty-seven self-identified former intimate stalking vic-tims volunteered for participation in the study as a result of newspaper advertisements, advertisements and referrals at victim service agencies and county courthouses, fliers at laundromats and supermarkets, and word of mouth. All participants lived within 150 miles of Philadel-phia, Pennsylvania. Participants were screened to ensure that they had been stalked (i.e., repeatedly followed, harassed, threatened) within the past five years by someone with whom they had previously had a relationship. To participate, the victims must also have indicated that they experienced emotional distress, fear of bodily harm, actual phys-ical harm, or the belief that the stalker intended one or more of these effects.[5]

Each respondent received ten dollars[6] for participating in an exten-sive (1–3–hour) semistructured face-to-face interview. The interview elicited from the respondents information about their former relation-ships with their stalkers and the nature of their stalking experiences. Demographic data were also gathered through a brief questionnaire.

The respondents' ages ranged from 18 to 74 ($M = 34.5$, $SD = 9.3$, median = 34).[7] Most of the women in the sample were nonHispanic White (74.5%), while 23.4% were African American, and only 2% were Hispanic or Asian. The respondents' education ranged from some elementary school through completion of a doctoral program. Ninety percent reported having completed high school and 69% reported having completed at least some college. Seventy percent of the respon-dents reported working outside the home, and annual household in-comes for all respondents ranged from no income through $130,000 ($M = \$31,115$, $SD = \$26,725$, median = $24,000). Former intimate relationships with the stalkers included marriage (37%), cohabitation (25%), engagement or serious dating (24%), and casual dating (6%).

Characteristics of Stalkers and Stalking

According to the respondents, their stalkers ranged in age from 17 through 57 at the time of the stalking ($M = 31.2$, $SD = 8.9$, median = 30). The majority of the stalkers were nonhispanic White (57%) and African American (37%), with fewer than 6.5% classified as other racial minorities. Only 100 of the victims specified the educational background of their stalkers, ranging from some elementary school through the completion of a doctoral program. Seventy-seven percent had completed at least high school and 45% at least some college. The majority of the stalkers were employed (43% in blue-collar positions, 26% in white-collar positions). About a fifth were reportedly unemployed (22.5%), and a few (5%) were incarcerated.

The length of time the women reported having known their stalkers ranged from 1 to 456 months ($M = 97$, $SD = 79.6$, median = 72), with the stalking period also lasting from between 1 to 456 months ($M = 28, SD = 50$, median = 12 months).[8] Behaviors that occurred during the stalking period often included making telephone calls ($n = 169$, 90.4%), sending letters or cards ($n = 111$, 59.4%), watching/spying on ($n = 147$, 78.6%), following the victim ($n = 128$, 68.4%), driving or walking by the victim's home or workplace ($n = 101$, 54%), causing property damage ($n = 82$, 44%), and making verbal threats of violence ($n = 136$, 72.7%).

Data Collection

As stated above, extensive semistructured interviews were conducted with the respondents. Most of the interview consisted of open-ended questions eliciting information about the victim-stalker relationship prior to the stalking, the commencement of the stalking, and characteristics of the stalking. In addition, several objective scales were utilized to obtain more specific information in each of those areas.[9]

Dependent Variable: Physical Violence During Stalking

Most of the women who suffered physical violence during the stalking period discussed that occurrence in response to the first open-ended question of the interview, "Can you tell me about your victimization experience?," or to later open-ended questions such as, "Was there any violence during the stalking period?" and "Did you suffer from any physical injuries at the hands of your stalker?" Other follow-up questions elicited greater detail about the physical violence that occurred, including its frequency, the type of violence, and types of physical injury suffered, if any. Analyses here focus on three violence-related variables:

1. whether violence occurred at all during the stalking—a dichotomous variable (yes/no) based on whether any violence reportedly took place, ranging from pushing, slapping, kicking, and biting, to rape, assault with a weapon, etc.;
2. the number of separate incidents of violence during the stalking—coded as "none," "one or two," "three or more"; and
3. whether or not victims suffered physical injury as a result of stalker violence—an ordinal level variable coded as "no violence or injury," "no injury despite violence," and "injury as a result of violence." A range of injuries from small cuts and bruises through wounds requiring stitches and broken bones is included here.

Independent Variables: Possible Predictors of Violence

Based on prior research on violence and available data gathered from the present sample, the independent variables included in the various analyses included victim's age at the time the stalking began, education,[10] whether or not the stalker used drugs or alcohol, whether violence took place during the prior relationship, whether verbal threats of physical violence were made during the stalking,[11] and the frequency of various stalking characteristics (i.e., telephone calls, letters, and following). The independent variables were all based on data collected through the victim interviews. The specific variables were coded as follows:

1. Victim's age at commencement of stalking—measured in years;
2. Victim's education—an ordinal level, 10-category variable, ranging from no formal education to completion of a doctoral program;
3. History of violence in the prior relationship—a dummy variable based on whether the victim reported the occurrence of violence during her prior intimate relationship with the stalker;
4. Stalker's use of drugs—dummy variable (yes/no);

5. Stalker's abuse of alcohol—dummy variable (abuse/nonabuse of alcohol);
6. Frequency of phone calls during stalking—an ordinal level, 8-category variable, ranging from "never" to "daily or more";
7. Frequency of letters—an ordinal level, eight-category variable, ranging from "never" to "daily or more";
8. Frequency of following—an ordinal level, eight-category variable, ranging from "never" to "daily or more"; and
9. Stalker's use of verbal threats of physical violence during stalking—coded as no threats, implied threats, and direct threats.

Direct threats were those that specified types of violence (i.e., "I'm gonna kill you." "I'm gonna run you down with my car." "I'll break your arms and legs."). Implied threats were those threats that were veiled in nature (i.e., "Do you have a will in case anything should happen to you?" "Is your life insurance paid up?" "Where would you like to be buried?" "You should draw up a will just in case you should get killed or something.").

ANALYSIS OF THE DATA

Summary Statistics

Descriptive statistics for the dependent variables and the covariates included in the regression models are provided in Table 13.1. Close to half (46%) of the stalking victims reported stalker on victim violence, with most (66%) of those who experienced violence reporting one or two incidents. Of the total sample of victims, 15.5% reported at least three violent incidents during the stalking. Although most of the sample (54%) did not suffer physical violence, most of those who did experience violence (81%) also suffered some type of physical injury.

Physical injuries

At the time of the stalking, most of the respondents were in their 20s or 30s (72%). Nearly 90% of the respondents had completed at least high school. The majority (65%) of the victims reported a history of violence during their former relationship with the stalker, and most indicated that their stalkers abused drugs (51%) and/or alcohol (58%).

Table 13.1 Summary Statistics for Variables Included in Regression Models

Variable	N and percentage	
Stalker on victim violence		
No	101	(54%)
Yes	86	(46%)
Number of violent incidents		
None	101	(54%)
one or two incidents	57	
(30.45%)		
Three or more incidents	29	(15.5%)
Physical injuries		
None (no violence)	101	(54%)
None (despite violence)	16	(8.6%)
Yes, physical injuries	70	(37.4%)
Age at time of stalking (x = 31, SD = 8.64)		
Under 20 years of age	20	(10.7%)
20–29	70	(37.4%)
30–39	65	(34.8%)
40–49	27	(14.4%)
50–59	5	(2.7%)
Victim's educational level		
Less than high school	19	(10.2%)
Completed high school through some college	106	(57.3%)
Bachelor's degree +	60	(32.4%)
History of violence in former intimate relationship		
No	65	(34.8%)
Yes	122	(65.2%)
Stalker abused alcohol		
No	79	(42.2%)
Yes	108	(57.8%)
Stalker drug use		
No	91	(48.6%)
Yes	96	(51.3%)
Frequency of phone calls		
Never	18	(9.6%)
More than one time but less than once a week	10	(5.3%)
At least once a week but less than daily	63	(33.7%)
Daily or more	96	(51.3%)
Frequency of letters		
Never	76	(40.6%)
More than one time but less than once a week	81	(43.4%)
At least once a week but less than daily	22	(11.6%)
Daily or more	8	(4.3%)

Table 13.1 *(Continued)*

Variable	N and percentage	
Frequency of following		
Never	59	(31.6%)
More than one time but, less than once a week	77	(41.1%)
At least once a week but less than daily	31	(16.6%)
Daily or more	32	(10.7%)
Verbal threats of physical violence		
Direct threats	99	(52.9%)
Implied threats	37	(19.8%)
No threats	51	(27.3%)

Most respondents reported phone calls during the stalking (90%), many indicating the occurrence of daily phone calls (51%). Letters from the stalker were less common, although 59% reported having received at least one letter from their stalker. Only 16% received letters at least once a week from their stalker. "Following" by the stalker was reported by 68% of the respondents, and 37% of the women were followed at least weekly. Finally, direct verbal threats of violence reportedly took place in over half (52.9%) of the stalking situations, implied threats occurred in 19.8% of the cases, and no threats were made by 27.3% of the stalkers.

Regression Models

Three regression models (two linear and one logistic) were used to assess the strength and statistical significance of the following variables as predictors of physical violence during stalking: victim's age at commencement of stalking, victim's education, whether or not there was a history of violence in the prior relationship, the stalker's use of drugs, the stalker's use of alcohol, the frequency of phone calls, the frequency of letters, the frequency of following, and the stalker's use of verbal threats of physical violence.

A logistic regression model was used to analyze the impact of the independent variables on whether or not the stalker was violent during the stalking. The coefficients, presented in Table 13.2, reveal that only "verbal threats of violence" had a statistically significant independent effect on the likelihood of violence.[12] That is, when verbal threats occurred, the likelihood of violence occurring significantly increased.

Table 13.2 Logistic Regression Results: Whether or Not Violence Occurred During Stalking

Variables	b	SE	bSE	Sig.
Victim age	−.0027	.0218	−.1239	.9002
Victim education	−.0958	.1340	−.7149	.4757
Stalker alcohol abuse	.5492	.4014	1.3682	.1712
Stalker drug use	.4710	.3965	1.1879	.2349
Freq. of phone calls	.0051	.0862	.0592	.9524
Freq. of following	.0383	..0756	.5066	.6130
Freq. of letters	−.0129	.0938	−.1375	.8910
Prior violence during relationship	.0187	.4086	.0458	.9636
Verbal threats of violence	.9255*	.2287	4.0468	.0001
Constant	−1.4426	1.2300	.2409	

*p = .0001.

(Model chi-square = 35.854, df = 9, sig. < .0001)

None of the coefficients for the other covariates in the equation was statistically significant at the .05 level.

A second model was used to estimate the coefficients of a linear regression equation in predicting the variable "number of violent occurrences during the stalking." The coefficients presented in Table 13.3 indicate, again, that "verbal threats of violence" was the only

Table 13.3 Regression Results for Number of Violent Incidents During Stalking

Variables	b	SE	Beta	Sig.
Victim age	−.0042	.0065	−.0491	.5158
Victim education	−.0063	.0401	−.0114	.8754
Stalker alcohol abuse	.1822	.1255	.1198	.1484
Stalker drag use	.0720	.1233	.0481	.5598
Freq. of phone calls	.0150	.0254	.0425	.5570
Freq. of following	.0176	.0229	.0541	.4434
Freq. of letters	−.0092	.0281	−.0235	.7443
Violence during prior relationship	.0863	.1241	.1198	.4882
Verbal threats of violence	.3221*	.0664	.3605	.0000
Constant	.0417	.3641	.9090	

*p < .0001.

(Multiple R = .46872, R square = .21970, standard error = .67812, F = 5.09933, p < .0001).

Table 13.4 Regression Results for Violence/Physical Injuries During Stalking

Variables	b	SE	Beta	Sig.
Victim age	.0015	.0085	.0134	.8629
Victim education	−.0349	.0520	−.0498	.5033
Stalker alcohol abuse	.2868	.1628	.1488	.0800
Stalker drug use	.2104	.1599	.1109	.1903
Freq. of phone calls	−.0091	.330	−.0205	.7821
Freq. of following	.0250	.0297	.0607	.4009
Freq. of letters	−.0082	.0281	−.0166	.8220
Prior violence during relationship	.0313	.1610	.0155	.8459
Verbal threats of violence	.3199*	.0862	.2827	.0003
Constant	.2832	.4723	.5496	

*sig. = .0003.

(Multiple R = .42627, R square = .18170, standard error = .87953, F = 4.02156, p = .0001).

variable in the equation that had a significant independent effect on number of violent incidents. Again, verbal threats were associated with a higher frequency of violent incidents.

Finally, a third regression model assessed the importance of the covariates in predicting the "violence/injury" variable, coded as no violence/no injury, no injury despite violence, or injury as a result of violence. Coinciding with the results of the two other regression models, "threats of physical violence" was again the only variable in the model with a statistically significant coefficient (Table 13.4).

Due to the potential for collinearity between alcohol abuse and drug abuse by the stalker (see Appendix for bivariate correlations), the three regression models were rerun, first without the alcohol abuse variable and then again without the drug abuse variable. When one was included in the regression equation without the other, alcohol and drug abuse were each statistically significant predictors (p < .05) only in the linear regression model predicting physical injury, as presented in Table 13.5. That is, the situation where the stalker was reportedly abusing drugs or abusing alcohol was significantly more likely to result in injury than the situation where no alcohol or drug abuse occurred.

Table 13.5 Regression Results for Violence/Physical Injuries During Stalking, Alternating the Inclusion of Alcohol Abuse and Drug Abuse in the Model

Variables	b	SE	Beta	Sig.	b	SE	Beta	Sig.
Victim age	−.0014	.0077	−.0127	.8565	.0033	.0085	.0298	.7003
Victim educ.	−.0380	.0483	−.0570	.4318	−.0419	.0522	−.0598	.4230
Stalker alc. abuse	.3173*	.1489	.1662	.0345	—	—	—	—
Stalker drug use	—	—	—	—	.3050*	.1516	.1608	.0459
Freq. of phone calls	−.0036	.0309	−.0083	.9081	−.0056	.0331	−.0125	.8666
Freq. of following	.0198	.0290	.0475	.4950	.0269	.0299	.0653	.3690
Freq. of letters	−.0108	.0354	−.0216	.7595	.0017	.0362	.0035	.9620
Prior violence during relationship	.0876	.1547	.0442	.5717	.1042	.1566	.0517	.5066
Threats of violence	.3252**	.0815	.2953	.0001	.3432**	.0857	.3033	.0001

$*p < .05$; $**p = .0001$.

(Multiple $R = .42627$, R square $= .18170$, standard error $= .87953$, $F = 4.02156$, sig. $F = .0001$).

APPENDIX. Bivariate Correlation Matrix for Covariates

	Age	Educ.	Prior Viol.	Alcohol	Drugs	Phone	Follow	Letters	Threats
Age	.125	−.062	.065	−.281*	.129	.085	.050	−.014	
Educ.		−.236*	−.195*	−.155	−.031	−.084	.029	−.193	
Pr.Viol.			.376*	.252*	.177	.006	−.123	.258*	
Alcohol				.408*	.209*	.053	−.078	.319*	
Drugs					.117	−.084	−.095	.240*	
Phone						.069	.108	.167	
Follow							.119	.019	
Letters								−.032	

$*N = 187$, $p < .01$.

DISCUSSION

The results of the regression analyses described above emphasize the important role that verbal threats play in predicting physical violence against stalking victims. Threats of violence were significantly correlated with actual physical violence in every model. These findings are consistent with Ryan's (1995) findings; that is, threats are predictive of violence.[13] Despite the limitations of the study (i.e., sample size, sampling approach, etc.), these results call for a closer look at the relationship between threats and violence, particularly in stalking situations.

It is apparent that threats of violence are better predictors of violence during stalking than is a past history of violence. Reiss and Roth (1993, p. 223) suggest that, due to the ongoing relationship between intimate partners, "[i]t is quite likely that the victim will be violated repeatedly." The former intimate stalking situation is different from the domestic violence situation, however, in that in the stalking situation, the victim and perpetrator are no longer in the intimate relationship and are not sharing a home. The increased physical distance and difficulty in making physical contact with the victim may partially explain why the history of physical violence in the prior relationship is not a predictor of violence during stalking.[14]

The results pertaining to drug and alcohol abuse are also consistent with findings from other research on violence, at least in one regression model. When alcohol and drug use were included in separate regression equations along with other covariates, each was a statistically significant predictor of injury during stalking. These findings coincide with those of a study of domestic violence incidents involving 72 victims, where "92 percent of assailants used drugs or alcohol during the day of the assault (Brookoff, 1997)." In another study, Shuckitt and Russell (1984) found that a sample of alcoholics had a high rate of committing serious violence and inflicting injuries. Similarly, Fagan (1990), Sherman (1992), and Leonard and Senchak (1996) suggest a link between alcohol/drug abuse and violence.

It is interesting to note that characteristics of stalking such as the frequency of phone calls, letters, and following are not predictive of violence. Although these behaviors may be viewed as threatening by the victims, they are not significant predictors of violence when controlling for verbal threats, drug and alcohol abuse, history of violence in the relationship, victims' age, and victims' education.

Finally, victims' age and education were not predictive of violence during the stalking. These findings are inconsistent with National Crime Victimization Survey (NCVS) results, which indicate that as age and education increase, the occurrence of violence decreases (U.S. Department of Justice, 1995). This discrepancy is likely due to the use of a small, voluntary availability sample in the present study while the NCVS sample is nationally representative. Stalking victims' motivations for participating in the present study were not known. Those victims who were willing to participate may not represent all former intimate stalking victims.[15]

CONCLUSIONS

The results of the analysis of data collected through interviews with 187 female former intimate stalking victims indicate that verbal threats are a strong and statistically significant predictor of violence. These findings reinforce the need to take verbal threats seriously. However, as Meloy (1996) points out in his discussion of obsessional stalkers, there are both false positives (where threats are made and not followed through) and false negatives (where violence occurs without any verbal threat beforehand). Although there are fewer false negatives than false positives, researchers should explore factors other than threats which may serve as forewarnings of subsequent violence. Results of this study coincide with Meloy's (1996) study of obsessional followers to the extent that both studies reveal that physical violence did not usually occur if there were no threats made, and that the likelihood of violence increased when threats were made. Unlike Meloy's study, however, this study of a former intimate sample revealed that nearly two-thirds of those who were threatened also suffered violence during the stalking. Meloy found only a 25% rate of violence following threats among the obsessional followers.[16]

The findings with respect to drug and alcohol abuse lend some additional support to the link between substance abuse and violence established by earlier researchers (e.g., Fagan, 1990; Sherman, 1992; Shuckitt & Russell, 1984). Additional research needs to be conducted to establish specifically which drugs and combinations of drugs are most predictive of violence in stalking.

While threats during stalking are clearly related to violence, other stalking behaviors failed to make a contribution to the predictive model of violence during stalking. In addition, the history of violence during the former intimate relationship was not predictive of stalking violence when controlling for threats and the other covariates.

The results of this research have implications for criminal justice professionals and policymakers. Law enforcement professionals may want to use these findings to determine the potential for violence against a stalking victim and react accordingly. The response of those in the criminal justice system to stalking should be one that reflects the seriousness of threats, and the subsequent increased likelihood of violence. An example of one such response is the Threat Management Unit (TMU) established by the Los Angeles Police Department as a strategy for dealing with "individuals [who] have demonstrated an abnormal fixation and generated an identifiable, long-term pattern of unsolicited acts of visitation and/or telephonic or written correspondence in an annoying or threatening manner towards a specific person (Lane, 1992, p. 27)." The TMU handles stalking cases where verbal and/or nonverbal threats are made.

Future researchers may want to examine more closely the link between specific threats (e.g., assault, stabbing, homicide, property damage, blackmail) and the specific corresponding behaviors.[17] Other research should be conducted to attempt to more extensively identify predictors of violence in stalking situations where no verbal threats have been made. Additionally, researchers may want to investigate predictors of violence against indirect victims of stalking (e.g., family, friends, and coworkers of the stalking victim). Future investigators should also assess the predictors of violence for each of the various types of stalking (e.g., former intimate, psychopathic, erotomanic), since the characteristics of each may vary (see e.g., Hazelwood & Warren, 1990; Leong et al., 1994; Shore et al., 1989), as may the relationship between threats and violence in the different situations. Finally, those conducting future research on stalking might attempt to identify a more representative sample of victims and/or stalkers in order to broaden the understanding of the nature and dynamics of stalking incidents, the escalation of behaviors in stalking, and the motivations behind those behaviors. Researchers should pay particular attention to the stalkers' motivations for the stalking, threats, and violence (i.e., instrumental versus expressive) to determine which motivations are likely to result in violence. More specifically the motivations behind specific degrees of violence (e.g., lethal and nonlethal) should be examined.[18]

NOTES

1. See also Burgess et al. (1997).
2. See Sohn, 1994, p. 204, footnote 2 for a list of state statutes pertaining to stalking.
3. Roberts (1996) is one of the few who does address the prevalence of

death threats. Based on data collected from 210 battered women, Roberts claims that death threats were made against approximately two-thirds of the women.

4. See also Daly & Wilson (1997).

5. Stalking victim screening criteria were based upon the Pennsylvania stalking statute. See Brewster (1997) for additional information regarding sampling and screening of respondents.

6. Several victims requested that this nominal payment be donated to a variety of recipients including an elementary school, the SPCA, and a battered women's shelter.

7. The subjects' ages at the time the stalking began ranged from 15 through 58 ($M = 30.5$, $SD = 8.8$, median = 29).

8. The mean is skewed as a result of one victim who dated someone for less than a month, terminated the relationship, and was subsequently stalked for 38 years (456 months).

9. Although a fairly narrow focus is taken in this analysis, a more detailed description of data collection and findings regarding the nature of stalking and the experiences of victims can be found in Brewster (1997).

10. Originally, income was also included in the analysis. It was removed because of a collinearity problem with education.

11. The researcher chose to use mainly demographic characteristics of the victims as opposed to the stalkers to reduce the numbers of missing values and because earlier research supports victim characteristics as predictors of violence. Victim demographic characteristics were also correlated to stalker demographic characteristics, therefore the use of both in the same analyses would have also led to a multicollinearity problem.

12. Similar results (not presented here) occurred when a stepwise approach was used to build the predictive model.

13. Ryan (1995), however, focuses on current intimates while this study focuses on former intimates.

14. This issue is also raised by Edleson and Grusznski (1988), who also suggest that some batterers replace violence with threats.

15. See Follingstad (1990) for more on this sampling problem in domestic violence research.

16. This is likely due to the differences between the samples used for the two studies. The sample for this study was a self-selected sample of female former intimate stalking victims. Meloy's "obsessional followers" included both males and females, many of whom had had no prior relationship or contact. Most of Meloy's stalkers had also been clinically diagnosed erotomanics. Findings in a study by Schwartz-Watts and Morgan (1998) also indicate that stalkers who have had prior attachment to their victims were more likely than other stalkers to become violent.

17. Felson and Steadman (1983, p. 66) touch upon this by stating that threats are more likely to occur prior to assaults than prior to homicides.

18. See Daly and Wilson (1997) and Decker (1996) for more on expressive versus instrumental violence.

ACKNOWLEDGMENT

This project was supported under award number 95–WT-NX-0002 from the National Institute of Justice, Office of Justice Programs, U.S. Department of Justice. Points of view in this document are those of the author and do not necessarily represent the official position of the U.S. Department of Justice.

REFERENCES

Aldarondo, E., & Sugarman, D. B. (1996). Risk marker analysis of the cessation and persistence of wife assault. *Journal of Consulting and Clinical Psychology, 64,* 1010–1019.

Bachman, R., & Saltzman, L. E. (1995, August). *Violence against women: Estimates from the redesigned survey.* Washington, DC: U.S. Department of Justice, Bureau of Justice Statistics.

Brewster, M. (1997). *An exploration of the experiences and needs of former intimate stalking victims.* Unpublished manuscript.

Brookoff, D. (1997, October). *Drugs, alcohol, and domestic violence in Memphis.* Washington, DC: U.S. Department of Justice, National Institute of Justice.

Burgess, A. W., Baker, T., Greening, D., Hartman, C. R., Burgess, A. G., Douglas, J. E., & Halloran, R. (1997). Stalking behavior within domestic violence. *Journal of Family Violence, 12,* 389–403.

Daly, M., & Wilson, M. (1997). Crime and conflict: Homicide in evolutionary psychological perspective. *Crime and Justice: A Review of the Research, 22,* 51–100.

Decker, S. (1996). Deviant homicide: A new look at the role of motives and victim-offender relationships. *Journal of Research in Crime and Delinquency, 33,* 427–449.

Dutton, D. G., vanGinkel, C., & Landolt. M. A. (1996). Jealousy, intimate abusiveness, and intrusiveness. *Journal of Family Violence, 11,* 411–423.

Edleson, J. L., & Grusznski, R. J. (1989). Treating men who batter: Four years of outcome data from the Domestic Abuse Project. *Journal of Social Service Research, 12* (1/2), 3–22.

Fagan, J. (1990). Intoxication and aggression. *Crime and Justice: A Review of the Research, 13,* 241–320.

Felson, R. B., & Steadman, H. J. (1983). Situational factors in disputes leading to criminal violence. *Criminology, 21* (1), 59–74.

Follingstad, D. (1990). Methodological issues and new directions for research on violence in relationships. In D. J. Besharov (Ed.), *Family violence: Research and public policy issues* (pp. 13–25). Washington, DC: AEI Press.

Follingstad, D. R., Laughlin, J. E., Polek, D. S., Rutledge, L. L., & Hause, E. S. (1991). Identification of patterns of wife abuse. *Journal of Interpersonal Violence, 6* (2), 187–204.

Hazelwood, R. R., & Warren, J. W. (1990, February). The criminal behavior of the serial rapist. *FBI Law Enforcement Bulletin, 1990,* 11–16

Hough, M. (1990). Threats: Findings from the British Crime Survey. *International Review of Victimology, 1,* 169–180.

Lane, J. C. (1992, August). Threat management fills void in police service. *The Police Chief,* 27–31.

Leonard, K. E., & Senchak, M. (1996). Prospective prediction of husband marital aggression within newlywed couples. *Journal of Abnormal Psychology, 105,* 369–380.

Leong, G. B., Silva, J. A., Garza-Trevino, E. S., Oliva, D., Jr., Ferrari, M. M., Komanduri, R. V., & Cladwell, J. C. B. (1994). The dangerousness of persons with the Othello syndrome. *Journal of Forensic Sciences, 39,* 1445–1454.

McAnaney, K. G., Curliss, L. A., & Abeyta-Price, C. E. (1993). From imprudences to crime: Antistalking laws. *Notre Dame Law Review, 68,* 819–909.

Meloy, J. R. (1996). Stalking (obsessional following): A review of some preliminary findings. *Aggression and Violent Behavior, 1* (2), 147–162.

Murphy, C. M., & O'Leary, K. D. (1989). Psychological aggression predicts physical aggression in early marriage. *Journal of Consulting and Clinical Psychology, 57,* 579–582.

Perez, C. (1993). Stalking: When does obsession become a crime? *American Journal of Criminal Law, 20,* 263–280.

Reiss, A. J., Jr., & Roth, J. A. (Eds.). (1993). *Understanding and preventing violence.* Washington, DC: National Academy Press.

Roberts, A. R. (1996). Battered women who kill: A comparative study of incarcerated participants with a community sample of battered women. *Journal of Family Violence, 11,* 291–304.

Roberts, A. R., & Dziegielewski, S. F. (1996). Assessment typology and intervention with the survivors of stalking. *Aggression and Violent Behavior, 1,* 359–368.

Ryan, K. M. (1995). Do courtship-violent men have characteristics associated with a "battering personality?" *Journal of Family Violence, 10* (1), 99–120.

Schwartz-Watts, D., & Morgan, D. W. (1998). Violent versus nonviolent stalkers. *Journal of the American Academy of Psychiatry and the Law, 26* (2), 241–245.

Shore, D., Filson, C. R., Johnson, W. E., Rae, D. S., Muehrer, P., Kelley, D. J., Davis, T. S., Waldman, I. N., & Wyatt, R. J. (1989). Murder and assault arrests of White House cases: Clinical and demographic correlates of violence subsequent to civil commitment. *American Journal of Psychiatry, 146,* 645–651.

Sherman, L. W. (1992). *Policing domestic violence: Experiments and dilemmas.* NY: Free Press.

Shuckitt, M. A., & Russell, J. W. (1984). An evaluation of primary alcoholics with histories of violence. *Journal of Clinical Psychiatry, 45,* 3–6.

Sohn, E. F. (1994). Anti-stalking statutes: Do they actually protect victims? *Criminal Law Bulletin, 29* (2), 124–136.

Sugarman, D. B., & Hotaling, G. T. (1989). Violent men in intimate relationships: An analysis of risk markers. *Journal of Applied Social Psychology, 19,* 1034–1048.

Thomas, K. R. (1993). How to stop the stalker: State anti-stalking laws. *Criminal Law Bulletin, 29* (2), 124–136.

U.S. Department of Justice, Bureau of Justice Statistics. (1995, August). *Violence between intimates: Domestic violence.* Washington, DC: Author.

Wilson, M., & Daly, M. (1993). Spousal homicide risk and estrangement. *Violence and Victims, 8* (1), 3–16.

14

Negative Family-of-Origin Experiences: Are They Associated With Perpetrating Unwanted Pursuit Behaviors?

Jennifer Langhinrichsen-Rohling and Martin Rohling

Unwanted pursuit behaviors have been defined as activities that constitute the ongoing and unwanted pursuit of a romantic relationship (Langhinrichsen-Rohling, Palarea, Cohen, & Rohling, this volume). When perpetrated by intimates, these behaviors are thought to be most likely to occur after a consensual romantic relationship has ended or before a consensual relationship has been initiated (Cupach & Spitzberg, 1998). Theoretically, unwanted pursuit behaviors are expected to vary in severity (e.g., hang-up call to unwanted in-person visit), frequency (once to numerous times), and impact (e.g., positive and negative). It is likely that perpetrating repeated, threatening, and severe unwanted pursuit behaviors will meet the legal definitions of harassment, stalking, and/or assault (Spitzberg, Nicastro, & Cousins, 1998; Tjaden & Thoennes, 1998).

The literature on unwanted pursuit behaviors and stalking has only recently advanced from anecdotal to empirically descriptive (Spitzberg et al., 1998). Consequently, relatively little is known about the risk factors for perpetrating unwanted pursuit. In general, the existing research has focused on delineating individual factors that may predispose one toward stalking perpetration (e.g., Meloy & Gothard, 1995; Zona, Sharma, & Lane, 1993). More recently, research has shown that relationship factors are associated with unwanted pursuit behavior perpetration (Langhinrichsen-Rohling et al., this volume). The current study seeks to extend what is known by considering whether negative family-of-origin factors are also associated with unwanted pursuit behavior perpetration after the termination of a romantic relationship.

Previous research has substantiated that stalking by intimates often occurs after a dating relationship ends (Tjaden & Thoennes, 1998). Furthermore, emotional abuse and domestic violence co-occur frequently in relationships that end with stalking (Langhinrichsen-Rohling et al., this volume; Tjaden & Thoennes, 1998). Past research has also demonstrated that several specific types of negative family-of-origin experiences are associated both with the perpetration of relationship violence and with negative outcomes in relationship (e.g., poorly resolved or unsolicited relationship dissolution). In particular, parental divorce, a history of parental separation, experiences with parental marital conflict (as measured by the Children's Perception of Parental Conflict Scale) and a history of parental marital violence (as measured by versions of Straus's Conflict Tactics Scale; Straus, 1979) have all been shown to predict relationship violence and/or relationship difficulties (Amato & Keith, 1991; Dostal & Langhinrichsen-Rohling, 1997; Langhinrichsen-Rohling & Neidig, 1995). By extension, it was hypothesized that these four types of family-of-origin experiences would also emerge as significant correlates of unwanted pursuit behavior perpetration at the end of a romantic relationship.

The intergenerational transmission of relationship instability and the intergenerational transmission of violence hypotheses have generally formed the basis for choosing these family-of-origin variables for consideration (Amato, 1996; Mueller & Pope, 1977; Widom, 1989). These family-of-origin hypotheses postulate that children who have endured parental marital instability (generally manifested by parental separation, and/or divorce) or who have witnessed interparental violence or intense marital conflict are more likely to experience instability, violence, and intense conflict in their own adult relationships. Social learning theory is the main theoretical rationale proposed for the transmission process (Bandura, 1973; Mihalic & Elliott, 1997). This theory posits that children learn both by absorbing and processing what they have personally experienced and by direct imitation of others. According to social learning theory, children who observe their parents arguing, separating, and/or divorcing are likely to learn that high levels of conflict and instability in relationships are acceptable and to a certain extent normative. Some specificity to the intergenerational transmission models has been assumed (i.e., experiencing child abuse is most likely to create child abusers; witnessing parental marital violence will lead to perpetrating relationship violence as an adult). Thus, we predict, a priori, that the strongest associations will be found between a history of parental separations, parental marital violence, and intense and unresolved marital conflict and the perpetration of unwanted pursuit after the dissolution of an important romantic relationship.

The majority of previous tests of intergenerational transmission processes have focused exclusively on one negative family-of-origin event at a time. For example, there is an extensive body of research that substantiates the notion that parental divorce is a risk factor for divorce in the next generation (e.g., Amato & Keith, 1991). There is also considerable research which has studied the degree to which family-of-origin violence begets violence in the next generation of relationships (e.g., Widom, 1989). However, the most current reviews within these literatures highlight the need for more complex understandings of the interrelationships between family-of-origin experiences and adult intimate relationship behavior (Downs, Smith, & Miller, 1996; Holtzworth-Munroe & Stuart, 1994; Tolman & Bennett, 1990). Specifically, researchers have suggested the importance of considering several different kinds of negative family-of-origin experiences simultaneously because these experiences tend to co-occur within families and multiple negative events may have additive or potentiating effects (Cummings & Davies, 1994; David, Steele, Forehand, & Armistead, 1996; Jackson, 1999). Thus, the current study was designed to assess several important types of family-of-origin experiences concurrently.

In addition, the necessity of considering the gender-specificity of any obtained associations has also been suggested as both the gender of the parent who is viewed as the perpetrator and the gender of the child may alter the impact of the family-of-origin event (Black & Sprenkle, 1991; Langhinrichsen-Rohling & Neidig, 1995; O'Keefe, 1998). In particular, the associations between negative family-of-origin experiences and subsequent perpetration in dating relationships may be stronger for males than females (Foo & Margolin, 1995). In a study by Mangold and Koski (1990), for both genders, an association was found between witnessing father-to-mother marital violence and perpetrating stranger violence. However, higher levels of witnessing father-to-mother physical violence was associated with perpetrating stranger violence for males only (Mangold & Koski,1990). Along the same lines, Langhinrichsen-Rohling and Neidig (1995) found that witnessing parental violence suppressed female but not male Job Corps residents' violence toward parents. Research focused on children's reactions to simulated conflict has also demonstrated that boys from violent homes responded to certain types of marital conflict with more intense sadness and anger than other children (Adamson & Thompson, 1998). Related research has also shown that males may be more likely than females to perpetrate severe forms of unwanted pursuit behavior perpetration such as stalking (Tjaden & Thoennes, 1998). Some have theorized that while males and females may be equally distressed by negative family-of-origin events, males may be more likely than females to respond to this distress with violence. Females may be more predisposed to internalizing disorders as a consequence (Cummings & Davies, 1994). Therefore, we predict that the associations between negative family-of-origin experiences and severe forms of unwanted pursuit behavior perpetration will be stronger for males than for females in the current study.

Overall, this project was undertaken to determine which of a variety of negative family-of-origin experiences would associate with perpetrating unwanted pursuit behavior after the termination of an important romantic relationship. The following family-of-origin experiences (e.g., parental divorce, parental separation, parental marital conflict, and interparental violence) were chosen for measurement because they have been well studied in the literature, have documented associations with relationship violence and dissolution, and can be theoretically related to the production of unwanted pursuit behavior at the end of a romantic relationship. Gender specificity in these associations was hypothesized. Unwanted pursuit behaviors were chosen as the important outcome variable because these behaviors are likely to reflect the success of the dissolution process and because they have been conceptually linked both to domestic violence and to stalking (Burgess et al., 1997).

METHOD

Participants

The sample consisted of 212 college students (109 males and 103 females) who were enrolled in introductory psychology courses either at a large public midwestern university (56%) or a large public university in the South (44%). All students participated in this study for partial fulfillment of a research requirement. Prior to the study, all participating students indicated that they had experienced the unwanted termination of an important romantic dating relationship (i.e., they were Breakup sufferers). Their ended relationship must have lasted longer than one month to meet eligibility criteria. All participants also reported on their level of experience with family-of-origin violence, their perceptions of interparental conflict, their parents' history of marital separation, and whether their parents were currently separated or divorced.

Overall, the sample was predominantly Caucasian (84.0%). The remaining students were African American (6.1%), Asian American (4.7%), Hispanic (1.4%), Native American (1.9%) and other (1.4%). Average age at time of breakup was 18.6 years. The modal student was reporting on a relationship that had broken up within the past 12 months. The mean duration of the romantic relationship being reported on was 15.2 months ($SD = 12.7$ months). The majority (92.5%) were dating relationships, although 7.5% had been engaged prior to the breakup. Eight percent of the sample indicated that they had lived together and 2.8% had a child with their ex-partner. More than 40% of the sample had brokenup at least once before the final breakup.

Procedure

Informed consent was obtained from all participants. Each participant was asked to focus exclusively on his/her most significant past relationship. Only participants who indicated that their partner had ended the relationship (i.e., they were Breakup Sufferers) were retained for the current study. Each consenting participant was then given a two-page demographic questionnaire that consisted of 22 items. These items assessed demographics (e.g., age, gender, ethnicity), family-of-origin structure (e.g., current parental divorce or separation) as well as specifics about their broken-up romantic relationship (e.g., the duration of the relationship, the extent of their emotional involvement, how much time had elapsed since the breakup had occurred, etc.).

Measures

Independent Variables

FAMILY-OF-ORIGIN EXPERIENCES: CURRENT PARENTAL DIVORCE/SEPARATION

Parental divorce and current separation was assessed with one categorical "yes" or "no" question. It was "Are your parents currently separated or divorced?"

HISTORY OF PARENTAL SEPARATION

A known history of parental separation was assessed via two questions. Potential responses were "yes," "no," and "don't know." The first question was "Before your parents got married, did they ever break up with one another?" The second question was "After your parents got married, did they ever separate or threaten to separate?" All individuals that answered "yes" to either one or both of these two questions were considered to have a known history of parental separation.

HISTORY OF WITNESSING INTERPARENTAL MARITAL VIOLENCE

A history of witnessing interparental violence was assessed via two "yes" or "no" questions. All acts that comprised the physical assault subscale of the Revised Conflict Tactics Scales (CTS2; Straus, Hamby, McCoy, & Sugarman, 1996) were included in this 2–item modification. This physical assault subscale was reported to have a coeffcient alpha of .86 in a college student sample. The first question included all acts of mild physical violence as defined by Straus's (1979) Conflict Tactics Scale. It was "Have you ever seen or heard your parents or step-parents do any of the following things to one another: throw something that could hurt, twist the other's arm or hair, push or shove the other, grab the other, or slap the other?" The second question assessed for witnessing acts of severe physical violence. The question was "Have you ever seen or heard your parents or step-parents do any of the following things to one another: use a knife or a gun against the other, punch or hit the other with something that could hurt, choke the other, slam the other against a wall, beat the other up, burn or scald the other, or kick the other?" The coefficient alpha for these two items was .74 in the current sample.

EXPERIENCING INTERPARENTAL MARITAL CONFLICT

The extent to which the participant had experienced interparental marital conflict was assessed via the Children's Perception of Interparental Conflict Scale (CPICS; Grych, Seid, & Fincham, 1992). This instrument measures offspring's perceptions about conflict observed between parents. The CPICS has eight subscales reflecting different aspects of parental conflict. They are: Frequency, Intensity, Resolution, Content, Perceived Threat, Coping Efficacy, Self-Blame, and Triangulation. The wording of the items in the CPICS was modified slightly in the current study in order to accommodate the retrospective nature of the reporting. Previous research has substantiated the internal consistency of the subscales, with coefficient alpha's ranging from .61 to .82 (Grych et al., 1992). Similarly, in the current sample, all the subscales except the coping subscale (coefficient alpha = .66) were shown to have excellent internal consistency (coefficient alpha's ranging from .81 to .93). Furthermore, all of the subscale scores were shown to meet assumptions of normality (skewness of less than one, kurtosis less than two). Correlational analyses revealed that these subscales were significantly intercorrelated in the current sample (range .63 to .88). A participant gender by CPIC subscales MANOVA was conducted to determine if there were gender differences in overall reports of marital conflict. No significant gender differences in reports were revealed. Finally, the coefficient alpha for the total score in the current sample was .97 which indicates excellent internal consistency for the scale as a whole.

Dependent Variable: Reports of Unwanted Pursuit Behaviors

PURSUIT BEHAVIOR INVENTORY

The Pursuit Behavior Inventory (PBI; Palarea & Langhinrichsen-Rohling, 1998) is a 26–item instrument that assesses the presence, frequency, impact, and motivation underlying a full range of unsolicited pursuit behaviors that can occur after a romantic relationship has terminated (e.g., leaving phone messages and hang-up calls, contacting the ex-partner's friends and family without permission, following, threatening, committing violence toward the victim and/or his/her property). The coefficient alpha for this scale in the current sample was .70. The internal consistency of the scale was improved somewhat if the item *talked with your ex-partner unwantedly in an internet chat room* was removed from the scale (coefficient alpha = .75). All participants included in the current study reported on their unwanted pursuit behavior perpetration after the breakup. Pursuit behavior total scores were then created by summing reports of all perpetrated acts endorsed, regardless of the perceived impact of the behavior on the ex-partner.

A second total score was created from responses to the Pursuit Behavior Inventory. This score was called the Unwanted Pursuit Behavior Severity Index. This index was derived to reflect the overall severity of the unwanted pursuit behaviors that were perpetrated. Clinically, it was expected that this measure would most closely approximate the phenomena of stalking. For this score, only perpetrated acts that were reported to have a negative impact on the ex-partner were included in the summary score; items perceived to have a positive impact were eliminated. Second, all negative impact pursuit acts were weighted by their reported frequency of occurrence, prior to creating the perpetration severity summary score. As expected, this derived score was skewed because of the large number of individuals reporting no acts of perpetration (skew = 3.3).

Previous research has shown these two indices to be only mildly correlated for Breakup Sufferers (Langhinrichsen-Rohling et al., this volume). Consistent with these findings, the total acts' score and the severity index were correlated .28 for males and .25 for females in the current sample.

RESULTS

Prevalence of Negative Family-of-Origin Experiences

Current parental divorce or separation was reported by 25.9% of the sample (*n* = 55; 25 males and 30 females), whereas any known history of parental breakup or separation was reported by 49.3% of the sample (*n* = 102; 47 males and 55 females). Witnessing acts of mild parental violence was reported by 17.5 % of the sample (*n* = 37) whereas witnessing at least one act of severe interparental violence was reported by 8.5% of the sample (n = 18). Overall, any act of parental marital violence was witnessed by 18.2% of the sample (23 females and 15 males). Chi-square analyses revealed no significant gender differences in any of the reported prevalence of these family-of-origin experiences (p > .10). For both acts of mild and severe violence, the most frequently identified perpetrators were either the father only or both the mother and father (52.8% and 30.6% of the witnessed acts of mild violence and 55.6% and 33.3% of the witnessed acts of severe violence, respectively).

Overall, the mean score on the PBI total score was 5.66 (SD = 3.33). The mean for males was 5.97 while the mean for females was 5.33. This difference failed to meet significance, F (1, 210) = 1.99, p = .16. The mean score on the Unwanted Pursuit Behavior Severity Index was 1.87 for the sample as a whole (SD = 4.03). The mean for males on the index was 2.19. The mean for females was 1.52. Again, this gender difference was not statistically significant, F (1, 210) = 1.46, p = .23.

Associations Between the Three Dichotomous Negative Family-of-Origin Experiences and Unwanted Pursuit Behavior Perpetration

To test the relationship between the three dichotomized family-of-origin experiences and the experience of unwanted pursuit behavior perpetration, three ANOVAs were conducted. In each ANOVA, one of the negative family-of-origin experiences served as an independent variable, while participants' gender was included as a second independent variable. In these analyses the Unwanted Pursuit Behavior Severity Perpetration Index served as the dependent measure. This measure was chosen because theoretically it was expected to be most closely related to the phenomena of stalking.

In the first ANOVA, current parental divorce and/or separation was the primary independent variable. Results from this analysis indicated that there was no main effect for parental divorce status, F (1, 204) < 1. There was also no significant main effect for gender, F (1, 204) = 2.67, p = .10. However, a gender by parental divorce status interaction was revealed, F (1, 204) = 4.67, p < .05. As shown in Table 14.1, males from currently divorced or separated parental homes reported significantly higher levels of unwanted pursuit behavior perpetration than did males from intact homes or females from either family situation.

In the second ANOVA, a known history of parental breakup or separation served as the primary independent variable. No main effect for the history of parental breakup and/or separation variable was

Table 14.1 Mean Differences in Unwanted Pursuit Behavior Perpetration Reported by Male and Female Break-up Sufferers From Various Types of Family Backgrounds.

| | Gender of Break-up Sufferer | |
	Male	Female
Parent's Current Marital Status		
Intact	1.43[b] (.40)	1.73[b] (.42)
	(*n* = 80)	(*n* = 73)
Divorced/Separated	3.20[a] (.72)	1.03[b] (.66)
	(*n* = 25)	(*n* = 30)
History of Parental Relationship Separations		
None Known	1.21[b] (.47)	2.11[a,b] (.53)
	(*n* = 58)	(*n* = 47)
History of Separation	2.65a (.53)	1.06[b] (.49)
	(*n* = 47)	(*n* = 55)
Level of Interparental Violence Witnessed		
None	1.84 (.38)	1.43 (.42)
	(*n* = 91)	(*n* = 80)
Any Physical Violence	2.80 (1.35)	1.87 (.67)
	(*n* = 15)	(*n* = 23)

Note. Means with different superscripts are significantly different at the $p < .05$ level using Tukey's Least Significant Different Post-Hoc Test.

revealed, $F (1, 203) < 1$ and there was no main effect for gender either, $F < 1$. However, a significant gender by parental breakup and separation history interaction was obtained, $F (1, 203) = 6.03$, $p < .05$. As shown in Table 14.1, males with a history of parental breakup and separation had the highest means on the Unwanted Pursuit Behavior Severity Perpetration Index.

In the third ANOVA, witnessing parental violence was the primary independent variable. Breakup sufferers were categorized into two groups: those who reported no parental violence witnessed ($n = 172$), and those who witnessed at least one act of physical violence between parents ($n = 38$). Again, gender of participant was included as an independent variable. No significant main effects (gender, $F < 1$ and violence, $F (1, 205) = 1.08$, $p = .30$) or interaction effects ($F < 1$) were obtained for this analysis.

Although ANOVA has been shown to be relatively robust in response to violations in assumptions of normality, the above analyses were rerun with the PBI Total scores as the dependent variable to determine if the skew of the severity index was responsible for the findings. These results revealed that the reported findings remained substantially unchanged. There was still a significant gender by history of parental separation interaction. There were still no significant findings with the parental violence independent variable. However, in these analyses, the gender by parental divorce interaction was reduced to nonsignificance (F (1, 204) = 1.45, p = .23.

Finally, correlation analyses were conducted to consider whether the fourth family-of-origin variable was associated with unwanted pursuit behavior perpetration. The subscales of the CPIC were used to determine which particular aspects of parental marital conflict might be associated with unwanted pursuit behavior perpetration. The correlational analyses were conducted using both the Unwanted Pursuit Behavior Severity Index and the Pursuit Behaviors Total Score as dependent variables as these two indices were only mildly correlated for male and female Breakup Sufferers (.28 for males and .25 for females in the current sample). The CPIC subscales were used as the independent variables. These results are also shown in Table 14.2. For both males and females, many significant associations were obtained between the CPIC subscale scores and the pursuit behavior total score measure (which includes both positive and negative impact pursuit behaviors). Specifically, for males and females, all indices of negative parental conflict were associated with increased numbers of acts of unsolicited pursuit after the relationship had ended. More acts of unwanted post-dissolution pursuit were engaged in by individuals who had experienced frequent, intense, child-focused, unresolved, and threatening parental arguments. More acts of unwanted pursuit were also reported by males and females who indicated that they had trouble coping with parental arguments, blamed themselves for their parent's conflicts, and experienced triangulation when their parents fought.

A similar set of analyses was conducted with the Unwanted Pursuit Behavior Severity Index. Because this index evidenced considerable skew, Spearman rho's were used for this set of correlational analyses. Results revealed significant associations between parental conflict and severe unwanted pursuit behavior perpetration, for females only. Specifically, females who reported parental conflict which was intense (r = .25, p < .01) and threatening (r = .23, p < .05) reported perpetrating more severe unwanted pursuit behavior. Likewise, difficulty coping with parental conflict (r = .20, p < .05), triangulation during parental

Table 14.2 Correlations Among the Predictor Variables

Parental Conflict	f	Intense	Content	Unresolved	Threat	Cope	Self-Blame	Triangulation
Total # of Acts Perpetrated (Pearson r's were computed)								
Female (n = 103)	.33***	.32***	.38***	.26**	.32***	.27***	.31***	.31***
Male (n = 109)	.23***	.22*	.31***	.24**	.20*	.26**	.30***	.17*
z-score of difference	.71	.79	.57	.14	.93	.07	.07	1.07
Unwanted Pursuit Behavior Perpetration Severity Index (Spearman rho's were computed)								
Female (n = 103)	.13	.25**	.13	.15	.23*	.20*	.18*	.16*
Male (n = 109)	-.02	.04	.08	.02	-.05	-.02	.03	.04
z-score of difference	1.08	1.54	.36	.93	2.03*	1.59	1.09	.86

Note. N's vary slightly across analyses due to missing data. f = frequency of parental arguments, Intense = intensity of parental arguments, Cont = degree content of parental arguments was child focused, Unresolved = degree parental arguments were unresolved, Threat = perceived threat from parental arguments, Cope = perceived lack of ability to cope with parental arguments, Self-blame = extent of self-blame for parental arguments, and Triangulation = triangulation in parental arguments.

* $p < .05$. ** $p < .01$. *** $p < .001$.

conflict ($r = .16$, $p < .05$), and degree of self-blame for parental arguments ($r = .18$, $p < .05$) were also associated with severe unwanted
pursuit behavior perpetration, for females only. Differences in the
magnitude of correlation obtained for males and females were compared using an r to z transformation. These results revealed that there
was a stronger association between experiencing parental arguments
as threatening and severe unwanted pursuit behavior perpetration for
females than for males ($r = .23$ for females and $r = -.05$ for males, $z =$
2.03, $p < .05$.

DISCUSSION

A variety of pursuit behaviors is common after the termination of
college students' dating relationships (Langhinrichsen-Rohling et al.,
this volume). Previous research has also substantiated that the occurrence of unwanted pursuit behaviors and stalking is associated with
individual (Meloy & Gothard, 1995; Zona, Sharma, & Lane) and
relationship-specific factors (i.e, love styles experienced, partner-specific dependency, and the presence of relationship violence; Langhinrichsen-Rohling et al., this volume; Spitzberg et al., 1998). The current
study was undertaken to determine the degree to which perpetration
of unwanted pursuit behaviors might also be associated with various
types of family-of-origin experiences (e.g., parental conflict, witnessing
interparental violence, and a history of parental separation and/or
divorce). The rationale for this study was derived from social learning
theory and is an extension of the intergenerational transmission of
relationship dysfunction hypotheses (Amato, 1996; Bandura, 1973;
Mihalic & Elliott, 1997; Widom, 1989).

As predicted, findings obtained in the current study revealed some
gender-specific associations between various types of family-of-origin
experiences and unwanted pursuit behavior perpetration. Overall, these
results are consistent with other research that has documented long-
term effects of negative family-of-origin experiences such as increased
likelihood of relationship violence perpetration, higher levels of depression and suicidal behavior, and increased risk of divorce (Langhinrichsen-Rohling, Monson, Meyer, Caster, & Sanders, 1998; Maker,
Kemmelmeier, & Peterson, 1998; McNeal & Amato, 1998). These
results are also consistent with previous findings that indicate that
family-of-origin experiences may have a gender-specific impact. Specif-

ically, some of the obtained relationships were primarily for males. Males from divorced and/or currently separated parental homes reported perpetrating more severe unwanted pursuit behavior than did males from intact parental homes or females from either type of family. A similar gender-specific pattern was found for the history of parental relationship separation variable. Males who reported a history of parental separation also reported the highest levels of severe unwanted pursuit behavior perpetration. These results are consistent with previous research that has shown that the associations between negative family-of-origin experiences and subsequent perpetration in dating relationships may be stronger for males than females (Foo & Margolin, 1995).

Several possible mechanisms for these male-specific results are proposed. For example, males may be more impacted than females by some of the assessed family-of-origin experiences because of male's same-sex identification with their fathers. Fathers are more likely to perpetrate severe interparental violence than mothers (Cascardi, Langhinrichsen, & Vivian, 1992), and fathers may also be more likely to leave the family after parental divorce or separation. Conversely, it is possible that mediating relationships are more utilized by females from difficult family situations than males (i.e., females may have more protective relationships with their mothers or with other extended family members or friends), and these relationships may protect them from later perpetration. It is also possible that negative family-of-origin experiences are more related to problematic externalizing behaviors for males and to problematic internalizing behaviors, such as depression, for females (Cummings & Davies, 1994; McNeal & Amato, 1998).

Findings with the Children's Perception of Interparental Conflict Scale revealed some different gender-specific effects, however. For both males and females, all negative aspects of parental conflict were associated with perpetrating acts (with either positive or negative impact) of unsolicited pursuit behavior. No gender differences in the strength of these associations were revealed. However, when the Unwanted Pursuit Behavior Severity Index was used as the dependent variable in the correlational analyses, a different picture emerged. Significant correlations emerged between perceptions of parental conflict and severe unwanted pursuit behavior perpetration, only for females. In particular, stronger associations were obtained between perceptions of threat from parental conflict and perpetration for females than for males. There are several possible interpretations of these female-specific findings. One possibility is that the perception of parental conflict scale may be the most sensitive index of parental discord used in the current study. Females may be more impacted by continuous and threatening parental discord than males. They may see their mother as more of an equal participant in continuing, threatening, intense, and on-going marital conflict than in cases of divorce or marital violence. Ongoing conflict would also allow for more opportunities for females to observe their same-sex parent engaged in negative relationship behaviors. Another possibility, however, is that there is a reporting effect occurring such that females who are willing to admit that they experienced their parents' conflict as threatening, intense, and difficult to cope with, are also more willing to disclose that their unwanted pursuit behavior was repeated and had negative impact on their ex-partner. Future research will be needed to replicate these findings and to clarify our understanding of these gender-specific associations. Taken as a whole, these results highlight the importance of considering gender as an important variable linking negative family-of-origin experiences and perpetration of negative relationship behavior.

While the obtained findings also support the notion that many different types of family-of-origin experiences (e.g., conflict characteristics, interparental violence, parental separation and/or divorce) continue to exert influence on young adult's relationship behavior, additional research that considers the specific impact of multiple familial stressors is needed (Maker et al., 1998). This type of research will help develop more complex models of the intergenerational process as some family-of-origin experiences may predispose young adults to depression, victimization, and internalizing disorders while other types of family experiences may be a risk factor for aggression and perpetration. Certainly, results from the current study indicate that several different types of negative family-of-origin experiences may be risk factors for perpetrating severe unwanted pursuit behaviors. Theoretically, one could expect that these same negative family-of-origin experiences might also be risk factors for ex-partner harassment, assault, and stalking (e.g., Belknap & Erez, 1995; Cupach & Spitzberg, 1998). Consistent with this assumption, some research has already substantiated that childhood physical abuse is a risk factor for domestic violence stalking (Burgess et al., 1997). Future research is needed to assess the nature and strength of the particular associations between various family-of-origin experiences and types of pursuit, harassment, and stalking in clinical populations that include both males and females.

Limitations to the current findings must also be noted. These results were obtained via a cross-sectional design. Consequently, reports of family-of-origin experiences are retrospective in nature. The current affective state of the participant may have impacted their retrospective reports. Furthermore, this study relies on correlating reports given by one individual. Shared method variance may have changed the nature of the results. Finally, all the perpetration experiences are self-reports. It is likely that social desirability concerns led some individuals to not disclose their perpetration behavior or to minimize the extent or negative impact of their unwanted pursuit. Reports from multiple informants, longitudinal designs, and non-college student samples will be important directions for future research to take.

ACKNOWLEDGMENT

We would like to acknowledge the research assistance provided by Melissa Fredenberg, Jennifer Cohen, Russell Palarea, Melanie Marler, and Jaquese James.

REFERENCES

Adamson, J. L., & Thompson, R. A. (1998). Coping with interparental verbal conflict by children exposed to spouse abuse and children from nonviolent homes. *Journal of Family Violence, 13*, 213–232.

Amato, P. R. (1996). Explaining the intergenerational transmission of divorce. *Journal of Marriage and the Family, 58*, 628–640.

Amato, P. R., & Keith, B. (1991). Parental divorce and adult well being: A meta-analysis. *Journal of Marriage and the Family, 53*, 43–58.

Bandura, A. (1973). *Aggression: A social learning analysis.* Englewood Cliffs, NJ: Prentice Hall.

Belknap, J., & Erez, E. (1995). The victimization of women on college campuses: Courtship violence, date rape, and sexual harassment. In B. S. Fisher and J. J. Sloan (Eds.). *Campus crime: Legal, social, and policy perspectives* (pp. 156–178). Springfield, IL: Charles C. Thomas.

Black, L. E., & Sprenkle, D. H. (1991). Gender differences in college students' attitudes toward divorce and their willingness to remarry. *Journal of Divorce and Remarriage, 14*, 47–60.

Burgess, A. W., Baker, T., Greening, D., Hartman, C. R., Burgess, A. G.,

Douglas, J. E., & Halloran, R. (1997). Stalking behaviors within domestic violence. *Journal of Family Violence, 12,* 389–403.

Cascardi, M., Langhinrichsen, J., & Vivian, D. (1992). Impact, injury and health correlates for husbands and wives. *Archives of Internal Medicine, 152,* 1178–1184.

Cummings, E. M., & Davies, P. (1994). *Children and marital conflict.* Guilford Press, NY.

Cupach, W. R., & Spitzberg, B. H. (1998). Obsessive relational intrusion and stalking. In B. H. Spitzberg and W.R. Cupach (Eds.). *The dark side of close relationships* (pp. 233–263). Hillsdale, NJ: Lawrence Erlbaum Associates.

David, C., Steele, R., Forehand, R., & Armistead, L. (1996). The role of family conflict and marital conflict in adolescent functioning. *Journal of Family Violence, 11,* 81–91.

Downs, W. R., Smith, N. J., & Miller, B. A. (1996). The relationship between childhood violence and alcohol problems among men who batter: An empirical review and synthesis. *Aggression and Violent Behavior, 1,* 327–344.

Dostal, C., & Langhinrichsen-Rohling, J. (1997). Relationship-specific cognitions and family-of-origin divorce and abuse. *Journal of Divorce and Remarriage, 27,* 101–120.

Foo, L., & Margolin, G. (1995). A multivariate investigation of dating violence. *Journal of Family Violence, 10,* 351–375.

Grych, J. H., Seid, M., & Fincham, F. D. (1992). Assessing marital conflict from the child's perspective: The Children's Perception of Interparental Conflict Scale. *Child Development, 63,* 558–572.

Holtzworth-Munroe, A., & Stuart, G. L. (1994). Typologies of male batterers: Three subtypes and the differences among them. *Psychological Bulletin, 116,* 476–497.

Jackson, S. M. (1999). Issues in the dating violence research: A review of the literature. *Aggression and Violent Behavior, 4,* 233–247.

Langhinrichsen-Rohling, J., Monson, C. M., Meyer, K. A., Caster, J., & Sanders, A. (1998). The associations among family-of-origin violence and young adults' current depressed, hopeless, suicidal, and life-threatening behavior. *Journal of Family Violence, 13,* 243–261.

Langhinrichsen-Rohling, J., & Neidig, P. (1995). Violent backgrounds of economically disadvantaged youth: Risk factors for perpetrating violence? *Journal of Family Violence, 10,* 379–397.

Maker, A., Kemmelmeier, M., & Peterson, C. (1998). Long-term psychological consequences in women of witnessing parental physical conflict and experiencing abuse in childhood. *Journal of Interpersonal Violence, 13,* 574–589.

Mangold, W. D., & Koski, P. R. (1990). Gender comparisons in the relationship between parental and sibling violence and nonfamily violence. *Journal of Family Violence, 5,* 225–235.

McNeal, C., & Amato, P. R. (1998). Parents' marital violence: Long-term consequences for children. *Journal of Family Issues, 19,* 123–139.

Meloy, J. R., & Gothard, S. (1995). Demographic and clinical comparison of obsessional followers and offenders with mental disorders. *American Journal of Psychiatry, 152,* 258–262.

Mihalic, S. W., & Elliott, D. (1997). A social learning theory model of marital violence. *Journal of Family Violence, 12,* 21–47.

Mueller, C. W., & Pope, H. (1977). Marital instability: A study of its transmission between generations. *Journal of Marriage and the Family, 48,* 319–326.

O'Keefe, M. (1998). Factors mediating the link between witnessing interparental violence and dating violence. *Journal of Family Violence, 13,* 39–57.

Palarea, R. E., & Langhinrichsen-Rohling, J. (1998). *Pursuit Behavior Inventory.* Unpublished measure.

Spitzberg, B. H., Nicastro, A. M., & Cousins, A. V. (1998). Exploring the interactional phenemon of stalking and obsessive relational intrusion. *Communication Reports, 11,* 33–47.

Straus, M. A. (1979). Measuring intrafamily conflict and violence: The Conflict Tactics Scales. *Journal of Marriage and the Family, 41,* 75–88.

Straus, M. A., Hamby, S. L., Boney-McCoy, S., & Sugarman, D. (1996). The Revised Conflict Tactics Scale (CTS2). *Journal of Family Issues, 17,* 283–316.

Tjaden, P., & Thoennes, N. (1998). *Stalking in America: Findings for the National Violence Against Women Survey.* Washington, DC: National Institute of Justice and Centers for Disease Control and Prevention (NCJ 169592).

Tolman, R. M., & Bennett, L. W. (1990). A review of quantitative research on men who batter. *Journal of Interpersonal Violence, 5,* 87–118.

Westrup, D., Fremouw, W. J., Thompson, R. N., & Lewis, S. F. (1999). The psychological impact of stalking on female undergraduates. *Journal of Forensic Sciences, 44,* 554–557.

Widom, C. (1989). Does violence beget violence? A critical examination of the literature. *Psychological Bulletin, 106,* 3–28.

Zona, M. A., Sharma, K. K., & Lane, J. (1993). A comparative study of erotomanic and obsessional subjects in a forensic sample. *Journal of Forensic Sciences, 38,* 894–903.

15

The Role of Stalking in Domestic Violence Crime Reports Generated by the Colorado Springs Police Department

Patricia Tjaden and Nancy Thoennes

Although stalking research is still in its infancy, several studies have established a link between stalking and violence in intimate relationships. Meloy (1998) conducted a profile of known stalkers and found that stalkers who had been sexually intimate with their victims were most likely to be violent toward their victims. Tjaden and Thoennes (1998) found that 81 percent of the women in the National Violence Against Women (NVAW) Survey, who were stalked by a current or former husband or cohabiting partner, also were physically assaulted by that partner, while 31 percent were raped by that partner. Tjaden and Thoennes (1998) also found that ex-husbands who stalked their partners were significantly more likely than ex-husbands who did not stalk to have engaged in emotionally abusive (e.g., shouting or swearing) and controlling behavior (e.g., limiting contact with others, jealousy, possessiveness, denying access to family income). Moracco and colleagues (1998) found that nearly a quarter (23.4 percent) of femicide victims in North Carolina who were murdered by a current or former intimate partner had been stalked prior to the fatal incident. And most recently, McFarlane and associates (1999) found that 76 percent of partner femicide victims and 85 percent of attempted partner femicide victims in 10 cities were stalked by their assailant in the

12 months preceding their victimization. McFarlane and colleagues (1999) also found a statistically significant association between intimate partner physical assault and stalking for both femicide and attempted femicide victims. Given these findings, it is not surprising that several researchers have recommended that stalking be considered a risk factor for further physical abuse or lethality in cases of involving violence perpetrated against women by intimates (Felder & Victor, 1997; Jacobson & Gottman, 1998; McFarlane et al., 1999; Schaum & Parrish, 1995; Walker & Meloy, 1998).

In light of the apparent link between stalking and physical violence in intimate relationships, the U.S. Department of Justice encourages state and local jurisdictions to train police officers and other justice system officials about the potential risks associated with intimate partner stalking and the efficacy of implementing collaborative efforts to respond more effectively to domestic violence and stalking (Violence Against Women Grants Office, 1998). However, because antistalking laws have been enacted only recently (Hunzeker, 1992), there is no systematic information about the prevalence of stalking allegations in domestic violence crime reports or the use of antistalking statutes to respond to these allegations. Thus, it is unclear how often domestic violence crime reports involve stalking and whether suspects in these cases are charged with stalking. An anecdotal survey of criminal justice practitioners commissioned by the Office of Justice Programs found that stalkers continue to be charged and sentenced under harassment, intimidation, or other related laws instead of under a state's antistalking statute (Violence Against Women Grants Office, 1998). But empirical data have been lacking on the prevalence of stalking in domestic violence crime reports or the ways in which justice system officials respond to reports with stalking allegations.

Empirical information also is limited on the characteristics of stalkers and their victims, especially in cases of intimate partner stalking. Tjaden and Thoennes (2000a) found that 4.8 percent of the women in the NVAW survey reported being stalked by a current or former intimate partner at some time in their lifetime, compared with 0.6 percent of the men. Thus, women are at greater risk of intimate partner violence than men. Tjaden and Thoennes (1998) also found that women were more likely to report being stalked by a former rather than a current intimate partner, and that the majority of stalking victims were between 18 and 29 years of age. However, Tjaden and Thoennes (2000a) found no significant differences in the rates of intimate partner stalking among women and men of specific racial backgrounds or between women and men of Hispanic/non-Hispanic origin. Burgess and associates (1997) profiled domestic violence perpetrators by whether or not they stalked and found that domestic violence stalkers, compared to nonstalkers, tended to live alone, were less likely to be married, and used more alcohol. While these studies provide a starting point for understanding risk factors associated with intimate partner stalking, there is clearly a need for more research on the correlates and causes of intimate partner violence.

This article presents findings from a study that examined the role of stalking in domestic violence crime reports in one jurisdiction, Colorado Springs, Colorado. The study consists of a case file review of domestic violence crime reports that were initiated by the Colorado Springs Police Department (CSPD) during a nine-month period. The CSPD serves a metropolitan area which is located 70 miles south of Denver and consists of a population of about 350,000. According to 1990 Census data, the ethnic/racial composition of the Colorado Springs Metropolitan Statistical Area (which encompasses El Paso County) is 86 percent White, 7.2 percent African American, 0.8 percent American Indian, 8.7 percent Hispanic (of any race), 2.5 percent Asian, and 3.5 percent Other (Greater Colorado Springs Economic Development Corporation Fact Sheet). Thirty-two percent of the population is employed by military bases (Greater Colorado Springs Economic Development Corporation Web Site) and 60 percent of the population has a college degree (Encyclopedia Britannica Online).

Colorado Springs is unique to other metropolitan settings in that it is home to the Domestic Violence Enhanced Response Team (DVERT), a nationally recognized, one-of-a-kind domestic violence prevention program that provides a multi-disciplinary system response to cases of domestic violence that have a high risk for lethality. The DVERT primary case management team consists of local law enforcement officials and detectives, representatives from the District Attorney's Office, and representatives from The Center for Prevention of Domestic Violence. The goal of DVERT is to provide seamless, systematic community response to domestic violence through a multi-disciplinary collaboration focusing on pro arrest policies and procedures, case investigation and prosecution, and implementation of innovative forms of outreach, advocacy, and services to victims.

Using data from the study, this article addresses the following questions:

1. How prevalent is stalking in domestic violence crime reports?
2. What are risk factors associated with domestic violence stalking?
3. How often are intimate partner stalkers charged with stalking?
4. Do presenting conditions in domestic violence crime reports with stalking allegations differ significantly from those in domestic violence crime reports without stalking allegations?
5. Do law enforcement outcomes in domestic violence crime reports with stalking allegations differ significantly from those in domestic violence crime reports without stalking allegations? To better understand how victim gender impacts these questions, separate analyses were conducted for female and male victims.

STUDY METHODS[1]

Sample Generation

The sample consists of misdemeanor and felony crimes reported to the CSPD during April-September, 1998, that involved victims and suspects who were current and former spouses, cohabiting partners, dates, boyfriends and girlfriends. All types of misdemeanor and felony domestic violence crime reports are included in the sample, including those involving allegations of attempted murder, kidnaping, robbery, simple and aggravated assault, rape, arson, burglary, vandalism, trespassing, disorderly conduct, menacing, intimidation, harassment, and stalking. The sample includes domestic violence crime reports with male and female suspects, male and female victims, and same-sex and opposite-sex intimates.

The sample was generated from CSPD Domestic Violence Summons and Complaint (DVSC) forms. These forms are used by CSPD officers to investigate crime reports of victims and suspects who are or have been in an intimate relationship and where there is probable cause to believe a crime was committed. Information from all 1998 DVSC forms was entered into a computerized database as part of the evaluation process for DVERT. A subfile of 1,788 reports for which a DVSC was initiated by the CSPD during April-September, 1998, was generated from this database and formed the basis for the study sample. Three of these reports were subsequently eliminated from the sample because they were lost or destroyed and could not be reviewed by data collectors. Thus, the sample for the present study consists of 1,785 DVSC crime reports.

Data Collection

The DVSC case file review was conducted from January to September, 1999. Data collectors reviewed DVSC forms and entered coded information directly into a computerized data base. The DVSC forms contained detailed information about the violation, including date of the violation; date of the report; victim-suspect relationship; age, race, sex, and employment status of the victim and suspect; type of violation committed; specific criminal charges made by the police officer; whether the alleged violations constituted misdemeanor or felony crimes; whether a suspect was arrested; whether the victim sustained injuries; whether the victim received medical attention; whether the suspect used a firearm or other type of weapon; whether items were placed in evidence; whether the victim and suspect were using drugs and/or alcohol at the time of the incident; number and ages of children in the household; whether children were in the home at the time of the incident; and whether there was a no-contact or restraining order in effect against the suspect at the time of the incident. The DVSC forms also contained written narratives by both the victim and the investigating officer. These narratives provided detailed information about the events precipitating the report, including whether the suspect stalked the victim.

Data Processing and Analysis

Once data collection was completed, the case extraction data were merged into one comprehensive SPSS data file and subjected to extensive editing. Missing information was assigned non-response codes or corrected from other case record information. The data were analyzed using SPSS base 7.0 for Windows software. The prevalence of stalking allegations was estimated using information extracted from the victim and police narratives. For purposes of the study, a domestic violence crime report was classified as having stalking allegations if the victim and/or police narrative specifically stated that the victim was stalked by the suspect, or if the victim and/or police narrative mentioned that the suspect engaged in stalking-like behaviors. Stalking-like behaviors included repeated following, face-to-face confrontations, or unwanted communications by phone, page, letter, fax, e-mail, or a combination thereof, with *repeated* meaning on two or more occasions.

The definition of stalking used in the study is similar to the definition of stalking used in the model antistalking code for States developed by the National Criminal Justice Association for the National

Institute of Justice. The model antistalking code defines stalking as a course of conduct directed at a specific person that involves repeated visual or physical proximity, non-consensual communication, or oral, written, or implied threats, or a combination thereof, that would cause a reasonable person to fear bodily injury or death, with *repeated* meaning on two or more occasions (National Criminal Justice Association, 1993). The model antistalking code does not require stalkers to make a credible threat of violence against victims, but it does require victims to feel a high level of fear (i.e., fear of bodily injury or death). The definition of stalking used in the present study does not require suspects to overtly threaten the victim. Nor does it require victims to expressly state that they feared bodily injury or harm at the hands of the suspect. It was assumed that persons who were identified as victims in a domestic violence crime report had experienced fear as a result of behaviors perpetrated against them by the suspect. It should be noted that the definition of stalking used in the present study was not based on the Colorado antistalking statute because the statute was in a state of legal flux at the time of the study. The Colorado antistalking statute faced three constitutional challenges during 1998. Moreover, the statute was amended in July 1998.

To identify risk factors associated with intimate partner stalking, a series of bivariate analyses were conducted to determine whether the prevalence of stalking allegations in CSPD domestic violence crime reports varied significantly by select victim and suspect characteristics. The specific characteristics included in the analyses were: victim gender (male vs. female); victim age (≤ 30 vs. 30+); victim race (White vs. non-White); victim employment status (employed vs. unemployed); suspect gender (male vs. female); suspect age (≤ 30 vs. 30+); suspect race (White vs. non-White); suspect employment status (employed vs. unemployed); and victim-suspect relationship (married vs. separated or divorced vs. living together vs. dating but not living together vs. former dates or cohabitants). These characteristics were selected for analysis because they represented attributes of the victim and suspect that preceded the incident leading to the crime report and could therefore be considered predictors of stalking.

In addition, a logistic regression was conducted in which several independent variables representing characteristics of the victim and suspect were regressed against the dependent variable, *the crime report contained allegations that the suspect stalked the victim.* The goals of the logistic regression were to provide a measure of the relative importance of these variables and to determine which independent variables increased the odds that a domestic violence victim reported being stalked by his or her partner. Logistic regression was used because of the dichotomous and unevenly distributed nature of the dependent variable (Hutcheson & Sofroniou, 1999). In order to check for multicollinearity among the independent variables, each variable's tolerance level was calculated using linear regression. Variables with a tolerance of less than .600 were examined to determine which should be removed from the analysis (Menard, 1995).

The following 10 independent variables were initially included in the logistic regression: whether the victim was female; whether the suspect was male; whether the victim was 30 years of age or less; whether the victim was White; whether the victim was employed; whether the suspect was over 30 years of age; whether the suspect was White; whether the suspect was unemployed; whether the victim and suspect were former intimates; and whether the victim and suspect were same-sex. The independent variable *whether the suspect was male* was removed from the analysis because it was highly correlated with the variable *whether the victim was female*.

To determine whether presenting conditions and outcomes in CSPD domestic violence crime reports with stalking allegations differed significantly from those in domestic violence crime reports without stalking allegations, another series of bivariate analyses was conducted in which characteristics of the presenting incident and the investigation were compared in crime reports with and without stalking allegations. Presenting conditions included: whether the victim was physically assaulted; whether a weapon was used; whether the victim was injured; whether the suspect was using drugs; whether the suspect was using alcohol; whether the victim was using drugs; whether the victim was using alcohol; the emotional state of the victim; whether the victim was the person who called the police; whether the victim signed a release form; whether the victim signed a request to be notified of further action; whether children were living in the home; whether witnesses were present; and whether the victim had an active restraining order against the suspect. Investigation outcomes included: whether the officer issued a companion summons; whether the officer placed items in evidence; whether the suspect was charged with a felony; and whether the police officer made an arrest or issued an arrest warrant.

In each of the bivariate analyses, measures of association were calculated between nominal-level independent and dependent variables, and the chi-square statistic was used to test for statistically significant differences between domestic violence crime reports with stalking allegations and domestic violence crime reports with no stalking allegations (*p*-value .05).

Any estimates based on information from less than five crime reports were deemed unreliable and were not presented in the tables. Estimates with a minimum expected frequency of less than five were not tested for statistically significant differences between groups. Because estimates presented in this article generally exclude "don't know," "missing" and other invalid responses, sample and subsample sizes (n's) vary from table to table.

RESULTS

Stalking Prevalence in CSPD Domestic Violence Crime Reports

Of the 1,785 domestic violence crime reports included in the sample, only one resulted in the police officer formally charging the suspect with stalking. Based on this evidence, one might conclude that incidents of domestic violence that are reported to the CSPD almost never involve stalking. However, this conclusion contradicts findings from previous studies that have documented a strong link between stalking and other forms of lethal and nonlethal violence in intimate relationships (McFarlane et al., 1999; Meloy, 1998; Moracco et al., 1998; Tjaden & Thoennes, 1998).

To more accurately estimate the prevalence of stalking in CSPD domestic violence crime reports, the frequency with which the victim and/or officer stated in the narrative section of the crime report that the suspect had stalked the victim or had engaged in stalking-like behaviors was examined. Of the 1,785 domestic violence crime reports included in the sample, 1,731 (97 percent) had a victim narrative, a police narrative, or both, and therefore could be used to estimate the prevalence of stalking in domestic violence crime reports.[2]

In 285 (16.5 percent) of these reports, either the victim or the police officer mentioned in their respective narratives that the suspect had stalked the victim or had engaged in stalking-like behaviors (see Table 15.1). Thus, 1 in 6 domestic violence crime reports that were made to the CSPD during the study time period contained allegations in the victim and/or officer narrative that the suspect had stalked the victim. Stalking allegations were significantly more prevalent in crime reports with female versus male victims (18.3 vs. 10.5 percent).

It should be noted that in most of the domestic violence crime reports that were determined to have stalking allegations, there was no mention of the word stalking in either the victim narrative or the police narrative. Of the 285 reports that were determined to have

Table 15.1 Percentage of Reports With Stalking Allegations by Victim Gender

	Percentage of Reports[a]		
Stalking was mentioned in narrative[b]	Female Victims (n = 1,327)	Male Victims (n = 400)	Total (n = 1,727)
Mentioned	18.3	10.5	16.5
Not mentioned	81.7	89.5	83.5

[a]Estimates are based only on reports with a victim and/or officer narrative.
[b]Differences between female and male victims are statistically significant: χ^2 = 13.61, df = 1, $p \le$ .000.

stalking allegations, only 14 (2.9 percent) contained the word *stalking* in the victim narrative, while 21 (7.4 percent) contained the word stalking in the officer narrative. Thus, most of the victims who were stalked did not self-identify as stalking victims on the crime report— nor were they identified as stalking victims by police officers.

Risk Factors Associated With Intimate Partner Stalking

Among female victims, stalking allegations were significantly more prevalent if the woman was White rather than non-White (19.9 vs. 15.2 percent), if the woman was employed versus unemployed (21.1 vs. 15.1 percent), and if the suspect was unemployed versus employed (22.3 vs. 16.9 percent). Stalking allegations were also significantly more prevalent if the woman and suspect were former rather than current intimates. Nearly half (47.8 percent) of the reports involving women who were victimized by former dates/cohabitants and about a third (33.7 percent) of the reports involving women and suspects who were divorced or separated contained stalking allegations. In comparison, 10.9 percent of the reports involving women and suspects who were married, 8.0 percent of the reports involving women and suspects who were living together, and 22.4 percent of the reports involving women and suspects who were dating but not living together, contained stalking allegations. No significant relationship was found between stalking allegations and the woman's or suspect's age. Although stalking allegations were more prevalent if the suspect was a female rather than a male partner (22.7 vs. 18.3 percent), this finding must be viewed with caution given the small number of women (n = 22) who were victimized by a current or former female partner (see Table 15.2).

Table 15.2 Percentage of Reports With Stalking Allegations by Select Characteristics of the Report and Victim Gender

Characteristic	Percentage of Reports With Stalking Allegations			
	Female Victims[a]		Male Victims	
Total	18.3		10.5	
Victim Age				
30	18.0	(634)	11.5	(183)
31+	18.6	(672)	9.8	(214)
Victim Race				
White	19.9[i]	(851)	11.7	(231)
Non-White	15.2	(461)	9.0	(167)
Victim Employment Status				
Employed	21.1[ii]	(749)	12.3	(285)
Unemployed	15.1	(344)	___b	(55)
Suspect Gender				
Male	18.3[c]	(1,304)	20.6[c]	(34)
Female	22.7	(22)	9.6	(366)
Suspect Age				
30	16.7	(575)	10.1	(199)
31+	19.7	(747)	11.0	(200)
Suspect Race				
White	19.1	(721)	11.3	(240)
Non-White	17.3	(601)	9.6	(157)
Suspect Employment Status				
Employed	16.9[iii]	(152)	12.0	(242)
Unemployed	22.3	(269)	8.1	(123)
Victim-suspect relationship				
Married	10.9[iv]	(396)	6.2	(145)
Separated/divorced	33.7	(183)	27.9	(43)
Living together	8.0	(399)	___b	(137)
Dating, not living together	22.4	(152)	___b	(33)
Former dates/cohabitants	47.8	(113)	45.8	(24)

Note. Numbers in parentheses indicate subsample size (n).

[a]Differences between female victims with and without characteristic are statistically significant: [i]$\chi^2 = 4.34$, $df = 1$, p $\leq$ .05; [ii]$\chi^2 = 5.43$, $df = 1$, $p \leq$ .05; [iii]$\chi^2 = 3.99$, $df = 1$, $p \leq$ .05; [iv]$\chi^2 = 141.14$, $df = 4$, $p \leq$ .000.

[b]Estimates not presented on less than 5 victims.

[c]Minimum expected frequency less than 5; statistical tests not conducted.

With respect to male victims, the study found no significant relationship between the prevalence of stalking allegations and the victim's age, race, and employment status, or between the prevalence of stalking allegations and the suspect's age, race, and employment status. Like women, men were more likely to allege stalking by former rather than current dates, cohabitants, and spouses. They were also more likely to allege stalking by male rather than female partners, although these findings must be viewed with caution given the small number of men (n = 34) who were victimized by male partners (see Table 15.2).

Results of the logistic regression reveal that stalking allegations were significantly more prevalent in CSPD domestic violence crime reports involving female victims and victims and suspects who were former intimates (see Table 15.3). The variable that was most likely to in-

Table 15.3 Logistic Regression Analysis Predicting the Likelihood that the Crime Report Contained Allegations of Stalking

Independent Variable	B	SE	P-value	Exp(b)
Victim was female	.5634	.2210	.0108*	1.7566
Victim was ≤ 30	−.0630	.2108	.7650	.9389
Victim was White	.2330	.2159	.2805	1.2624
Victim was employed	.2358	.1929	.2215	1.2659
Suspect was 30+	.2058	.2132	.3344	1.2285
Suspect was White	−.0371	.2038	.8855	.9636
Suspect was unemployed	.1743	.1885	.3550	1.1905
Victim and suspect were former intimates	1.6503	.1682	.0000*	5.2083
Victim and suspect were the same sex	−.0577	.4369	.8949	.9439
Constant	−3.0252	.3132	.000	

Note. Several statistics are presented in Table 2. The model chi-square statistic (χ^2) (see below) provides an indication of the overall fit of the data to the model. A significant chi-square indicates that the variables as a group contribute significantly to the dependent variable (crime report contains stalking allegations). In addition, the exhibit reports the logistic coefficients (B) and their standard errors (SE). The logistic coefficient can be interpreted as the change associated with a unit change in the explanatory variable when all other variables in the model are held constant. The regression coefficients can be more easily understood if quoted as odds ratio. The odds ratio (Exp [b]) provides the ratio of the odds of the p (the probability of an event happening) which is associated with a unit change in the explanatory variables (x) whilst all other variables are held constant. For example, an odds ratio of 1 indicates that changes in the explanatory variable do not lead to changes in the odds of p; a ratio of less than 1 indicates that the odds of p decrease as x increases; and a ratio of greater than 1 indicates that the odds of p increase as x increases. Variables are considered significant if they have a p-value of < .05.

Model χ^2 = 114.341; df = 9; p ≤ .0000; n = 1,217.

*Coefficient is significant: p-value .05.

crease the likelihood that a crime report would contain stalking allegations was whether the victim and suspect were former intimates. In fact, as the odds ratio (Exp (b) = 5.2083) indicates, crime reports involving former intimates were about five times more likely to contain stalking allegations than were crime reports involving current intimates even when other variables were controlled. The following variables did not predict whether a crime report would contain stalking allegations: whether the victim was 30 years of age or less; whether the victim was White; whether the victim was employed; whether the suspect was over 30 years of age; whether the suspect was White; whether the suspect was employed; and whether the victim and suspect were a same-sex couple.

Presenting Conditions in CSPD Domestic Violence Crime Reports With and Without Stalking Allegations

As Table 15.4 shows, CSPD domestic violence crime reports with stalking allegations differed significantly from those without stalking allegations with respect to several key presenting conditions. Crime reports with stalking allegations were significantly less likely than crime reports without stalking allegations to identify physical abuse or victim injury in the presenting condition, to involve suspects and victims who were using alcohol at the time of the report, and to involve households with children regardless if the victim was male or female. Conversely, crime reports with stalking allegations were significantly more likely to involve victims who were the person who called the police and who signed a form releasing information they provided to investigators. In addition, women who alleged stalking by their partners were significantly less likely than women who did not allege stalking to be emotionally distraught at the time of the report. Moreover, women who alleged stalking were significantly more likely than women who did not allege stalking to sign a form requesting notification of further action on the case. They were also nearly three times more likely to have an active retraining order against the suspect at the time of the report.

Law Enforcement Outcomes in CSPD Domestic Violence Crime Reports With and Without Stalking Allegations

A comparison of law enforcement outcomes in CSPD domestic violence crime reports with and without stalking allegations revealed very

Table 15.4 Percentage of Reports With Select Presenting Conditions by Presence of Stalking Allegations and Victim Gender

Characteristic	Female Victims[a]		Male Victims[b]	
	Stalking	No Stalking	Stalking	No Stalking
Victim was physically assaulted	30.5 (243)	83.2[i] (902)	31.0 (42)	87.4[i] (358)
Weapons were used	5.0 (239)	8.9[ii] (1,054)	__[c] (39)	16.6 (349)
Victim was injured/in pain	18.5 (238)	57.7[iii] (1,055)	23.7 (38)	62.9[ii] (348)
Suspect was using drugs	3.7 (243)	3.0 (1,084)	__[c] (42)	__[c] (358)
Suspect was using alcohol	21.0 (243)	38.4[iv] (1,084)	21.4 (42)	36.9[iii] (358)
Victim was using drugs	__[c] (243)	1.0 (1,084)	__[c] (42)	__[c] (358)
Victim was using alcohol*	11.9 (243)	31.1[v] (1,084)	11.9 (42)	38.0[iv] (358)
Victim's emotional state				
Calm	58.0 (243)	48.0[vi] (1,084)	64.3 (42)	66.5 (358)
Hysterical	2.5 (243)	6.8[vii] (1,084)	__[c] (42)	__[c] (358)
Angry	14.4 (243)	17.6 (1,084)	19.0 (42)	15.4 (358)
Withdrawn	4.1 (243)	8.6[viii] (1,084)	__[c] (42)	4.5 (358)
Apologetic	__[c] (243)	5.8 (1,084)	__[c] (42)	3.6 (358)
Crying	21.8 (243)	40.1[ix] (1,084)	__[c] (42)	7.8 (358)
Yelling	__[c] (243)	4.4 (1,084)	__[c] (42)	2.8 (358)
Belligerent	__[c] (243)	1.8 (1,084)	__[c] (42)	2.2 (358)
Combative	__[c] (243)	1.2 (1,084)	__[c] (42)	1.7 (243)
Victim was caller	85.7 (238)	62.0[x] (1,043)	80.5 (41)	50.4[v] (341)
Victim signed release form	56.4 (243)	52.1[xi] (1,084)	57.1 (42)	41.9[vi] (358)
Victim signed request to be notified	66.7 (243)	54.7[xii] (1,084)	45.2 (42)	32.7 (358)
Children were living in the home	33.7 (243)	41.4[xiii] (1,084)	14.3 (42)	38.0[vii] (358)
Other witness(es) present	44.4 (243)	39.1 (1,084)	57.1 (42)	30.2[viii] (358)
Active restraining order	39.1 (243)	14.6[xiv] (1,084)	21.4 (42)	8.1[d] (358)

Note. Numbers in parentheses indicate subsample size (n).

[a]Differences between female victims with and without stalking allegations are statistically significant: [i]$x^2 = 284$, $df = 1$, $p \le .000$: [ii]$x^2 = 3.93$, $df = 1$, $p \le .05$; [iii]$x^2 = 119.74$; $df = 2$, $p \le .000$; [iv]$x^2 = 26.32$, $df = 1$, $p \le .000$; [v]$x^2 = 36.46$, $df = 1$, $p \le .000$; [vi]$x^2 = 8.03$, $df = 1$, $p \le .01$; [vii]$x^2 = 6.65$, $df = 1$, $p \le .01$; [viii]$x^2 = 5.53$, $df = 1$, $p \le .05$; [ix]$x^2 = 28.65$, $df = 1$, $p \le .000$; [x]$x^2 = 48.73$, $df = 1$, $p \le .000$; [xi]$x^2 = 19.36$, $df = 3$, $p \le .000$; [xii]$x^2 = 21.88$, $df = 3$, $p \le .000$; [xiii]$x^2 = 4.87$, $df = 1$, $p \le .05$; [xiv]$x^2 = 77.34$, $df = 1$, $p \le .000$.

[b]Differences between male victims with and without presenting condition are statistically significant: [i]$\chi^2 = 79.52$, $df = 1$, $p \le .000$; [ii]$\chi^2 = 21.84$, $df = 2$, $p \le .000$; [iii]$\chi^2 = 3.93$, $df = 1$, $p \le .05$; [iv]$\chi^2 = 11.21$, $df = 1$, p 001; [v]$\chi^2 = 13.29$, $df = 1$, $p \le .000$; [vi]$\chi^2 = 6.9$, $df = 2$, $p \le .05$; [vii]$\chi^2 = 9.22$, $df = 1$, $p \le .01$; [viii]$\chi^2 = 12.37$, $df = 1$, $p \le .000$.

[c]Estimates not presented on less than 5 victims.

[d]Minimum expected frequency less than 5; statistical tests not conducted.

Table 15.5 Percentage of Reports With Select Law Enforcement Outcomes by Presence of Stalking Allegations and Victim Gender

| | Percentage of Reports With Law Enforcement Outcome | | | |
| | Female Victims | | Male Victims | |
Outcome	Stalking	No Stalking	Stalking	No Stalking
Officer issued companion summons	13.6 (243)	17.2 (1,084)	11.9 (42)	34.6[a] (358)
Officer placed items in evidence	16.5 (243)	21.2 (1,084)	26.2 (42)	19.6 (358)
Suspect charged with felony	10.8 (241)	7.8 (1,075)	___[b] (42)	5.6 (356)
Suspect was arrested	81.1 (243)	84.9 (1,084)	81.0 (42)	90.8[c] (358)

Note. Numbers in parentheses indicate subsample size (*n*).

[a]Differences between men with and without stalking allegations are statistically significant: $\chi^2 = 8.89$, $df = 1$, $p \leq .01$.

[b]Estimates not presented on less than 5 victims.

[c]Minimum expected frequency less than 5; statistical tests not conducted.

little differences. Police officers were significantly less likely to issue a companion summons if a man alleged stalking by his current or former partner. However, whether a male or female victim alleged stalking had no significant impact on whether police placed items in evidence, charged a suspect with a felony, or arrested a suspect (see Table 15.5).

It is important to note that relatively few domestic violence crime reports generated by the CSPD resulted in the suspect being charged with a felony offense, regardless if the report involved a male or female victim or if the victim alleged stalking. Although crime reports involving women who alleged stalking were somewhat more likely to result in the suspect being charged with a felony , the difference was not statistically significant.

As Table 15.6 shows, domestic violence crime reports with stalking allegations tended to result in different types of charges than those without stalking allegations. If a woman alleged stalking, the suspect was significantly more likely to be charged with violation of a restraining order and bail bond violation, and significantly less likely to be charged with harassment, assault, or intimidation. If a man alleged stalking, the suspect was significantly less likely to be charged with assault and intimidation.

Table 15.6 Percentage of Reports With Specific Types of Charges by Presence of Stalking Allegations and Victim Gender

| | Percentage of Reports With Charge | | | |
| | Female Victims[a] | | Male Victims[b] | |
Charge	Stalking (n = 243)	No Stalking (n = 1,084)	Stalking (n = 42)	No Stalking (n = 358)
Harassment	61.3	69.1[i]	71.4	72.9
Violation of restraining order	37.0	9.4[ii]	21.4	3.4[c]
Assault/intimidation	13.2	43.7[iii]	19.0	48.3[i]
Criminal mischief	5.8	7.1	11.9	8.1[c]
Menacing	4.1	5.4	___[d]	3.1
Bail bond violation	4.1	1.7[iv]	___[d]	___[d]
Burglary/breaking and entering	2.9	1.5[c]	___[d]	___[d]

[a]Differences between female victims with and without stalking allegations are statistically significant: [i]$\chi^2 = 5.49$, $df = 1$, $p \leq .05$; [ii]$\chi^2 = 122.43$, $df = 1$, $p \leq .000$; [iii]$\chi^2 = 78.57$, $df = 1$, $p \leq .000$; [iv]$\chi^2 = 5.79$, $df = 1$, $p \leq .05$.

[b]Differences between male victims with and without stalking allegations are statistically significant: [i]$\chi^2 = 13.00$, $df = 1$, $p \leq .000$.

[c]Minimum expected frequency less than 5; statistical tests not conducted.

[d]Estimates not presented on less than 5 victims.

CONCLUSIONS

Because the study is based on information from only one police department, the results should not be extrapolated to the experiences of police departments nationally. Nonetheless, results from the study provide much needed empirical data on the prevalence of stalking in domestic violence crime reports, risk factors associated with intimate partner stalking, and police responses to reports of intimate partner stalking. Results from the study also provide a benchmark for future research.

Results from this study confirm previous research (McFarlane et al, 1999; Meloy, 1998; Moracco et al., 1998; Tjaden & Thoennes, 1998) that found a link between stalking and violence in intimate relationships: 1 in 6 of the domestic violence crime reports (16.5 percent) initiated by the CSPD during the study time period contained evidence in the victim and/or police narrative that the suspect stalked the victim. Because this estimate represents stalking allegations that were made spontaneously by the victim and/or police officer and were not in response to any systematic questioning about stalking victimization by investigating officers, it probably underestimates the true amount of intimate partner stalking that occurred in the context of domestic violence crime reports initiated by the CSPD. To generate more reliable information about the prevalence of stalking in domestic violence crime reports, police departments should train their investigating officers to ask questions about possible stalking victimization when investigating reports of domestic violence. By doing so, police departments will undoubtedly uncover more incidents of intimate partner stalking than are being uncovered by current investigatory practices. In turn, awareness of this serious social problem will be increased among the justice system community and the public at large.

Results from the study clearly show that police officers almost never charge a domestic violence stalking suspect with stalking. Only 1 of the 285 domestic violence crime reports in the study sample that contained evidence of stalking resulted in the suspect being charged with the crime of stalking. Thus, stalking prevalence estimates that are based on formal charges made by police officers during the investigation of a domestic violence crime report substantially underestimate the role stalking plays in domestic violence cases that are reported to the police. Given these findings, researchers and policy makers should consider the number of stalking charges generated by police officers during their investigation of domestic violence crime reports an accurate measure of the prevalence of stalking in domestic violence crime reports.

The study found that in the vast majority of reports that were determined to have stalking allegations, neither the victim nor the police officer used the word stalking in their narratives. Instead, they mentioned that the suspect had engaged in stalking-like behaviors. These findings suggest that most domestic violence victims who have been stalked by their intimate partners do not self-identify as stalking victims during the initial stages of the police investigative process. Similarly, many police officers do not define intimate partner stalking cases as stalking cases during the initial stages of the investigative process. Further research is needed to understand why intimate partner stalking victims who come to the attention of law enforcement tend not to self-identify as stalking victims and under what circumstances these victims come to perceive of themselves as stalking victims and use language that reflects their perceptions. Research is also needed to understand the processes by which law enforcement officers identify and label domestic violence crime reports that contain evidence of stalking as stalking cases.

The present study confirms previous research that shows women are the primary victims of intimate partner stalking (Tjaden & Thoennes, 1998; Tjaden & Thoennes, 2000a; Tjaden & Thoennes, 2000b). While nearly a fifth (18.3 percent) of the female victims alleged stalking by their partners, only about a tenth (10.5 percent) of the men did so. Furthermore, results of a logistic regression show that CSPD domestic violence crime reports involving female victims were significantly more likely to contain allegations that the suspect stalked the victim, even when the effects of other socio-demographic variables were controlled. Given these findings, research and intervention strategies should focus on stalking perpetrated against women by male intimates. Results of a logistic regression also show that the variable most likely to predict that a CSPD domestic violence crime report contained stalking allegations was whether the suspect was a former rather than a current intimate partner. These findings support the theory that when women are stalked by an intimate partner the stalking typically occurs after the women attempt to leave the relationship (National Institute of Justice, 1996). Given these findings, police officers should be made aware that domestic violence crime reports involving suspects and victims who are former intimates pose the highest risk for stalking.

The study produced clear evidence that domestic violence crime reports with stalking allegations exhibit significantly different presenting conditions during the initial interview with the police than do crime reports without such allegations. Both women and men who were stalked by their partners were significantly more likely to have been the person who made the report to the police and to sign a form releasing the information they provided to investigators. These findings suggest that domestic violence victims who have been stalked by their partner may be more eager to see their perpetrator prosecuted than are domestic violence victims who have not been stalked. These findings also support anecdotal evidence from a survey of justice system practitioners that found victims are the principal source of information and evidence that stalking is occurring, particularly at the earliest stages of case development (Violence Against Women Grants Office, 1998).

CSPD domestic violence crime reports with stalking allegations were significantly less likely to identify physical abuse and victim injury in the presenting condition or to involve suspects and victims who were using alcohol at the time of the incident. And if the victim was a woman, they were significantly more likely to involve an active restraining order against the suspect. Moreover, women who alleged stalking were significantly less likely to be emotionally distraught (e.g., crying, yelling, angry, withdrawn) at the time of the initial interview. These findings are important because they suggest that domestic violence cases with a stalking component have distinctively different presenting conditions than do domestic violence cases without a stalking component. Further research is needed to verify these findings and to identify other presenting conditions that are characteristic of domestic violence stalking cases. Results of this type of research should be disseminated to police departments nationally so that investigating officers can be trained to recognize the specific characteristics of domestic violence stalking cases and the specific needs of domestic violence stalking victims.

The study found that domestic violence crime reports with stalking allegations did not result in significantly different law enforcement outcomes than did domestic violence crime reports without stalking allegations. Police officers were significantly less likely to issue a companion summonses if a man alleged stalking by his partner. This finding is difficult to explain without additional information. It is possible that police officers issued fewer companion summons because domestic violence crime reports with stalking allegations were less likely to involve victims and suspects who were mutually abusive. However, more research is needed to determine whether this explanation is valid.

The study confirms previous anecdotal evidence from criminal justice practitioners that stalkers tend to be charged and sentenced under harassment and related charges rather than under a state's antistalking statute (Violence Against Women Grants Office, 1998). As previously noted, only 1 of the 285 CSPD domestic violence crime reports that contained stalking allegations resulted in the police officer charging the suspect with stalking. Instead, CSPD police officers tended to charge suspects who were alleged to have stalked their victim with harassment and, in cases involving female victims, violation of a restraining order.

There are many possible reasons why CSPD police officers failed to charge intimate partner stalkers with the crime of stalking. The Colorado antistalking statute was in a state of legal flux at the time of the study. The statute faced three constitutional challenges during the year the sample was drawn (1998). The Colorado antistalking statute was also amended halfway during the study time frame (July 1998). CSPD investigating officers may have been aware of these legal fluctuations and been reluctant to charge suspects under a statute that was in the process of being amended and whose constitutionality was in question. Lack of familiarity with the law also may have impeded CSPD investigating officers from charging suspects with the crime of stalking. Anecdotal information suggests that few police officers are familiar with or understand their state antistalking statute, and that few have received training on how to investigate stalking cases. As CSPD police officers receive more training and become more familiar with the stalking statute, they may use it more frequently. In addition, the credible threat requirement in the old Colorado antistalking statute may have impeded CSPD officers from charging suspects with stalking. The amended Colorado antistalking statute does not require stalkers to make a credible threat against the victim and according to at least one CSPD official, as a result it is much easier to prosecute stalking cases (Hethcock, 1999). Finally, CSPD officers may have charged intimate partner stalkers with harassment or violation of a restraining order rather than stalking because they wanted to intervene in the case at the earliest possible opportunity. Stalking cases are very time-consuming to put together (Violence Against Women Grants Office, 1998). In contrast, documenting a harassment or violation of a restraining order is easier and less time consuming.

It is important to note that these explanations for why CSPD police officers failed to charge most stalkers with the crime of stalking are based on hunches, not scientific evidence. Research of a more qualitative nature is needed to determine how and under what circumstances police officers and other criminal justice practitioners come to define and label domestic violence crime reports with stalking allegations as stalking cases. Research also is needed to determine how representative the findings from this study are of police departments nationally.

NOTES

1. The study was conducted jointly by The Justice Studies Center at the University of Colorado at Colorado Springs (JSC) and the Center for Policy Research (CPR) in Denver. JSC staff generated the sample, conducted the police case file review, and coded and entered the case file extraction

data into a computerized data base. CPR staff conducted the analysis and wrote the final report.

2. It is unclear why some CSPD DVSC forms were missing a victim and/or police narrative. Presumably victims and police officers failed to complete their respective narratives for a variety of reasons. Some victims may not have been able to read or write; others may have been too emotionally distraught or in too much physical pain to fill out a narrative; still others may not have been willing to cooperative with the investigation. With respect to officers, some may have had too little time to complete the narrative; others may have had no additional information to include in the narrative; and still others may have simply overlooked the narrative section of the DVSC form.

ACKNOWLEDGMENT

This research was supported by National Institute of Justice grant number 97–WT-VX-0002. The opinions and conclusions expressed in this document are solely those of the authors and do not necessarily reflect the views of the funding agency.

REFERENCES

Burgess, A. W., Baker, T., Greening, D., Hartman, C. R., Burgess, A. G., Douglass, J. E., & Halloran R. (1997). Stalking Behaviors within Domestic Violence. *Journal of Family Violence, 12,* 389–402.

Felder, R., & Victor, B. (1997). *Getting away with murder: Weapons for the war against domestic violence.* New York: Touchstone.

Hethcock, W. (1999, November 3). Going after stalkers: Tougher approach gets credit for rise in filings, *The Gazette News.*

Hunzeker, D. (1992, October). Stalking Laws. *National Conference of State Legislatures, 17*(19), 1–6.

Hutcheson, G., & Sofroniou, N. (1999). *The Multivariate Social Scientist.* Thousand Oaks, CA: Sage Publications.

Jacobson, N., & Gottman, J. M. (1998). *When men batter women: New insights into ending abusive relationships.* New York: Simon and Schuster.

McFarlane, J. M., Campbell, J. C., Wilt, S., Sachs, C., Ulrich, Y., & Xiao Xu. (1999, November). Stalking and intimate partner femicide, *Homicide Studies, 3* (4), 300–316.

Meloy, J. R. (Ed.). (1998). *The psychology of stalking: Clinical and forensic perspectives.* San Diego, CA: Academic Press.

Menard, S. (1995). *Applied logistic regression analysis*. Series no. (07–106). Thousand Oaks, CA: Sage Publications.

Moracco, K., Runyan, C. W., & Butts, J. D. (1998). Femicide in North Carolina, 1991–1993: A statewide study of patterns and precursors, *Homicide Studies, 2*, 422–446.

National Criminal Justice Association. (1993, October). *Project to develop a model anti-stalking code for states* (NCJ 144477). Washington, DC: U.S. Department of Justice, National Institute of Justice.

National Institute of Justice. (1996, April). *Domestic violence, stalking, and antistalking legislation: An annual report to Congress under the Violence Against Women Act* (NCJ 160943). Washington, DC: U.S. Department of Justice, Office of Justice Programs.

Schaum, M., & Parrish, K. (1995). *Stalked: Breaking the silence on the crime of stalking in America*. New York, NY: Pocket Books.

Tjaden, P., & Thoennes, N. (1998, April). *Stalking in America: Findings from the National Violence Against Women Survey* (NCJ 169592). Washington, DC: U.S. Department of Justice, National Institute of Justice.

Tjaden, P., & Thoennes, N. (2000a). Prevalence and consequences of male-to-female and female-to-male intimate partner violence as measured by the National Violence Against Women Survey. *Violence Against Women, 6*(2), 140–159.

Tjaden, P., & Thoennes, N. (2000b, May). *Extent, nature, and consequences of intimate partner violence: Findings from the National Violence Against Women Survey*. Washington, DC: U.S. Department of Justice, National Institute of Justice.

Violence Against Women Grants Office. (1997, July). *Domestic violence and stalking: The second annual report to Congress under the Violence Against Women Act*. Washington, DC: U.S. Department of Justice, Office of Justice Programs.

Violence Against Women Grants Office. (1998, July). *Stalking and domestic violence: The third annual report to Congress under the Violence Against Women Act* (NCJ Report no. 172204). Washington, DC: U.S. Department of Justice, Office of Justice Programs.

Walker, L., & Reid Meloy, J. (1998). Stalking and domestic violence. In J. R. Meloy (Ed.), *The psychology of stalking: Clinical and forensic perspective*, (pp. 139–160). San Diego, CA: Academic Press.

III

Overview

16

Research on Stalking: What Do We Know and Where Do We Go?

Keith E. Davis and Irene Hanson Frieze

In this chapter, we want to look at how our knowledge of stalking victims and perpetrators has been extended by the contributors to this volume. We also want to examine how stalking fits into the context of research and theory about relationship violence. An understanding of several aspects of stalking has been developed in this collection. These include perpetrator and victim characteristics (including gender), dyadic, social/family networks, and developmental histories of relationships as factors in stalking but, with the exception of White, Kowalski, Lyndon, and Valentine's chapter, our contributors have had little to say about the cultural context of stalking. We will organize our review by victims, perpetrators, theories, and methods.

VICTIMS OF STALKING

The major work on victimization is the National Violence Against Women (NVAW) Survey jointly funded by the National Institute of Justice and the Centers for Disease Control and Prevention and reported by Tjaden and Thoennes (1998) and Tjaden, Thoennes, and Allison (this volume). Data from the NVAW Survey suggest that using either a behavioral definition or a self-classification scheme, women reported more stalking victimization than did men (8.1% vs. 2.2% with a behavioral definition and 12.1% vs. 6.2% with a self-classification scheme). Differences in results using the behavioral definition and the self-classification scheme were due primarily to the fact that about 60% of the persons who self-classified as stalked did not meet the fear criterion of the behavioral definition—either they did not feel very frightened or they did not think that they or someone close to them would be seriously harmed. Male respondents' increased reluctance to express fear may also explain the gender differences reported by Tjaden and colleagues (this volume)—a difference not consistently seen in the other articles in the volume. Both women and men who had been intimate with the perpetrator were more likely to self-classify as stalked than those who had not.

Results from the national survey data (Tjaden & Thoennes, 1998) indicate that women—but not men—tend to be stalked in the context of current or former intimate relationships (marriage, cohabitation, or dating). Stalking, particularly of women by ex-husbands, was strongly related to physical abuse in the relationship. The levels of distress reported by women and men were quite substantial, and the psychological impact was great. Both male and female victims of stalking were more likely to report that they were very concerned about their safety than non-victims (42% vs. 24%). They also tended to carry something to protect themselves (45% vs. 29%). Over a quarter of all victims sought counseling during the process. And many were provoked to take extreme actions such as getting a gun (17%), changing addresses (11%), or moving out of town (11%), to deter the stalker (Tjaden & Thoennes, 1998). There are thus several major themes to explore: How are prevalence rates for stalking connected to the specific behavioral definitions used? How is stalking related to gender? To physical and psychological abuse in the relationships? To its emotional and life-changing consequences?

PREVALENCE AND SPECIFIC DEFINITIONS

In Table 16.1, we have arranged all five of the indices of stalking that play a major role in this volume. The starting point for almost all of them is the NVAW Survey, which uses eight types of behaviors with two additional criteria. A behavior had to be engaged in more than one time (consistent with the legal requirement of a pattern of behavior), and "only respondents who were very frightened or feared bodily harm [to themselves or someone close] were counted as stalking vic-

Table 16.1 Comparing Measures of Stalking Behavior

	C&S	T&T	L-R	S&F	LLW	DAA
Spying on you	*	*		*	*	
Follow you	*	*	*	*	*	
Sending notes	*	*	*	*	*	*
Unwanted phone calls	*	*	*		*	*
Left messages on telephone	*		*			
Recorded conversations w/you secretly	*					
Send gifts		*		*C	*	*
Sent (offensive) photos	*				*	
Waited (in car) for you	*		*	*		
Left notes on your windshield	*					
Left notes at home	*					
Staying outside home, work (or driving by)	*	*	*	*	*	
Waited around when you conversed w/person	*					
Showing up where you are	*	*	*	*		*
Visit at work	*			*	*	
Called at work	*					
Leaving items for you to find		*		*		
Communicating verbally against your will		*				*
Damaging your property	*	*	*	*	*	*
Do unrequested favors				*C		
Family contact		*				
Ask others about you	*		*	*	*	
Knocked on your window	*					
Ask out as friends				*C		
Ask out on a date				*C		
Threaten or release harmful information about you				*		
Find your info				*		
Take up an activity to be closer to you				*		
Manipulate into dating				*		
Scare you				*		*
Secretly taking belongings			*	*	*	*
Give unusual parcels				*		
Attempt to, or verbally abuse you				*		
Harass you				*		
Broke into house/car		*	*			
Visited your home	*		*		*	
Threaten or attempt to hurt you	*		*	*	*	
Physically violent to you	*			*		
Threaten emotional harm				*		
Threaten or attempt to hurt someone you know		*		*	*	*
Threaten or harm pet		*	*			

Table 16.1 *(Continued)*

	C&S	T&T	L-R	S&F	LLW	DAA
Force sexual contact	*			*	*	
Took photos of you	*					
Release harmful info			*			
Kidnap you			*			
Use profanity about you	*					
Argue in public places	*					
Spread false rumors	*					
Claim to still be in relationship	*					
Violate restraining order					*	
Will not take hints he/ she was not welcome	*					
Tried to keep you away from the opposite sex						*
Harm new partner or his/her property					*	*
Threaten to hurt him/herself				*	*	*
Told others stories about you	*			*		
Constantly apologize for past wrongs	*					
Exaggerated claims of affection for you	*					*
Described acts of sex to you	*					

C&S = Cupah & Spitzberg; T&T = Tjaden & Thoennes; L-R = Langhinrichsen-Rohling et al.; S&F = Sinclair & Frieze (*C = "Normal" courtship approach behavior); LLW = Logan, Leukefeld & Walker; DAA = Davis, Ace & Andra.

tims" (Tjaden & Thoennes, 1998, p. 17). At the other end of the spectrum is Cupach and Spitzberg's (1998) Obsessional Relational Intrusion (ORI) measure, which contained 63 items. While one can see that many of the ORI items could be seen as specific instances of the eight NVAW items, the ORI intentionally sampled far beyond the NVAW Survey by inquiring about highly threatening, coercive, vandalizing, and intrusive behaviors. The ORI can be factored into four clusters of items that have been labeled *pursuit, violation, violence,* and *hyper-intimacy.* Except for item 8 (the vandalism item) in the NVAW survey, it deals largely with behaviors that fall into Cupach and Spitzberg's *pursuit* factor or into the milder forms of stalking harassment identified by others (Coleman, 1997; Davis, Ace, & Andra, this volume; Sinclair & Frieze, this volume). In between these two measures are Sinclair and Frieze's Courtship Persistence Inventory, which has 43 items, loading on six conceptually distinct clusters, Palarea and Langhinrichsen-Rohling's (1998) Pursuit Behavior Inventory which has

26 items that yield 3 separate scores (mild, severe, and total stalking); Coleman's 26–item measure that distinguishes stalking harassment from stalking violence; and Davis, Ace, and Andra's (this volume) inventory which has 16 items to identify three clusters of stalking-like behaviors and four items to index expressions of love. Logan, Leukefeld, and Walker (this volume) used a slightly modified version of Coleman's measure.

The ORI generated much higher rates of stalking victimization which were found in three separate samples of college students than did the NVAW survey (Cupach & Spitzberg, this volume). In their initial instructions, Cupach and Spitzberg did not require persistent or repeated instances of the ORI behaviors and their data have been reported in terms of percent "ever," not multiple events as in the NVAW. Their broader definition turns up more cases, but their recent directions emphasize that the behaviors must be persistent. Logan and colleagues (this volume) and Davis, Ace, and Andra (1999) both required multiple events of stalking-like behavior for the person to be classified as having been stalked. For the Stalking Harassment items, Logan and associates reported a stalking victimization rate that ranged from 62% (for "called at home") to 9% (for "drove by home" and "sent photos") with a median of 22%. For the stalking violence or more severe items, the range was from 20% ("damaged property of new partner") to 0% (several items) with a median of 6.2%.

Davis, Ace, and Andra (1999), in two separate samples of college students, used the exact wording of the NVAW survey, with slightly different response alternatives ("Never, a few times, or several times"). The findings were quite consistent in the two samples. Using the criterion of "a few times," 53.7% reported receiving unsolicited phone calls, and 9.4% reported being vandalized. With the criterion of "several times," these prevalence rates dropped to 11.5% for unsolicited phone calls and 1.4% for vandalism. Averaging across all eight items, 5.8% of the two samples reported stalking victimization at the level of "several times." Two factors—other than specific item wording and the frequency of occurrence—are probably relevant to the levels of stalking victimization found among the different samples. Researchers are beginning to establish that victims feel afraid rather than that some potentially harassing behaviors have occurred (Bjerregaard, this volume; Cupach & Spitzberg, this volume). With the criterion of being "very afraid," only 9.5% (study 1) and 10.8% (study 2) could be classified as having been stalked (Davis et al., 1999). These figures are much closer to the NVAW findings. The other factor that is probably at work is cohort/age. Seventy-four per cent of women victims reported that they were first stalked at the age of 39 or earlier (52% at 29 or younger). The cohorts becoming teenagers in the 1980's and 1990's have had the chance to learn about the crime of celebrity stalking, and to know that it could happen to them (Schaum & Parrish, 1995). Rather than giving such behaviors a benign interpretation, they are probably more likely to classify it as stalking and to consider reporting it to the authorities (Tjaden, Thoennes, & Allison, this volume).

Even this very brief survey suggests that the specific definitions of stalking used by researchers affects the reported frequency. Definitions can be primarily legal (e.g., Tjaden & Thoennes, 1998) or more related to clinical cases that include physical and sexual threats (e.g., Coleman, 1997; Cupach & Spitzberg, this volume; and Langhinrichsen-Rohling et al., this volume). Sinclair and Frieze (this volume) and White and associates (this volume) have made the case that behavioral research cannot be limited entirely to the legal definition, but must look at courtship persistent behaviors and milder forms of stalking to fully understand the phenomenon. Conceptually, there is a good reason to continue research on measures of stalking victimization that maintain a finer range of distinctions than those embodied in the original NVAW items. To the degree that one issue is how full-blown dangerous stalking develops out of the milder harassment cases, we need measures of the distinct stages or types of stalking-like behaviors (Emerson et al., 1997). Maintaining finer distinctions—such as those in Cupach and Spitzberg's ORI, Langhinrichsen-Rohling and colleagues' Pursuit Behavior Inventory (this volume), or Sinclair and Frieze's Courtship Behavior Scale (this volume)—should allow one to detect differences in which behaviors are seen as normative versus those that cross the line to intrusion and harassment. Furthermore, the correlates and risk factors for stalking threat and vandalism may be quite different from those for courtship persistence and milder stalking harassment.

GENDER AND STALKING VICTIMIZATION

Stalking that reaches police attention and stalking as defined by the NVAW survey usually involves female victims (78%) and male perpetrators (86%). Campus surveys with large convenience samples also show that pattern (Fremouw, Westrup, & Pennypacker, 1996). But Cupach and Spitzberg (1998, this volume; Spitzberg, Nicastro, &

Cousins, 1998) consistently do not find gender differences in being victimized on the individual ORI items.[1] And Langhinrichsen-Rohling, Palarea, Cohen, and Rohling (this volume) also failed to find a gender difference. How does one reconcile these findings? One possibility is that the *same behaviors are appraised differently as a function of gender,* such that when a man follows, engages in vandalism, or in threats, the behaviors are taken more seriously by a woman than when a woman engages in similar behaviors toward a man. Magdol and associates (1997) have offered a similar interpretation of the differences in reported partner violence in their birth cohort sample of New Zealand youth. In that sample, women report a significantly higher level of physical violence than men, but the women who were abused were more anxious about violence and more likely to get hurt. Magdol and coworkers (1997) suggest that the correlates and thus the meaning of violence are quite different for women and men in these relationships. Except for the most extreme case, women were unlikely to really hurt their partners; they can thus express their anger and irritation physically without fear of damaging consequences. In contrast, when men lose control, they violate their status as protectors of their partner and are much more likely genuinely to hurt their partner. For men, physical aggression within relationships is correlated with a much different pattern of variables than for women—a pattern that points toward psychopathology, substance abuse, and status/power inequalities as characteristics of violent men, according to Magdol and colleagues (1997).

Bjerregaard's (this volume) study of a representative sample of a large southeastern university found that, although there were no gender differences in the frequency of stalking victimization, women had significantly higher levels—almost 3 times as high—of "fear of physical safety" and "fear for emotional safety" than did men.

In two studies, Davis, Ace, and Andra (1999) examined the same issue with respect to stalking victimization. Using the eight items from the NVAW survey, no consistent differences were found between men and women students in the overall experience of stalking—harassment behaviors, but women (stalked by men) were significantly more afraid in both samples. To the degree that males see threats as more acceptable in the context of romantic rejection (as the data on perpetrators gathered by Sinclair and Frieze [this volume] show), they may give off cues of threat without making explicit threats. In effect, the same behaviors may be more dangerous and hence more fear-provoking when exhibited by a man.

Cupach and Spitzberg (this volume) also have critically examined the meaning of gender differences and their lack among ORI clusters. They found that "men were likely to experience milder forms of ORI (*privacy invasion* and *hyper-intimacy*) than women, while women may be more likely to be victims of severe and violent intrusions. The size of differences was quite small [but] women perceived *all* types of intrusion to be more distressing [as indicated by the four ratings of annoyance, upset, threatened, and privacy violated] than did men" (Cupach & Spitzberg, this volume). A direct test of the different implication of being stalked as a woman or as a man needs to be made, but these studies suggest that an interpretation similar to that of Magdol and associates (1997) would integrate seemingly disparate findings.

Threatened and Actual Abuse by Stalkers

The early consensus was that most stalkers, while disturbing to victims, are not physically violent (Zona et al., 1993; where they reported a 2.3% violence rate). But recent studies, which take advantage of distinctions among types of stalkers and which have used multivariate statistical techniques all agree that former intimate partner stalkers—particularly sexually intimates—are much more dangerous to their ex-partners than non-intimate stalkers (Meloy, in press; Mullen, Pathé, & Purcell, 2000; Palarea, Zona, Lane, & Langhinrichsen-Rohling, 1999). Indeed, Meloy (in press) now sums the implications of these studies as follows: "Risk management of prior sexually intimate stalking cases should assume that an act of interpersonal violence toward the object of pursuit will occur at some point in the stalking crime" (p. 23).

In addition to the NVAW which found 81% of women who were stalked by an ex-husband were physically assaulted by that person and 31% were sexually assaulted (Tjaden & Thoennes, 1998), four chapters to this volume bring additional information to bear on the connection among stalking, psychological violence, and physical abuse.

In the Mechanic, Weaver and Resick study (this volume) the level of stalking acknowledged was 20 to 30 times higher than Coleman (1997) found in his study of college students. In contrast with the NVAW sample, where explicit verbal threats were made to only 45% of the women stalked, 94% of the Mechanic et al. sample of abused women received threats. In their sample, psychological abuse prior to separation was the strongest predictor of violent stalking and of the victim's subsequent fear, controlling for physical violence. Brewster (this volume), in a study of volunteers for a study of stalking, found that 46% were physically attacked after leaving an intimate relationship, and that 86% of these suffered physical injury as a result. The best predictor of physical violence as part of stalking was a threat of violence and physical harm by the perpetrators. The use of alcohol or drugs by the perpetrators also predicted injury. Both Davis and his associates (this volume) and Logan and associates (this volume) have shown that psychological abuse in a relationship that ultimately ends in a difficult breakup is a very strong predictor of subsequent stalking victimization for both men and women. However, for the male perpetrators, alcohol use was much more predictive of both stalking and psychological abuse than for female stalking perpetrators.

IMPACT OF STALKING VICTIMIZATION

Systematic case studies of stalking victims (Orion, 1997; Pathé & Mullen, 1997) document the pervasiveness of fear, anger, and distress at not being able to control one's privacy. The NVAW survey (Tjaden & Thoennes, 1998) documents the range of behaviors that victims take to deal with their experience of victimization and the impact of the experience. The levels of distress reported by women and men were quite substantial. Thirty per cent of the women and 20% of the men victims sought counseling. The psychological impact was equally great, for it seemed to affect feelings of personal safety (68% saw it as having gotten worse), their level of concern about personal safety (42% were very concerned), and their tendency to carry something to protect themselves (45%). Hall (1996, 1998) in a study of male and female stalking victims found that both (83%) reported that their personalities had changed as a result of the experience. They had become more cautious (85%), more paranoid (40%), felt more easily frightened (53%), and had become much more aggressive (30%). Spitzberg, Nicastro, and Cousin (1998) developed a 30–item measure of relevant symptoms, and created 3 scales (angst, fear, and hopelessness) after-factor to analyze the items. Angst items reflected "general stress" and "depression;" fear items included "paranoia" and "feelings of being watched;" hopelessness items included a "loss of faith" in aspects of the justice system and a related world. Students who self-categorized themselves as having been stalked had significantly higher symptom reports on all three scales. The number and duration of stalking incidents were also predictive of levels of angst and fear.

Mechanic, Uhlmansiek, Weaver, and Resick (this volume) used the Posttraumatic Diagnostic Scale (PDS), developed by Foa, Cashman, Jaycox, and Perry (1997), to assess the impact of violent stalking on their sample of battered women. Relentlessly stalked battered women reported more severe PTD symptoms than did those who were infrequently stalked. Since all of the women in the sample had been battered, a partial control for that variable has been introduced. Still, it must be acknowledged that the co-occurrence of physical violence and stalking makes it hard to disentangle these variables.

All of the studies that have examined the issue support the conclusion that stalking that is accompanied by assaults and verbal threats is strongly connected to serious emotional consequences for victims. The consequences are revealed in the victims' emotional liability as indicated by the PDS arousal scale, in their background levels of fear, and in the view that their world has become a more dangerous place in which to live—one that requires much more caution and protective action on their parts. The patterns are reminiscent of those described by Janoff-Bulman (1992) in her discussion of *Shattered Assumptions*. In more than 20 years of work with trauma victims, she found that trauma, such as rape, threat of death, and untimely loss of a partner, tends to shatter a person's assumptions that they are safe and not vulnerable to harm. Most persons take it for granted that they are worthy, that the world is benevolent, and that whatever happens to them makes sense. Becoming a trauma victim can undermine all of these assumptions. Stalking, unlike some traumas, continues over significant periods of time—the average case occurred over 1.8 years (Tjaden & Thoennes, 1998). One has to continue dealing with it, often with the strong sense that nothing can prevent the stalker from continuing his or her intrusion into one's life (Orion, 1997). Thus, one might expect reactions to be more severe than might be expected by looking at the severity of the acts committed. Stalking victims may be analogous to hostages or even to incest victims. (See Mechanic's chapter in this volume for a detailed review of issues related to impact, coping, and the clinical management of stalking.)

COPING

The pervasiveness of stalking experiences and their potential to become quite troubling and problematic for the victims takes us to the next issue: What is known about the ways in which people try to cope with stalking and what is their relative effectiveness? The identification of patterns of coping has been one of Cupach and Spitzberg's (this volume, 1996; Spitzberg, Nicastro, & Cousin's [1998]) major contributions. Starting with 50s self-report items, they developed a five-factor structure. The factors are *interactional coping* (e.g., had a serious talk, told the person that what he/she was doing was wrong, or cursed at them and used obscenities), *retaliation* (threats), *protection* (e.g., call the police, seek a restraining order), *evasion* (e.g., moving, changing jobs or schools), or *technology* (e.g., obtaining caller ID or the call-back feature for the telephone).

The number, duration, and intensity of stalking experiences is related to the number and frequency of coping attempts. The more one attempts to cope in one way, the more one also uses other methods of coping. All forms of coping are moderately to strongly interrelated (rs from .20 to .70) with each other. The more symptoms of distress at being stalked, the more forms of coping that one uses. One interpretation of these findings is: "the more a person is obsessively pursued, the more this person attempts to cope, and the increased coping is merely a barometer of the stalking and its disruptiveness, rather than a method of effectively diminishing the negative effects of the stalking" (Spitzberg, Nicastro, & Cousins, 1998, p. 43). As these authors note, other interpretations are also plausible, and the most interesting questions may well concern how and when coping is attempted rather than the frequency of attempts. Certainly, we have very little systematic work on the effectiveness of various methods of dealing with stalkers.

Perpetrators of Stalking

While the clinical and forensic literature on aspects of stalking perpetration is quite large, systematic empirical research is only beginning. Three of the articles in this volume make major contributions by first conceptualizing stalking as a continuum from normal but persistent courtship behaviors to various forms of harassment ending in violent stalking (Davis et al., Langhinrichsen-Rohling et al.; Sinclair & Frieze). The clinical and forensic literature has been carefully summarized by Meloy (1998) and by White and associates (this volume), but it is worth touching on the highlights as they provide a context for the research reported below. In the case of women and men victims, their stalkers were more likely to be male. The majority of stalkers are not mentally disturbed, but rather obsessionally focused on a specific person with whom they have had some previous relationship. The NVAW survey suggests that at least 59% of the stalkers who stalked women had been husbands, ex-husbands or boyfriends. In the study based on the files of the Los Angeles Police Department, Zona, Palarea, and Lane (1998) have found that 65% of their sample had a prior, often intimate, relationship with the stalker. Thus stalking is often related to a failed or blocked relationship in which a stalker feels rejected by a desired love object. A subset of stalkers has, however, a history of limited and unsuccessful relationships, and they tend to live alone and to be underemployed. According to Zona and colleagues (1998), stalkers are more likely to have used physical or verbal abuse in the relationship (before it broke up) than do nonstalkers. Likewise, the clinical data indicate that a subset of stalkers has a history of alcohol or drug abuse (Hall, 1998) and, for men, this finding has been supported by Logan and associates' data (this volume). The NVAW study indicates that victims' perception of why they were stalked included control (21%), to keep the victims in the relationship (20%), and to scare the victims (16%). The exercise of control is perceived by victims as central to the stalker's purposes as indicated by the original Tjaden and Thoennes report (1998) and by Langhinrichsen-Rohling and associates (this volume).

SELF-REPORTED INCIDENTS OF STALKING

In the Fremouw and colleagues (1997) study of college students, only 3 males (2.3%) reported engaging in stalking defined as "knowing and repeatedly following, harassing, or threatening someone." No females acknowledged engaging in stalking. Both theoretical work and empirical work by Baumeister, Wotman, and Stillman (1993) suggest that stalking is more likely to develop in the context of an unrequited love or the experience of being rejected by a previous lover.

Sinclair and Frieze (this volume) chose to focus on the assessment of courtship and stalking-like behaviors in the context of unrequited loves. Participants were recruited for a study of "Loving when your partner does not love back," and the instructions for the survey asked them to "report on crushes, love interests or passionate love they felt for another that was not reciprocated" (Sinclair & Frieze, this volume). In this context, 18% of the students acknowledged "[being] aggressive to get his/her attention" and 18% acknowledged going "too far in trying to get his/her attention." Using the factor—derived scales rather than single items, 29% reported intimidation, 24% verbal or mild physical aggression, and 13% threat or attempted physical harm. In no case did they find gender differences in self-report of these stalking-like activities, but their sample of men was small (N = 44).

Within a large convenience sample of undergraduates, Langhinrichsen-Rohling, Palarea, Cohen, and Rohling (this volume) distinguished between initiators of relationship breakups and receivers of the breakup. Men were slightly more likely than women to claim to have initiated the breakup. As expected, almost all receivers acknowledged engaging in at least one pursuit behavior, and 27.5% admitted having done at least one thing that had a negative impact on the former partner. However, only 3.3% reported engaging in a severe pursuit behavior such as threats or damage to property. Breakup initiators, however, reported receiving a much higher level of severe stalking (14%). They did not find gender differences in self-reported Pursuit Behaviors.

In the Davis and colleagues' studies (this volume), a criterion of six stalking behaviors was used as an index of significant stalking. Ten and seven-tenths percent of those in Study 1 and 7.6% in Study 2 acknowledged engaging in 6 or more stalking activities after breakups. Stalking was more likely after being rejected in a relationship, after multiple breakups, and was markedly greater among those breakups where the person felt a combination of anger, jealousy, and obsessiveness. These estimates fall in the same range as those from Langhinrichsen-Rohling and colleagues (this volume) and Logan and coworkers (this volume), but are lower than the estimates reported by Sinclair and Frieze (this volume) who used a criterion of "ever" versus "never" in the scoring of the courtship persistence.

Not only do rejected or unrequited lovers not see themselves as engaging the level and severity of stalking that those who initiate the breakups report, but they seem blind to the impact of even their milder stalking behaviors. Langhinrichsen-Rohling et al. asked for comments about the partner's reaction to any incidents reported, and also got ratings of the degree to which the partner may have changed in love, anger, fear, sadness, or guilt. Receivers who initiated various Pursuit Behaviors gave them much lower ratings on negative impact on the ex-partner than did persons rating the impact of getting such attention. It is important to remember that the receivers and initiators are not reporting on the same breakups, and thus perfect correspondence would not be expected, but discrepancies of this magnitude are suggestive of motivated distortion by stalkers or the conscious giving of socially desirable responses.

Sinclair and Frieze (this volume) found a similar pattern. Perpetrators placed a largely positive interpretation on their behaviors. They report low levels (2% to 16%) of real threatening and damaging behaviors. Only 18% viewed themselves as having gone too far in their pursuit of the wished-for partner.

To what extent are these findings relevant to stalking perpetrators as legally defined? That is not entirely clear because each research team has used its own definition, and also because the base-rate of self-acknowledged severe or violent stalking is quite low. But substantial proportions of the participants in both studies acknowledge engaging in surveillance, in unwanted persistence in contact, and in verbal abuse and threats. This provides a situation in which one can meaningfully examine the correlates of stalking-like behavior, and it is that to which we now turn.

PREDICTORS OF STALKING-LIKE BEHAVIOR AFTER BREAKUPS OR UNREQUITED LOVES

Kurt (1995) reminds us that stalking is part of the constellation of behaviors associated with domestic violence. White and colleagues (this volume) also have used that insight as one foundation for their overview of current literature on interpersonal aggression and stalking. Logan, Leukefeld, and Walker (this volume) have conducted one of the first studies to examine whether stalking after a "difficult break up with an intimate partner" was related to the degree of psychological and physical violence in that relationship. When they examined the correlates of stalking perpetration, they found that, for men, stalking perpetration was associated with heavy drinking, the use of alcohol or drugs during sex, or the perception of self as having been a victim of stalking and psychological abuse. For women, none of the correlates of stalking perpetration was as strong as for men, and only stalking victimization, psychological abuse victimization, and the use of drugs or alcohol during sex were significantly related to stalking perpetration. The pattern suggested that male stalkers tended to justify their own stalking (and aggression) by blaming their partners much more than did women. The data from Mechanic and associates' (this volume) sample of acutely abused women also fit. Psychological abuse (specifically the dominance/isolation subscale of Tolman's [1989] PMWI scale) during the relationship was the strongest predictor of subsequent stalking behavior. A tentative interpretation is that men are much more likely to see stalking as a way of continuing to control the ex-partner than are women. This interpretation is supported by the consistently strong relationship between need for control as measured by Follingstad, Rutledge, McNeill-Harkins, and Polek (1988) in the two samples collected by Davis and coworkers (this volume). Differences in strength and willingness to engage in the use of force may be part of the story, but, in a culture with some vestiges of patriarchal ideology, men may feel more entitled to attempt to control a woman who was once "theirs."

From the victim's perspective, the NVAW data are particularly revealing. Exhibit 13 in their Research Brief (Tjaden & Thoennes, 1998) showed that victims thought that their stalkers wanted to control them (21%), to keep them in the relationship (20%), or to scare them (16%). Among ex-husbands who stalked, there was a strong connection with control, emotional abuse, and jealousy (see Exhibit 14 in Tjaden & Thoennes, 1998). When Langhinrichsen-Rohling and associates (this volume) asked their respondents who had initiated breakups about the kinds of things the stalkers did and their characteristics, a similar cluster appeared. Degree of pursuit behavior was related to the perception of the partner as jealous, controlling, and emotionally abusive prior to the breakup.

Spitzberg and Cupach (1999, May) have reported strong connections among jealousy-based restrictiveness and aggressive jealousy and behaviors of both an aggressive sort and pursuit or harassing sort. Guerrero (1998) has shown that attachment insecurity is connected to several aspects of jealousy and that together they predict engaging in surveillance and stalking-like behaviors. In the studies by Davis and coworkers (this volume), the constellation of anger-jealousy-obsessiveness was consistently predictive of stalking, and the degree to which individuals had these feelings at the time of a breakup was correlated with anxious attachment.

Summary of Perpetrator Results

What do these studies suggest about the psychology of stalkers? The early insight that stalking had to do with pathologies of love (Mullen & Pathé, 1994) has been borne out. Some stalkers want more than anything else to reestablish or initiate intimate relationships. In this context, the predictors and correlates of the milder form of stalking are those that related to intensity and characteristics of romantic love relationships. Thus, erotic and manic love styles, and the degree of anxious attachment were predictors of courtship persistence and the milder forms of stalking. But some stalking is driven more by control and revenge than by merely reestablishing a love relationship. In Sinclair and Frieze (this volume), feelings of vengefulness, wanting to hurt, and feelings of being deceived were the strongest emotional correlates of stalking for both men and women. And in both the Logan and colleagues (this volume) and Mechanic and associates (this volume) studies, psychological abuse during the relationship was the strongest predictor of subsequent stalking of a serious and potentially dangerous sort.

TYPOLOGIES AND THEORETICAL FRAMEWORKS FOR UNDERSTANDING INTIMATE PARTNER VIOLENCE AND STALKING

Typologies

By distinguishing among types of batterers (and stalkers), one is likely to have a more adequate and practically useful set of categories. Furthermore, evidence is beginning to develop that stalking during and after an intimate relationship is related to psychological and physical violence within the relationship prior to breakup (Davis et al., this volume; Emerson et al., 1998; Logan et al., this volume; Tjaden & Thoennes, 1998). With respect to batterers, Holtzworth-Munroe and Stuart (1994) reviewed the existing studies and proposed that three general types could be distinguished in terms of severity of violence, generality of violence, and nature of the psychopathology exhibited. *Family-only* batterers committed the least and less severe violence toward their partners of the other two groups; they were more likely to fall in the passive-dependent personality disorder. Their violence tended to be only within the family—not general, and they had less involvement with drugs and with other crimes. *Borderline/dysphoric* batterers engaged in moderate to severe marital violence and were more likely to have used both psychological abuse and sexual abuse than family-only batterers. They were much more likely to qualify with a psychopathology—most often of the borderline personality, dysphoria, or the emotional volatility type. This group was more likely to use either alcohol or drugs to cope with distress than the family-only batterers were.

Antisocial batterers used moderate to severe physical violence in relationship as well as psychological and sexual abuse. But they also have a history of violence outside the family, of trouble with the law, and a pattern of alcohol and drug use. As the label indicates, this group is most likely to be classified as suffering from antisocial personality disorder or being psychopaths. Several studies have supported the soundness of these distinctions (Hamberger, Lohr, Bonge, & Tolin, 1996; Holtzworth-Munroe, Meehan, Herron, & Stuart, 1999). These typologies are also beginning to inform treatment programs for batterers (Saunders, 1996).

Gottman and Jacobson (1998) offer support for the importance of several of these dimensions. In a sample of 201 couples, they identified 63 in which the wives were repeatedly beaten and emotionally abused— thus eliminating low-level common couple violence from their analysis. Within the 63 couples, they identified two types of batterers—*pit bulls* and *cobras*. These two show a marked similarity to the *borderline/dysphoric* and *antisocial* batterers of Holtzworth-Munroe. Pit bulls were described as jealous, fearful of abandonment, and determined to reduce the independence of their partners. They were prone to rage at threats to the relationship, and likely to engage in stalking to re-assert control. They were unlikely to have criminal records and tended to confine their violence to people whom they love. *Cobras,* in contrast, were not emotionally dependent upon the partner, but rather determined to have their way. They were capable of violence to pets and nonfamily members. They were more likely to threaten or use weapons and to have a history of crime. One striking contrast between the two groups was the tendency of *cobras* to become physiologically calm before and during violence, whereas the *pit bulls* became physiologically aroused.

Just as students of interpersonal violence have found it important to distinguish subtypes, the same applies to the case for stalking. Zona, Palarea, and Lane (1998) have continued to refine a three-category distinction—simple obsessional, love obsessional, and erotomanic— which is based on clinical judgments of files from the Los Angeles Police Department's Threat Management Unit. Simple obsessional stalkers may also be divided into two subgroups—those who had had a previous intimate relationship with the victim (the largest category in their studies) and those who knew the victim from a work or professional setting, but who had not dated or been intimate. Within each of these groups, two motives seemed paramount in stalking. The first was a desire to coerce the victim into (or back into) a relationship and the second was revenge for some real or imagined act of mistreatment. Obsessional and erotomanic stalkers are both out of touch with reality in that the former develops an obsession with a public figure who has power, status, beauty, or is a celebrity, and the latter has an obsession with someone in his personal network. Many of these stalkers meet criteria for serious psychopathology, such as schizophrenia or bipolar disorder. They have seldom had meaningful intimate relationships and tend to be prone to alcohol and substance abuse. Erotomanics are more likely to be female, and to have a firm delusion of having a real relationship with a high-status male whom they know but with whom there is no such relationship.

Recently Mullen, Pathé, and Purcell (2000) have made a major contribution to the classification of types of stalkers. Three dimensions are considered in the typology: the motivational functions of stalking, the previous relationship with the victim, and the type and degree of psychopathology. The motivational typology is novel and supported by a careful study of 168 cases. They separate stalkers into the rejected, the intimacy seekers, the resentful, the predatory, and the incompetent. The rejected have been prevented from establishing or continuing a relationship that they desired, and they want either to reconcile or force the victim to suffer. Intimacy seekers are lonely persons who want to have a relationship. The resentful stalkers see themselves as having been insulted and want revenge and vindication. The predatory are attempting to gain control and sexual gratification. The incompetents are would be suitors whose approaches are counter-productive. "The typology alone, and when taken together with the prior relationship and psychiatric diagnosis, enabled predictions to be made about the duration of stalking, the nature of the stalking behaviors, the risks of threatening and violent behavior, and to some extent the response to management strategies" (2000, p. 76).

Because stalking is an instrumental behavior which can have several different goals—not just reestablishment of a relationship or revenge when one is rejected—it is clearly important to gain greater insight into what stalkers are trying to accomplish. Further studies such as those of Mullen et al. (2000) are highly desirable because of their implications both for theory and for clinical practice. A promising research technique for identifying motives and cognitions about the targets of stalking are laboratory simulations of conflict and rejection between couples. Eckhardt, Barbour, and Davison (1998) have used audiotaped stimuli designed to elicit jealousy and anger and asked the male participants to imagine themselves in the situations, and to talk out loud about their thoughts and feelings as they listened to the tapes. Their recorded thoughts were analyzed for irrational beliefs, for hostile attributions, cognitive biases, and anger control statements. The coding of the spontaneous thoughts was much more sensitive as a tool for separating marital violent from nonviolent men than was any of the self-report measures. This procedure could be adapted with slight modifications to assess the cognitions and motives relevant to stalking. The use of projective measures and the analysis of spontaneous verbal behavior may allow one to circumvent the inhibitions about the acknowledgment of stalking and related emotions that now yield quite low rates of self-reported stalking.

SUMMARY

Although the systematic study of stalking—both of victims and perpetrators—is in its infancy, we can already see some consistent themes in the research. The early clinical and forensic work that emphasized the conceptualization of stalking as pathology of love has borne fruit. One line of investigation that has appeared to be quite productive is the examination of stalking as a form of domestic violence, occurring most often in the context of failed or desired-but-unreciprocated intimate relationships. Many of the same variables that have been implicated in physical and psychological abuse also are implicated in the early studies of stalking: A history of childhood abuse, attachment insecurity that involves anxiety over abandonment or mania and jealousy, and need for control.

Both the clinical-forensic research on stalking and the research on types of aggressors indicate the need for differentiation. Not all stalkers are alike in their motives, their degree of reality contact and specific psychopathologies, or their willingness to engage in physical violence. Related to this effort would be an effort to standardize the assessment of stalking by examining the validity of self-report instruments such as those used in the research in this issue against police and victim reports.

The relationship between gender and stalking remains unclear. The national survey shows many more women victims and a greater emotional impact on women victims. Many other studies of moderately large convenience samples on college campuses have found no or only small gender differences in rates of victimization reported or in self-reported perpetration of stalking. One possibility is that both the different criteria of stalking victimization used and the possibility that the same activities when engaged in by a man rather than by a woman are appraised as more dangerous, may account for the findings.

There are some clear indications of needed research. Victim reports of stalking need to include both the NVAW Survey items and a broader set that allows the distinctions between courtship persistence, stalking harassment, threats, and stalking violence to be detected. Victim reports of the impact of stalking on their worldviews, their perception of personal safety and mental health, such as symptoms of posttraumatic stress and depression, need to be brought together so that a more systematic and refined statement of the impact of stalking victimization can be made. The outline of such an assessment is contained in the NVAW Survey, Cupach and Spitzberg's research, and in Mechanic's contributions to this volume.

We also want to endorse the suggestion made by Emerson and coworkers (1998), Cupach and Spitzberg (this volume) and White and associates (this volume) that we need to move beyond static analyses of stalking and delve into the developmental-interactional history of stalking. We do not know how many cases of courtship persistence or mild stalking turn into more serious harassment or violence vs. those that stop. Nor do we know if there are critical events that can pinpoint such changes. To what degree is the outcome of a rejection dependent upon how it is delivered and whether or not it triggers a sense of humiliation? Reconstructing the history of failed rejections that have led to stalking and of those that successfully ended the relationship would be important. We believe that the articles in this issue provide important data about both the perpetrators and victims of stalking, develop significant conceptual resources for the integration of findings, and identify substantive questions and methodological issues that need to be addressed.

REFERENCES

Baumeister, R. F., Wotman, S. R., & Stillwell, A. M. (1993). Unrequited love: On heartbreak, anger, guilt, scriptlessness, and humiliation. *Journal of Personality and Social Psychology, 64,* 377–394.

Burt, M. R. (1980). Cultural myths and supports for rape. *Journal of Personality and Social Psychology, 38,* 217–230.

Coleman, J. R. (1997). Stalking behavior and the cycle of domestic violence. *Journal of Interpersonal Violence, 12,* 420–432.

Cupach, W. R., & Spitzberg, B. H. (1998). Obsessional relational intrusion and stalking. In B. H. Spitzberg & W. R. Cupach (Eds.), *The dark side of close relationships* (pp. 233–263). Mahwah, NJ: Lawrence Erlbaum Associates.

Davis, K. E., Ace, A., & Andra, M. (1999).[Stalking victimization data]. Unpublished raw data.

Eckhardt, C. I., Barbour, K. A., & Davison, G. C. (1998). Articulated thoughts of maritally violent and nonviolent men during anger arousal. *Journal of Consulting and Clinical Psychology, 66,* 259–269.

Emerson, R. M., Ferris, K. O., & Gardner, C. B. (1998). On being stalked. *Social Problems, 45,* 289–314.

Foa, E. B., Cashman, L., Jaycox, L., & Perry, K. (1997). The validation of a self-report measure of posttraumatic stress disorder: The posttraumatic diagnostic scale. *Psychological Assessment, 9,* 445–451.

Fremouw, W. J., Westrup, D., & Pennypacker, J. (1997). Stalking on campus: The prevalence and strategies for coping with stalking. *Journal of Forensic Sciences, 42,* 664–667.

Gottman, J. & Jacobson, N. (1998). *When men batter women.* NY: Simon & Schuster.

Guerrero, L. K. (1998). Attachment-style differences in the experience and expression of romantic jealousy. *Personal Relationships, 5,* 273–291.

Hall, D. M. (1998). The victims of stalking. In J. R. Meloy (Ed.), *The psychology of stalking* (pp. 113–137). San Diego, CA: Academic Press.

Hamberger, L. K., Lohr, J. M., Bonge, D., & Tolin, D. F. (1996). A large sample empirical typology of male spouse abusers and its relationship to dimensions of abuse. *Violence & Victims, 11,* 277–292.

Holtzworth-Munroe, A., Meehan, J. C., Herron, K., & Stuart, G. L. (1999) A typology of male batterers. In X. B. Arriaga & S. Oskamp (Eds.), *Violence in intimate relationships* (pp. 45–71). Thousand Oaks, CA: Sage.

Holtzworth-Munroe, A., & Stuart, G. L. (1994). Typologies of male batterers: Three subtypes and differences among them. *Psychological Bulletin, 116,* 476–497.

Janoff-Bulman, R. (1992). *Shattered assumptions: Toward a new psychology of trauma.* NY: The Free Press.

Johnson, M. P. (1995). Patriarchal terrorism and common couple violence: Two forms of violence against women. *Journal of Marriage and the Family, 57,* 283–294.

Kurt, J. L. (1995). Stalking as a variant of domestic violence. *Bulletin of the Academy of Psychiatry and the Law, 23,* 219–223.

Magdol, L., Moffitt, T. E., Caspi, A., Newman, D. N., Fagan, J., & Silva, P. A. (1997). Gender differences in partner violence in a birth cohort of 21–year-olds: Bridging the gap between clinical and epidemiological approaches. *Journal of Consulting and Clinical Psychology, 65,* 68–78.

Meloy, J. R. (2001). Stalking and violence. In J. Boon & L. Sheridan (Eds.), *Stalking and psychosexual obsession.* London: Wiley.

Meloy, J. R. (1998). The psychology of stalking. In J. R. Meloy (Ed.), *The psychology of stalking* (pp. 1–27). San Diego, CA: Academic Press.

Mullen, P. E., Pathé, M., & Purcell, R. (2000). *Stalkers and their victims.* NY: Cambridge University Press.

Orion, D. (1997). *I know you really love me.* NY: MacMillan.

Pathé, M., & Mullen, P. E. (1997). The impact of stalkers on their victims. *British Journal of Psychiatry, 170,* 12–17.

Saunders, D. G. (1996). Feminist-cognitive-behavioral and process-psychodynamic treatments for men who batter: Interaction of abuser traits and treatment models. *Violence and Victims, 11,* 393–414.

Schaum, M., & Parrish, K. (1995). *Stalked: Breaking the silence on the crime of stalking in America.* NY: Pocket Books.

Spitzberg, B. H., Nicastro, A. M., & Cousins, A. V. (1998). Exploring the interactional phenomenon of stalking and obsessive relational intrusion. *Communications Reports, 11,* 33–47.

Spitzberg, B. H., & Cupach, W. R. (1999, May). *Jealousy, suspicion, possessiveness and obsession as predictors of obsessive relational intrusion.* Paper presented at the International Communication Association Convention, San Francisco, CA.

Straus, M. A., & Gelles, R. J. (1990). *Physical violence in American families.* New Brunswick, NJ: Transaction Publishers.

Tjaden, P., & Thoennes, N. (1998). *Stalking in America: Findings from the National Violence Against Women Survey* (NCJ Report no. 169592). Washington, DC: National Institute of Justice and Centers for Disease Control and Prevention.

Tolman, R. M. (1989). The development of a measure of psychological maltreatment of women by their male partners. *Violence and Victims, 4,* 159–177.

Zona, M., Palarea, R. E., & Lane, J. C. (1998). Psychiatric diagnosis and the offender-victim typology of stalking. In J. R. Meloy (Ed.), *The psychology of stalking: Clinical and forensic perspectives* (pp. 69–84). NY: Academic Press.

Zona, M., Sharma, K. K., Lane, J. (1993). A comparative study of erotomanic and obsessional subjects in a forensic sample. *Journal of Forensic Sciences, 38,* 894–903.

Index